"Anyone interested in delving into the riches of the Old Testament in the original languages will welcome this impressive volume. The author succeeds admirably in his attempt to introduce the sometimes dizzying world of Hebrew and Aramaic scholarship to the intermediate student. In light of advances being made in current investigations of these ancient languages, this volume will find a wide readership among students and teachers alike for many years to come."

Bill T. Arnold
Paul S. Amos Professor of Old Testament Interpretation,
Asbury Theological Seminary

"Trying to keep up with the volume and pace of new developments in the linguistic study of Biblical Hebrew and Aramaic can be overwhelming. Thanks to Benjamin Noonan, we now have an up-to-date volume that orients students to these advances. Noonan concisely describes the methods and terminology being used and insightfully assesses the bewildering array of conclusions being proposed. In addition to his helpful summaries and evaluations, Noonan provides ample, up-to-date bibliographies for those who want to pursue specific subjects. The book is an ideal supplemental text for advanced master's level courses."

Robert B. Chisholm, Jr.
Chair and Senior Professor of Old Testament Studies,
Dallas Theological Seminary

"*Advances in the Study of Biblical Hebrew and Aramaic* is a helpful and succinct guide to the complex landscape of recent study of Biblical Hebrew and Aramaic grammar. Noonan provides a brief orientation to the linguistic theories that have animated many of these recent studies but also hinder easy access to them. Noonan's surveys of key advances and debates in the fields provides the 'lay of the land' and key resources for further study. This book is a useful initiation to the recent study of Biblical Hebrew and Aramaic grammar for students and biblical scholars alike."

John A. Cook
Professor of Old Testament and Director of Hebrew Language Instruction,
Asbury Theological Seminary

"This book will help intermediate students, pastors, and even scholars to keep abreast of current linguistic research. Noonan makes the material easy to grasp and provides helpful summaries. I heartily recommend this work."

Peter J. Gentry
Donald L. Williams Professor of Old Testament,
The Southern Baptist Theological Seminary

D1546122

"The last century and a half witnessed numerous seismic shifts in the study of language. Most students find understanding these changes challenging, others fail to understand the importance of different linguistic theories, and even biblical scholars have a difficult time keeping up with the everchanging nuances of the various discussions. Noonan provides an indispensable resource to help navigate the current state of linguistics for biblical studies. *Advances in the Study of Biblical Hebrew and Aramaic* balances accessible, informed descriptions of the major linguistic movements with helpful evaluations of recent language-specific developments in Hebrew and Aramaic. Students at every level will find this work both enlightening and valuable."

H. H. Hardy II
Associate Professor of Old Testament and Semitic Languages,
Southeastern Baptist Theological Seminary, Wake Forest, North Carolina

"Ben Noonan has provided a remarkable service in providing a survey of not only the theoretical discussions in Biblical Hebrew and Aramaic but most especially elucidating the relationships between theories, scholars, and publications. For a field that has become so fragmented and specialised in which no scholar can master all the literature, this book provides an outstanding resource. The student will acquire an awareness of the field and find a well curated yet manageable bibliography. The scholar will find an overarching network of relationships that bring both coherence and cohesion where they have been much needed."

Elizabeth Robar
Tyndale House, Cambridge, UK

"*Advances in the Study of Biblical Hebrew and Aramaic* is just that, another advance! The author is to be commended for his collation and analysis of modern scholarship in a single, accessible volume. From philology to pedagogy, readers will encounter the origins, major contributors, and analyses of some of the more significant topics in Biblical Hebrew and Aramaic research. We are guided through the controversies and debates, shown how far we have come, and pointed in the right direction for further study. Readers may not agree at every point, but that is half the fun. Anyone interested in the academic study of Biblical Hebrew and Aramaic will certainly appreciate and even enjoy this work."

Miles V. Van Pelt
Alan Hayes Belcher, Jr. Professor of Old Testament and Biblical Languages
and Director of the Summer Institute for Biblical Languages,
Reformed Theological Seminary

ADVANCES *IN THE* STUDY *OF* BIBLICAL HEBREW *AND* ARAMAIC

NEW INSIGHTS *for* READING *the* OLD TESTAMENT

BENJAMIN J. NOONAN

ZONDERVAN ACADEMIC

Advances in the Study of Biblical Hebrew and Aramaic
Copyright © 2020 by Benjamin James Noonan

ISBN 978-0-310-59601-1 (softcover)

Requests for information should be addressed to:
Zondervan, *3900 Sparks Dr. SE, Grand Rapids, Michigan 49546*

All Scripture quotations, unless otherwise indicated, are the author's own translations. Scripture quotations noted as NIV are taken from The Holy Bible, New International Version®, NIV®. Copyright © 1973, 1978, 1984, 2011 by Biblica, Inc.® Used by permission of Zondervan. All rights reserved worldwide. www.Zondervan.com. The "NIV" and "New International Version" are trademarks registered in the United States Patent and Trademark Office by Biblica, Inc.®

Any internet addresses (websites, blogs, etc.) and telephone numbers in this book are offered as a resource. They are not intended in any way to be or imply an endorsement by Zondervan, nor does Zondervan vouch for the content of these sites and numbers for the life of this book.

No part of this publication may be reproduced, stored in a retrieval system, or transmitted in any form or by any means—electronic, mechanical, photocopy, recording, or any other—except for brief quotations in printed reviews, without the prior permission of the publisher.

Art direction: Tammy Johnson
Interior design: Kait Lamphere

Printed in the United States of America

19 20 21 22 23 24 25 26 27 28 29 /LSC/ 15 14 13 12 11 10 9 8 7 6 5 4 3 2 1

For all students of Biblical Hebrew and Biblical Aramaic who strive to be faithful in their exegesis and effective in their ministry

CONTENTS

EXPANDED TABLE
of CONTENTS

ABBREVIATIONS

AASOR	Annual of the American Schools of Oriental Research
AB	Anchor Bible
ABD	*Anchor Bible Dictionary.* Edited by David Noel Freedman. 6 vols. New York: Doubleday, 1992
ABRL	Anchor Bible Reference Library
AbrNSup	Abr-Nahrain Supplements
AIL	Ancient Israel and Its Literature
AION	*Annali dell'Istituto Orientale di Napoli*
AJSL	*American Journal of Semitic Languages and Literatures*
AKM	Abhandlungen für die Kunde des Morgenlandes
ANEM	Ancient Near Eastern Monographs
AOAT	Alter Orient und Altes Testament
AOS	American Oriental Series
AS	*Aramaic Studies*
AS	Assyriological Studies
ATJ	*Ashland Theological Journal*
BDB	Brown, Francis, S. R. Driver, and Charles A. Briggs. *A Hebrew and English Lexicon of the Old Testament*
BHRG	*A Biblical Hebrew Reference Grammar.* Christo H. J. van der Merwe, Jacobus A. Naudé, and Jan H. Kroeze. 2nd ed. London: Bloomsbury T&T Clark, 2017
Bib	*Biblica*
BibInt	Biblical Interpretation Series
BibOr	Biblica et Orientalia
BO	*Bibliotheca Orientalis*
BSac	*Bibliotheca Sacra*
BSL	*Bulletin de la Société de Linguistique de Paris*

BSOAS	*Bulletin of the School of Oriental and African Studies, University of London*
BZAW	Beihefte zur Zeitschrift für die alttestamentliche Wissenschaft
CahRB	Cahiers de la Revue biblique
CBET	Contributions to Biblical Exegesis and Theology
ConBOT	Coniectanea Biblica: Old Testament Series
DCH	*Dictionary of Classical Hebrew.* Edited by David J. A. Clines. 8 vols. Sheffield: Sheffield Phoenix, 1993–2011
EHLL	*Encyclopedia of Hebrew Language and Linguistics.* Edited by Geoffrey Khan. 4 vols. Leiden: Brill, 2013
EncJud	*Encyclopaedia Judaica.* Edited by Fred Skolnik and Michael Berenbaum. 2nd ed. 22 vols. Jerusalem: Keter, 2007
FAT	Forschungen zum Alten Testament
FO	*Folia Orientalia*
GKC	*Gesenius' Hebrew Grammar.* Edited by Emil Kautzsch. Translated by A. E. Cowley. 2nd ed. Oxford: Clarendon, 1910
HALOT	*The Hebrew and Aramaic Lexicon of the Old Testament.* Ludwig Köhler, Walter Baumgartner, and Johann J. Stamm. Translated and edited under the supervision of Mervyn E. J. Richardson. 2 vols. Leiden: Brill, 2001
HAR	*Hebrew Annual Review*
HdO	Handbuch der Orientalistik
Hen	*Henoch*
HS	*Hebrew Studies*
HSM	Harvard Semitic Monographs
HSS	Harvard Semitic Studies
HTR	*Harvard Theological Review*
HUCA	*Hebrew Union College Annual*
IBHS	*An Introduction to Biblical Hebrew Syntax.* Bruce K. Waltke and Michael O'Connor. Winona Lake, IN: Eisenbrauns, 1990
ICC	International Critical Commentary
IEJ	*Israel Exploration Journal*
IOS	*Israel Oriental Studies*
JANES	*Journal of the Ancient Near Eastern Society*
JAOS	*Journal of the American Oriental Society*
JBL	*Journal of Biblical Literature*
JBS	Jerusalem Biblical Studies
JCS	*Journal of Cuneiform Studies*
JEOL	*Jaarbericht van het Vooraziatisch-Egyptisch Gezelschap Ex Oriente Lux*

JETS	*Journal of the Evangelical Theological Society*
JHebS	*Journal of Hebrew Scriptures*
JJS	*Journal of Jewish Studies*
JNES	*Journal of Near Eastern Studies*
JNSL	*Journal of Northwest Semitic Languages*
JOTT	*Journal of Translation and Textlinguistics*
Joüon	Joüon, Paul. *A Grammar of Biblical Hebrew.* Translated and revised by T. Muraoka. 2nd ed. SubBi 27. Rome: Pontificio Istituto Biblico, 2006
JPOS	*Journal of the Palestine Oriental Society*
JQR	*Jewish Quarterly Review*
JSem	*Journal for Semitics*
JSNTSup	Journal for the Study of the New Testament Supplement Series
JSOTSup	Journal for the Study of the Old Testament Supplement Series
JSS	*Journal of Semitic Studies*
LANE	Languages of the Ancient Near East
LBHOTS	Library of Hebrew Bible/Old Testament Studies
Leš	*Lešonénu*
LSAWS	Linguistic Studies in Ancient West Semitic
NIDOTTE	*New International Dictionary of Old Testament Theology and Exegesis.* Edited by Willem A. VanGemeren. 5 vols. Grand Rapids: Zondervan, 1997
OLA	Orientalia lovaniensia analecta
Or	*Orientalia*
OtSt	Oudtestamentische Studiën
PHSC	Perspectives on Hebrew Scriptures and Its Contexts
PLO	Porta Linguarum Orientalium
RBL	*Review of Biblical Literature*
REJ	*Revue des études juives*
RevQ	*Revue de Qumran*
SAHD	*Semantics of Ancient Hebrew Database*
SAOC	Studies in Ancient Oriental Civilization
SBFA	Studium Biblicum Franciscanum Analecta
SBLDS	Society of Biblical Literature Dissertation Series
SBLMS	Society of Biblical Literature Monograph Series
SBT	Studies in Biblical Theology
ScrHier	Scripta Hierosolymitana
SDBH	*Semantic Dictionary of Biblical Hebrew*
SemeiaSt	Semeia Studies

SJOT	*Scandinavian Journal of the Old Testament*
SSN	Studia Semitica Neerlandica
StBibLit	Studies in Biblical Literature (Lang)
STDJ	Studies on the Texts of the Desert of Judah
SubBi	Subsidia Biblica
TDOT	*Theological Dictionary of the Old Testament.* Edited by G. Johannes Botterweck and Helmer Ringgren. Translated by John T. Willis et al. 15 vols. Grand Rapids: Eerdmans, 1974–2006
TGUOS	*Transactions of the Glasgow University Oriental Society*
Them	*Themelios*
TLOT	*Theological Lexicon of the Old Testament.* Edited by Ernst Jenni, with assistance from Claus Westermann. Translated by Mark E. Biddle. 3 vols. Peabody, MA: Hendrickson, 1997
TUGAL	Texte und Untersuchungen zur Geschichte der altchristlichen Literatur
VT	*Vetus Testamentum*
VTSup	Supplements to Vetus Testamentum
ZAH	*Zeitschrift für Althebraistik*
ZAW	*Zeitschrift für die alttestamentliche Wissenschaft*
ZDMG	*Zeitschrift der deutschen morgenländischen Gesellschaft*
ZECOT	Zondervan Exegetical Commentary on the Old Testament
ZKT	*Zeitschrift für katholische Theologie*

FOREWORD

A *dvances in the Study of Biblical Hebrew and Aramaic* is a masterpiece that reveals the complexities of Biblical Hebrew and Aramaic and the various approaches through which scholars have attempted to uncover the most accurate meaning of the text. This volume includes the latest and best scholarship on the study of Biblical Hebrew and Aramaic. The tome is well-written, thorough, current, and a must-read for all serious students of Semitic languages.

I met Ben Noonan at Hebrew Union College–Jewish Institute of Religion, Cincinnati, while serving in the position of Director of Hebrew Language Instruction. Ben and his wife Jenn were pursuing graduate studies under the guidance of Professor Stephen A. Kaufman, who had also served as my doctoral advisor. Since Ben, Jenn, and I were fascinated by the field of comparative Semitics, our interests brought us together numerous times over the years to work on scholarly projects and participate in academic conferences together. I had the pleasure of having Ben and his wife Jenn in my home and loved to engage with them on topics related to the field of Semitic languages.

Ben, Jenn, and I co-edited the Festschrift *"Where Shall Wisdom Be Found:" A Grammatical Tribute for Stephen A. Kaufman*. This collaborative project revealed Ben as a serious researcher, an excellent writer, and a thorough editor. I will never forget working on the manuscript overseas while teaching Biblical Hebrew to seminarians in India. Ben, Jenn, and I communicated almost daily via email while I was teaching at the Hyderabad Institute of Theology and Apologetics (HITHA). At the time, I was living in an apartment that had no internet connection. It was in the school's office that I downloaded and printed the documents. I edited the chapters between classes and returned them to him the next day or as quickly as I could. Ben and Jenn worked tirelessly to advance the project, communicate with contributors, edit the manuscript, write their own chapters, and bring it to completion by the due date.

In this new publication, *Advances in the Study of Biblical Hebrew and Aramaic*, Ben Noonan covers topics central to the field of Semitic studies: the long history of scholarship on Biblical Hebrew and Biblical Aramaic, lexicology and lexicography, the verbal system—morphology, stems, voice, aspect, *Aktionsart*, and mood—discourse analysis, word order, linguistic variations, dating of texts, and pedagogy for biblical languages. I know of no other publication that brings together as comprehensively and as cohesively these important topics in Biblical Hebrew and Aramaic as the present volume.

Linguistics is a term that often creates tension in language learners. As the author notes, it frequently "conjures up bad memories of learning grammar in grade school" (p. 31). In this volume, Ben successfully elucidates the complexities of linguistic terminology and establishes the value of linguistics for the study of Biblical Hebrew and Aramaic. The author defines the terms with precision. He provides a clear description of each approach and presents each view with care and accuracy. Although the field of linguistics is multifaceted and complex, it is certainly crucial for the study of Biblical Hebrew and Aramaic. In the section entitled Relevance for Biblical Hebrew and Biblical Aramaic, Ben connects the various linguistic theories to Hebrew and Aramaic and demonstrates how each theory contributes in one form or another to a deeper understanding of the biblical text.

Ben's overview of verbal stems is exemplary in that it presents a clear synopsis of modern scholarly views. For example, in his important discussion on the Piel stem, Ben elaborates on the views of prominent scholars on the functions of the Piel (Hebrew) and Pael (Aramaic)—i.e., intensive, causative, complex active, resultative, pluralitive, factitive, iterative, denominative, or a combination of these. He highlights and adopts the typological nature of the Piel stem based on Kaufman's work on Afro-Asiatic languages, "the major language family to which the Semitic languages belong" (p. 103). Ben adopts Kaufman's important insight that "any overarching paradigm for the verbal stems should be limited to the active-stative dichotomy" (p. 116) rather than attributing a single primary function to each stem.

The origin and functions of the *qatal*, *yiqtol*, *wayyiqtol*, and *weqatal* have been visited and revisited numerous times over the past decades. Recent scholarly studies of these verbal forms—including studies on tense, aspect, and mood (TAM)—are plentiful and represent several views. These include the long-standing tense-prominent theory, the common aspect-prominent theory, and the less common mood-prominent theory. The impressive bibliography that appears at the end of this volume attests to the attention these verbal forms and theories have received over the past century.

Discourse analysis, also known as text-linguistics, is beginning to take root in the study of Biblical Hebrew and Aramaic. Scholars of biblical languages have recently turned to its three foundational notions, i.e., coherence and cohesion, discourse units and relations, and information structure, for the study of Hebrew and Aramaic. Highlighting the use of discourse markers such as conjunctions, deictic particles, lexical and morphosyntactic patterns, thematic groupings, and other such features, Ben shows the importance of discourse analysis for the study of Biblical Hebrew and Aramaic. It "falls within the realm of pragmatics because it looks at language in use rather than language as an abstraction" (p. 145).

In recent scholarship, issues related to word order in Biblical Hebrew and Aramaic have been addressed under markedness, dominance, frequency, distribution, and pragmatics. Traditionally, the VSO word order in Biblical Hebrew has been identified as dominant due to its statistically high frequency in narrative prose. However, this view has been challenged by scholars such as Robert Holmstedt who argues that since the *wayyiqtol* (that requires a VSO word order) appears primarily in a delineated environment, a pragmatically marked SVO seems to be the predominant word order in Biblical Hebrew. In Biblical Aramaic, although SVO seems to be the predominant word order, scholars who have treated this topic have mostly advocated for a free word order rather than a fixed pattern.

During the past two decades, the field of biblical studies has witnessed new advances in the teaching of Biblical Hebrew and Aramaic. Pedagogy for biblical languages has welcomed communicative approaches based on Second Language Acquisition practices—listening, speaking, reading, and writing— Total Physical Response Storytelling (TPRS), Content-Based Instruction, and Processing Instruction. New textbooks include visuals, audio files, interactive activities, websites, comic-strips, color-coded features, visual vocabulary PowerPoints, and much more. Proponents of these pedagogies offer intensive workshops for instructors who wish to learn living language approaches for the teaching of biblical languages. Ben is a practitioner of the communicative approach for Biblical Hebrew and Aramaic. His participation in sessions on applied linguistics at the Evangelical Theological Society (ETS) and Society of Biblical Literature (SBL) attests to his commitment to this new pedagogy for biblical languages.

Ben Noonan is a serious scholar of Biblical Hebrew and Aramaic whose understanding of comparative Semitics is wide-ranging. The application of his knowledge to the study of Biblical Hebrew and Aramaic will no doubt be far-reaching. The production of this magnificent tome shows the seriousness of Ben's commitment to the field of Semitic studies. The volume will greatly benefit academics and students of Biblical Hebrew and Aramaic for years to come.

Hélène Dallaire, PhD
Earl S. Kalland Professor of Old Testament and Semitic Languages,
Denver Seminary

PREFACE

This book grew out of a commitment to the scholarly study of Biblical Hebrew and Biblical Aramaic, a commitment I want as many others as possible to share. My dedication to biblical language scholarship was first instilled in me by my Hebrew teachers, especially Stephen A. Kaufman. Through my classes with him I came to see the benefits of studying Biblical Hebrew and Biblical Aramaic as real languages, within their ancient Semitic context. It was largely as a result of his teaching that I have fallen in love with the academic study of Hebrew and Aramaic, and I hope readers will see his influence throughout.

I want to thank my students at Columbia International University. I am grateful for their interest in the biblical languages and for encouraging me to continue to grow in my understanding of Biblical Hebrew and Biblical Aramaic. Their questions and insights challenge me to think more deeply about the biblical languages and to become the best teacher and scholar I can be. My students serve daily as a reminder of why I do what I do, and for this I am very thankful.

I am also grateful to Zondervan for making the publication of this book possible. It has been a pleasure to work with a publisher who is committed to producing excellent resources in the service of the academy and the church. I am especially thankful to Nancy Erickson for her support of this book and her expert guidance in bringing this book to publication. It is because of her dedication to this project that it has become a reality. A special thanks also goes to Hélène Dallaire for writing the foreword to this book.

I dedicate this book to all students of Biblical Hebrew and Biblical Aramaic. It is my hope that this book helps them to become better interpreters of the Hebrew Bible so that they may be more faithful in their exegesis and more effective in their ministry.

INTRODUCTION

You cannot read the Bible for yourself unless you know the languages
in which it was written. . . . Hence if we want to know the Scriptures,
to the study of Greek and Hebrew we must go.

—J. Gresham Machen[1]

Many would agree that the study of Biblical Hebrew and Biblical Aramaic is necessary for those who want to interpret the Hebrew Bible faithfully. But, to truly study Hebrew and Aramaic requires an understanding of the way these languages work, which in turn requires familiarity with scholarship on these languages. This presents a challenge to many readers of the Hebrew Bible. They face the unfortunate fact that such scholarship is often technical, filled with unfamiliar terms and theories, and inaccessible to those outside the guild. Given these difficulties, they may even wonder why linguistic scholarship matters for reading the Hebrew Bible.

This book addresses this dilemma by providing an accessible introduction to the world of Biblical Hebrew and Biblical Aramaic scholarship.[2] My aim is that this book will introduce anyone who engages with the Hebrew and Aramaic of the Bible—students, pastors, professors, and scholars—to current issues of interest on these languages. The desired goal is a better understanding of what the key issues are in Hebrew and Aramaic scholarship and why they matter.

---

1. Machen, "Purpose and Plan," 6.
2. As such, this book serves as the Hebrew Bible counterpart to Campbell, *Advances in the Study of Greek.*

0.1 WHAT IS THIS BOOK ABOUT?

As already mentioned, this book surveys issues of interest in Biblical Hebrew and Biblical Aramaic scholarship. By this I mean that it explores issues that set new directions for interpretation and scholarship of the Hebrew Bible. I have intentionally selected the issues I address in this book because they reflect significant advances—and in some cases, controversy—in the field. I have not selected issues that have not seen much development or controversy in recent years because these issues do not represent genuine advances in the field. This book is not intended to be a general introduction to Biblical Hebrew and Biblical Aramaic scholarship but a survey of developments in the study of these languages.

Throughout, this book focuses on advances in the study of *Biblical* Hebrew and *Biblical* Aramaic. In other words, its concern is not with more general scholarship on Hebrew and Aramaic because I have a particular readership in mind: those who seek to understand the Hebrew Bible. At the same time, it is not possible to completely separate the study of Biblical Hebrew and Biblical Aramaic from their broader Semitic context. Accordingly, as necessary I situate Biblical Hebrew and Biblical Aramaic within what is known of the Semitic languages, and Hebrew and Aramaic in particular. I hope that this makes the book useful to others whose primary interest may not be the Hebrew Bible.

0.2 WHY IS THIS BOOK NEEDED?

No other book surveying modern advances in the study of Biblical Hebrew and Biblical Aramaic currently exists. This is true despite the many exciting developments that have taken place in the field over the past several decades. As a result of the application of modern linguistic approaches, we have a better understanding of what Biblical Hebrew and Biblical Aramaic words mean, the function of specific verbal forms, the structure of discourse, the Hebrew Bible's linguistic diversity, and even teaching Biblical Hebrew and Biblical Aramaic. Unfortunately, the scattered studies that treat these topics individually tend to be inaccessible for the average reader.

This book presents the most important areas of development for students, pastors, professors, and scholars so that they might apply these advances to their study of the Hebrew Bible. This is important because the study of Biblical Hebrew and Biblical Aramaic ultimately affects everyone interested in the Hebrew Bible, whether they know it or not. The advances that have taken place lead us to new insights, enhance our exegesis, and correct misunderstandings.

If knowledge of the biblical languages truly is necessary for understanding the Hebrew Bible, then we ignore any advances to our peril, as the history of Biblical Hebrew and Biblical Aramaic scholarship confirms.

0.3 WHAT TOPICS DOES THIS BOOK INCLUDE, AND WHY?

The first chapter addresses linguistics and the major schools of linguistic thought. The complexity of linguistic terminology and ideas has played a large role in making Biblical Hebrew and Biblical Aramaic scholarship inaccessible. So, chapter one explains and clarifies many of the key concepts and theories in linguistics. The topics addressed in this chapter thereby provide the reader with the knowledge base necessary to understand the rest of the book.

The second chapter also sets the stage for the remainder of the book. It does so by surveying the history of Biblical Hebrew and Biblical Aramaic scholarship, especially as it relates to the concepts and theories discussed in chapter one. By knowing the history of scholarship, we can better comprehend modern trends in Biblical Hebrew and Biblical Aramaic scholarship, understand where they have come from, and appreciate current issues of debate and controversy.

Chapter three examines lexicology (the meaning of words) and lexicography (the making of dictionaries). Despite many advances in lexicology, biblical scholars have been particularly slow to incorporate them. This necessarily impacts exegesis, which directly depends on the meaning of words, and word studies in particular. Advances in lexicology, in turn, affect the use of dictionaries, which are crucial tools for anyone reading Hebrew and Aramaic.

The next several chapters discuss the Biblical Hebrew and Biblical Aramaic verbal systems. Chapter four surveys recent scholarship on the verbal stems. Especially significant developments have taken place in our understanding of the Niphal and Piel. These developments, which deal in part with grammatical voice, are analogous to the rejection of deponency in Biblical Greek. Like this advance, these developments are controversial but important because they directly impact the way we understand the function of these stems.

Chapter five examines tense, aspect, and mood in both Biblical Hebrew and Biblical Aramaic. For nearly 2000 years the dominant view was that the verbal conjugations primarily expressed tense. Within the last one-hundred years, however, much scholarship has advanced the idea that aspect is most important. This has generated significant discussion regarding the function of the verbal conjugations and the role that modern linguistic concepts like grammaticalization play in our understanding of their meaning.

Chapter six deals with an especially popular topic, discourse analysis. Current interest in discourse analysis reflects a broader trend within linguistics to explore meaning within real-life contexts of usage. Not only are there a variety of approaches to discourse analysis of Biblical Hebrew and Biblical Aramaic texts, there are also a growing number of resources for applying discourse analysis to the Hebrew Bible. Discourse analysis ultimately enhances our understanding of what the Hebrew Bible's authors were trying to do with their words.

Chapter seven treats the related topic of word order in Biblical Hebrew and Biblical Aramaic. Although traditionally Hebrew has been understood as a verb-subject-object language, recent years have seen proponents of the order subject-verb-object. There has also been much discussion in the past few decades of word order in Biblical Aramaic. The word order debate directly impacts exegesis because departure from standard word order can draw attention to a particular word or clause, but we cannot know what words are highlighted without first knowing what that standard word order is.

The next two chapters investigate linguistic variation within the Hebrew Bible. Chapter eight discusses register, dialect, style-shifting, and code-switching. Although perhaps lesser known issues, these topics have significant exegetical implications for the language choices made by the biblical authors. These topics also reflect the current popularity of sociolinguistics, or the study of linguistic variation, within the field of linguistics.

Chapter nine examines the question of whether some of the Hebrew Bible's linguistic variation is chronological in nature. Traditionally, scholars have argued that older linguistic features in the Hebrew Bible can be distinguished from newer ones. Challenges to this view have led to refinement in the way we understand the dating of biblical texts. This ongoing debate has a very practical application in that dating biblical texts can help establish the historical context of specific passages, a necessary part of exegesis.

The tenth, and final, chapter explores pedagogy of the biblical languages. This important topic does not relate to the study of Biblical Hebrew and Biblical Aramaic, at least not properly speaking. However, how we view pedagogy has obvious impact on anyone learning them or teaching them to others. Insights from the field of second language acquisition have produced some exciting advances in how we go about learning the biblical languages.

0.4 HOW SHOULD THIS BOOK BE USED?

This book can be used by students, pastors, professors, and scholars for both personal study and classroom use. Its accessibility makes it ideal for anyone interested in learning more about the study of Biblical Hebrew and Biblical Aramaic and how this study impacts our interpretation of the Hebrew Bible. In the classroom, it would serve well as a textbook in second-year Hebrew courses, especially as a supplement to other textbooks treating advanced Hebrew grammar. Those interested in pursuing further study of Biblical Hebrew and Biblical Aramaic, those presently involved in postgraduate study, and current scholars will especially benefit from using this book.

With these potential uses in mind, I have tried to strike a helpful balance between presenting developments as comprehensively as possible without sacrificing accessibility. Each chapter sketches a basic outline of the topic it covers, evaluating the strengths and weaknesses of the different advances that have taken place. I strive to present this information as objectively as possible, but I do not keep from making my own opinions and conclusions known; my own views should not dissuade the reader from forming their own conclusions. The "Modern Linguistic Framework" sections found after the introduction in each chapter as well as the "Further Reading" resources listed at the end of each chapter provide excellent starting points for those wishing to dig deeper.

0.5 WHAT ARE THE INTENDED OUTCOMES OF THIS BOOK?

My overarching goal is that whoever reads this book will gain a meaningful understanding of the key issues in Biblical Hebrew and Biblical Aramaic scholarship, and why they matter. This entails several outcomes related to biblical interpretation, teaching, and scholarship. Each of these outcomes is, furthermore, practical in nature. They aim to encourage faithful exegesis of the Hebrew Bible and to foster more effective ministry in whatever contexts readers serve.

Regarding biblical interpretation, I hope that readers of this book will be better equipped to read the Hebrew Bible in its original languages with linguistic sensitivity and an accurate understanding of what it communicates. Regarding teaching, I hope that readers of this book will be empowered to communicate the Hebrew Bible to others more accurately and to teach the biblical languages in an informed way. Finally, regarding scholarship, I hope that readers of this book will come to grasp the foundational issues in current scholarship, empowering them to engage with that scholarship and perhaps even contribute to it.

CHAPTER 1

A SHORT INTRODUCTION *to* LINGUISTICS *and* LINGUISTIC THEORIES

All scholars interested in biblical language owe it to themselves to acquire a basic competence in linguistics.

—ADINA MOSHAVI AND TANIA NOTARIUS[1]

1.1 INTRODUCTION

Many students, pastors, and even scholars of the Hebrew Bible shudder at the mention of the term *linguistics*. For some, linguistics conjures up bad memories of learning grammar in grade school. They ask, "If I struggled so much with grammar in school, how can I ever understand linguistics?" For others, linguistics seems irrelevant. They ask, "Why does linguistics matter? I can understand the Hebrew and Aramaic of the Old Testament just fine without it."

Questions like these reflect a long-standing tension. Traditionally we have done a good job learning Biblical Hebrew and Biblical Aramaic, but a not so good job of understanding these languages in light of linguistics. This is a problem because—as this book will demonstrate—linguistics directly impacts exegesis. Whether we realize it or not, we each have our own understanding of linguistics that we bring to the table when we read Hebrew and Aramaic. An informed understanding will produce good results, but a poor understanding will produce bad results. To ignore linguistics is to bring harm to our understanding of the Hebrew Bible, which then weakens our effectiveness in ministry and the academy.

---

1. Moshavi and Notarius, "Biblical Hebrew Linguistics," 16.

Nevertheless, the fact remains that linguistics is a relatively specialized, technical field. To remedy this situation, in this chapter I sketch a selective outline of linguistics and key linguistic theories. I begin by defining linguistics and presenting its various subfields. Then I survey the most important approaches to linguistics and discuss their relevance for Biblical Hebrew and Biblical Aramaic. This chapter thereby lays the necessary foundation for understanding the concepts explored in more detail throughout this book.

1.2 WHAT IS LINGUISTICS?

1.2.1. Defining Linguistics

Linguistics can be defined as the scientific study of language,[2] and a linguist is someone who studies linguistics.[3] As a scientific field of study, linguistics uses empirical research to investigate the languages of the world. Furthermore, its primary goal is descriptive rather than prescriptive. Linguistics does not aim to say how language should be used but to describe what language is like and how language is used in actual practice.[4]

1.2.2 Core Branches of Linguistics

The field of linguistics has many different branches, or levels of organization. Linguists relate these branches in different ways and have varying perspectives on which ones represent the core of linguistic analysis.[5] But, many linguists represent the core of linguistic study with some variation of the following branches: phonetics, phonology, morphology, syntax, semantics, and pragmatics.[6] Each branch directly relates to the study of Biblical Hebrew and Biblical Aramaic in its own way.

Phonetics and phonology both relate to the physical sounds of a language. *Phonetics* deals with the physical way that speech sounds are produced (i.e., pronounced) and heard, whereas *phonology* deals with the way that languages pattern their sounds.[7] Every language has its own set of sounds pronounced in a particular way and puts those sounds together in particular ways. For example,

---

2. Crystal, *Dictionary of Linguistics and Phonetics*, 283; McGregor, *Linguistics*, 2; Akmajian et al., *Linguistics*, 5.

3. Crystal, *Dictionary of Linguistics and Phonetics*, 282.

4. McGregor, *Linguistics*, 2–3.

5. Crystal, *Cambridge Encyclopedia of Language*, 84–85.

6. In the broadest sense, all these branches together describe grammar. More properly, though, in linguistics the term *grammar* subsumes only morphology and syntax. See Crystal, *Dictionary of Linguistics and Phonetics*, 218.

7. McGregor, *Linguistics*, 4; Crystal, *Dictionary of Linguistics and Phonetics*, 363, 365.

in Hebrew a *shewa* will be either silent or vocal depending on where it occurs in a word and the type of vowel (short or long) it follows. Furthermore, when vocal, the *shewa* is pronounced as a short, reduced vowel.

Morphology deals with the way that word units are structured and patterned.[8] Many words can be analyzed in terms of their various components, called *morphemes*, that have a specific grammatical function. Likewise, Hebrew and Aramaic use different morphemes to mark key features of nouns and verbs. For example, the final ָה- on the noun מַלְכָּה ("queen") represents the feminine singular morpheme, which tells us that מַלְכָּה is feminine singular. As another example, the ending תִּי- on the verb אָמַרְתִּי ("I spoke") represents the *qatal* first-person common singular morpheme, which tells us that אָמַרְתִּי is a *qatal* first-person common singular verb.

Syntax deals with the way that words are patterned to form phrases and sentences.[9] Words can be categorized according to their role in a sentence or clause and often have different positions depending on their function. Hebrew and Aramaic are no different, and we can examine syntax at both the phrasal and sentence level. For example, in the phrase אִשָּׁה חֲכָמָה ("wise woman"), the adjective חֲכָמָה modifies the noun אִשָּׁה. As another example, in the sentence בָּרָא אֱלֹהִים אֵת הַשָּׁמַיִם וְאֵת הָאָרֶץ ("God created the heavens and the earth"), בָּרָא is the verb, אֱלֹהִים serves as the subject, and הַשָּׁמַיִם and הָאָרֶץ serve as the direct objects.

Finally, semantics and pragmatics deal with meaning. *Semantics* examines the encoding of meaning through individual words or through grammatical (i.e., morphological or syntactical) features, whereas *pragmatics* looks at how a particular context determines meaning.[10] Hebrew and Aramaic both express meaning through words and grammatical constructions, and that meaning will naturally depend on the specific context of usage. For example, the word סֵפֶר in Hebrew refers generally to a written document. Depending on the context, however, the type of written document it denotes may take the form of a scroll (e.g., Jer 36:8), letter (e.g., 2 Sam 11:14–15), legal deed or certificate (Deut 24:1, 3), or royal edict (e.g., Esth 9:25).

1.2.3. Other Branches of Linguistics

Beyond these core levels, several other key branches are important for linguistics, many of which overlap with other disciplines. These include language typology, historical linguistics, sociolinguistics, discourse analysis, and

---

8. McGregor, *Linguistics*, 4; Crystal, *Dictionary of Linguistics and Phonetics*, 314.

9. McGregor, *Linguistics*, 4; Crystal, *Dictionary of Linguistics and Phonetics*, 471.

10. McGregor, *Linguistics*, 4; Crystal, *Dictionary of Linguistics and Phonetics*, 428.

language acquisition.[11] As is the case with the core branches, each of these additional branches is important in its own way for the study of Biblical Hebrew and Biblical Aramaic.

Language typology, also known as *typological linguistics*, is the study of structural similarities between languages, regardless of their history. The goal of this branch of linguistics is to establish a classification, or typology, of language.[12] Language typology is important for Hebrew and Aramaic because we can compare proposed functions with the way that languages typically work across the world. Particularly of interest here are the verbal system and word order.

Historical linguistics is the study of how languages change over time. It explores the reasons for language change. It also tries to reconstruct the past histories of and relationships between different languages.[13] Placing Hebrew and Aramaic within their broader Semitic context can enhance our understanding of these languages. Specific areas of application include determining the meaning of Hebrew and Aramaic words, tracing the development of the verbal system, and distinguishing between earlier and later stages of the Hebrew and Aramaic preserved in the Bible.

Sociolinguistics is the study of language in its social context. It examines the variation in languages that can be explained through social, rather than purely historical, factors. Thus, it deals with topics such as register, dialect, and stylistic variation.[14] This branch of linguistics is relevant for Hebrew and Aramaic because the Hebrew Bible contains much evidence for sociolinguistic variation. A knowledge of sociolinguistics can help us to identify this variation, to determine the reason for it, and to distinguish it from variation due to historical language change.

Discourse analysis is the study of patterns in language and how those patterns affect meaning. It therefore deals with the way that stretches of languages—spoken or written—are connected together and structured.[15] Discourse analysis is especially important for the study of Hebrew and Aramaic because the Hebrew Bible consists of extended texts put together in a certain way. Understanding the way these texts have been put together and structured can enhance our comprehension of their meaning.

---

11. Many other branches could be discussed here, such as anthropological linguistics, computational linguistics, forensic linguistics, neurolinguistics, psycholinguistics, quantitative linguistics, statistical linguistics, and text and corpus linguistics (cf. Crystal, *Dictionary of Linguistics and Phonetics*, 285). The list here is naturally selective and focuses on the branches most directly relevant for linguistic study of Hebrew and Aramaic.

12. McGregor, *Linguistics*, 5; Crystal, *Dictionary of Linguistics and Phonetics*, 499.

13. McGregor, *Linguistics*, 5; Crystal, *Dictionary of Linguistics and Phonetics*, 440–41.

14. McGregor, *Linguistics*, 5; Crystal, *Dictionary of Linguistics and Phonetics*, 229.

15. McGregor, *Linguistics*, 5; Crystal, *Dictionary of Linguistics and Phonetics*, 148.

Language acquisition is the study of the process of acquiring comprehension and production of a language. It can deal with either how children learn their first language or how adults learn languages other than their native tongue.[16] Learning Biblical Hebrew and Biblical Aramaic falls within the latter category, known as *second language acquisition*. This branch of linguistics is relevant for Hebraists and Aramaicists because it can provide insight into how we should, or should not, teach and learn these languages.

1.3 MAJOR APPROACHES TO LINGUISTICS

Language has been studied for more than four millennia, beginning in antiquity. Grammatical discussions from ancient Mesopotamia, India, and China testify to the study of language from a very early period, and the Greeks and Romans laid the foundation for Western linguistics.[17] But the modern study of language finds its origins much later in the eighteenth and nineteenth centuries, and modern linguistics during the twentieth century.

The past several centuries attest to several key linguistic approaches: Comparative Philology, Structuralism, Generative Grammar, Functionalism, and Cognitive Linguistics. Each of these approaches has its own unique characteristics that set it apart, although naturally some theories exhibit overlap. Furthermore, each of these linguistic approaches is important for understanding modern linguistics and its application to Hebrew and Aramaic.

1.3.1 Comparative Philology
1.3.1.1 Overview and History of Comparative Philology

Beginning with the sixteenth century, Europeans were exposed to many different languages through voyages, conquests, trade, and colonization. This prompted language comparison for both grammar and the lexicon.[18] By the eighteenth century, interest had shifted from comparison of various native African, Asian, and American languages to comparison of Indo-European languages. Individuals like Sir William Jones (1746–1794), Christian Jacob Kraus (1753–1807), Rasmus Rask (1787–1832), Franz Bopp (1791–1867), and Jacob Grimm (1785–1863) explored the implications of these comparisons for relating the languages to each other.[19]

---

16. McGregor, *Linguistics*, 5; Crystal, *Dictionary of Linguistics and Phonetics*, 8.

17. Bodine, "Linguistics and Biblical Studies," 4:327.

18. Campbell, "History of Linguistics," 100–1; Jankowsky, "Comparative, Historical, and Typological Linguistics," 635–37.

19. Campbell, "History of Linguistics," 101–5; Jankowsky, "Comparative, Historical, and Typological Linguistics," 637–50; Seuren, *Western Linguistics*, 79–89.

These explorations led to the development of Comparative Philology, which came to dominate linguistic study until the twentieth century. This approach sought to learn about history and culture through the study of ancient written texts like the Hebrew Bible and classical literature. It also sought to reconstruct the history of the languages in which these texts were written, all with the goal of better understanding those texts. Thus, Comparative Philology emphasizes the diachronic nature of language and uses linguistic comparison as a means of better understanding grammar and the lexicon.[20]

Comparative Philology largely gave way to other linguistic approaches around the beginning of the twentieth century. This was mainly due to that era's growing emphasis on synchronic rather than diachronic language study. However, the historical-comparative approach continues to remain important; even today, more linguists list historical linguistics—the branch of linguistics that shares much of Comparative Philology's approach—as one of their areas of specialization than any other subfield of linguistics.[21] This approach's enduring influence is evident, for example, in recent interest in grammaticalization.[22]

1.3.1.2 Key Tenets of Comparative Philology

Comparative Philology emphasizes the diachronic study of language. It entails three tenets: philology, the importance of language change, and use of the comparative method. These three notions directly relate to one another in that the comparative method permits reconstruction of past language change as attested in written documents.

1.3.1.2.1 PHILOLOGY

As its name implies, Comparative Philology gives primacy to philology. Although originally the term *philology* (from Greek φιλολογία) meant "love of learning and literature," it has since come to refer to the historical study of texts.[23] It focuses especially on ancient texts, which pose a unique set of challenges because no living speakers of their languages exist today. One way that philology addresses these challenges is through linguistic reconstruction. This entails attention to historical linguistics as well as other fields of study, like textual criticism and literary criticism.[24]

---

20. Jankowsky, "Comparative, Historical, and Typological Linguistics," 648; Seuren, *Western Linguistics*, 79.

21. Campbell, *Historical Linguistics*, 2.

22. Campbell, "History of Linguistics," 113–14.

23. Koerner, "Linguistics vs Philology," 168.

24. Campbell, *Historical Linguistics*, 391–92.

1.3.1.2.2 The Comparative Method

Comparative Philology also holds to the importance of the comparative method. The similarities between some languages (e.g., between English and German) are best explained by a common origin. The image of a family tree is helpful and therefore commonly used: these languages, said to be within the same language family, are "genetically descended" from a single original language (i.e., a protolanguage). The comparative method compares genetically related languages to reconstruct their history, including the various changes that have taken place in those languages. This process of reconstruction, the task of philology, helps us to understand ancient texts better.[25]

1.3.1.2.3 Language Change

Comparative Philology's final foundational notion is the importance of language change. Language change may originate within a language due to physical or psychological factors or may be prompted by contact with another language. Regardless of the cause, linguists identify many different kinds of language change. These can affect language at various levels, including phonology, morphology, syntax, and semantics.[26] One type of syntactic change that has become an important topic of study in recent years is grammaticalization, or the process by which words are given a grammatical function (e.g., English *will*, originally meaning "want," is now a future-tense marker).[27]

1.3.1.3 Relevance for Biblical Hebrew and Biblical Aramaic

Comparative Philology is less popular today than it was during the eighteenth and nineteenth centuries. Yet, it has significantly influenced the study of Hebrew and Aramaic because academic study of the biblical languages emerged while Comparative Philology was flourishing.[28] Furthermore, a good number of modern Hebrew and Aramaic scholars have been trained in Comparative Philology. They point to the importance of comparative Semitics for understanding the Hebrew Bible. Well-known Semiticists like J. A. Emerton, John Huehnergard, and Stephen A. Kaufman belong to this mold.[29]

The historical-comparative tradition also lies behind many modern grammars

---

25. Campbell, *Historical Linguistics*, 107–44; Hock and Joseph, *Language History, Language Change, and Language Relationship*, 427–54.

26. Hock and Joseph, *Language History, Language Change, and Language Relationship*, 8–14.

27. Campbell, *Historical Linguistics*, 281–85.

28. Thompson and Widder, "Major Approaches to Linguistics," 91–93.

29. E.g., Emerton, "Comparative Semitic Philology and Hebrew Lexicography," 1–24; Kaufman, "Classification of the North West Semitic Dialects," 41–57; idem, "Semitics," 273–82; Huehnergard, "Early Hebrew Prefix-Conjugations," 19–23; idem, "Hebrew Relative šɛ-," 103–25.

and lexicons. This is in part due to the enduring influence of Wilhelm Gesenius, whose grammar (*Hebräische Grammatik*) and lexicon (*Hebräisches und aramäisches Handwörterbuch über das Alte Testament*) still serve as standard reference works today. Comparative Philology's influence does not stop with Gesenius, however. In terms of grammar, Comparative Philology lies behind many current discussions of the Hebrew verbal system. In terms of the lexicon, two of the most popular Hebrew dictionaries—Francis Brown, S. R. Driver, and Charles A. Briggs's *A Hebrew and English Lexicon of the Old Testament* and Ludwig Köhler and Walter Baumgartner's *The Hebrew and Aramaic Lexicon of the Old Testament*—are based on Comparative Philology.

1.3.2 Structuralism
1.3.2.1 Overview and History of Structuralism

Structuralism emerged as a reaction against Comparative Philology. Two structuralist schools of thought arose, one in Europe and one in the United States. Although different, both viewed language as a system to be studied and described scientifically. They emphasized study of the structures—linguistic elements like phonemes and morphemes—that make up languages. This approach serves as a major turning point in linguistic thought because it shifted the focus from diachronic to synchronic analysis.[30]

In Europe, Structuralism can be traced to the work of the Swiss linguist Ferdinand de Saussure (1857–1913). His *Cours de linguistique générale* (*Course in General Linguistics*) was compiled from student notes on his general linguistics course offered at the University of Geneva between 1906 and 1911.[31] For Saussure, a linguistic structure can be defined only through the system of relations it has with other units. Thus, Saussure's Structuralism can be summarized in terms of several dichotomies that I discuss more below, including synchrony versus diachrony, *langue* "language" versus *parole* "speaking," and syntagmatic versus associative relations.[32]

In the United States, the linguist-anthropologists Franz Boas (1858–1942) and Edward Sapir (1884–1939) were the first to develop structuralist thought, but it was Leonard Bloomfield (1887–1949) who gave American Structuralism—also known as Descriptivism—its basic form. Like his predecessors, he emphasized the scientific description of language structure, but he was also influenced by behaviorism and denied a connection between language

---

30. Campbell, "History of Linguistics," 107.
31. Seuren, *Western Linguistics*, 146–47.
32. Graffi, "European Linguistics since Saussure," 470–71; Campbell, "History of Linguistics," 107–8.

and mentalism. Accordingly, Bloomfield argued that language was a response to external stimuli rather than something innate to the brain.[33]

Structuralism had enormous impact on linguistics during the first half of the twentieth century. In Europe, linguists like Émile Benveniste (1902–1976) adopted and further developed Saussure's ideas. Several schools of linguistics influenced by Saussure's thought also emerged in Europe, including the Geneva School, the Prague School, and the Copenhagen School.[34] In the United States, linguists like Charles Francis Hockett (1916–2000), Zellig S. Harris (1909–1992), and Bernard Bloch (1907–1965) popularized forms of Bloomfield's Structuralism.[35] Today, almost all approaches to linguistics exhibit at least some influence from Structuralism, especially as formulated by Saussure.[36]

1.3.2.2 Key Tenets of Structuralism

Structuralism's key tenets are best presented through the dichotomies established by Saussure. The most relevant for our purposes are *langue* versus *parole*, synchrony versus diachrony, and syntagmatic versus associative relations.[37] These tenets all relate to Structuralism's view of language as a system in which linguistic structures are defined in relation to one another.

1.3.2.2.1 *Langue* "Language" versus *Parole* "Speaking"

The starting point of Saussure's dichotomies is his distinction between *langue* and *parole*. On the one hand, *langue* (French for "language") refers to an abstract language system, or the common code shared by all the speakers of a given language. On the other hand, *parole* (French for "speaking") refers to the actual use of a language by specific individuals. According to Saussure, the abstract linguistic system—*langue*—rather than its specific usage—*parole*—should be the object of linguistic study.[38]

1.3.2.2.2 Synchrony versus Diachrony

. Saussure also distinguished between synchrony and diachrony. The difference between these two concepts relates to time. Synchronic analysis views a language as a whole system at a specific point in time, whereas diachronic analysis traces the development of a language through time.[39] In reaction to Comparative

---

33. Campbell, "History of Linguistics," 109–11; Sampson, *Schools of Linguistics*, 57–64.

34. Graffi, "European Linguistics since Saussure," 473–81; Seuren, *Western Linguistics*, 157–67.

35. Blevins, "American Descriptivism," 419–37; Seuren, *Western Linguistics*, 207–19.

36. Campbell, "History of Linguistics," 108.

37. Cf. Robins, *Short History of Linguistics*, 224–25.

38. Graffi, "European Linguistics since Saussure," 471.

39. Graffi, "European Linguistics since Saussure," 471–72.

Philology, Saussure argued that synchronic analysis, not diachronic analysis, is primary in linguistic analysis: "The synchronic point of view predominates, for it is the true and only reality to the community of speakers. . . . [If a linguist] takes the diachronic perspective, he no longer observes language [*langue*] but rather a series of events that modify it."[40]

1.3.2.2.3 SYNTAGMATIC VERSUS ASSOCIATIVE RELATIONS

Saussure's final dichotomy distinguishes between syntagmatic and associative relations. On the one hand, a syntagmatic relation is the relationship between two or more signs that go together; for example, the words *a*, *good*, and *teacher* in the phrase *a good teacher*. On the other hand, an associative relation is the relationship between a sign and others that are similar; for example, the word *teacher* can be associated with other words like the plural noun *teachers*, the verb *teach*, and the synonym *professor*. Associative relations like these relate linguistic structures to one another abstractly within a language system (*langue*) rather than actual use (*parole*). Thus, Saussure contended that associative relations are the proper object of linguistic study.[41]

1.3.2.3 Relevance for Biblical Hebrew and Biblical Aramaic

Structuralism has substantially impacted the linguistic study of Hebrew and Aramaic. One of its biggest proponents was James Barr. Although he saw a proper use for Comparative Philology, he critiqued the common abuse of this approach in his *Comparative Philology and the Text of the Old Testament* and *The Semantics of Biblical Language*. Barr argued for a primarily synchronic approach to the biblical languages; he also contended that language is an abstract system, separate from one's worldview. In this Barr clearly follows Saussure's emphasis on *langue* (rather than *parole*) and synchrony (rather than diachrony). One of Barr's students, Moisés Silva, promoted a similar structuralist understanding of linguistics in his *God, Language, and Scripture*.

Much of Hebrew and Aramaic studies today displays influence from Structuralism.[42] Two of the most commonly used reference grammars, Bruce K. Waltke and Michael O'Connor's *An Introduction to Biblical Hebrew Syntax* and Paul Joüon and Takamitsu Muraoka's *A Grammar of Biblical Hebrew*, apply general structuralist principles.[43] However, Structuralism has had the most impact on lexical analysis, which is not surprising given Saussure's focus

---

40. Saussure, *Course in General Linguistics*, 90.
41. Graffi, "European Linguistics since Saussure," 472; Seuren, *Western Linguistics*, 243–44.
42. Merwe, "Some Recent Trends," 14–15.
43. Cf. *BHRG* §3.4.

on words as the object of linguistic analysis.[44] David J. A. Clines's widely used lexicon, *Dictionary of Classical Hebrew*, is structuralist, as is evident from its lack of comparative data and its focus on how words are used in relation to one another. Silva has done much to popularize structuralist semantics, especially among Christians, in his *Biblical Words and Their Meaning*.

1.3.3 Generative Grammar
1.3.3.1 Overview and History of Generative Grammar

Generative Grammar originated in the United States as an alternative to Bloomfield's Structuralism. Its primary proponent was Noam Chomsky (born 1928), who revolutionized the linguistics world when he published his *Syntactic Structures* in 1957. Chomsky argued that, contra Bloomfield, language does stem from some internal, innate ability. Every person possesses a basic linguistic "competence" in their language without having been taught. This competence enables everyone to generate a potentially infinite number of linguistic combinations.[45]

The task of linguistics, according to Chomsky, is to determine a "universal grammar." This universal grammar represents the internal, innate ability in the brain. For Chomsky, only an underlying universal grammar shared by all humanity can explain why a person can possess competency in their language without any formal training.[46] In this, Chomsky departs sharply from Structuralism—not only Bloomfield's descriptivism, but also Structuralism as formulated by Saussure—because he sees language as part of the mind and not simply an external, autonomous system.

The significance of Chomsky's work cannot be overstated. Chomsky himself produced several different iterations of his Generative Grammar throughout his career: Standard Theory, Extended Standard Theory (The Lexicalist Hypothesis), Trace Theory, Government and Binding (Principles and Parameters), and the Minimalist Program. Many other spin-off theories sharing Chomskyan principles have also emerged (e.g., Head-Driven Phase Structure Grammar, Lexical-Functional Grammar, and Relational Grammar).[47] Today, Chomsky is "among the ten most-cited writers in all of the humanities (beating out Hegel and Cicero and trailing only Marx, Lenin, Shakespeare, the Bible, Aristotle, Plato, and Freud)."[48]

---

44. Thompson and Widder, "Major Approaches to Linguistics," 100.
45. Campbell, "History of Linguistics," 111.
46. Wasow, "Generative Grammar," 122–23.
47. Campbell, "History of Linguistics," 113.
48. Pinker, *Language Instinct*, 23.

1.3.3.2 Key Tenets of Generative Grammar

Generative Grammar as first formulated by Chomsky can be characterized in terms of three basic tenets: universal grammar, transformations, and competence versus performance. These ideas are logically related to one another and naturally follow from Chomsky's view of language as innate to the human brain. Although Generative Grammar has many varieties today, these three tenets remain foundational to this linguistic approach.

1.3.3.2.1 UNIVERSAL GRAMMAR

First, as already noted, Generative Grammar is based on the premise of a universal grammar. The idea here is that all languages have certain features in common (e.g., the existence of verbs or the ability to give commands). Beneath the world's variety of languages, then, there lies a set of language universals, or features that all languages have in common. These universals together make up a universal grammar, and any differences that exist between languages can be explained through a set of rules.[49] According to Chomsky, the existence of a universal grammar explains why a child without any formal training can speak their native language.[50]

1.3.3.2.2 TRANSFORMATIONS

A second tenet foundational to most theories of Generative Grammar is the importance of transformations. Not only do languages themselves share certain universal features, but so do many sentences within a language. For example, the sentences *I read the book* and *The book was read by me* express the same basic idea—reading a book—even though they each use a different grammatical voice. These sentences' similarities represent an underlying deep structure whereas the differences reflect different surface structures. This is where transformations come in. Each language possesses a set of transformations, or mathematical-like rules, that determine how a single deep structure can manifest itself in various surface structures. Speakers of the language innately know those transformations, which is what enables them to generate a potentially infinite number of sentences.[51]

1.3.3.2.3 PERFORMANCE VERSUS COMPETENCE

A third tenet of Generative Grammar is its distinction between competence and performance. Competence describes people's innate ability to produce a

---

49. Wasow, "Generative Grammar," 122.
50. Wasow, "Generative Grammar," 124–25; Freidin, "Noam Chomsky's Contribution," 453.
51. Wasow, "Generative Grammar," 122–23; Freidin, "Noam Chomsky's Contribution," 447–51.

potentially infinite number of different linguistic expressions. Performance describes the actual output of real speakers, which due to errors of human speech can be messy in practice. According to Chomsky, competence—the idealized, potentially infinite language ability—rather than performance represents the proper object of linguistic study.[52] Any understanding of how a language is actually used therefore requires understanding speakers' unconscious knowledge of that language.[53]

1.3.3.3 Relevance for Biblical Hebrew and Biblical Aramaic

Generative Grammar has not impacted Hebrew and Aramaic studies as much as some other approaches, despite the enormous influence it has had on the field of linguistics. However, the few Hebraists actively promoting Generative Grammar have been quite prolific and have significantly impacted our understanding of Hebrew grammar.[54] In accordance with Generative Grammar's interest in syntax, their work has especially focused on word order and the placement of constituents in clauses. Key scholars here include Vincent DeCaen, Robert D. Holmstedt, and Jacobus A. Naudé.[55] Only a few scholars have explored generative approaches to other topics, like Hebrew phonology.[56]

In addition, generative concepts appear in several key resources for the study of Hebrew and Aramaic. Generative Grammar appears in some standard reference works. For example, Waltke and O'Connor's *Introduction to Biblical Hebrew Syntax* highlights the importance of surface structure versus deep structure for Hebrew syntax and seems to support universal grammar.[57] Various other important resources exhibit influence from Generative Grammar. An example in this category is the Holmstedt-Abegg Syntactic Database of Ancient Hebrew. This resource, an electronic database of Hebrew syntax, is explicitly based on generative principles.[58]

---

52. Chomsky's distinction between competence and performance is somewhat analogous to Saussure's distinction between *langue* and *parole*. Furthermore, like Saussure, Chomsky argues that the abstract language system takes priority over actual language use. See Thompson and Widder, "Major Approaches to Linguistics," 113.

53. Wasow, "Generative Grammar," 121.

54. Cf. Merwe, "Some Recent Trends," 15–17; *BHRG* §3.4.

55. E.g., DeCaen, "Hebrew Linguistics and Biblical Criticism," 1–32; idem, "Unified Analysis of Verbal and Verbless Clauses," 109–31; Holmstedt, *Relative Clause in Biblical Hebrew*; idem, "Word Order and Information Structure," 111–39; Naudé, "Government and Binding," 2:72–76; idem, "Syntactic Analysis of Dislocations," 115–30.

56. E.g., Malone, *Tiberian Hebrew Phonology*.

57. *IBHS* §§3.5c, e.

58. http://individual.utoronto.ca/holmstedt/Ancient_Hebrew_Syntax_Database.html.

1.3.4 Functionalism
1.3.4.1 Overview and History of Functionalism

Functionalism's roots lie in the structuralist Prague School, especially the work of Vilém Mathesius (1882–1945).[59] He and other Prague School members highlighted the function that a language's components have when used to communicate.[60] Linguists in Eastern Europe continued to develop this line of thought after World War II, but Functionalism also spread farther west, particularly in Europe. The work of scholars like Simon C. Dik (born 1940) in the Netherlands and M. A. K. Halliday (born 1925) in England helped to popularize it. Today, Functionalism remains most popular in Europe, although it also has many practitioners on the West Coast of the United States.[61]

True to its origins, Functionalism asserts that the role of language in communication is central to linguistic study and analysis.[62] Functionalists examine the way languages express different speech acts—such as conveying information, asking questions, or giving commands—in different ways. They explore the meaning of and conditions for using different speech acts. They also explore how grammar and word choice are used to say one thing over another. To help them determine why one speech act or construction might be used over another, functionalists often turn to cross-linguistic comparison and linguistic typology.[63]

This brief description demonstrates that Functionalism differs from both Structuralism and Generative Grammar. Functionalism's attention to language use in real-life contexts diverges from Structuralism's focus on language as an abstract system, apart from actual use.[64] Functionalism's view that the purpose of language is communication provides a very different starting point than that of Generative Grammar, which instead sees the communicative functions of language as irrelevant for analysis.[65] In this way, Functionalism exists as an alternative to the two approaches that have dominated much of linguistic thought since the twentieth century.

1.3.4.2 Key Tenets of Functionalism

Today there are three main varieties of Functionalism: Functional Grammar and its newer version, Functional Discourse Grammar; Systemic Functional

---

59. Siewierska, "Functional and Cognitive Grammars," 485–86.
60. Sampson, *Schools of Linguistics*, 103.
61. Siewierska, "Functional and Cognitive Grammars," 486.
62. Van Valin, "Functional Linguistics," 141.
63. Van Valin, "Functional Linguistics," 142–45.
64. Van Valin, "Functional Linguistics," 146–47.
65. Van Valin, "Functional Linguistics," 152–54.

Grammar; and Role and Reference Grammar.[66] The existence of these three varieties demonstrates the diversity that exists within Functionalism. Yet, despite this diversity functionalist thought can be summarized by at least three central tenets: language as communication, the non-autonomy of grammar, and the centrality of meaning.[67]

1.3.4.2.1 LANGUAGE AS COMMUNICATION

First, Functionalism claims that the primary purpose of language is communication. Functionalism does not deny that some uses of language may be non-communicative, but it does contend that the primary function of language is to communicate. All linguistic acts have a variety of functions in common, each of which relate to communication. Language's functions are informative (language makes a particular reality relevant to a communicative situation), intentional (language allows a user to pursue communicative intentions with respect to that reality), and social-contextual (language can be adapted to the specific setting in which communication occurs).[68]

1.3.4.2.2 NON-AUTONOMY OF GRAMMAR

Second, Functionalism contends that grammar is non-autonomous. A language system cannot be abstracted from the real world because it is shaped by various external factors related to how we communicate. These factors—which can be cognitive, socio-cultural, physiological, and diachronic—reflect actual language use in the real world. The analogy of an ecosystem is helpful here. An ecosystem like a rainforest cannot exist or even be understood autonomously because it is interdependent with other ecosystems. In the same way, grammar cannot be isolated from other linguistic systems but must be viewed in relationship to those other systems.[69]

1.3.4.2.3 CENTRALITY OF MEANING

Finally, Functionalism asserts that human language primarily communicates meaning. Functionalism therefore focuses especially on the realms of semantics (what words and sentences mean) and pragmatics (what speakers intend to communicate by using specific forms and constructions). Syntax is subordinate to these two realms because it simply provides one possible way of communicating meaning. Syntax is therefore also subordinate to higher-level

---

66. Van Valin, "Functional Linguistics," 149.
67. Butler, *Structure and Function*, 29.
68. Butler, *Structure and Function*, 2–4.
69. Butler, *Structure and Function*, 5–15.

concerns like discourse analysis. This is because communication of meaning takes place within the context of discourse rather than isolated sentences.[70]

1.3.4.3 Relevance for Biblical Hebrew and Biblical Aramaic

Out of all the linguistic approaches, Functionalism has had the most significant impact on modern Biblical Hebrew and Biblical Aramaic studies. The two primary applications of Functionalism to Hebrew and Aramaic—in both general and specific form—have been pragmatics and discourse analysis. These are natural applications given Functionalism's emphasis on language as communication. Over the past several decades, many scholars have explored these topics and assigned functionalist labels to different grammatical constructions. Other scholars have applied specific models of Functionalism, like Dik's Functional Discourse Grammar, to the linguistic study of the Hebrew Bible.[71] Key scholars here include Randall Buth, Christo H. J. van der Merwe, and Nicolai Winther-Nielsen.[72]

Although Functionalism has appeared in many recent studies of Hebrew and Aramaic, few of the standard reference works incorporate Functionalism to any substantial degree. The noteworthy exception is Christo H. J. van der Merwe, Jacobus A. Naudé, and Jan H. Kroeze's *A Biblical Hebrew Reference Grammar*. This grammar is the first to devote significant attention to issues of discourse analysis and word order. Although it seeks to present Hebrew grammar in as theory-neutral a way as possible, its reliance on functionalist concepts of discourse analysis and word order is evident.[73]

1.3.5 Cognitive Linguistics
1.3.5.1 Overview and History of Cognitive Linguistics

Cognitive Linguistics has no single founder or theory but gradually emerged as a linguistic school of thought during the mid-1970s. It was at this time that George Lakoff (born 1941) used the term "cognitive" to describe his linguistic approach[74] and began work on his foundational *Metaphors We Live By*, co-authored with Mark Johnson (born 1949). It was also around this time

---

70. Butler, *Structure and Function*, 27–28.

71. Merwe, "Some Recent Trends," 17–20; *BHRG* §3.4.

72. E.g., Buth, "Word Order in Aramaic"; idem, "Functional Grammar, Hebrew and Aramaic," 77–102; Merwe, "Discourse Linguistics and Biblical Hebrew Grammar," 13–49; idem, "Overview of Hebrew Narrative Syntax," 1–20; idem, "Explaining Fronting in Biblical Hebrew," 173–86; Winther-Nielsen, *Functional Discourse Grammar of Joshua*.

73. *BHRG* §§46–48.

74. Lakoff and Thompson, "Introducing Cognitive Grammar," 295–313. The term "Cognitive Linguistics" first appears in Lakoff, *Women, Fire, and Dangerous Things*.

that other scholars like Ronald W. Langacker (born 1942) and Leonard Talmy (born 1942) began to lay important foundations for Cognitive Linguistics. Since then, Cognitive Linguistics has developed into a flourishing school of thought.[75]

The basic principle behind Cognitive Linguistics is that linguistics is not just knowledge of a language but is itself a form of knowledge. Cognitive Linguistics sees language as a psychologically real phenomenon and takes the processing and storage of information in the brain as crucial to language.[76] In other words, language encompasses the way that the brain processes and categorizes our interaction with the world.[77] Thus, in Cognitive Linguistics language is all about meaning.[78]

As this brief summary indicates, Cognitive Linguistics departs significantly from both Structuralism and Generative Grammar. Both of these linguistic models see language as an autonomous entity—an abstraction—that exists apart from the brain, but Cognitive Linguistics considers language inextricably linked with cognition.[79] This perspective closely aligns Cognitive Linguistics with Functionalism, which also connects language with its concrete usage. Cognitive Linguistics and Functionalism share significant overlap, although Functionalism has a broader focus on the communicative usage of language, generally speaking.[80]

1.3.5.2 Key Tenets of Cognitive Linguistics

Cognitive Linguistics entails many different research topics, including Prototype Theory, Conceptual Metaphor Theory, and Frame Semantics. Furthermore, several different cognitive frameworks (e.g., Cognitive Grammar) for bringing these concepts together exist, but uniting these concepts and perspectives are at least three basic tenets: perspectival meaning, encyclopedic meaning, and usage-based meaning.[81]

1.3.5.2.1 Perspectival Meaning

Cognitive Linguistics's first tenet is that meaning is not just an objective reflection of the world, but actually shapes the world. Language's categorization

---

75. Nerhlich and Clarke, "Cognitive Linguistics and the History of Linguistics," 591–92.
76. Geeraerts, "Rough Guide to Cognitive Linguistics," 3.
77. Geeraerts and Cuyckens, "Introducing Cognitive Linguistics," 5.
78. Geeraerts, "Rough Guide to Cognitive Linguistics," 3.
79. Taylor, "Cognitive Linguistics and Autonomous Linguistics," 574–81.
80. Cf. Nuyts, "Cognitive Linguistics and Functional Linguistics," 548–52.
81. Geeraerts and Cuyckens, "Introducing Cognitive Linguistics," 5; Geeraerts, "Rough Guide to Cognitive Linguistics," 4–6; cf. Croft and Cruse, *Cognitive Linguistics*, 1–4.

function actually gives a structure to the world, or "embodies" a perspective onto the world.[82] Consider the two sentences, which describe the same situation: *The bicycle is behind the house* and *The bicycle is in front of the house.* Both of these sentences embody a different perspective on the world. On the one hand, the bicycle appears behind the house from your perspective if you're looking at your back yard toward your front yard, where the bicycle is. On the other hand, the bicycle appears in front of the house from the perspective of the house because a house is thought to face the direction of the front yard.[83]

1.3.5.2.2 ENCYCLOPEDIC MEANING

A second tenet of Cognitive Linguistics is that meaning does not exist abstractly apart from the brain. This follows naturally from the tenet that meaning is perspectival. If language meaning is perspectival, then meaning must have a connection with humanity's perspective on the world. Meaning therefore cannot be reduced to a simple dictionary definition. Rather, it is encyclopedic in that it incorporates our understanding of the world. Furthermore, that encyclopedic knowledge is directly impacted by one's life experience. For example, the word *house* will have a different meaning for different people, depending on their life experience with houses.[84]

1.3.5.2.3 USAGE-BASED MEANING

A third tenet of Cognitive Linguistics is its understanding of meaning as usage based. In Cognitive Linguistics, grammar and the lexicon can never be abstracted because they do not simply exist "out there." Rather, grammatical constructions and words are always used as part of actual utterances and actual conversations. They have no meaning apart from their usage in the real world. Thus, in Cognitive Linguistics the study of language must entail the real-life use of grammatical constructions and words, rather than some abstract, idealized system (i.e., Saussure's *langue* and Chomsky's competence).[85]

1.3.5.3 Relevance for Biblical Hebrew and Biblical Aramaic

Although young compared with other approaches, Cognitive Linguistics has a substantial following in Hebrew and Aramaic studies. Naturally, given its

---

82. Geeraerts and Cuyckens, "Introducing Cognitive Linguistics," 5; Geeraerts, "Rough Guide to Cognitive Linguistics," 4.

83. Geeraerts, "Rough Guide to Cognitive Linguistics," 4.

84. Geeraerts and Cuyckens, "Introducing Cognitive Linguistics," 5; Geeraerts, "Rough Guide to Cognitive Linguistics," 4–5.

85. Geeraerts and Cuyckens, "Introducing Cognitive Linguistics," 5; Geeraerts, "Rough Guide to Cognitive Linguistics," 5–6.

focus on meaning, Cognitive Linguistics has primarily impacted Hebrew and Aramaic studies in terms of the lexicon.[86] Both Christo H. J. van der Merwe and Reinier de Blois have pointed out the value of cognitive linguistic concepts, especially encyclopedic and usage-based meaning, for understanding Hebrew word meaning.[87] Blois's online Hebrew lexicon, *The Semantic Dictionary of Biblical Hebrew*, takes as its starting point a cognitive approach to word meaning.[88] Various other applications of Cognitive Linguistics to Hebrew and Aramaic word meaning—especially ones incorporating Prototype Theory, Frame Semantics, and Conceptual Metaphor Theory—have also appeared in recent years.[89]

Cognitive Linguistics has also had some impact on the study of Hebrew and Aramaic grammar. Perhaps the most notable scholar to apply Cognitive Linguistics to Hebrew grammar is Ellen J. van Wolde. She proposes a cognitive approach to Biblical Hebrew grammar and syntax founded on Cognitive Grammar.[90] Other scholars have applied cognitive-based approaches to various aspects of Hebrew and Aramaic studies, such as the verbal system and discourse analysis.[91] As more biblical scholars become familiar with Cognitive Linguistics, we will hopefully continue to see more applications of Cognitive Linguistics to the study of Hebrew and Aramaic.

1.4 Conclusion

The topics treated in this chapter are essential for understanding many of the issues discussed later in the book. Before delving into these issues, though, we also need to explore the history of Hebrew and Aramaic study. Throughout the years the study of Biblical Hebrew and Biblical Aramaic has been directly impacted by different approaches to linguistics and a changing understanding of linguistic concepts. So, with the linguistic framework established by this chapter in mind, let us now examine the history of Hebrew and Aramaic study.

---

86. Cf. Thompson and Widder, "Major Approaches to Linguistics," 131–32; Blois, "Cognitive Linguistic Approaches," 1:471–72.

87. E.g., Merwe, "Biblical Hebrew Lexicology," 87–112; idem, "Lexical Meaning," 85–95; Blois, "New Tools and Methodologies," 203–16.

88. http://www.sdbh.org/dictionary/main.php?language=en.

89. E.g., Shead, *Radical Frame Semantics and Biblical Hebrew*; Kotzé, "Cognitive Linguistic Methodology," 105–17.

90. E.g., Wolde, *Reframing Biblical Studies*, 104–200.

91. E.g., Robar, *Verb and the Paragraph in Biblical Hebrew*.

1.5 Further Reading

Akmajian, Adrian, Ann Kathleen Farmer, Lee Bickmore, Richard A. Demers, and Robert M. Harnish. *Linguistics: An Introduction to Language and Communication.* 7th ed. Cambridge: MIT Press, 2017.

Allan, Keith, ed. *The Oxford Handbook of the History of Linguistics.* Oxford: Oxford University Press, 2013.

Aronoff, Mark and Janie Rees-Miller, eds. *The Handbook of Linguistics.* 2nd ed. Blackwell Handbooks in Linguistics. Malden, MA: Wiley-Blackwell, 2017.

Bodine, Walter R. "Linguistics and Biblical Studies." *ABD* 4:327–33.

Campbell, Lyle. "The History of Linguistics: Approaches to Linguistics." Pages 97–117 in *The Handbook of Linguistics.* Edited by Mark Aronoff and Janie Rees-Miller. 2nd ed. Blackwell Handbooks in Linguistics. Malden, MA: Wiley-Blackwell, 2017.

Cook, John A. and Robert D. Holmstedt. *Linguistics for Hebraists.* LSAWS. University Park, PA: Eisenbrauns, forthcoming.

Goldenberg, Gideon. "The Contribution of Semitic Languages to Linguistic Thinking." *JEOL* 30 (1987–1988): 107–15.

Heine, Bernd and Heiko Narrogk, eds. *The Oxford Handbook of Linguistic Analysis.* 2nd ed. Oxford Handbooks in Linguistics. Oxford: Oxford University Press, 2015.

McGregor, William B. *Linguistics: An Introduction.* 2nd ed. London: Bloomsbury Academic, 2015.

Robins, Robert H. *A Short History of Linguistics.* 4th ed. Longman Linguistics Library. London: Routledge, 1997.

Sampson, Geoffrey. *Schools of Linguistics.* Stanford, CA: Stanford University Press, 1980.

Seuren, Pieter A.M. *Western Linguistics: An Historical Introduction.* Oxford: Blackwell, 1998.

Silva, Moisés. *God, Language, and Scripture: Reading the Bible in the Light of General Linguistics.* Foundations of Contemporary Interpretation 4. Grand Rapids: Zondervan, 1990.

Thompson, Jeremy P. and Wendy Widder. "Major Approaches to Linguistics." Pages 87–133 in *Linguistics and Biblical Exegesis.* Edited by Douglas Mangum and Joshua R. Westbury. Lexham Methods Series 2. Bellingham, WA: Lexham, 2017.

CHAPTER 2

A SHORT HISTORY *of* BIBLICAL HEBREW *and* BIBLICAL ARAMAIC STUDIES

The language of the Old Testament has been intensively studied for the most part of two millennia, and every detail has been subjected to multiple scrutiny. . . . Within such a subject, can anything new arise? In fact, on the contrary, the pace of new research is increasing.

—JAMES BARR[1]

2.1 INTRODUCTION

The past is the key to the present. Who we are in the present is largely shaped by our past—our backgrounds, experiences, and so on. It is similar for academic fields of study, and the study of Biblical Hebrew and Biblical Aramaic is no exception. If we are to understand the advances that have taken place in the study of Hebrew and Aramaic, we must first understand the history of Hebrew and Aramaic studies.

So, in this chapter I sketch a short history of Biblical Hebrew and Biblical Aramaic studies, beginning with medieval Jewish scholarship, when the linguistic study of Hebrew and Aramaic originated. From there I trace the emergence of this study as an academic discipline during the Renaissance and Enlightenment eras, the historical-comparative study of Hebrew and Aramaic during the nineteenth and early twentieth centuries, and finally trends during

---

1. Barr, "Semitic Philology and the Interpretation of the Old Testament," 31.

the modern era. Along the way I highlight key resources that integrate linguistics into the study of these languages.

This chapter is necessarily selective. Since most scholarship has concerned Biblical Hebrew rather than Biblical Aramaic, I naturally focus more on the former than the latter. Furthermore, my goal is not to be comprehensive but instead to capture the most important developments in Biblical Hebrew and Biblical Aramaic studies, especially as they follow developments in linguistics as discussed in the last chapter. Doing so will set the stage for the rest of the book and provide a context for the different topics it discusses.

2.2 BIBLICAL HEBREW AND BIBLICAL ARAMAIC STUDIES FROM THEIR BEGINNINGS TO THE PRESENT DAY

The *Encyclopaedia Judaica*'s article on linguistic literature presents an excellent overview of linguistic scholarship on the Hebrew Bible, although short surveys can be found in the standard Hebrew reference grammars.[2] In what follows, I rely closely, although not exclusively, on *Encyclopaedia Judaica*'s survey of biblical linguistic literature from its origins in the medieval period to the present day.

2.2.1 Medieval Jewish Scholarship (Tenth–Sixteenth Centuries CE)
2.2.1.1 First Attempts (Tenth Century)

Rabbinic literature contains sporadic grammatical and lexical observations on features such as directional *he* and the different meanings of the particle כִּי (*b. Yebam.* 13b; *Giṭ.* 90a).[3] Proper linguistic study of Biblical Hebrew and Biblical Aramaic, however, did not begin until the tenth century CE. This is because it was not possible to have true linguistic discussion prior to the establishment of a vocalized, fixed text by the Masoretes ca. 1000 CE. Their work produced an authoritative vocalization of the biblical text that could serve as a faithful source for grammars and lexicons of the biblical languages. The influence of Arabic linguistic literature upon the Jewish scholars of this time further encouraged the linguistic study of Hebrew and Aramaic, as did the Jews' growing realization that study of the Bible required a linguistically informed understanding of what the Bible said.[4]

As a result, during the tenth century the first genuine linguistic literature began to appear in both Arabic (in the East and in North Africa) and in Hebrew

---

2. Téné, Maman, and Barr, "Linguistic Literature," 13:29–61; cf. GKC §3; Joüon §4; *IBHS* §2; *BHRG* §3. The titles in this section are, in part, taken from *Encyclopaedia Judaica*'s survey.

3. *IBHS* §2.1b.

4. Téné, Maman, and Barr, "Linguistic Literature," 13:30, 34–35.

(in Spain). The linguistic literature that emerged included both grammar and lexicography but focused primarily on the latter. Saadiah ben Joseph Gaon (882–942) produced the first grammar of Biblical Hebrew, his *Kutub al-Lugha* (*Books on the [Hebrew] Language*), as well as the first Biblical Hebrew lexicon, his *Sefer ha-Egron* (*Book of the Vocabulary*). Two of Saadiah's contributions remain significant for our understanding of grammar today: the division of words by part of speech (i.e., noun, verb, and particle) and the need to relate the different forms and functions of a grammatical feature.[5]

Saadiah's scholarship set the standard for subsequent linguistic literature during the tenth century. In particular, Saadiah's lexical studies—which also included a study of *hapax legomena* known as *Kitāb al-Sabʿīn Lafẓa al-Mufrada* (*Book of the Interpretation of Seventy Words*)—generated significant interest in biblical vocabulary and prompted the publication of other lexicons. Among these were Judah Ibn Quraysh's *Risāla* (*Epistle*) and Dunash ibn Tamim's lexicon (of unknown name because it is now lost), both of which compared Biblical Hebrew words with their Aramaic and Arabic cognates.[6] These early lexicons focused exclusively on Biblical Hebrew vocabulary, but some works encompassing Biblical Aramaic also appeared, including David ben Abraham Alfāsi's *Kitāb Jāmiʿ al-Alfāẓ* (*Book of Collected Meanings*) and Menaḥem ben Saruq's *Maḥberet* (*Notebook*).[7]

2.2.1.2 The Creative Period (1000–1150)

Building on Saadiah's legacy, a new set of Jewish scholars emerged during the eleventh century. Most of them lived in Spain and wrote in Arabic. The first scholar of this new era was Judah ben David Ḥayyuj (ca. 945–1010). About 1000 CE Ḥayyuj wrote two important works on the Hebrew verb: *Kitāb al-Afʿāl Dhawāt Ḥurūf al-Līn* (*The Book of Weak Letter Verbs*) and *Kitāb al-Afʿāl Dhawāt al-Mithlayn* (*The Book of Geminate Verbs*). In these studies, Ḥayyuj introduced the concept of the three-letter root that had been popular in Arabic linguistic literature since the eighth century. He also formulated the classification of weak verbs by the letters they contain.[8] These two concepts remain very important to this very day, as any student of Biblical Hebrew will recognize.

Ḥayyuj's work was controversial and generated several responses. His main opponent was Jonah ibn Janāḥ (ca. 990–1050), who produced a complete

---

5. Téné, Maman, and Barr, "Linguistic Literature," 13:31, 38–39.
6. Téné, Maman, and Barr, "Linguistic Literature," 13:31.
7. Téné, Maman, and Barr, "Linguistic Literature," 13:31.
8. Téné, Maman, and Barr, "Linguistic Literature," 13:32, 39–40; Valle Rodríguez, "Grammarians: Medieval Spain," 2:95–96.

description of Biblical Hebrew in his two-part *Kitāb al-Tanqīḥ* (*Book of Minute Research*). The grammar portion, *Kitāb al-Lumaʿ* (*Book of Colored Flowerbeds*), represents the first comprehensive Hebrew grammar due to its scope of coverage. The lexicon portion, *Kitāb al-Uṣūl* (*Book of [Hebrew] Roots*), was the first dictionary to group words by their three-letter root and present its entries in alphabetical order, a tradition that continues in most Biblical Hebrew lexicons today.[9]

The works of Ḥayyuj and ibn Janāḥ set a trajectory for subsequent linguistic literature of the eleventh and twelfth centuries, most of which focused on grammar rather than the lexicon. The significance of this period is summarized by David Téné: "The authors of this period are the great creators of Hebrew linguistics. It is they who determined its scope, consolidated its system, and formulated its rules. It is they who fixed its terminology and phraseology."[10]

2.2.1.3 The Period of Dissemination (1150–1250)

When the Almohad Caliphate conquered southern Spain in 1148 CE, many Jewish intellectuals fled to Italy and southern France. There they spread the ideas of their predecessors by translating and adapting previous linguistic writings, especially those of Ḥayyuj and ibn Janāḥ. The most influential scholars of this period include Abraham ben Meir ibn Ezra (1089–1164) and members of the Kimḥi family, including Joseph (ca. 1105–1170) and his sons Moses (died ca. 1190) and David (ca. 1160–1235).[11]

Of their works, the most important is probably David Kimḥi's *Sefer Mikhlol* (*Book of Completeness*). Following the tradition of Ibn Janāḥ's *Kitāb al-Tanqīḥ* this work is arranged into two parts: a grammatical portion titled *Ḥeleq ha-Diqduq* (later known independently as *Mikhlol*) and a lexical portion titled *Ḥeleq ha-ʿInyan* (later known independently as *Sefer ha-Shorashim*, or the *Book of the [Hebrew] Roots*). As its name implies, Kimḥi's *Mikhlol* is comprehensive and complete. Its major contribution was its systemization of the presentation of grammar, with the verb at the center. It focused especially on the various verbal stems (*binyanim*) and conjugations and the presentation of their forms in paradigms.[12]

Although the works of this period made very few original contributions to linguistic thought, this period is crucial for our modern understanding of Hebrew and Aramaic. As Téné summarizes:

---

9. Téné, Maman, and Barr, "Linguistic Literature," 13:32, 37, 40–41; Valle Rodríguez, "Grammarians: Medieval Spain," 2:96–97.

10. Téné, Maman, and Barr, "Linguistic Literature," 13:33.

11. Téné, Maman, and Barr, "Linguistic Literature," 13:33; Valle Rodríguez, "Grammarians: Medieval Spain," 2:98–100.

12. Téné, Maman, and Barr, "Linguistic Literature," 13:33, 41–42; Valle Rodríguez, "Grammarians: Medieval Spain," 2:99–100.

It was the translators and adaptors who saved Hebrew linguistics from oblivion and made it a permanent branch in the history of Jewish literature. They also translated into Hebrew the Arabic grammatical terms used in the works of Ḥayyuj and ibn Janāḥ, and they fixed a mode of exposition for grammatical and lexicographical issues, that has existed until today in the study and teaching of the Hebrew language and in Hebrew biblical exegesis.[13]

2.2.1.4 The "Standstill" (1250–1500)

The publication of David Kimḥi's *Mikhlol* serves as the transition to the final period of Jewish medieval scholarship. Throughout this period the *Mikhlol* largely dominated Hebrew and Aramaic studies, whether through copying, adaptation, or reliance on it. The result was a standstill, with little advancement in the field.[14] Nevertheless, this period saw several important developments that continue to impact Hebrew and Aramaic studies today. These developments are particularly evident in the works of Profiat Duran (died ca. 1414) and Abraham de Balmes (ca. 1440–1523).

Duran's major contribution was his comprehensive Hebrew grammar entitled *Maʿaseh Efod* (*Work of Ephod*, "Ephod" being a pseudonym of Duran). Duran criticized Kimḥi's *Mikhlol*, reacting against its mechanical understanding of language. In its place Duran argued for a more theoretical view of language, as was characteristic of Ibn Janāḥ's *Kitāb al-Lumaʿ*. Duran's reframing of the linguistic enterprise placed more emphasis on the linguistic study of logic, which highlighted the role that theory plays in linguistic analysis.[15]

De Balmes incorporated concepts of Latin grammar in his *Miqneh Avram* (*Collection of Abram*). This was a significant development because, up until de Balmes, the categories of Arab grammarians had shaped the linguistic understanding of Hebrew and Aramaic. Another major contribution of de Balmes's *Miqneh Avram* was its establishment of a tripartite system—following the Indo-European tradition—of linguistic study: phonology, morphology, and syntax. These three categories remain the basic categories of Hebrew and Aramaic grammar to this day.[16]

---

13. Téné, Maman, and Barr, "Linguistic Literature," 13:33.

14. Téné, Maman, and Barr, "Linguistic Literature," 13:33–34.

15. Téné, Maman, and Barr, "Linguistic Literature," 13:34, 42; Valle Rodríguez, "Grammarians: Medieval Spain," 2:100.

16. Téné, Maman, and Barr, "Linguistic Literature," 13:34, 42–43; Charlap, "Grammarians: Medieval Italy," 2:91–92.

2.2.2 Emerging Academic Study of Biblical Hebrew and Biblical Aramaic (1500–1800)

The early sixteenth century saw a major shift in Hebrew and Aramaic linguistics. The Reformation emphasized the need for individual study of Scripture, and the Renaissance's concern for ancient civilization generated interest in original sources and their languages. The result was that Biblical Hebrew and Biblical Aramaic, which had been largely ignored in the medieval Christian world, emerged as a key component in Christian scholarship. No longer, then, was the linguistic study of Hebrew and Aramaic an exclusively Jewish enterprise.[17]

The first important Christian Hebraist of this period was Johann Reuchlin (1455–1522).[18] In 1506 he published his *Rudimenta linguae hebraicae*. This work consisted of both a grammar and a lexicon and was influenced by David Kimḥi in that it was attached to the *Mikhlol*. At the same time, Reuchlin applied Latin terminology to Hebrew grammatical phenomena, some of which is still in use today (e.g., the *status absolutus* "absolute state" of nouns). The primary contribution of Reuchlin, though, was his popularization of Hebrew and Aramaic among Christians. He wrote his *Rudimenta linguae hebraicae* for the purpose of teaching Hebrew to Christians, and subsequent church leaders—perhaps even Martin Luther—learned Hebrew from this foundational work.[19]

The Jew Elijah Levita (1468 or 1469–1549) also significantly influenced Christian Hebraists during this period. He wrote his own grammar, *Sefer ha-Baḥur* (*Book of the Baḥur*, "Baḥur" representing one of Levita's nicknames). Levita was well integrated within the humanist movement of the time and taught his Kimḥian understanding of Hebrew to Sebastian Münster (1489–1552). Münster, who served as professor at Basel, Switzerland from 1529 until his death, translated Levita's work into Latin and published it alongside his own *Melekhet ha-Diqduq ha-Shalem* (*Work of Complete Grammar*). In this way, Münster popularized medieval Jewish views of Hebrew grammar among Christians.[20]

Jewish influence on the Christian Hebraists was also evident in the works of Johann Buxtorf the Elder (1564–1629) and Johann Buxtorf the Younger (1599–1664).[21] Nevertheless, Jewish influence upon Christian Hebraists began

---

17. Téné, Maman, and Barr, "Linguistic Literature," 13:54.
18. Campanini, "Christian Hebraists: Medieval Period," 1:443.
19. Téné, Maman, and Barr, "Linguistic Literature," 13:34, 53, 55.
20. Téné, Maman, and Barr, "Linguistic Literature," 13:54–55; Campanini, "Christian Hebraists: Medieval Period," 1:446–47.
21. E.g., Buxtorf, *Epitome grammaticae hebraeae*; idem, *Tiberias*.

to wane as the persecution of Jews in Europe hindered Jewish academic study. This era also saw the establishment of the study of Hebrew and Aramaic in European universities. For example, the Regius chairs at Oxford and Cambridge—later occupied by giants in the field such as S. R. Driver, J. A. Emerton, and James Barr—were established by Henry VIII in 1540. These developments resulted in the emergence of Western academic study of Hebrew and Aramaic apart from Jewish tradition.[22]

The academic study of other ancient Near Eastern languages also developed during this time. Syriac and Classical Ethiopic (Geʿez) came to be studied alongside Aramaic and Arabic in the university. The result was the gradual reconnection of Hebrew and Aramaic with their Semitic context, something that had largely been lost when de Balmes and his successors began using Latin categories.[23] By the end of the eighteenth century, influential professors of Oriental languages like Albert Schultens (1686–1750), Johann David Michaelis (1717–1791), and Nikolaus Wilhelm Schröder (1721–1798) had fully situated Hebrew and Aramaic within their ancient Near Eastern context.[24] They emphasized that these languages belonged to the Semitic language family and that knowledge of other Semitic languages was necessary to understand Hebrew and Aramaic.[25]

James Barr well summarizes the status of Hebrew and Aramaic studies by the end of the eighteenth century:

> The academic Hebraist was now expected to be an Orientalist; this meant not only knowledge of Arabic, but also an awareness of the new information brought by travelers from the East about customs, the physical surroundings of life, and now—in its first rudimentary form—archaeology. By this time the Christian Hebraist was less involved in traditional dogmatism, and was likely, on the contrary, to be something of a rationalist.[26]

2.2.3 Comparative Philology and the Study of Biblical Hebrew and Biblical Aramaic (1800–1950)

These developments set the stage for the work of Wilhelm Gesenius (1786–1842), one of the greatest Hebraists of the nineteenth century who remains

---

22. Téné, Maman, and Barr, "Linguistic Literature," 13:55.
23. Téné, Maman, and Barr, "Linguistic Literature," 13:56–57.
24. Schultens, *Institutiones ad fundamenta linguae Hebraea*; Michaelis, *Grammatica Chaldaica*; Schroeder, *Institutiones ad fundamenta linguae Hebraeae*.
25. Téné, Maman, and Barr, "Linguistic Literature," 13:57.
26. Téné, Maman, and Barr, "Linguistic Literature," 13:57.

highly influential today. Gesenius taught at the University of Halle and, among many other contributions, published both a grammar and lexicon that remain standard reference works to this day. His work—especially his grammatical and lexical work—exemplifies the comprehensive and empirical study that distinguish this period. Today, Gesenius is known for freeing Biblical Hebrew study from theological dogmatism and instead situating it within rational linguistic description.[27]

Gesenius's Hebrew grammar was first published in 1813 under the title *Hebräische Grammatik*. It was subsequently revised numerous times by Gesenius himself as well as others. The most recent English edition, entitled *Gesenius' Hebrew Grammar* and published in 1910, represents A. E. Cowley's translation of the twenty-eighth German edition produced by Emil Kautzsch. The later editions of Gesenius's grammar, including this one, exemplify the many historical-comparative insights of the nineteenth century. The end product is a comprehensive grammar that describes the Hebrew language as fully as possible in light of Hebrew's historical development.

Gesenius's lexicon, which includes both Biblical Hebrew and Biblical Aramaic, first appeared in German in 1810–1812 under the title *Hebräisch-deutsches Handwörterbuch über die Schriften des Alten Testaments*. It was subsequently revised by several different individuals,[28] eventually serving as the basis for Francis Brown, S. R. Driver, and Charles A. Briggs's *A Hebrew and English Lexicon of the Old Testament*. Like his grammar, Gesenius's lexicon exemplifies careful presentation of linguistic data. It focuses especially on the presentation of etymology and cognate information, in accordance with the Comparative Philology of his day.

Gesenius's influence is reflected in the grammars and lexicons that appeared throughout the latter nineteenth century. Among the Biblical Hebrew grammars following the historical-comparative tradition are those of Heinrich Ewald (1803–1875), Justus Olshausen (1800–1882), Julius Friedrich Böttcher (1801–1863), Bernhard Stade (1848–1906), and Eduard König (1846–1936);[29] among the most important Biblical Aramaic grammars are those

---

27. Téné, Maman, and Barr, "Linguistic Literature," 13:57–58; Merwe, "Major Contributions," 162–64; Rabin, "Hebrew," 308.

28. The last edition to derive entirely from Gesenius's hand was the two-volume German *Hebräisches und chaldäisches Handwörterbuch über das Alte Testament* (1834), although the four-volume Latin *Thesaurus philologicus criticus linguae Hebraeae et Chaldaeae Veteris Testamenti* (1829–1858), completed by Gesenius's pupil Emil Rödiger, also comes primarily from his hand. The most recent German edition is the eighteenth edition, edited by Rudolf Meyer and Herbert Donner.

29. Ewald, *Kritische Grammatik der hebräischen Sprache*; Olshausen, *Lehrbuch der hebräischen Sprache*; Böttcher, *Ausführliches Lehrbuch der hebräischen Sprache*; Stade, *Lehrbuch der hebräischen Grammatik*; König, *Historisch-kritisches Lehrgebäude der hebraischen Sprache*.

of Emil Kautzsch (1841–1910), H. L. Strack (1848–1922), and Karl Marti (1855–1925).[30] Like Gesenius, these grammars rely on empirical observation and historical-comparative reconstruction of the Semitic languages for their grammatical descriptions. They utilize Latin-based categories and are arranged into the same three parts—phonology, morphology, syntax—popularized during the standstill period.[31]

Carl Brockelmann (1868–1956) brought the comparative Semitic enterprise to its full fruition in the early twentieth century.[32] His study laid the groundwork for the Hebrew and Aramaic grammars of this period. The most influential include the grammars of Hans Bauer (1878–1937) and Pontus Leander (1872–1935), as well as Gotthelf Bergsträsser (1886–1933).[33] Bauer and Leander co-wrote grammars of both Biblical Hebrew and Biblical Aramaic that offered detailed grammatical description—especially of the verb—as informed by comparative reconstruction of Proto-Semitic.[34] Bergsträsser's grammar, based on Gesenius, is similar to, but more historically oriented than, Bauer and Leander's.[35] Also in the historical-comparative tradition, but with more attention to syntax, is the descriptive grammar of Paul Joüon (1871–1940).[36]

Comparative Philology continued to dominate Biblical Hebrew and Biblical Aramaic studies even after Structuralism emerged around the turn of the twentieth century. This was partially due to Hebraists' and Aramaicists' reluctance to adopt new linguistic theories.[37] However, the decipherment and discovery of new Semitic languages like Ugaritic (discovered and quickly deciphered ca. 1930) also contributed to this trend, as did the discovery of new Hebrew texts like the Dead Sea Scrolls (discovered in 1948). The giants of this era, who largely embraced Comparative Philology, are still well-known today: William Foxwell Albright (1891–1971) in America, Godfrey Rolles Driver (1892–1975) in Britain, and Naphtali Herz Tur-Sinai (1886–1973) in Israel.[38]

---

30. Kautzsch, *Grammatik des Biblisch-Aramäischen*; Strack, *Grammatik des Biblisch-Aramäischen*; Marti, *Kurzgefasste Grammatik*.

31. Rabin, "Hebrew," 308–9.

32. Brockelmann, *Grammatik der semitischen Sprachen*. Another important comparative Semitic grammar of this period, though less detailed and of a slightly different nature than Brockelmann's, is Bergsträsser, *Einführung in die semitischen Sprachen*.

33. Téné, Maman, and Barr, "Linguistic Literature," 13:58; Merwe, "Major Contributions," 165–66; Rabin, "Hebrew," 309.

34. Bauer and Leander, *Historische Grammatik der hebräischen Sprache*; idem, *Grammatik des biblisch-Aramäischen*.

35. Bergsträsser et al., *Hebräische Grammatik*.

36. Joüon and Muraoka, *Grammar of Biblical Hebrew*.

37. Merwe, "Major Contributions," 168.

38. Téné, Maman, and Barr, "Linguistic Literature," 13:59–60.

The enduring influence of the historical-comparative approach—and specifically the work of Gesenius—demonstrates the significance of this period. Gesenius's grammar remains a standard reference work today and has essentially determined the structure and content of all modern grammars of Biblical Hebrew. This era's focus on the verb laid the foundation for modern discussions of the verbal stems and especially tense, aspect, and mood.[39] Furthermore, Gesenius's historical-comparative approach to lexicography serves as the basis for the two most popular lexicons today: *A Hebrew and English Lexicon of the Old Testament* (by Francis Brown, S. R. Driver, and Charles A. Briggs) and *The Hebrew and Aramaic Lexicon of the Old Testament* (by Ludwig Köhler and Walter Baumgartner).

2.2.4 The Modern Era of Biblical Hebrew and Biblical Aramaic Studies (1950–Present)

2.2.4.1 The Application of Modern Linguistic Approaches

Despite continued attention to Comparative Philology, about halfway through the twentieth century Hebraists and Aramaicists began to adopt other linguistic methods. The earliest scholars to do so were linguists who were also in part Hebraists, such as Zellig S. Harris (1909–1992) and Noam Chomsky (born 1928).[40] Because they had a linguistic background, these scholars did not have the same fear of applying linguistic theories to the biblical languages that many Hebraists and Aramaicists did. However, eventually Hebraists and Aramaicists without any formal linguistic training also began to apply modern linguistic approaches to the study of their languages.

These scholars first applied Structuralism, the major alternative to Comparative Philology at the time, to Hebrew and Aramaic phonology.[41] They encountered difficulty, though, when trying to apply Structuralism to the Semitic verbal system. This was because it is difficult to fully disconnect the diachronic development of the verbal system from its synchronic usage. This challenge, combined with ongoing study of Ugaritic and Amarna Akkadian, generated many studies on the Biblical Hebrew verbal system. Some of these studies concerned the verbal stems (*binyanim*), but the vast majority focused on the question of tense, aspect, and mood.[42] Key scholars contributing to this debate include William L. Moran (1921–2000), Jan Joosten (born 1959), and John A. Cook (born 1968).

---

39. Cf. Driver, *Tenses in Hebrew*.

40. Téné, Maman, and Barr, "Linguistic Literature," 13:60.

41. E.g., Birkeland, *Akzent und Vokalismus*; Harris, "Linguistic Structure of Hebrew," 143–67; Cantineau, "Phonologie de l'hébreu biblique," 82–122.

42. Rabin, "Hebrew," 310–12; Emerton, "Hebrew Language," 191–93.

In contrast to the grammar of verbs, Structuralism found easy application to the realm of lexicography. James Barr (1924–2006) served as the primary champion of this approach. He argued against too much reliance upon the historical-comparative approach for determining words' meanings, beginning in his *The Semantics of Biblical Language* (published 1961). Barr's influence on biblical lexicography cannot be overstated, and recent dictionaries like the *Dictionary of Classical Hebrew* (published 1993–2011) largely adopt a structuralist approach. Nevertheless, the rise of Cognitive Linguistics has also produced a significant minority of scholars who rely more on Cognitive Linguistics instead. The *Semantic Dictionary of Biblical Hebrew* (launched online in 2000)[43] is representative of this recent trend.

Another important development in modern Biblical Hebrew and Biblical Aramaic studies is interest in discourse analysis.[44] Many recent Hebraists and Aramaicists, particularly those influenced by Functionalism and Cognitive Linguistics, have shown concern for the meaning that words have within the broader context of their discourse. They investigate the way meaning is expressed at the macro level, particularly through use of specific verbal forms, and within the sentence through word order. This development, which parallels more general linguistic interest in discourse analysis, has been pioneered by scholars like Robert E. Longacre (1922–2014), Randall Buth (born 1950), and Robert D. Holmstedt (born 1972).

Modern interest in sociolinguistics has led to the investigation of linguistic variation within the Hebrew Bible.[45] Prior to the decline of Comparative Philology, most Hebraists understood this variation in chronological terms. However, in recent times scholars such as Gary A. Rendsburg (born 1954) and Ian Young (born 1962) have postulated alternative understandings. They have explained at least some of the Hebrew Bible's linguistic variation through sociolinguistic variables like social status, dialect, and style-shifting. The existence of sociolinguistic variation in the Hebrew Bible has in turn generated much discussion over whether linguistic features can indicate a biblical text's date of composition. Along with Young, several others like Robert Rezetko (born 1967) have challenged the linguistic dating of biblical texts in recent years.[46]

Since 1950, only a few significant reference grammars of Biblical Hebrew and Biblical Aramaic have appeared. Important Biblical Hebrew reference grammars include Bruce K. Waltke and Michael O'Connor's *An Introduction*

---

43. http://www.sdbh.org/dictionary/main.php?language=en.

44. *BHRG* §3.4.

45. Emerton, "Hebrew Language," 173–75.

46. Emerton, "Hebrew Language," 175–90; *BHRG* §3.4.

to Biblical Hebrew Syntax (published 1990), Christo H. J. van der Merwe, Jacobus A. Naudé, and Jan H. Kroeze's *A Biblical Hebrew Reference Grammar* (published 1999),[47] and Takamitsu Muraoka's *A Grammar of Biblical Hebrew* (published in 1991 as a translation and revision of Joüon's *Grammaire de l'hébreu biblique*).[48] The most important Biblical Aramaic reference grammar to appear is Franz Rosenthal's *A Grammar of Biblical Aramaic* (published 1961).[49] Most of these grammars are primarily structuralist and ignore more recent linguistic approaches, such as discourse analysis.[50] The exception is *A Biblical Hebrew Reference Grammar*, the sole grammar from this era to devote special attention to discourse analysis.

2.2.4.2 Modern Resources on Biblical Hebrew, Biblical Aramaic, and Linguistics

The use of modern linguistic approaches to describe Biblical Hebrew and Biblical Aramaic represents one important aspect of modern Hebrew and Aramaic studies. Another significant trend is the emergence of resources devoted to Biblical Hebrew, Biblical Aramaic, and linguistics. These resources exist in at least three different forms: monographs, academic journals, and Brill's *Encyclopedia of Hebrew Language and Linguistics*.

2.2.4.2.1 MONOGRAPHS

The past twenty-five years have seen the publication of several works on linguistics and the biblical languages.[51] These monographs encompass both the Old and New Testaments and therefore cover Biblical Greek in addition to Biblical Hebrew and Biblical Aramaic. Nevertheless, they serve as helpful resources to the Hebraist and Aramaicist for understanding developments in linguistics and how those developments impact exegesis. Of these, most helpful is the recent *Linguistics and Biblical Exegesis*, edited by Douglas Mangum and Joshua Westbury and part of the Lexham Methods Series. This invaluable resource explains linguistic fundamentals, covers the major linguistic schools of thought, and discusses current issues in the application of linguistics to the biblical languages.

---

47. A second edition was published in 2017.
48. A revised edition was published in 2006.
49. The most recent edition is the seventh edition, published in 2006.
50. Cf. *BHRG* §3.4.
51. E.g., Mangum and Westbury, *Linguistics and Biblical Exegesis*; Cotterell and Turner, *Linguistics and Biblical Interpretation*; Silva, *God, Language, and Scripture*; Silzer and Finley, *How Biblical Languages Work*.

In recent years several monographs have also sought to apply modern linguistic methodology specifically to the study of Biblical Hebrew. The most accessible of these is Susan Groom's *Linguistic Analysis of Biblical Hebrew*, which provides a survey of the application of linguistics to select issues in Biblical Hebrew. In addition, various collections of essays such as *The Study of Linguistics and Biblical Hebrew* (edited by Walter R. Bodine) and *Advances in Biblical Hebrew Linguistics: Data, Methods, and Analyses* (edited by Adina Moshavi and Tania Notarius) apply modern linguistic methodology to the study of Biblical Hebrew. Finally, many of the volumes in Eisenbrauns's Linguistic Studies in Ancient West Semitic (LSAWS) series explore issues in Biblical Hebrew and Biblical Aramaic within a modern linguistic framework.[52] Monographs like these demonstrate modern interest in applying linguistic theory to the biblical languages.

One of the most important monographs in the LSAWS series is *Linguistics for Hebraists*, co-edited by John A. Cook and Robert D. Holmstedt. This book aims to advance understanding of contemporary linguistic theories and model their application to the Hebrew Bible. Each of its essays presents a major linguistic theory (e.g., Historical-Comparative Linguistics, Functionalism, and Cognitive Linguistics) in a clear and understandable way, then discusses several case studies using that linguistic theory. *Linguistics for Hebraists* is intentionally aimed at those with a minimal background in linguistics. It is accessible and represents an invaluable resource to everyone—students and pastors included—wanting to understand linguistics' relevance for the Hebrew Bible.

2.2.4.2.2 Academic Journals

Several academic journals also attest to a growing interest and application of linguistics to Biblical Hebrew and Biblical Aramaic.[53] The sole journal devoted specifically to linguistics and Biblical Hebrew is *Lešonénu*, published by the Academy of the Hebrew Language in Israel, but many other journals contain academic articles on Hebrew, Aramaic, and linguistics. Especially included among them are journals devoted to the study of the Semitic languages and the ancient Near East: *Aramaic Studies, Hebrew Abstracts, Hebrew Studies, Journal of Near Eastern Studies, Journal of Northwest Semitic Languages, Journal of Semitic Studies, Journal of the Ancient Near Eastern Society of Columbia University, Maarav, Tarbiz*, and *Zeitschrift für Althebraistik*. However, other journals more broadly devoted to biblical studies also frequently include articles of value:

---

52. https://www.eisenbrauns.org/books/series/book_SeriesLinguisticStudiesinSemitic.html.
53. Cf. Waldman, *Recent Study of Hebrew*, 2.

Biblica, Catholic Biblical Quarterly, Journal of Biblical Literature, Revue biblique, Vetus Testamentum, and *Zeitschrift für die alttestamentliche Wissenschaft.*

2.2.4.2.3 BRILL'S *ENCYCLOPEDIA OF HEBREW LANGUAGE AND LINGUISTICS* (*EHLL*)

Finally, a monumental recent resource for all students and scholars of Biblical Hebrew is Brill's *Encyclopedia of Hebrew Language and Linguistics* (*EHLL*). It was edited by Geoffrey Khan, Regius Professor of Hebrew at the University of Cambridge, and his team of associate editors. *EHLL* contains over 950 entries available in both online and print format. These entries cover history of scholarship, major grammatical features (phonology, morphology, and syntax), lexicon, stylistics and sociolinguistics, discourse analysis, Hebrew in relation to other languages, and the major periods of the Hebrew language.

EHLL is limited to the Hebrew language, and as such it does not contain entries devoted to Biblical Aramaic or even the Aramaic language in general. Yet, it contains a plethora of entries invaluable for Hebraists. Even the entries covering topics related to other periods of Hebrew are helpful because they situate Biblical Hebrew within its broader context. Given its scope and comprehensiveness, *EHLL* is rightfully self-described as "the authoritative reference work for students and researchers in the fields of Hebrew linguistics, general linguistics, Biblical studies, Hebrew and Jewish literature, and related fields."[54] All students, pastors, and scholars interested in Hebrew and linguistics need to familiarize themselves with and regularly consult this monumental resource.

2.3 CONCLUSION

The study of Biblical Hebrew and Biblical Aramaic has a long history that goes back to the Middle Ages. Medieval Jewish grammarians and lexicographers established a tradition of describing Hebrew and Aramaic that continues to this day. Beginning with the Renaissance era, the study of Hebrew and Aramaic further developed and found solid academic footing. This led to the historical-comparative study of Hebrew and Aramaic, which continues to influence the field today. Finally, since the 1950s scholars have sought to apply other linguistic theories to the study of Hebrew and Aramaic. The result has been the publication of various resources that describe Hebrew and Aramaic in a linguistically informed way.

The historical developments discussed in this chapter set the stage for the rest of this book. Specifically, the linguistic theories, major figures, and trends

---

54. https://referenceworks.brillonline.com/browse/encyclopedia-of-hebrew-language-and-linguistics.

provide a context for the topics discussed in the following chapters: lexicology and lexicography (chapter 3); the verbal stems (chapter 4); tense, aspect, and mood (chapter 5); discourse analysis (chapter 6); word order (chapter 7); register, dialect, style-shifting, and code-switching (chapter 8); dating Biblical Hebrew and Biblical Aramaic texts (chapter 9); and finally, teaching and learning the languages of the Hebrew Bible (chapter 10). Keeping the history of scholarship presented by this chapter in mind, let us now explore each of these fascinating issues.

2.4 FURTHER READING

Barr, James. "Semitic Philology and the Interpretation of the Old Testament." Pages 31–64 in *Tradition and Interpretation: Essays by Members of the Society for Old Testament Study.* Edited by G. W. Anderson. Oxford: Clarendon, 1979.

Campanini, Saverio. "Christian Hebraists: Renaissance Period." *EHLL* 1:440–49.

Delgado, José Martínez. "Lexicography: Middle Ages." *EHLL* 2:510–14.

———. "Phonology in Medieval Grammatical Thought." *EHLL* 3:122–30.

Emerton, J. A. "The Hebrew Language." Pages 171–99 in *Text in Context: Essays by Members of the Society for Old Testament Study.* Edited by Andrew D. H. Mayes. Oxford: Oxford University Press, 2000.

Hirschfeld, Hartwig. *Literary History of Hebrew Grammarians and Lexicographers, Accompanied by Unpublished Texts.* Jews' College Publications 9. London: Oxford University Press, 1926.

Kutscher, E. Y. "Aramaic." Pages 347–412 in *Linguistics in South West Asia and North Africa.* Edited by Thomas A. Sebeok. Vol. 6 of *Current Trends in Linguistics.* 14 vols. The Hague: Mouton, 1970.

Maman, Aharon. "Morphology in the Medieval Rabbanite Grammatical Tradition." *EHLL* 2:712–21.

Merwe, Christo H. J. van der. "A Short Survey of Major Contributions to the Grammatical Description of Old Hebrew since 1800 A.D." *JNSL* 13 (1987): 161–90.

———. "Some Recent Trends in Biblical Hebrew Linguistics: A Few Pointers towards a More Comprehensive Model of Language Use." *HS* 44 (2003): 7–24.

Rabin, Chaim. "Hebrew." Pages 304–46 in *Linguistics in South West Asia and North Africa.* Edited by Thomas A. Sebeok. Vol. 6 of *Current Trends in Linguistics.* 14 vols. The Hague: Mouton, 1970.

Téné, David, Aharon Maman, and James Barr. "Linguistic Literature, Hebrew." *EncJud* 13:29–61.

Valle Rodríguez, Carlos del. "Grammarians: Medieval Spain." *EHLL* 2:94–101.

Waldman, Nahum M. *The Recent Study of Hebrew: A Survey of the Literature with Selected Bibliography.* Bibliographica Judaica 10. Cincinnati: Hebrew Union College Press, 1989.

CHAPTER 3

LEXICOLOGY *and* LEXICOGRAPHY

All biblical interpreters need exposure to and experience in lexicographic method if they would use the linguistic data in a responsible way.

—MOISÉS SILVA[1]

3.1 INTRODUCTION

The study of meaning, or semantics, represents one of the most fundamental areas of study within linguistics. Meaning can be represented at several levels, but one of the most basic levels is the word level. This is because words constitute a fundamental component of every language. They establish a bridge between abstract concepts and the real world, enabling us as humans to communicate with one another.

Yet, despite its importance, word meaning seems to present a particular challenge for scholars of the Hebrew Bible. Time and time again, it has been subject to abuse in sermons, popular-level books, and even scholarly publications. The situation was so dire in the early 1960s that James Barr called for significant reform in our understanding of word meaning and its application to the Hebrew Bible. We have made much progress since then, but many of the problems have not gone away. As a result, Hebrew Bible lexicology and lexicography continue to suffer from misunderstanding and abuse today. This is unfortunate because word meaning must be understood properly to carry out accurate exegesis and to avoid various exegetical fallacies and mistakes.[2]

---

1. Silva, *Biblical Words and Their Meaning*, 32.
2. Carson, *Exegetical Fallacies*.

So, in this chapter I examine the meaning of words and demonstrate this topic's relevance for understanding Biblical Hebrew and Biblical Aramaic. I begin with a survey of lexicology, the branch of linguistics that deals with lexical meaning. Then I explore various applications of lexicology to the meaning of biblical words. Finally, I discuss lexicography, or the practical application of lexicology through the writing of dictionaries, with reference to Biblical Hebrew and Biblical Aramaic lexicons.

3.2 A MODERN LINGUISTIC FRAMEWORK FOR LEXICOLOGY

This section explores key aspects of lexicology and its relevance for interpreting the Hebrew Bible. Specifically, I discuss lexical meaning, lexical relations, etymology and meaning change, and polysemy. These topics provide a framework for examining lexicology as it applies to Biblical Hebrew and Biblical Aramaic.

3.2.1 Lexical Meaning

Lexical semantics, or the study of word meaning, necessarily distinguishes word, reference, and sense. A *word* is a sequence of letters that together function as a symbol; it has no meaning in and of itself. This symbol points to its *reference*, or the thing in the world to which the word refers. A word and its reference are not directly equivalent to one another but are linked together by the *sense*, which is an abstract representation of what the word and its reference have in common.[3] Distinguishing between sense and reference explains how different words can designate the same reference. For example, a book can be designated as *book* in English, *Buch* in German, *livre* in French, and סֵפֶר in Hebrew because all legitimately express the sense of *book*.

Traditionally, lexical meaning has been described through *lexical entailment*. According to this notion, to know the meaning of a word is to know that something else about it is true—in other words, if *A* is true about a word, then *B* must also necessarily be true.[4] For example, a lexical entailment of the English word *book* is that of a written text because if something is a book, then it is a written text ("If it is a book, then it is a written text"). A word's lexical entailments are often expressed through componential analysis, which analyzes a meaning in terms of the presence or absence of certain binary features. For example, the English word *woman* could be analyzed via componential analysis

---

3. Murphy, *Lexical Meaning*, 34–37.
4. Murphy, *Lexical Meaning*, 31–32; Hovav, "Lexical Semantics," 2:499.

as [+HUMAN], [+FEMALE], and [+ADULT] whereas the English word *girl* could be analyzed as [+HUMAN], [+FEMALE], and [-ADULT].[5]

Although helpful, the notion of lexical entailment as traditionally understood is limited. It does not distinguish what elements are most important to a word's meaning, nor can it express the full sense of a word.[6] This is partly because meaning cannot be limited to a simple dictionary definition. Meaning also entails *concept*, or information derived from encyclopedic (i.e., experiential) knowledge of a word. For example, the English word *in-law* can have any number of mental associations, both good and bad. These associative meanings reflect common knowledge, a cultural "baggage" of sorts, that impacts one's understanding of the word *in-law* just as much as a dictionary definition does.

Given the limitations of lexical entailment, Cognitive Linguistics has instead advocated Prototype Theory, which uses a *prototype* (i.e., exemplar) of a semantic category as a point of reference for understanding the "fuzzy boundaries" of words.[7] For example, the meaning of the English word *bird* can be understood in light of its prototype. This approach enables expression of the central (e.g., having two legs and feathers) and peripheral (e.g., flying and living in trees) features of the word *bird* and thereby provides a better understanding of its meaning. Furthermore, unlike traditional lexical entailment, prototypes incorporate experiential knowledge in that prototypes differ from culture to culture. A bird like a robin or sparrow—but probably not a penguin or chicken—will serve as the prototype of the word *bird* for most English speakers in the United States, but other birds will serve as the prototype in other parts of the world.[8]

3.2.2 Lexical Relations

Lexical meaning can be further explored by comparing a word's meaning with those of other words, a concept known as *lexical relations* or *paradigmatics*. The primary concern of lexical relations is the classification of meanings according to their characteristics.[9] As such, lexical relations entail synonymy, antonymy, and inclusion relations as well as semantic field theory. The key idea behind lexical relations is that the meanings of different words mutually define one another.

---

5. Murphy, *Lexical Meaning*, 45–47; Geeraerts, *Theories of Lexical Semantics*, 70–80. Componential analysis was especially popularized by structuralist thought during the mid-twentieth century.

6. Cf. Taylor, *Linguistic Categorization*, 35–39.

7. Murphy, *Lexical Meaning*, 51–54; Geeraerts, *Theories of Lexical Semantics*, 183–203; Taylor, *Linguistic Categorization*, 41–83. Prototypicality can be traced back to the work of Elenaor Rosch during the mid-1970s ("Internal Structure," 111–44;"Principles of Categorization," 27–48).

8. Cf. Rosch, "Internal Structure," 131–34.

9. Murphy, *Lexical Meaning*, 108–9; Geeraerts, *Theories of Lexical Semantics*, 80–91.

A *synonym* has the same meaning as another word, whereas an antonym expresses a meaning incompatible with that of another word.[10] Rarely are two words *absolute synonyms* in that one can be exchanged for the other with no change in meaning. Much more common is *near-synonymy*, in which two words can substitute for each other in some contexts—but not every context—due to differences in sense, including connotation.[11] The natural implication is that authors choose a specific word, at the exclusion of all others, to express the particular meaning they have in mind. This requires that we pay close attention not only to what word is used in discourse, but to what words are not used.

Another aspect of paradigmatics is *inclusion relations*, or the hierarchical categorization of meanings that contain or are contained in other meanings.[12] For example, *tulip* is a subset of *flower* in that its meaning falls within the general meaning of *flower*, and *flower* is in turn a subset of *plant*.[13] In such a taxonomy, meanings that are subordinate are termed *hyponyms*, words that are superordinate are termed *hypernyms*, and the most general category is the *basic level item*. An important contribution of Cognitive Linguistics to our understanding of inclusion relations is the recognition that most people categorize words according to a popular-level *folk taxonomy* rather than a technical, scientific one.

Synonyms, antonyms, and inclusion relations all facilitate the classification of meaning according to *semantic field*, a notion that has its origins in Structuralism.[14] Words that can be grouped together based on similar meaning, such as *steam, boil, fry, broil, roast,* and *bake* make up a semantic field under the hypernym *cook*.[15] Our understanding of something is often enhanced by comparing and contrasting it with something else, especially that which is similar. So, by juxtaposing word meanings in this way, semantic field theory enhances our understanding of each individual meaning.[16]

3.2.3 Etymology and Meaning Change

Thus far I have discussed words and their meaning synchronically. However, it is important to consider words diachronically too. *Etymology* is the

---

10. Murphy, *Lexical Meaning*, 110–12, 117–22.

11. Murphy, *Lexical Meaning*, 108–13.

12. Murphy, *Lexical Meaning*, 113–17.

13. Lyons, *Semantics*, 1:291.

14. Murphy, *Lexical Meaning*, 125–27; Geeraerts, *Theories of Lexical Semantics*, 53–70. The first influential publication on this topic was that of Jost Trier (*Deutsche Wortschatz im Sinnbezirk des Verstandes*).

15. Lehrer, *Semantic Fields and Lexical Structure*, 30–35.

16. Componential analysis can also facilitate lexical relations in that a word's components can easily be expressed in terms of synonyms and antonyms and thereby compared with other words. Yet, such an approach can only go so far because it does not take into account the finer nuances of a word's meaning.

investigation of a word's history. It examines not only the origin of a word but any subsequent developments or changes that word may have undergone.[17] Because words and their meanings are connected, etymology naturally entails investigation of the history of a word's meaning. The study of etymology can be traced back to classical times (e.g., Plato, *Cratylus* 390e–427d), but as a modern discipline it emerged from Comparative Philology during the eighteenth and nineteenth centuries.[18]

Words originate in one of three different ways. First, a word can be inherited from a linguistic ancestor, known as a proto-language. Related words with related meanings, each derived from the same "parent" language, are known as *cognates* (e.g., English *house*, German *Haus*, Dutch *huis*, Danish, Norwegian, and Swedish *hus*, and Icelandic *hús* are all descended from Proto-Germanic *hūsa-* "house").[19] Second, a word can be created within a language through the process of *word formation*. Common means of forming words include adding affixes (e.g., the addition of the suffix -*ly* to English *slow* creates the adverb *slowly*) and compounding (e.g., English *skyscraper*, formed from *sky* and *scraper*).[20] Finally, a word can enter a language from the outside as a *loanword*. When a language has no word to express a new thing or concept, it often adopts a word from a language that already has a word to express the thing or concept (e.g., Europeans first encountered chocolate in the New World but had no word for it, so they adopted the native Nahuatl word for chocolate, *čokolātl*, hence English *chocolate*).[21]

Over the course of its history, a word often takes on meanings different from its original meaning. There are several different ways a word can acquire a new sense.[22] *Metonymy* occurs when a word takes on meanings of something related to it (e.g., *Hollywood* refers not only to a geographical location but also to the American film industry). *Metaphor* entails comparison between different things and describing one as if it were the other (e.g., the word *hands* in the phrase *hands of a clock* compares the pointers of a clock with people's hands). A word's senses can also be broadened (e.g., English *cupboard* originally referred to a place for storing dishes but now refers to any small storage cabinet) or narrowed (e.g., English *meat* originally meant "food" in general but now refers to animal flesh that is eaten).

---

17. Durkin, *Oxford Guide to Etymology*, 1–2.
18. Geeraerts, *Theories of Lexical Semantics*, 2–4.
19. Campbell, *Historical Linguistics*, 107–44.
20. Durkin, *Oxford Guide to Etymology*, 94–131; Campbell, *Historical Linguistics*, 238–45.
21. Durkin, *Oxford Guide to Etymology*, 132–78; Campbell, *Historical Linguistics*, 56–75.
22. Murphy, *Lexical Meaning*, 94–98; Campbell, *Historical Linguistics*, 222–38.

Because meanings can change like this, etymology cannot conclusively establish a word's present-day meaning.[23] For example, English *deer* comes from Proto-Germanic **deuza-*, which means "animal." Whereas German *Tier* and Dutch *dier* preserve the original general meaning, English has narrowed the definition to refer to a specific type of animal, namely one with four legs and antlers. Another problem with using etymology to determine a word's meaning is that a word is not always analyzable in terms of its components or root. For example, whereas the meaning of English *microbiology* makes good sense in light of its components *micro* and *biology*, such is not the case with English *butterfly*. Nevertheless, a key function of etymology is that it illuminates the formal and semantic relationships between words.[24] Especially in absence of other evidence, etymology can potentially play a role in clarifying—although not conclusively establishing—the meaning of a word.

3.2.4 Polysemy

Investigation of etymology enables us to explain why many words have multiple meanings. In some cases, a word has multiple meanings due to *homonymy*, which occurs when two different words of separate, unrelated origin have come to look the same for historical reasons.[25] In most cases, however, multiple meanings can instead be attributed to *polysemy*. This occurs when the multiple meanings arise from semantic change rather than differing etymologies. An example is English *coat*, which can mean "an outer garment with sleeves," "an animal's covering of fur," or "a covering of paint or similar material." The various meanings of *coat* can be explained by expansion of existing senses to include other senses. Specifically, the garment sense was broadened to include other types of coverings, including an animal's fur and a layer of paint.[26]

A single "core meaning" is rarely discoverable when polysemy occurs. In the case of *coat*, the original sense—a garment—no longer plays a significant role in the secondary meanings of this word. One could perhaps try to argue that each of its meanings entails the notion of covering. However, this idea cannot be abstracted as the core meaning because this word *coat* refers to specific kinds of coverings, and *coat* and *covering* are therefore not fully interchangeable.[27]

---

23. Durkin, *Oxford Guide to Etymology*, 26–30.
24. Durkin, *Oxford Guide to Etymology*, 24–26.
25. Murphy, *Lexical Meaning*, 87–88. Murphy gives the example of English *sole*, which can mean either "the bottom surface of a shoe" or "only." These two words are homonyms that just happen to look the same due to historical changes: *sole* ("the bottom surface of a shoe") derives from Latin *solea* ("sandal") whereas *sole* ("only") comes from Latin *solus* ("alone").
26. Murphy, *Lexical Meaning*, 88–89.
27. Murphy, *Lexical Meaning*, 89.

Thus, although certain senses are undoubtedly central to a polysemous word, it is often difficult, if not impossible, to determine a core meaning.

In light of this difficulty, Cognitive Linguistics offers a helpful perspective for understanding polysemy. In cognitive approaches like Frame Semantics (developed by Charles J. Fillmore)[28] and Cognitive Grammar (developed by Ronald W. Langacker),[29] encyclopedic meaning in the form of *frames* or *domains* creates a network for understanding a word's various meanings.[30] For example, the English word *mother* can be used with reference to giving birth, contributing genetic material, nurturing, and marriage to one's father. These different senses create a network, or frame, that establish the prototypical concept MOTHER. Not every usage of the English word *mother* will activate each of these meanings, but they provide a general framework that helps to explain its various usages, including non-prototypical ones.[31]

A significant corollary of all this is that a given word will rarely, if ever, possess all its possible meanings in a single usage. It is true that sometimes an expression contains a word with deliberate vagueness in order to create wordplay or a double entendre. However, this phenomenon is relatively rare. The only way to know which of a word's senses is intended in a particular usage is consideration of the context.[32] The context entails the *cotext*, which includes *syntagmatics*, or the relationships with other words in the utterance, as well as the *literary context*, or the placement of the word within the broader discourse. It also entails *context of situation*, or the historical-cultural background of the text.[33]

3.3 LEXICOLOGY AND THE HEBREW BIBLE

Moisés Silva's *Biblical Words and Their Meaning* and James Barr's *The Semantics of Biblical Language* provide an excellent starting point for summarizing some important implications of the above theories for understanding Hebrew Bible lexicology, and I draw largely from them in what follows. However, I also expand upon and even modify some of their conclusions in light of recent developments in lexicology, particularly those of Cognitive Linguistics.[34]

---

28. E.g., Fillmore, "Scenes-and-Frames Semantics," 55–81.

29. Langacker, *Cognitive Grammar*.

30. Murphy, *Lexical Meaning*, 101–4; Geeraerts, *Theories of Lexical Semantics*, 222–29; Taylor, *Linguistic Categorization*, 87–93.

31. Lakoff, *Women, Fire, and Dangerous Things*, 74–76.

32. Murphy, *Lexical Meaning*, 30–31.

33. Cf. Murphy, *Lexical Meaning*, 30–31.

34. Cf. Merwe, "Biblical Hebrew Lexicology," 87–112.

3.3.1 Determining Meaning

One of the most important areas in which lexicology impacts our understanding of the Hebrew Bible regards word meaning. Silva especially emphasizes the importance of context for determining the meaning of biblical words.[35] This is because, for words with various possible meanings, "the context does not merely help us understand meaning—it virtually *makes* meaning."[36] We cannot simply pick what we want a word to mean, nor can we assume that a word carries all of its possible meanings at the same time.[37] Rather, we must rely on the contextual clues that a biblical author has given us to know which of a word's possible meanings is intended.[38] In the Hebrew Bible, context exists at multiple levels, both linguistically (at the linguistic level) and extralinguistically (beyond the linguistic level).

Linguistically, we can investigate the cotext of a biblical word. This entails both the syntagmatic relationship between a biblical word and its surrounding words as well as the broader literary context of the word's textual unit. Ideally, the cotext is examined in terms of contextual circles, beginning with the most immediate context and expanding outward to other contexts, namely the paragraph, major literary unit, the entire composition, all of the author's works, and finally the entire Hebrew Bible.[39] For example, if we were interested in the meaning of the Biblical Hebrew word חֵן in Gen 6:8, we would begin by investigating all occurrences of the syntagm מָצָא חֵן בְּעֵינֵי "to find favor in the eyes of" within the book of Genesis. Then we would gradually work our way outward to occurrences outside the book, giving priority to those that are conceptually parallel (e.g., Exod 33:12–13, 16–17; 34:9) and therefore contextually closer.

Extralinguistically, we can examine the historical-cultural circumstances surrounding the production of that textual unit as well as the way that the word has been interpreted in the history of biblical exegesis. Returning to the example of חֵן in Gen 6:8, we would examine the cultural associations of generosity and favor within the ancient Near East, including ancient Israel. We would also examine the reception history, an important step because we

---

35. Silva, *Biblical Words and Their Meaning*, 137–69; cf. Cotterell and Turner, *Linguistics and Biblical Interpretation*, 175–78.

36. Silva, *Biblical Words and Their Meaning*, 139. The emphasis is original.

37. The assumption that all possible meanings of a word are present in a single use of the word is known as *illegitimate totality transfer* (Barr, *Semantics of Biblical Language*, 217–18). Consider the word חֶסֶד, which sometimes refers to faithfulness within the context of covenant making (e.g., Deut 7:9; Isa 55:3). It would be a mistake, however, to assume that the entailments of covenant are present in all usages of חֶסֶד. Such is clearly not the case in a number of passages (e.g., Gen 19:19; Ezra 7:28).

38. Cf. Widder, "Linguistic Fundamentals," 30–31; Cotterell and Turner, *Linguistics and Biblical Interpretation*, 175–78.

39. Silva, *Biblical Words and Their Meaning*, 156–59.

commonly understand theologically loaded concepts in light of past interpretation. In the case of חֵן, the Protestant Reformation's dichotomy between
grace and works-righteousness may or may not lead us astray from the biblical
author's understanding of this word.

Silva also discusses how the meaning of a biblical word can be investigated
in terms of lexical relations. This is especially true of synonyms. When a biblical
author has the option of using several different words to refer to the same
thing, his choice of a specific word over others naturally evokes a particular
association that the others do not.[40] Thus, for example, the use of תּוֹרָה in Josh
1:7–8 evokes the association of the law given at Sinai, connotations that terms
within the same general semantic field (e.g., מִצְוָה or חֹק) would not necessarily
have. In the same way, the meaning of טוֹב ("good") can be illuminated by
investigating one of its antonyms, רַע ("bad, evil"). The interpreter therefore
benefits from asking not only the question "What is the meaning of the word
used by the author?" but also "Why did the author use this particular word as
opposed to others?"

Silva's analysis rightly notes how lexical meaning is mutually defining, and
he rightly presents the importance of context for determining the meaning
of a biblical word. At the same time, such an approach primarily reflects
Structuralism, which views language as an internal system. Accordingly,
although Silva does discuss the importance of context of situation (i.e., the
text's historical-cultural background) for understanding a word, through his
emphasis on syntagmatics and paradigmatics he downplays the role that encyclopedic knowledge plays in determining meaning. This same shortcoming
is evident in many works on Biblical Hebrew and Biblical Aramaic semantics
of the second half of the twentieth century, particularly those that focus on
syntagmatics and the semantic fields of biblical words.[41]

Following Cognitive Linguistics, recent scholarship on biblical semantics
has sought to incorporate encyclopedic knowledge into meaning. These studies
do so through use of cognitive approaches like Prototype Theory and Frame
Semantics.[42] A potential problem with many of these works is that they require
a background in Cognitive Linguistics, rendering them inaccessible to most

---

40. Silva, *Biblical Words and Their Meaning*, 120–26, 159–61; cf. Cotterell and Turner, *Linguistics and Biblical Interpretation*, 159–61.

41. E.g., Botha, "Measurement of Meaning," 3–22; Brenner, "Semantic Field of Humour, Laughter and the Comic," 39–58; Fox, "Words for Wisdom," 149–65; idem, "Words for Folly," 4–15; Sawyer, *Semantics in Biblical Research*. A recent work advocating the traditional approach is Zanella, *Lexical Field of the Substantives of "Gift."*

42. E.g., Burton, *Semantics of Glory*; Peters, *Hebrew Lexical Semantics and Daily Life*; Shead, *Radical Frame Semantics and Biblical Hebrew*; Widder, *"To Teach" in Ancient Israel*.

scholars of the Hebrew Bible. Furthermore, since scholars have only recently begun to apply Cognitive Linguistics to Biblical Hebrew and Biblical Aramaic, their methodologies and application will necessarily require some refinement. Nevertheless, these works represent significant advances in our understanding of lexical meaning, especially because they rightfully incorporate encyclopedic knowledge.[43] We look forward to more contributions along these lines.

3.3.2 Lexicology and Biblical Theology

Whereas Silva focuses much on establishing a linguistic foundation for biblical semantics, Barr critiques scholarship's application of lexical semantics to Biblical Hebrew and Biblical Aramaic. One topic he examines is the identification of language with worldview.[44] He notes how it is common to hear "Hebrew thought" distinguished from "Greek thought" on the basis of language.[45] According to those who distinguish the two, the ancient Israelites' way of thinking was concrete and dynamic because Biblical Hebrew only possesses the masculine and feminine genders whereas the Greeks, who also used a neuter gender, were supposedly more abstract and static. Identification of language with worldview is quite ancient but has been popularized in the modern era as the so-called Sapir-Whorf hypothesis, which argues that language actually determines worldview.[46] However—with all due respect to science fiction movies like *Arrival*—this perspective has largely been discredited by various scientific studies.[47] Accordingly, no significant link can be established between a particular way of thinking and the languages of the Hebrew Bible.

After establishing that there is no direct link between language and worldview, Barr turns to a critique of the use of words to construct biblical theology. Here Barr severely criticizes theological dictionaries, especially the *Theological Dictionary of the New Testament*.[48] His critique focuses on these dictionaries' failure to adequately distinguish between words and concepts, as is evident by their discussion of concepts under single words or word-groups. For example, the standard theological dictionaries for the Hebrew Bible all discuss the

---

43. Cf. Merwe, "Biblical Hebrew Lexicology," 87–112.

44. Barr, *Semantics of Biblical Language*, 8–20; cf. Silva, *Biblical Words and Their Meaning*, 18–19; Cotterell and Turner, *Linguistics and Biblical Interpretation*, 110–13.

45. Boman, *Hebrew Thought Compared with Greek*.

46. Hoijer, "Sapir-Whorf Hypothesis," 92–105. Despite its name, the Sapir-Whorf hypothesis did not originate—at least as commonly formulated—with the American linguists Edward Sapir and Benjamin Lee Whorf.

47. Cf. McWhorter, *Language Hoax*.

48. Barr, *Semantics of Biblical Language*, 8–45, 263–87; idem, "Semantics and Biblical Theology," 11–19; cf. Silva, *Biblical Words and Their Meaning*, 22–28; Cotterell and Turner, *Linguistics and Biblical Interpretation*, 115–23.

concepts of faith and faithfulness under a single entry for the word-group אמן, giving the impression that there is a one-to-one correspondence between the word-group אמן and these concepts.[49] This, however, is not true because these concepts can be associated with other words (e.g., בטח) and may even be present contextually in a passage that does not explicitly use אמן or its derivatives.

This critique is important and certainly worth our attention. Nevertheless, Barr's strict distinction between words and concepts was largely influenced by the structuralist thought of his day. Structuralism overreacted to Comparative Philology, the linguistic school of thought that produced the first theological dictionaries.[50] With the advent of Cognitive Linguistics, however, the pendulum has swung back toward the middle as linguists once again recognize a connection between language and worldview.[51] It is true that words and concepts are not the same thing. However, they are not entirely unrelated either. This is because encyclopedic knowledge contributes to our understanding of what a word means, as already discussed.

These associations are largely connected with one's culture. Thus, for example, within ancient Israelite culture, Biblical Hebrew מֶלֶךְ ("king, ruler") would have mentally evoked a number of associations that are not necessarily evoked by modern English *king* in today's United States (and certainly in today's United Kingdom). Recognition of the link between language and culture reopens the door for exploration of the relationship between words and biblical theology.[52] Hopefully, some will take up this important task.

3.3.3 The Use of Etymology

A final way in which modern lexicology impacts our understanding of the Hebrew Bible regards etymology. Barr especially criticizes the use of etymology for establishing the meaning of biblical words.[53] He rightfully points out that usage—not etymology—determines a word's meaning, and that a Biblical Hebrew or Biblical Aramaic word cannot always be easily analyzed in terms of its compound or root elements. For example, Biblical Hebrew מַלָּח ("sailor")

---

49. Jepsen, "אָמַן 'āman; אֱמוּנָה 'emûnāh; אָמֵן 'āmēn; אֱמֶת 'emeth," 1:292–323; Wildberger, "אמן 'mn firm, secure," 1:134–57; Moberly, "אמן," 1:427–33.

50. The first theological dictionary was Cremer, *Biblisch-theologisches Wörterbuch*, written when Comparative Philology was the reigning paradigm in lexical semantics.

51. As noted by Geeraerts, Cognitive Linguistics represents a return to the psychological dimension of language, a dimension largely ignored by Structuralism (*Theories of Lexical Semantics*, 277–80).

52. Cf. Joosten, "Hebrew Thought and Greek Thought," 125–33.

53. Barr, *Semantics of Biblical Language*, 107–60; idem, "Etymology and the Old Testament," 1–28; idem, "Limitations of Etymology," 41–65; cf. Silva, *Biblical Words and Their Meaning*, 35–51; Cotterell and Turner, *Linguistics and Biblical Interpretation*, 131–35.

seems to be connected in terms of its root to the word מֶלַח ("salt") because both share the same three root letters. However, there is no connection between the two. Barr also notes that comparison with cognates in other Semitic languages can be misleading because a word may change meaning differently in those languages than in Biblical Hebrew and Biblical Aramaic. For example, whereas Biblical Hebrew אמר means "to say, think," its Akkadian cognate *amāru* means "to see." Both verbs ultimately relate to perception, but they have different meanings due to different semantic developments within their respective languages.

At the same time, Barr's point is not that etymology can never be useful. Rather, his point is that etymology is not always reliable and that scholars therefore need to utilize it carefully, especially given its history of abuse. As Barr admits, etymology remains a useful tool for determining the meaning of words that have little context. This is especially true for rare words, including the approximately 1500 *hapax legomena* that make up about 15 percent of the Hebrew Bible's vocabulary. With very few occurrences, and therefore little context, scholars are often forced to rely on comparative data to determine the meaning of rare words.[54] If a scholar is to use comparative data rightly in these cases, he or she should ideally possess a thorough knowledge of the other languages involved. Any proposed relationships, furthermore, should reflect attested sound correspondences to avoid fanciful proposals.[55]

A good example of etymology's value for understanding rare words is Hebrew תֻּכִּי, which occurs only in 1 Kgs 10:22 and its parallel, 2 Chr 9:21.[56] This word was taken by the ancient versions (cf. the Vulgate's *pavo*, the Peshitta's *ṭws̓*, and the Targum's טווס) as meaning "peacock," a rendering that found its way into the King James Version and persisted in many modern translations (e.g., ESV, NASB, NRSV). However, this does not make much sense because the other items imported by Solomon in 1 Kgs 10:22—gold, ivory, and apes— seem to be products from the Horn of Africa, and peacocks do not live there. This word's meaning was solved in the early twentieth century, when William Foxwell Albright first suggested a connection with Egyptian *t̠-ky*, which denotes a species of African ape.[57] Such a meaning makes good sense within the context of 1 Kgs 10:22 and thereby helps to establish the meaning of this rare Hebrew word.

---

54. Barr, "Etymology and the Old Testament," 2; Silva, *Biblical Words and Their Meaning*, 41–44.

55. Groom, *Linguistic Analysis of Biblical Hebrew*, 62–63.

56. Cf. Noonan, *Non-Semitic Loanwords in the Hebrew Bible*, 221.

57. Albright, "Ivory and Apes of Ophir," 144.

3.4 LEXICOGRAPHY OF THE HEBREW BIBLE

Lexicography puts the theoretical discipline of lexicology into practice in that it entails the making of dictionaries.[58] Below I outline some of the challenges involved in producing a Hebrew Bible lexicon and then evaluate the most important Hebrew Bible lexicons, semantic domain dictionaries, and theological dictionaries.

3.4.1 The Challenges of Producing a Hebrew Bible Lexicon

It may be an obvious point, but it is worth remembering that Hebrew Bible lexicons fall within the category of dictionaries of dead languages. This automatically presents a significant challenge. Typically, the users of a dictionary are users of the language treated in the dictionary. Such is not the case for Hebrew Bible lexicons, however, because they deal with languages that are no longer spoken. This presents a difficulty because ideally a lexicographer has direct access to speakers of the language treated in the dictionary.[59]

This fundamental problem is compounded by the practical decisions that face the biblical lexicographer. These decisions, which are encountered by all lexicographers of dead languages, entail issues of both extent and content.[60]

First is the question of the corpus. Should the lexicon be limited to words in the Hebrew Bible, or should it also include material from contemporaneous material? Hebrew and Aramaic inscriptions as well as texts like the Dead Sea Scrolls contain additional, non-biblical words that could be included in the lexicon.

Second is the question of form. How should the lexemes be presented? Some Biblical Hebrew and Biblical Aramaic words exhibit spelling variation (i.e., full versus defective writing), so the lexicographer must decide which form will serve as the headword. Another important decision here, especially pertinent to the Semitic languages, is whether to arrange the lexemes by three-letter root or entirely alphabetically by word.[61]

Third is the question of the meaning. How should word meaning be presented? Here the lexicographer is faced with a choice between two basic options.[62] Should a lexeme's meaning be listed by sense, starting with the most

---

58. Technically speaking, lexicography can be divided into two subfields: first, the theory behind producing dictionaries (*theoretical lexicography*), and second, the actual act of making dictionaries (*practical lexicography*).

59. Ashdowne, "Dictionaries of Dead Languages," 350–54.

60. Ashdowne, "Dictionaries of Dead Languages," 354–66; cf. Barr, "Hebrew Lexicography," 137–51; O'Connor, "Semitic Lexicography," 175–87; Clines, "Hebrew Lexicography Today," 87–98.

61. O'Connor, "Semitic Lexicography," 178–82; Barr, "Three Interrelated Factors," 33–36.

62. Ashdowne, "Dictionaries of Dead Languages," 362–65.

basic, prototypical senses followed by less frequent, metaphorical senses? Such an approach is arguably more in line with modern lexical semantics. Or should meaning be organized by syntactical constructions? Although not as linguistically sound, such an approach could be more helpful for the dictionary user.

Fourth is the question of additional information. What information should be included beyond that of the lexeme's meaning? Information that could be included to illuminate the lexeme's meaning are data on syntagmatics, context in situation, and stylistics. Other possible information to include are cognates (e.g., Akkadian, Ugaritic, and Arabic) and etymologies (in the case of loanwords and newly invented words).

Keeping these challenges in mind, I now turn to investigating the most common lexicons of Biblical Hebrew and Biblical Aramaic. These works include lexicons proper, semantic domain dictionaries, and theological dictionaries.[63]

3.4.2 Lexicons for Biblical Hebrew and Biblical Aramaic
3.4.2.1 A Hebrew and English Lexicon of the Old Testament (BDB)

A Hebrew and English Lexicon of the Old Testament, with an Appendix Containing the Biblical Aramaic (BDB) can be traced back to the work of Wilhelm Gesenius. The three authors of BDB—Francis Brown, S. R. Driver, and Charles A. Briggs—based their lexicon on Edward Robinson's English translation of Gesenius's *Hebräisches und chaldäisches Handwörterbuch über das Alte Testament*. BDB was published in both the United States (1906) and Britain (1907) just after the turn of the twentieth century, and a second edition appeared nearly half-a-century later (1952).[64] Jo Ann Hackett and John Huehnergard of the University of Texas-Austin are currently producing a revision of BDB that, when completed, will be available both in print and online.[65]

BDB falls within the tradition of Comparative Philology, as might be expected given its time of publication and its dependence on the work of Gesenius. The introduction states that the lexicon's purpose is to establish the "proper meanings" of Hebrew words in light of their "extra-Biblical history and relationship" and "cognate languages."[66] In accordance with this purpose,

---

63. Other important lexicons for the study of Biblical Hebrew and Biblical Aramaic, not treated here, include Alonso Schökel, Morla-Asensio, and Collado, *Diccionario bíblico hebreo-español*; Kaddari, מילון העברית המקראית [*Dictionary of Biblical Hebrew*]; Zorell, *Lexicon hebraicum et aramaicum*. In addition, a new revision of Gesenius has recently become available (*Hebräisches und aramäisches Handwörterbuch über das Alte Testament*).

64. On the publication of BDB and its dependence on Gesenius, see Hunziker-Rodewald, "Gesenius/Brown-Driver-Briggs Family," 219–23.

65. Hackett and Huehnergard, "Revising and Updating BDB," 227–34.

66. BDB vi.

each lexeme is arranged according to root, and most entries list pertinent ety-mological and cognate data after the headword. Word usages are grouped by meaning, with glosses and representative examples provided.

BDB remains a noteworthy lexicon for the study of Biblical Hebrew and Biblical Aramaic. It represents a significant accomplishment of scholarship for its time. Yet, its rendering of Biblical Hebrew and Biblical Aramaic words with glosses rather than definitions cannot adequately express their meaning. Furthermore, BDB's organization by root is problematic, especially in the cases of words that have no clear root. Finally, BDB's philological data is sorely out-dated because it was produced prior to the discovery of Ugaritic and the Dead Sea Scrolls, and at a time when our understanding of other Semitic languages (e.g., Akkadian) was still in its infancy.

3.4.2.2 *The Hebrew-Aramaic Lexicon of the Old Testament* (*HALOT*)

What is now known as *The Hebrew-Aramaic Lexicon of the Old Testament* (*HALOT*) has a long publication history. The first edition was published in German by Ludwig Köhler between 1948 and 1953. Then, in 1957, it was succeeded by a supplement of Biblical Aramaic words, compiled by Walter Baumgartner, and published as a second edition along with a list of additions and corrections. After Köhler's death in 1956, Baumgartner began work on a third edition, enlisting the work of other scholars (especially Johann Jakob Stamm) to help bring it to completion. The project was finally completed in 1995, by which point both Baumgartner and Stamm had died. Meanwhile, the need for an English translation prompted M. E. J. Richardson to prepare an English edition, which was published between 1994 and 2000.[67] A concise single-volume edition is presently being produced by a team at the University of Berne,[68] and a supplement to the full English edition is currently in preparation by Chaim Cohen of Ben-Gurion University.[69]

As indicated in the preface, *HALOT* seeks to "render accurately in mod-ern language the meaning of the Hebrew words."[70] *HALOT* also considers the "most important part of linguistics . . . the comparison of languages."[71]

---

67. On the publication history of *HALOT*, see Kaltner, "Koehler-Baumgartner Family," 235–36.

68. Hunziker-Rodewald, "KAHAL—the Shorter HALAT," 243–49. Concurrent to the production of the three German editions was the publication of an abridged English edition for students: Holladay, *Concise Hebrew and Aramaic Lexicon of the Old Testament*. However, this was prior to the publication of the significantly revised third edition, and Holladay's edition does not include comparative or etymological data.

69. Kaltner, "Koehler-Baumgartner Family," 239–40.

70. *HALOT* lxx.

71. *HALOT* lxxi.

Thus, *HALOT* adopts Comparative Philology's approach to lexicography, similar to BDB. However, because of its later publication date it incorporates comparative data not available when BDB was produced. Another significant difference is that *HALOT* organizes its lexical entries alphabetically by lexeme. Word usage within each entry is grouped by meaning, expressed as glosses.

HALOT's alphabetical arrangement of words gives it a distinct advantage over BDB in terms of ease of use. Its updated etymological data, presented in transliterated form rather than its original script, is also a significant strength. However, its etymological data is not without weakness. *HALOT* contains a number of questionable etymologies and comparisons, particularly with respect to Arabic, that sometimes overshadow semantic and syntactic evidence from the biblical text itself.[72] Finally, like BDB, *HALOT* suffers from use of glosses rather than definitions.

3.4.2.3 *Dictionary of Classical Hebrew* (*DCH*)

The eight-volume *Dictionary of Classical Hebrew* (*DCH*) was first conceived in 1983. Work on the project began in 1988, and as volumes were completed it was published by Sheffield Academic Press between 1993 and 2011. The project was produced under the editorial leadership of David J. A. Clines at the University of Sheffield and under the auspices of the Society for Old Testament Study, making it a predominantly British work.

DCH significantly differs from its predecessors in two key ways, as noted by Clines in the introduction to the first volume.[73] First, it covers the Hebrew language as attested in texts prior to 200 CE, which includes not only the Hebrew of the Old Testament but also Ben Sira, the Dead Sea Scrolls, and extrabiblical inscriptions. Thus, unlike BDB and *HALOT*, it does not include Biblical Aramaic. Second, in accordance with its belief that "the meaning of a word is its use in the language,"[74] *DCH* lists all word usages, expressed as glosses, according to their syntagmatic constructions rather than similar meaning. This exclusive focus on word usage means that *DCH* does not include any comparative or etymological data. The result is a lexicon that looks very different from BDB and *HALOT*.

DCH's focus on the usage of words within their context makes it a rich repository of data. However, because it lists every single occurrence of a word, the amount of data is overwhelming, difficult to sort through, and not necessarily helpful. These data are presented at the complete expense of philological

---

72. Kaltner, "Koehler-Baumgartner Family," 236–42.
73. Clines, *DCH*, 1:14.
74. Clines, *DCH*, 1:14.

information[75] and do not provide any information on possible encyclopedic meaning. Furthermore, *DCH*'s corpus is problematic. Including Hebrew from as late as 200 CE as if it fits alongside earlier material effectively disregards changes that have taken place in the language.[76] The exclusion of Biblical Aramaic neglects a relatively small, but nevertheless important, portion of the canon.

3.4.2.4 *Semantics of Ancient Hebrew Database (SAHD)*

The *Semantics of Ancient Hebrew Database (SAHD)* originated during three workshops, held from 1992 to 1994, that explored the theoretical and practical aspects of a semantic database for ancient Hebrew.[77] The project was officially launched in 1994 under the auspices of the European Science Foundation. Currently chaired by Holger Gzella of Leiden University, it operates out of a network of centers established at universities throughout Europe. According to the project website, its purpose is "to prepare a tool which can be a useful inducement to further semantic research" and to "provide a badly needed survey of the results and arguments found in the scholarly literature."[78] Like *DCH*, it includes Hebrew words from the Old Testament as well as inscriptions, Ben Sira, and the Dead Sea Scrolls, but does not encompass Biblical Aramaic.

Each entry of *SAHD* contains several items. These include comparative Semitic and etymological data, key morphological characteristics, syntagmatics, translation equivalents in the ancient versions, categorization according to semantic field, exegetical insights for specific occurrences, concluding summary, and a bibliography.[79] Although far from finished, the project is well underway, and a number of entries are complete and available online. The project has also resulted in a number of print publications.[80]

SAHD represents a significant accomplishment and a model for future Hebrew Bible lexicons. It strikes a good balance between traditional historical-comparative (e.g., etymological data and data from ancient versions) and structuralist (e.g., syntagmatic information and semantic field data) approaches to lexicography. However, in doing so it largely ignores encyclopedic knowledge. Furthermore, although the data are laid out clearly in each entry, the user may not know what to do with the quantity of information, especially when it is

75. Muraoka, "New Dictionary of Classical Hebrew," 89–90, 93–94.

76. Muraoka, "New Dictionary of Classical Hebrew," 88–89; O'Connor, "Semitic Lexicography," 193–94.

77. http://www.sahd.div.ed.ac.uk/info:lexeme_index.

78. http://www.sahd.div.ed.ac.uk/info:description.

79. Williamson, "Semantics and Lexicography," 328–32.

80. http://www.sahd.div.ed.ac.uk/info:publications.

provided without comment or evaluative judgment. Finally, *SAHD*'s usefulness is limited to Hebrew because the project excludes Biblical Aramaic.

3.4.2.5 *Semantic Dictionary of Biblical Hebrew* (*SDBH*)

The *Semantic Dictionary of Biblical Hebrew* (*SDBH*) was launched online in 2000 under the auspices of the United Bible Societies.[81] Reinier de Blois, now the chief editor of *SDBH*, conducted the preliminary research for the project that resulted in his Vrije Universiteit dissertation.[82] The goal of the project is to "build a new dictionary of biblical Hebrew that is based on semantic domains, comparable to Louw and Nida's *Greek-English Lexicon of the New Testament.*"[83] Although currently available, it is a work in progress and not yet completed.

Unlike Louw and Nida, *SDBH* is based on Cognitive Linguistics, which provides a better model for expressing word meaning than componential analysis.[84] Naturally, its semantic domains also differ from those of Louw and Nida because Biblical Hebrew contains a different range of vocabulary than New Testament Greek.[85] Each Hebrew word belongs to one of three classes of words—Objects, Events, or Relationals—and is further sub-grouped with other words of similar semantic domains. Furthermore, words belonging to the Objects and Events classes are assigned both a lexical (i.e., extralinguistic) and contextual (i.e., within specific occurrences) meaning. Semantic distinctions therefore take priority over grammatical classification by part of speech.[86]

One strength of *SDBH* is its use of actual definitions rather than glosses. *SDBH* also incorporates a number of insights from Cognitive Linguistics. Perhaps most notable is its distinction between lexical and contextual meaning, an attempt to account for both the dictionary definition of a word as well as encyclopedic knowledge. Nevertheless, it is questionable whether *SDBH*'s semantic domains accurately represent ancient Israelite categories as opposed to Blois's own categories.[87] Furthermore, due to its focus on semantic domains, *SDBH* pays little attention to syntagmatics and no attention to etymological data.[88]

---

81. http://www.sdbh.org/dictionary/main.php?language=en; cf. Blois, "Semantic Dictionary of Biblical Hebrew," 275–95.

82. Blois, "Towards a New Dictionary of Biblical Hebrew."

83. http://www.sdbh.org/home-en.html.

84. Cf. Blois, "Semantic Domains for Biblical Greek," 265–78.

85. Blois, "Semantic Domains for Biblical Hebrew," 214. As such, *SDBH* avoids the error of Swanson, *Dictionary of Biblical Languages.*

86. http://www.sdbh.org/framework/index.html.

87. Van Steenbergen, "Hebrew Lexicography and Worldview," 302; cf. Merwe, "Towards a Principled Working Model," 133.

88. Merwe, "Towards a Principled Working Model," 132–33.

3.4.2.6 Theological Dictionaries

The most-commonly used theological dictionaries are the *Theological Dictionary of the Old Testament* (*TDOT*), the *Theological Lexicon of the Old Testament* (*TLOT*), and the *New International Dictionary of Old Testament Theology and Exegesis* (*NIDOTTE*). Both *TDOT* and *NIDOTTE* are relatively comprehensive in terms of their scope, whereas *TLOT* is limited to key theological terms. Entries in each dictionary contain information on cognates, usage in the Hebrew Bible, and theological significance.

Each of these projects began after Barr's critique of theological dictionaries. Therefore, they exhibit at least some awareness of the pitfalls inherent to producing a theological dictionary, as is evident from the editors' introductory remarks. Overall *TDOT*, *TLOT*, and *NIDOTTE* maintain a distinction between word and concept. However, they do not always do so successfully, in part because their structure inherently associates specific concepts with each word set, rather than the other way around. At the same time, because words are ultimately not separable from concepts, and because we as interpreters lack encyclopedic knowledge of ancient Israel due to our historical and cultural distance, theological dictionaries remain useful repositories of data.[89]

More problematic is the issue of semantic fields. Although each project claims to offer a dictionary based on semantic fields, none fully delivers. *NIDOTTE* comes the closest to doing so in that it provides an index of semantic fields. Nevertheless, in each project semantic fields are not well defined, nor are they based on any clear criteria. Furthermore, entries do not always pay adequate attention to synonyms and antonyms.[90] Here especially there remains significant room for growth, and hopefully future theological dictionaries will give greater consideration to this area.

3.4.2.7 Evaluation

The above survey demonstrates the rich and varied history of Hebrew Bible lexicography. Traditional dictionaries such as BDB and *HALOT* remain useful tools, and the emergence of electronic databases such as *SADH* and *SDBH* is particularly encouraging. Theological lexicons, furthermore, are alive and well despite their potential pitfalls. At the same time, the above survey demonstrates some methodological problems in most Hebrew Bible lexicons.

---

89. The best theological dictionary to date, one that entails New Testament Greek in addition to Biblical Hebrew and Biblical Aramaic, is *The Lexham Theological Wordbook*, edited by Douglas Mangum. This resource analyzes various concepts found in the Bible, similar to a Bible dictionary, in that its entries are listed by concept with relevant Hebrew, Greek, and Aramaic lexemes listed under each concept.

90. Cf. Van Steenbergen, "Hebrew Lexicography and Worldview," 307–8.

First, a significant problem with most current Hebrew Bible lexicons is the use of glosses.[91] Glosses imply a one-to-one correspondence between the Biblical Hebrew or Biblical Aramaic word and the modern gloss. This can be misleading when their meanings do not match up entirely. It does not, furthermore, line up with current lexicographic practice. Especially when the dictionary user is unaware of the cultural world of the source language, lexicographers recommend giving an explanatory equivalent. This entails providing an extended definition that describes the word's meaning in encyclopedic terms.[92] The challenge here is to know how much description is necessary— and practical—for the user. Nevertheless, biblical lexicographers would do well to incorporate definitions with at least some encyclopedic knowledge into their lexicons.[93]

Second, in part following Barr's strong critiques of etymology, several recent Hebrew Bible lexicons ignore etymological data altogether. It is true that etymological data is typically only included in diachronic (i.e., historical or etymological) dictionaries, which Hebrew Bible lexicons are not. It is also true that biblical lexicographers have frequently misused etymological data, as BDB and even the recent *HALOT* demonstrate. However, as noted earlier, the Hebrew Bible's many rare words require the use of etymology, and abuse does not preclude proper use. Furthermore, etymology is helpful for distinguishing homonyms even in synchronic dictionaries,[94] and including etymological data facilitates the comparative method for the Semitic languages. It would therefore be rash to ignore etymological data altogether.[95] Nevertheless, there is room for debate on how best to include such data.[96]

Finally, at the practical level there is significant need for better attention to the structure and presentation of biblical lexicons. BDB, *HALOT,* and *DCH* each omit an introductory "guide to the dictionary" that facilitates use of the lexicon. Generally speaking, these lexicons also lack intuitive organization and microstructures (e.g., clearly divided entries and organization of data that reflects importance and contribution).[97] The online databases of *SAHD* and *SDBH,* on the other hand, contain many of these features and make good

---

91. Barr, "Hebrew Lexicography," 119–20.

92. Adamska-Sałaciak, "Explaining Meaning in Bilingual Dictionaries," 150–52; cf. Aitken, "Context of Situation in Biblical Lexica," 182–88.

93. Cf. Van Steenbergen, "Hebrew Lexicography and Worldview," 306–7.

94. Koskela, "Homonyms in Different Types of Dictionaries," 459.

95. Cf. Emerton, "Comparative Semitic Philology and Hebrew Lexicography," 1–24; Kogan, "Semitic Etymology in a Biblical Hebrew Lexicon," 83–102.

96. See some helpful suggestions for incorporating etymological data into Hebrew Bible lexicons in Barr, "Hebrew Lexicography," 140–43.

97. Imbayarwo, "Biblical Hebrew Lexicon for Translators," 108–41.

use of technology to facilitate rapid access of data. Hopefully, future lexicon projects will follow suit by utilizing an open-ended, online database format.[98]

Despite these critiques, I want to reiterate that existing Hebrew Bible lexicons are helpful resources. The key for us is to recognize lexicons for what they are—tools—and what they are not—the final authority on the meaning of words. Here we do well to heed the conclusions of Richard Ashdowne regarding dictionaries of dead languages:

> The lexicographer always strives for a fair account of the surviving evidence, and, if it is diligently analysed, this gives the dictionary a degree of authoritativeness; users can reasonably rely on the information provided. However . . . the compiler of such a dictionary is repeatedly invited to go beyond the evidence into territory for which perhaps native knowledge and competence would be the only true source of authority. In the absence of this, it is unsurprising that dictionary users may come to a dictionary assuming that it can and will provide the information needed and that this information is uniformly certain. In how such a dictionary presents itself, however, we have seen ways in which this attitude is carefully discouraged: lexicographers of dead languages instead encourage their users to approach their dictionaries with different expectations and to reach views about interpretation for themselves *aided* by rather than derived from the dictionary.[99]

3.5 THE WAYS FORWARD

James Barr's critique of scholars' application of lexical semantics to the Hebrew Bible was much-needed. His clarion call gave scholars of the Hebrew Bible a solid foundation for applying lexical semantics to Biblical Hebrew and Biblical Aramaic, and many others—most notably Moisés Silva—have continued in this vein. All this has led to the production of many helpful tools and resources for understanding the meaning of Biblical Hebrew and Biblical Aramaic words. The end result is more linguistically informed exegesis and, ultimately, a better understanding of the text of the Hebrew Bible.

Yet, as always, there is continued room for improvement. Cognitive Linguistics offers valuable refinement of Barr's and Silva's approaches, which were largely based in Structuralism and the trappings of their time. Of particular note is the recent reawakening to the notion that encyclopedic knowledge

---

98. Cf. Kaufman, "Semitics," 279.
99. Ashdowne, "Dictionaries of Dead Languages," 365–66. The emphasis is original.

plays an important role in word meaning. Hopefully, future scholarship will continue to explore the role of encyclopedic knowledge for the meaning of Biblical Hebrew and Biblical Aramaic words. Continued investigation along this line can only lead to refinement in method and improved understanding. As scholarship advances in this way, however, we must not forget the value of syntagmatics and pragmatics as well as etymology for understanding word meaning. Only combined with these traditional approaches can recent insights from Cognitive Linguistics enhance our understanding of lexical meaning and thereby better equip us for faithful exegesis and ministry.

3.6 FURTHER READING

Barr, James. *The Semantics of Biblical Language.* Oxford: Oxford University Press, 1961.

Clines, David J. A. "The Challenge of Hebrew Lexicography Today." Pages 87–98 in *Congress Volume: Ljubljana, 2007.* Edited by André Lemaire. VTSup 133. Leiden: Brill, 2010.

Holtz, Shalom E. "Lexicography: Biblical Hebrew." *EHLL* 2:507–10.

Hovav, Malka Rappaport. "Lexical Semantics." *EHLL* 2:499–504.

Kedar-Kopfstein, Benjamin. *Biblische Semantik: Eine Einführung.* Stuttgart: Kohlhammer, 1981.

Merwe, Christo H. J. van der. "Biblical Hebrew Lexicology: A Cognitive Linguistic Perspective." *Kleine Untersuchungen zur Sprache des Alten Testaments und seiner Umwelt* 6 (2006): 87–112.

———. "Towards a Principled Working Model for Biblical Hebrew Lexicography." *JNSL* 30.1 (2004): 119–37.

O'Connor, Michael. "Semitic Lexicography: European Dictionaries of Biblical Hebrew in the Twentieth Century." Pages 173–212 in *Semitic Linguistics: The State of the Art at the Turn of the Twenty-First Century.* Edited by Shlomo Izre'el. IOS 20. Winona Lake, IN: Eisenbrauns, 2002.

Silva, Moisés. *Biblical Words and Their Meaning: An Introduction to Lexical Semantics.* 2nd ed. Grand Rapids: Zondervan, 1994.

Tropper, Josef. "Lexikographische Untersuchungen zum Biblisch-Aramäischen." *JNSL* 23.2 (1997): 105–28.

Walton, John H. "Principles for Productive Word Study." *NIDOTTE* 1:161–71.

CHAPTER 4

THE VERBAL STEMS

The question [of] how the function of Piel in relation to other conjugations, notably Qal, should be defined still remains one of the major challenges facing Hebrew and Semitic linguistics.

—TAKAMITSU MURAOKA[1]

4.1 INTRODUCTION

One of the major features of the Semitic languages—including Biblical Hebrew and Biblical Aramaic—is the verbal stems, or *binyanim*. The primary role of the verbal stems is to form new words, and thereby to expand the lexicon, by modifying the three-letter verbal root. Specific combinations of preformatives, vowels, and reduplicated consonants alter the basic pattern of the root and create new meanings. Hebrew and Aramaic therefore differ significantly from a language like English, for example, which relies primarily on the addition of words (i.e., auxiliaries) to express changes in meaning.

Given their importance for the Semitic languages and their uniqueness compared with the Indo-European languages, it is not surprising that the verbal stems have occupied a significant place in research. During the heyday of Comparative Philology, scholars grew in their understanding of the verbal stems with the discovery of Semitic languages such as Akkadian and Ugaritic. Today, the verbal stems continue to be a common topic of discussion in research. Developments in modern linguistics have contributed to this conversation.

In this chapter I examine recent advances in our understanding of the verbal stems, focusing mostly on Biblical Hebrew because little scholarship has treated this topic for Biblical Aramaic. I discuss modern linguistic concepts that shed

---

1. Joüon §52d.

light on the Biblical Hebrew verbal stems and canvas key scholarship on the primary derived stems: the Niphal (the N stem), the Piel (the D stem), the Hiphil (the C stem), and the Hithpael (the tD stem). Then, I survey scholarship on the verbal stems in Biblical Aramaic. I offer evaluation and conclude, finally, with some suggestions for the ways forward.

4.2 THE MODERN LINGUISTIC FRAMEWORK FOR THE VERBAL STEMS

Steven W. Boyd provides an excellent summary of the modern linguistic framework for the verbal stems.[2] He discusses three topics relevant for the verbal stems: arguments and transitivity, semantic roles and grammatical voice, and situation aspect and phasal aspect. I now turn to these concepts, demonstrating their significance for Biblical Hebrew and Biblical Aramaic in the process.

4.2.1 Arguments and Transitivity

The concept of a linguistic *argument* has its origins in the Government and Binding framework of the 1980s, especially the research of linguists such as Edwin Williams.[3] An argument is a nominal component of a clause (i.e., a noun) associated with a predicate (i.e., a verb). All verbs have at least one argument, the grammatical subject, but some may also have a direct object or additional arguments. For example, the sentence *The girl drew a picture* has two arguments: the subject *girl* and the direct object *picture*. Linguists use the term *valency*, which originated with the French linguist Lucien Tesnière,[4] to refer to the number of arguments associated with a verb.

As I just noted, a verb may or may not possess arguments in addition to its subject. Whether or not the verb does depends on its transitivity, or ability to take a direct object. Some verbs (e.g., *He ran*) are *intransitive* and do not take a direct object. Other verbs are *transitive* and take one direct object (e.g., *She wrote a book*) or even multiple ones (e.g., *She gave the man the book*). Naturally, whether a verb is intransitive or transitive will depend on the kind of situation it describes.

These concepts are important for understanding the verbal stems because the Semitic languages distinguish between active verbs (i.e., verbs that express an action) and stative verbs (i.e., verbs that express a characteristic), both of which can be either transitive or intransitive. Furthermore, since the derived

---

2. Boyd, "*Binyanim* (Verbal Stems)," 85–125; cf. Widder, "Linguistic Issues in Biblical Hebrew," 138–40.

3. Williams, "Argument Structure and Morphology," 81–114.

4. Tesnière, *Éléments de syntavxe structurale*, 238–82.

verbal stems increase or decrease transitivity and the number of arguments by transforming the basic meaning of the verbal root, having a grasp of these concepts is important.[5]

4.2.2 Semantic Roles and Grammatical Voice

The concept of a *semantic role* (also known as a *thematic relation*) has its origins in Generative Grammar and was first introduced by Jeffery Gruber and Charles J. Fillmore in the 1960s.[6] But it is not bound to the generative approach and has since been developed significantly by functionalists like Robert D. Van Valin.[7] A semantic role describes the relationship that the arguments have to the verb. There are two broad categories of semantic roles. The Actor is the one that brings about a state or event, and the Undergoer is the one affected by the situation.

Closely related to semantic roles is *grammatical voice* or *diathesis*, which describes the grammatical function of a sentence's arguments. For an *active* construction, the verb's subject is the Actor and any direct object is the Undergoer (e.g., *The boy kicked the ball*), but for a *passive* construction the verb's subject is the Undergoer (e.g., *The ball was kicked*). In between the active and the passive are the *middle* and *reflexive* voices. The subject of a middle construction acts but does not actually bring about a situation (e.g., *The door opened*). In reflexive constructions, the Actor and Undergoer are the same because the subject affects itself (e.g., *The woman washed herself*).

These ideas are significant for understanding the verbal stems because one of the verbal stems' primary functions is to indicate the grammatical voice of the verbal root. For example, the Pual and Hophal both express the passive of the Piel and Hiphil, respectively. Grammatical voice is also frequently—but not always—expressed in the Qal stem's active versus stative dichotomy, in that active verbs naturally express the active voice whereas stative verbs instead are passive.[8]

4.2.3 Situation Aspect and Phasal Aspect

The idea of *situation aspect*, also known as *lexical aspect* and often identified with *Aktionsart* (a German word meaning "type of action"), can be found in the writings of Aristotle (*Metaphysics* 1048b.27–34). However, Zeno Vendler is largely responsible for our modern understanding of this concept.[9]

---

5. Boyd, "*Binyanim* (Verbal Stems)," 89; cf. Bjøru, "Transitivity and the Binyanim," 48–63.

6. Gruber, "Studies in Lexical Relations"; Fillmore, "Case for Case," 1–90.

7. Cf. Van Valin, "Semantic Macroroles," 62–82.

8. Boyd, "*Binyanim* (Verbal Stems)," 94–95. Active verbs are always active, regardless of whether they are transitive or intransitive. Stative verbs are frequently passive when intransitive, but when transitive they are instead active.

9. Vendler, "Verbs and Times," 143–60.

Situation aspect refers to the type of situation that a verb expresses. A verb may describe either an event or a state (dynamicity), and its situation may have an end point or not (telicity), and may occur over a period of time or instantaneously (durativity[10]). Linguists disagree on how to classify the possible combinations of these categories, but at most there can be seven different situation aspects.

Situation Class	Dynamicity	Telicity	Durativity	Example(s)
Property	-	-	+	*be small, be red*
Point State	-	+	-	*it is 12 o'clock*
Transitory State	-	+	-	*be young, be hot*
Semelfactive	+	-	-	*knock, tap, cough, sneeze*
Activity	+	-	+	*walk, read, play*
Accomplishment	+	+	+	*build a house, grow up*
Achievement	+	+	-	*realize, find, win a contest*

As indicated by its name, phasal aspect refers to a situation's phases of development and describes a situation's progression through time. A verb can be either punctiliar (i.e., instantaneous) or durative (i.e., non-instantaneous), with the possibility of progression at the beginning, middle, and end of a situation.

Phasal Aspect	Description	Example
Inchoative	entrance into a state	*become angry*
Inceptive	beginning of an event	*begin walking*
Punctiliar	instantaneous, non-durative event	*to knock*
Iterative	repetition of a non-durative event	*to knock for 30 seconds*
Frequentative	non-habitual repetition of a durative event	*walk back and forth*
Habitual	customary repetition of a durative event	*used to walk*
Cessative	end of a state	*stop being angry*
Completive	completion of an event	*finish walking*

---

10. The category of durativity is rejected by some linguists (e.g., Rothstein, *Structuring Events*, 28–29). However, many linguists consider it valid, in part because common sense suggests that some situations occur in an instant of time whereas others take place over an interval of time (e.g., Comrie, *Aspect*, 41–44; Smith, *Parameter of Aspect*, 41–42). See Boyd, "*Binyanim* (Verbal Stems)," 91.

Situation aspect is directly connected with lexical meaning, which lies behind the primary function of the verbal stems. Furthermore, the derived stems may express certain types of situations that fall within the category of phasal aspect. Possible types include inchoative and inceptive situations (the Niphal) as well as iterative and frequentative situations (the Piel).[11]

4.3 THE VERBAL STEMS IN BIBLICAL HEBREW

These linguistic concepts (arguments and transitivity, semantic roles and grammatical voice, and situation aspect and phasal aspect) directly relate to the verbal stems' different functions. With these concepts in mind, I now look at key studies on the derived verbal stems in Biblical Hebrew, specifically the Niphal, Piel, Hiphil, and Hithpael.

4.3.1 The Niphal

The most common view of the Niphal is that it represents several different diatheses, one of which is the reflexive voice. Many modern grammars hold to this perspective.[12] However, especially over the past few decades, a growing number of scholars have come to recognize that the Niphal expresses something other than the reflexive voice.

In this section I survey key studies of the Niphal, highlighting recent departures from the traditional notion that the Niphal is reflexive. The relevant scholarship can be categorized in terms of three different functions attributed to the Niphal: the passive-reflexive, the resultative, and the medio-passive.

4.3.1.1 The Niphal as Passive-Reflexive
4.3.1.1.1 MAYER LAMBERT

On the one side of the spectrum of those who think the Niphal functions reflexively is Mayer Lambert, who published one of the earliest studies of the Niphal.[13] Lambert systematically lists and discusses each of the roots for which the Niphal occurs. He classifies each usage of the Niphal and connects its different functions to the other stems in which a root is attested. Lambert concludes that the Niphal typically functions as the reflexive or passive of the Qal, Piel, and Hiphil but can sometimes have its own distinct nuance and

---

11. Boyd, "*Binyanim* (Verbal Stems)," 89–94.
12. E.g., GKC §51c; Bauer and Leander, *Historische Grammatik der hebräischen Sprache*, 289 (§238w'); Joüon §51c; *IBHS* §23.4.b.
13. Lambert, "Emploi du nifal en hébreu," 196–214.

behave like an active verb. He thinks that the basic sense of the Niphal is the reflexive voice and that its passive function developed from its reflexive sense.[14]

Lambert's study is important because it represents the first systematic analysis of the Niphal. Yet, Lambert's study was conducted prior to the advent of modern linguistics. Accordingly, Lambert's study does not attempt to understand the Niphal in light of modern insights on semantic roles and diathesis. As a result, Lambert gives little attention to the middle voice in his study. Furthermore, Lambert's classification of each usage of the Niphal is somewhat arbitrary and largely relies on translation possibilities.

4.3.1.1.2 GEORGE LINAM KLEIN

On the other side of the spectrum is George Linam Klein, who argues that the Niphal is primarily passive even if it is sometimes reflexive.[15] He classifies all the Hebrew Bible's Niphals into one of nine categories: reflexive, reciprocal, passive, middle, resultative, tolerative, denominative, active, and ambiguous. According to the resulting analysis, the Niphal expresses the passive voice in just over 50 percent of its occurrences, whereas it denotes the reflexive and middle in only 14.7 percent and 1.6 percent of its occurrences, respectively. Accordingly, Klein contends that the Niphal is primarily passive and that its usage as a reflexive—and more rarely, as a middle—both result from its original passive function.

Klein's study is essentially the first systematic analysis of the Niphal to incorporate insights from modern linguistics. However, he largely relies upon the debated theories of Joan Bresnan, who considers the passive to be lexical rather than syntactic.[16] Furthermore, his categorization schema lacks nuance in that his criteria for classifying a root as reflexive (intransitivity and possession of both an unspecified agent and animate subject) can equally apply to the middle voice.

4.3.1.1.3 P. A. SIEBESMA

At least one study on the Niphal avoids categorizing this stem as primarily passive or reflexive. P. A. Siebesma argues for a single core meaning of the Niphal that encompasses the passive and reflexive voices.[17] Siebesma's approach

---

14. Cf. Lambert, *Traité de grammaire hebraïque*, 233–34 (§663).

15. Klein, "Niphal in Biblical Hebrew."

16. Bresnan, "Passive in Lexical Theory," 3–86. The passive is arguably both lexical and syntactic in Biblical Hebrew, not solely lexical. Whether or not a verbal root can be passive depends on the word (lexical), but the passive voice is expressed at the level of syntax (syntactic). Cf. Keenan, "Passive is Phrasal," 181–213.

17. Siebesma, *Function of the Niphʿal in Biblical Hebrew*.

largely follows that of Lambert in that he relates each root semantically to the Qal, Piel, and Hiphil—even using Lambert's same categories—and defines that semantic connection in terms of grammatical voice. However, unlike Lambert, Siebesma compares this data with similar data for the Pual, Hophal, and Hithpael. Also, unlike Lambert, Siebesma rejects the notion that the Niphal was primarily reflexive. He contends that the Niphal can be both passive and reflexive because Hebrew did not distinguish between the two. Thus, according to Siebesma, neither the passive nor reflexive voice takes priority in the Niphal, even though both are possible senses of the Niphal.

Similar to Lambert's analysis, the primary contribution of Siebesma's work is its thorough summary of data related to the Niphal. Nevertheless, Siebesma does not conduct his analysis within any modern linguistic framework. He leaves several questions unanswered, particularly questions about the relationship between the Niphal and Qal stems.[18] Finally, although he argues that the traditional passive-reflexive distinction is irrelevant, he ultimately holds to both of these functions for the Niphal and does not consider the possibility that the Niphal might express other diatheses.

4.3.1.2 The Niphal as Resultative
4.3.1.2.1 BELINDA JEAN BICKNELL

Belinda Jean Bicknell examines the Niphal within the broader framework of all the passive stems in Hebrew (the Qal passive, Niphal, Pual, and Hophal).[19] She rejects the standard attempt to understand the passive in terms of the relationship between the subject and an action. Instead, she views the passive in light of verbal function. She argues that the Niphal is resultative in that it expresses the final state resulting from an action, without reference to agency (e.g., the Niphal of לחם means "to become engaged in battle"). Thus, Bicknell views the Niphal's function exclusively in terms of situation aspect rather than grammatical voice.

Bicknell's study provides some important conclusions regarding agency and passive constructions. Furthermore, Bicknell rightly recognizes that the verbal stems relate to situation aspect, a fact largely ignored by many works on the Niphal. At the same time, Bicknell is mistaken to privilege situation aspect at the exclusion of grammatical voice. Linguists note that situation aspect and diathesis—including resultative and passive constructions—are not mutually exclusive categories but naturally overlap and intersect.[20]

---

18. Cf. Boyd, review of *The Function of the Niphʿal in Biblical Hebrew*, 670.
19. Bicknell, "Passives in Biblical Hebrew."
20. Cf. Nedialkov and Jaxontov, "Typology of Resultative Constructions," 17.

4.3.1.2.2 RICHARD C. BENTON

Another scholar who argues that the Niphal expresses situation aspect is Richard C. Benton.[21] Observing apparent overlap between the Niphal and Hithpael for some roots, he thinks the Niphal expresses the state that results from an action whereas the Hithpael expresses the process that results in a state (e.g., ברך means "to be blessed" in the Niphal but "to become blessed" in the Hithpael). Benton rejects Bicknell's separation of the passive voice from situation aspect, arguing that many languages of the world (e.g., Spanish and Tagalog) demonstrate interaction between these two concepts.

Like Bicknell, Benton rightly notes the important role that situation aspect has in the verbal stems. He avoids a simplistic dichotomy between situation aspect and grammatical voice, recognizing that the two frequently intersect. He also attempts to understand the function of the Niphal in light of cross-linguistic observations. Nevertheless, Benton places too much emphasis on situation aspect at the expense of grammatical voice. Benton's analysis also does not interact with the role of the N stem within the Semitic languages more generally.

4.3.1.3 The Niphal as Medio-Passive

4.3.1.3.1 ERNST JENNI

A significant step forward in the understanding of the Niphal was taken by Ernst Jenni, who in 1973 addressed the plethora of translation options for the Niphal.[22] In accordance with his view that each of the verbal stems has a central meaning in opposition to the other stems, he contends that the Niphal is neither primarily passive nor reflexive. Rather, he argues that the Niphal marks an event experienced by (rather than affected by) the subject. He expresses the basic meaning of the Niphal as "to show oneself as something" (*sich als etwas erweisen*).[23] Thus, for example, according to Jenni the Niphal of קדש would mean "to show oneself as holy."

Jenni comes close to understanding the Niphal's function as that of the middle voice, even if he does not state it as such. Jenni also understands the Niphal as a detransitiver, or a stem that removes an argument by making its root intransitive, which well suits the middle voice.[24] He is to be commended for his desire to understand the Niphal apart from translation possibilities.

---

21. Benton, "Aspect and the Biblical Hebrew Niphal and Hitpael"; idem, "Verbal and Contextual Information," 385–99.

22. Jenni, "Zur Funktion der reflexiv-passiven Stammformen," 4:61–70; idem, "Nif'al und Hitpa'el," 131–303; cf. idem, "Reflexive-Passive Stems in Biblical Hebrew," 15–16.

23. Jenni, "Zur Funktion der reflexiv-passiven Stammformen," 4:64.

24. Notably, N. J. C. Kouwenberg makes a similar argument regarding the Akkadian N stem (*Akkadian Verb and Its Semitic Background*, 294).

Yet he does not offer much evidence for his conclusions, and his approach lacks a modern linguistic framework.

4.3.1.3.2 Steven W. Boyd

Stephen W. Boyd highlights the usage of the Niphal to express the middle voice.[25] Boyd contends that most studies on the Niphal largely rely on translation possibilities in modern Indo-European. To avoid this pitfall, Boyd turns to the concept of semantic roles. He defines the reflexive voice as an argument in which the Agent and Patient are the same and defines the middle voice as an argument in which the subject's role becomes that of Actor. Boyd concludes that the Niphal is rarely reflexive but instead commonly expresses the middle voice in addition to the passive voice. Thus, for active verbs the Niphal is inceptive (e.g., קבר means "to be buried" in the Niphal) whereas for stative verbs the Niphal is inchoative (e.g., מלא means "to become full" and ראה means "to appear, become seen" in the Niphal).[26]

Boyd's study represents a major breakthrough in our understanding of the Niphal. His research is thorough and founded on a cogent linguistic methodology rather than translation possibilities. Some may dispute Boyd's sharp distinction between the middle and the reflexive.[27] Nevertheless, it cannot be disputed that Boyd has placed our understanding of the Niphal on solid linguistic footing.

4.3.1.4 Evaluation

The above survey demonstrates the need for linguistic sensitivity and sound methodology when considering the function of the Niphal. In particular, the research of Boyd cautions against imposing non-Semitic categories upon Hebrew. The native language of most current scholars of Hebrew—and certainly of past scholars, who tended to be German and French—is Indo-European. This can present problems for analyzing the Niphal because the middle voice is not inflected in these languages, making it easy to rely on translation possibilities and ignore the evidence that the Niphal is medio-passive.[28]

---

25. Boyd, "Medio-Passive-Reflexive in Biblical Hebrew." According to Boyd, the Niphal can also express the passive, but this function arose from the gradual loss of the Qal passive and the natural connection between the middle and passive voices.

26. Such a conclusion is consistent with the conclusions of Stephen J. Lieberman, who argues that the N stem, C stem, and t-infixed stems each reflect distinct pronominal elements. In his view, the N stem's pronominal element refers to someone not visible to the speaker. See Lieberman, "Afro-Asiatic Background of the Semitic N-Stem," 577–628.

27. Linguists differ in their classification of the reflexive voice. Some distinguish it from the middle (e.g., Geniusiene, *Typology of Reflexives*), whereas others subsume the reflexive under the middle voice (e.g., Kemmer, *Middle Voice*; Klaiman, "Middle Verbs," 35–61).

28. Unfamiliarity with the middle voice has led to confusion in New Testament Greek studies

Moving forward, scholars should avoid imposing grammatical categories of their native tongues upon Hebrew. Rather, Hebrew should be understood for what it is, namely, a Semitic language. To do otherwise will only perpetuate the errors of the past, in which the Niphal was viewed through translation possibilities in modern Indo-European languages. Important for this task is acknowledgement of the key role that grammatical voice plays in the Hebrew verbal system.

Future studies on the Niphal should adopt a medio-passive, not reflexive, framework for this stem. There is need for further research on the interaction between the Niphal's medio-passive diathesis and other categories such as *Aktionsart*, agentivity, and transitivity. There is also the need to examine the Niphal in light of the function of the N stem and other medio-passive stems in the Semitic languages. One particularly interesting avenue of research on this topic regards roots that appear in the Niphal in Hebrew but occur in both the N stem and the Gt stem, or only in the Gt stem, in other Semitic languages.[29]

4.3.2 The Piel

The second verbal stem to be examined is the Piel. It is perhaps the most debated of all the verbal stems, as noted by Takamitsu Muraoka in his translation of Paul Joüon's grammar: "The question [of] how the function of Piel in relation to other conjugations, notably Qal, should be defined still remains one of the major challenges facing Hebrew and Semitic linguistics."[30]

It is no surprise, then, that scholars have proposed a variety of distinct functions for the Piel. Here I summarize their views according to four different categories: intensive, complex active, resultative, and pluralitive-factitive. By nature of the discussion, many of the studies mentioned below deal generally with the D stem, the Semitic languages' equivalent of the Hebrew Piel.

4.3.2.1 The Piel as Intensive
4.3.2.1.1 JACOB WEINGREEN

The characterization of the Piel as intensive, or expressing strong and energetic action, can be traced to European Semiticists of the nineteenth century such as Wilhelm Gesenius.[31] Yet, the first focused study to argue for an intensive

---

as well, particularly in the category of so-called deponent verbs. Rediscovery of the middle voice has led an increasing number of scholars to reject the notion of deponency (cf. Pennington, "Setting aside 'Deponency,'" 181–203).

29. Cf. Gzella, "Voice in Classical Hebrew," 309–11.

30. Joüon §52d.

31. GKC §52f; cf. Bauer and Leander, *Historische Grammatik der hebräischen Sprache*, 281 (§238g); Brockelmann, *Grammatik der semitischen Sprachen*, 1:508.

function is that of Jacob Weingreen.[32] Weingreen notes that the function of the Piel depends on whether the root is active or stative in the Qal. He contends that the Piel expresses energetic or habitual action for active roots (e.g., the Piel of שבר means "to shatter, completely break") and the active promotion of a state for stative roots (e.g., the Piel of קדש means "to promote holiness"). Thus, Weingreen unifies the meaning of the Piel under the concept of intensification even as he distinguishes between active and stative roots.

Overall, Weingreen does not advance the conversation much. His study of the Piel is by no means comprehensive, and he does not incorporate modern linguistic insights into his analysis of the Piel. But he is right to draw attention to the active-stative distinction for verbal roots, a distinction that is fundamental not only to Hebrew but also to the other Semitic languages. This is an important contribution.

4.3.2.1.2 N. J. C. KOUWENBERG

N. J. C. Kouwenberg examines the function of the D stem in Akkadian, but his observations are significant for understanding the Piel in Hebrew.[33] He postulates that Proto-Semitic adjectives existed in pairs, a simple adjective without reduplication (e.g., *rapašum* "wide") and an adjective with reduplication to indicate expressiveness or intensification (e.g., *rappašum* "very wide"). The D stem was formed from the second type of adjective, with its intensive function (e.g., *ruppušu* "to be very wide") broadening to encompass verbal plurality (e.g., *ruppušu* "to be wide repeatedly").[34] Eventually, D stem verbs were created directly from G stem verbs rather than derived from adjectives. Then, because verbal plurality is associated with increased transitivity, the D stem became the preferred way of expressing the factitive, which turns an intransitive verb into a transitive one.[35]

Kouwenberg's reconstruction builds on a modern linguistic understanding of semantic roles, and it is able to explain why the D stem can be both pluralitive and factitive. Moreover, Kouwenberg has rightly noted the role that increased transitivity can play in the D stem. However, his hypothesis for the D stem's

---

32. Weingreen, "Pi'el in Biblical Hebrew," 21–29.

33. Kouwenberg, *Gemination in the Akkadian Verb*; idem, *Akkadian Verb and Its Semitic Background*, 268–87.

34. Kouwenberg sees reduplication as iconic, which means that there is a logical and direct connection between a reduplicated form and what it signifies. According to Kouwenberg, reduplication arose as a logical means of making words expressive and intensive. This original sense, however, was grammaticalized early on to include other functions such as verbal plurality. See Kouwenberg, *Gemination in the Akkadian Verb*, 19–48.

35. According to Kouwenberg, both the G stem and D stem could originally express both stative and factitive meanings, with the D stem expressing the intensive of the G stem. However, the G stem lost its factitive function once the D stem became the preferred way of communicating the factitive, causing the D stem to lose most of its non-factitive (including intensive and pluralitive) functions.

origin is speculative. Furthermore, Kouwenberg assumes an original intensive function for the D stem that broadened to encompass plurality. We know from cross-linguistic studies that reduplication is used to mark verbal plurality, not intensification,[36] and among the world's languages the path goes from plurality to intensification, not the other way around.[37] Finally, although Kouwenberg's desire to connect verbal plurality and factitiveness is admirable, it must be asked whether the diverse functions of the D stem need to be—and can be—unified.

4.3.2.1.3 Jan Joosten

Jan Joosten also thinks an intensive function is original to the D stem.[38] However, unlike Kouwenberg, Joosten postulates two different G stems in Proto-Semitic, one expressing the active voice and another expressing the middle voice. The D stem originally expressed the intensive of both the active form (e.g., *ḥtt* "to dismay someone" meant "to dismay someone greatly" in the D stem) and middle form (e.g., *ḥtt* "to be dismayed" meant "to be greatly dismayed" in the D stem). Within Hebrew, subsequent developments took place that gave the Piel a variety of different functions. Specifically, the Piel lost its intensive nuance for roots that lost their active counterpart in the Qal, but the Piel remained intensive for roots that lost their active or middle counterpart in the Qal.

Joosten tests his hypothesis against all occurrences of the Piel in the Hebrew Bible, and his reconstruction provides a way of unifying the different functions of the Piel. However, it seems that Joosten often interprets the data to fit his hypothesis rather than vice versa. Furthermore, like the work of Kouwenberg, Joosten's reconstruction is speculative and suffers from the same assumption that intensification led to plurality rather than the other way around. Yet Joosten is to be thanked for his efforts to understand the development of the Piel within the context of comparative Semitics.

4.3.2.1.4 John C. Beckman

In his 2012 Harvard dissertation, John C. Beckman compares Kouwenberg's reconstruction of the D stem with the idea that the Piel is resultative.[39]

---

36. Rubino, "Reduplication," 19–20; Newman, "Pluractional Verbs," 193–94; Wood, "Semantic Typology of Pluractionality," 37–38.

37. Dressler's foundational study of verbal plurality includes intensification alongside iterative, distributive, and continuative action (*Studien zur verbalen Pluralität*, 62–84). However, intensive action has no inherent relationship to verbal plurality. There is a natural connection between the two because a repeated action can be intensified, but, in such cases, intensification is a secondary meaning of verbal plurality rather than the other way around (Wood, "Semantic Typology of Pluractionality," 14–15; Newman, "Pluractional Verbs," 187).

38. Joosten, "Semitic D-Stem," 202–30.

39. Beckman, "Meaning of the Biblical Hebrew Piel Stem."

He concludes that Kouwenberg's analysis is superior, in part because it is able to connect the different functions of the D stem. In the midst of his evaluation, Beckman provides further support for Kouwenberg's work by noting cross-linguistic connections between intensification and causativity.[40]

Beckman's attention to possible connections between intensification and causativity significantly advances the conversation on the Hebrew Piel. However, like the studies of Kouwenberg and Joosten, Beckman conflates the notions of plurality and intensification. Furthermore, the Piel is factitive, not causative, so any grammaticalization paths from intensification to causativity may not apply in the case of the Piel. Finally, it remains to be shown that the Piel's various functions need to be unified under a single meaning.

4.3.2.2 The Piel as Complex Active

A unique reconstruction of the Piel is found in Kenneth Laing Harris's dissertation completed at the University of Liverpool.[41] Harris characterizes the Piel as "complex active," which means that the Piel adds complexity to the action described in the Qal for active verbs (e.g., שלח means "to send" in the Qal but "to send away" in the Piel) and functions causatively for stative verbs (e.g., חזק means "to be strong" in the Qal but "to cause to be strong" in the Piel). He argues that the designation "complex active" provides unity to the Piel. However, he admits not all verbs will neatly agree with this function due to lexicalization, and he contends that sometimes the Piel's meaning overlaps with other verbal stems.

Harris's study analyzes each of the roots that occurs in the Piel stem and is therefore systematic. However, his designation of the Piel as "complex active" is quite nebulous, in part because he wants to maintain a flexible understanding of the Piel. Furthermore, Harris provides no coherent methodology or linguistic framework for his conclusions.

4.3.2.3 The Piel as Resultative
4.3.2.3.1 ALBRECHT GOETZE

A major break with the characterization of the Piel as intensive is found in the work of Albrecht Goetze, who analyzes the Semitic D stem.[42] He argues that the label "intensive" does not encompass all the nuances of the D stem. He contends, furthermore, that genuine D stem verbs are resultative in that they cause their direct objects to enter the state described by the root. This distinction, according to Goetze, applies to both active and stative verbs. Active verbs

---

40. E.g., Li, "Examination of Causative Morphology," 349–51.
41. Harris, "Function of the Pi'el."
42. Goetze, "So-Called Intensive," 1–8.

emphasize the result of the action (e.g., *šbr* means "to break" in the G stem but "to make broken" in the D stem), whereas the D stem of stative verbs places the direct object in the root's state (e.g., *qdš* means "to be holy" in the G stem but "to make holy" in the D stem). Goetze explains away exceptions by appealing to a hypothetical Gn stem, or G stem with infixed *n* before the second radical, that just so happens to look like the D stem.

Goetze rightly notes that intensification cannot account for all the different functions of the D stem. However, Goetze simply claims, rather than demonstrates, that the D stem is resultative. The fact that Goetze must appeal to a hypothetical, otherwise-unattested stem to sustain his theory does not support his reconstruction, especially since he seems to be motivated by a desire to find a uniform function for the D stem.[43]

4.3.2.3.2 ERNST JENNI

Goetze's understanding of the Piel is largely adopted by Ernst Jenni, who finds a uniform function for each of the Hebrew verbal stems, including the Piel.[44] Like Goetze, Jenni argues that the Piel is resultative, expressing the imposition of the state associated with the root. The Piel therefore differs from the Hiphil, which instead describes the imposition of a process (e.g., the Piel of קדש means "to consecrate, make holy" whereas the Hiphil of בוא means "to bring, cause to enter"). However, unlike Goetze, Jenni argues that all instances of the Piel fit the resultative mold in that the term "resultative" includes any action that is not a literal expression of an actual event.[45]

Jenni creates a clean and neat picture of the Piel in which this stem has a single, uniform function. The problem is that this picture is just a little too perfect. The category of resultative loses its meaning when Jenni redefines it so that he can include exceptions. Furthermore, in his attempt to impose a uniform meaning on the Piel, Jenni loses sight of the active-stative dichotomy fundamental to the Hebrew verbal system.

4.3.2.3.3 STUART A. RYDER

In the published version of his 1966 dissertation, Stuart A. Ryder agrees with Goetze and Jenni that the D stem is primarily resultative rather than intensive.[46] However, unlike Goetze and Jenni, he is willing to allow for exceptions

---

43. Cf. Kaufman, "Semitics," 281.

44. Jenni, *Hebräische Pi'el*; idem, "Piel in verbesserter Sicht," 67–90.

45. Unlike the other standard Hebrew grammars, Waltke and O'Connor largely adopt Jenni's perspective on the Piel (*IBHS* §24.1).

46. Ryder, *D-Stem in Western Semitic*.

and does not attempt to explain all instances of the Piel as resultative. This is because Ryder does not view the D stem in opposition to the G stem but instead thinks that the D stem is denominative in origin (i.e., it is a verbal stem derived from nouns) and came about independently of the G stem.

Ryder's work improves upon the studies of Goetze and Jenni in that he is willing to allow for exceptions to the resultative paradigm. Ryder is also thorough in his research. However, Ryder's conclusions are not convincing. His contention that the D stem is denominative in origin is especially unpersuasive because it is difficult to explain the D stem's different functions via grammaticalization of a denominative stem.

4.3.2.4 The Piel as Pluralitive-Factitive
4.3.2.4.1 Arno Poebel

Goetze's rejection of the D stem as intensive dominated much of the latter part of the twentieth century, but Arno Poebel was actually the first modern scholar to deny the D stem's intensive function.[47] Poebel suggests that the Semitic D stem expresses verbal plurality, or repeated verbal action or results of the action (e.g., *šbr* means "to break into many pieces, break many times" in the D stem),[48] as well as factitiveness, or the imposition of a state (e.g., *qdš* means "to consecrate, make holy" in the D stem). He arrives at this conclusion primarily through lexical evidence but attempts to support it through a hypothetical reconstruction of the Proto-Semitic verbal system.[49]

Poebel is right to observe from the lexical evidence that the D stem is frequently associated with verbal plurality and factitiveness. This is an especially important contribution. However, Poebel provides little evidence for his speculative reconstruction of the Proto-Semitic verbal system, and his methodological approach lacks linguistic sophistication.

4.3.2.4.2 Joseph H. Greenberg

Joseph H. Greenberg approaches the topic of the Semitic D stem from the perspective of a linguist rather than a Semiticist.[50] He points to the existence of verbal plurality in other language families, most notably Native American and

---

47. Poebel, *Studies in Akkadian Grammar*, 65–68.

48. Paul Newman has coined the term "pluraction" to refer to verbal plurality ("Pluractional Verbs," 187–88).

49. According to Poebel (*Studies in Akkadian Grammar*, 65–68), Proto-Semitic originally possessed two G stems, one intransitive and the other transitive, and two D stems, one factitive and the other pluralitive, derived from these two G stems. The gradual lexicalization of the G stem caused the D stems to merge, so what were originally two separate D stems became one.

50. Greenberg, "Semitic 'Intensive,'" 577–87.

African languages, and observes that reduplication is commonly used cross-linguistically to express verbal plurality. He argues that the Semitic D stem is characterized by reduplication and is also pluralitive, as should be expected typologically but as is also evident in its usage in the Semitic languages.

The main contribution of Greenberg's article is his treatment of the Semitic D stem from a typological, cross-linguistic framework. Although his study is by no means comprehensive, his work is clear, logical, and straightforward. Accordingly, he places the pluralitive function of the D stem on solid linguistic footing.

4.3.2.4.3 STEPHEN A. KAUFMAN

In an article assessing the state of Semitic studies, Stephen A. Kaufman points to the Semitic D stem as a case study of how Semiticists and linguists can learn from one another.[51] He rejects Poebel's methodological approach and Proto-Semitic reconstruction, but he does agree with Poebel that the D stem is pluralitive and factitive, not intensive. Like Greenberg, Kaufman appeals to the broader phenomenon of verbal plurality, especially as attested in the Chadic and Cushitic languages.[52] He notes that in these and other languages, verbal plurality is quasi-ergative in that transitive roots possess plural objects and intransitive roots express repeated action.[53] Kaufman rejects the need to find a single function for the D stem in light of the active-stative dichotomy characteristic of the Semitic languages, contending that the D stem is factitive rather than pluralitive for stative roots.

Kaufman's discussion of the D stem is not comprehensive, and some may not appreciate Kaufman's refusal to unify the various functions of the D stem under a single meaning. Nevertheless, Kaufman grounds his conclusions clearly in linguistic typology and comparative data from Afro-Asiatic, the major language family to which the Semitic languages belong.

4.3.2.4.4 ABDELKADER FASSI FEHRI

Abdelkader Fassi Fehri approaches the function of the D stem from the perspective of an Arabic scholar.[54] He categorizes the D stem as both pluralitive and factitive. However, unlike Kaufman, he tries to explain how these two different functions are connected through transitivity. Fehri notes how verbal plurality increases transitivity in that it adds a direct object; he observes that a

---

51. Kaufman, "Semitics," 280–82.
52. Cf. Newman, *Nominal and Verbal Plurality in Chadic.*
53. Cf. Newman, "Pluractional Verbs," 193.
54. Fehri, "Verbal Plurality, Transitivity, and Causativity," 151–85.

factitive construction also increases transitivity because it makes an intransitive verb transitive by giving it a direct object.

Fehri's study engages well with contemporary linguistics and theories of transitivity. However, like other scholars who argue for a unifying function for the Piel, it is questionable whether such an approach is even necessary, much less possible. Although Fehri can connect the verbal plurality of transitive verbs and factitiveness, his hypothesis does not easily account for verbal plurality of intransitive verbs, nor can it explain the D stem's frequent denominative usage.

4.3.2.5 Evaluation

As the above discussion makes evident, the Piel's function is highly debated. Yet, the above views can be largely categorized according to those who seek to find a unified explanation for the Piel's diverse meanings and those who do not. The views that consider the Piel to be intensive and resultative seem to be driven largely by the former. However, these attempts ultimately fall short, in part because the labels "intensive" and "resultative" must be generalized so much that they lose any significant meaning. As indicated by Kaufman, the shortcoming of these approaches is not surprising because the Semitic verbal system does not require that each stem's functions be unified.

Thus, rather than assuming that the Piel must have a unified function, it is more profitable to examine the Piel typologically. Because reduplication frequently indicates verbal plurality, including in the Afro-Asiatic languages,[55] and because the Piel is marked by reduplication of the second radical, scholars would benefit from incorporating verbal plurality into their perspective of the Piel. An important area of research here is the quasi-ergative nature of verbal plurality and how it relates to transitivity and multiplication of the argument. Our understanding of the Piel's factitive function could be improved by comparison with the Hiphil's causative sense and by typological comparison of factitives and causatives.

4.3.3 The Hiphil

The Hiphil, of all the verbal stems, has attracted the least amount of attention in the scholarly literature. The Hiphil is traditionally considered causative in that the subject of the verb causes the object to perform a certain action (e.g., the Hiphil of בוא means "to bring, cause to enter").[56] However, the Hiphil can also express functions other than causativity, and scholars have struggled

---

55. In this regard, it is noteworthy that verbal plurality is frequently derivational and an inherent property of verbal stems (Newman, "Pluractional Verbs," 192–93).

56. E.g., GKC §53c; Joüon §54d; *IBHS* §27.1.e.

to understand how these other senses relate to one another. Another key issue regarding the Hiphil is how its causativity relates to the factitiveness of the Piel.

In what follows I examine the few noteworthy works on the Hiphil. Throughout I especially highlight how scholars have understood the non-causative functions of the Hiphil and the Hiphil's relationship to the Piel. I classify their approaches according to four different categories: causative, causative-factitive, force dynamic, and causative-elative.

4.3.3.1 The Hiphil as Causative

Ernst Jenni's desire to find a single meaning for each stem leads him to characterize the Hiphil as solely causative.[57] Yet, Jenni argues for several other features that characterize the Hiphil in opposition to the Piel, including imposition of an action (rather than a state) by the subject, durative (rather than momentary) action, occasional (rather than habitual) participation of the subject in the verbal action, and substantial (rather than accidental) action toward the object.[58] For Jenni, these characteristics are a by-product of the Hiphil's causative function. This allows him to subsume any non-causative senses under the broader category of causativity.

Jenni takes his sharp distinction between the Hiphil and Piel a little too far, and his resulting analyses of many Hiphils are debatable.[59] He also ignores the possibility that the Hiphil does not have a unifying function and may even occasionally overlap with the Piel. Yet Jenni correctly argues that causativity must be distinguished syntactically from factitiveness in that the former denotes the imposition of an action whereas the latter denotes the imposition of a state.

4.3.3.2 The Hiphil as Causative-Factitive

The sole monograph-length study of the Hiphil is W. T. Claasen's University of Stellenbosch dissertation.[60] Under the influence of James Barr, who served as one of his readers, he strictly adheres to a synchronic rather than diachronic approach. Claasen rejects Jenni's sharp distinction between the functions of the Piel and Hiphil. Instead, he argues that the Hiphil is frequently factitive, like the Piel, as well as causative, delocutive, and even expressive of simple action

---

57. Jenni, "Faktitiv und Kausativ," 143–57; cf. idem, *Hebräische Pi'el*, 33–119.

58. Under the influence of Jenni, the same is argued for Classical Arabic by Leemhuis, *D and H Stems in Koranic Arabic*.

59. Cf. Claasen, "Distinction between Pi'el and Hiph'il," 3–10.

60. Claasen, "Hiph'il Verbal Theme in Biblical Hebrew." Claasen published two articles based on his dissertation work: "Distinction between Pi'el and Hiph'il," 3–10; "Declarative-Estimative Hiph'il," 5–16.

like the Qal. Claasen concludes that the Hiphil often has an unpredictable meaning, especially when considered in opposition to both the Qal and Piel.

Claasen refutes many of Jenni's subjective distinctions between the Hiphil and Piel. He is right to note the importance of synchronic analysis; he also correctly cautions against trying to fit Hebrew into a predictable and uniform mold. But, Classen goes too far in viewing so many Hiphils as factitive when other explanations are possible. Furthermore, his approach emphasizes synchronic analysis at the expense of diachrony and possible insights from comparative Semitics.

4.3.3.3 The Hiphil as Force Dynamic

W. Randall Garr presents a very unique perspective on the Hiphil.[61] He agrees that the Hiphil is often causative but tries to find a more unifying function. For Garr, this function is evident in denominative Hiphils (i.e., Hiphils created from nouns) and certain roots for which the Hiphil is non-causative (e.g., בין, קשׁב, and ערד). According to Garr, the Hiphil can be understood in terms of force dynamics, a linguistic concept that analyzes expressions in light of force-exerting elements.[62] The subject of denominative Hiphils is directly responsible for a verbal action with immediate effect (e.g., the Hiphil of זעק means "to let out a cry"), and non-causative Hiphils express action that is more agentive and complex than that of the Qal (e.g., בין means "to perceive" in the Qal but "to deeply understand" in the Hiphil).

Garr bases his understanding of the Hiphil on a modern cross-linguistic perspective of causativity. However, Garr's interpretation of specific Hiphil forms is sometimes questionable. He seems to allow force dynamics to influence his understanding of the Hiphil rather than permitting the data to speak for themselves. Furthermore, Garr seeks to find a unifying function for the Hiphil, but the Semitic languages do not necessarily require that each stem has a single meaning.

4.3.3.4 The Hiphil as Causative-Elative

E. A. Speiser offers the most fruitful perspective on the Hiphil.[63] He takes his cue from Comparative Philology in that he explores the Hiphil's function

---

61. Garr, "Denominal, Lexicalized *Hiphil* Verbs," 51–58; idem, "Semantics of בי״ן in the *Qal* and *Hiphil*," 536–45.

62. The concept of force dynamics originated with the cognitive linguist Leonard Talmy ("Force Dynamics in Language and Cognition," 409–70; "Force Dynamics as a Generalization over 'Causative,'" 67–85).

63. Speiser, "'Elative' in West-Semitic and Akkadian," 81–92; cf. idem, "Studies in Semitic Formatives," 23–33.

within the Semitic languages as a whole. Speiser draws attention to what he calls the "elative" function of the Hiphil. Pointing to the similarity between the third-person personal pronouns and the C stem's preformative across the Semitic languages, Speiser argues that the C stem often expresses an action or state characterized by a particular quality in an exemplary way. According to Speiser, this is evident in the C stem's use to express colors, other lasting qualities or conditions, and superlative-like constructions.

Speiser makes a plausible connection between the third-person personal pronoun and the C stem's preformative, especially because the N and *t*-infix stems also seem to contain pronominal elements.[64] Speiser convincingly shows that the elative is a common function of the C stem in Semitic, especially for stative forms. The only disadvantage is that he does not interact with modern linguistic theories on the elative, but this is a relatively minor critique considering the strength of his argumentation otherwise.

4.3.3.5 Evaluation

As this survey indicates, the most cogent framework for understanding the Hiphil is Speiser's causative-elative approach. Only this theory considers comparative Semitics and adequately accounts for all the data. Moving forward, scholars should investigate how the elative is connected morphologically with the C stem and how elatives function typologically. Related, additional topics for research include the relationship between elatives and delocutive Hiphils as well as the connection between elative Hiphils and the adverbial Hiphil infinitive absolute.

The relationship between the Hiphil and the other verbal stems remains an important one. There is still need for comparison of the Hiphil with the Piel, avoiding the rigidness of Jenni while maintaining a linguistically informed distinction between causativity and factitiveness. The relationship of the Hiphil to other stems is especially significant for roots that do not occur in the Qal stem and for roots in which the Piel has a lexicalized rather than factitive function.

As these and other topics are researched, scholars should keep in mind that it is not necessary to find a single unifying function for the Hiphil stem. Linguistic theories such as force dynamics will undoubtedly be helpful as our understanding of the Hiphil's causativity is refined, but the Semitic languages never require that the functions of both active and stative verbs must be the

---

64. Lieberman, "Afro-Asiatic Background of the Semitic N-Stem," 604–10. The same connection is evident in Arabic, which uses the pattern *'afʿal* to form elatives, as well as Akkadian, in which words with prefixed *ša-* or *šu-* (the same preformative as that of the Š stem) have the elative sense.

same. In many cases the Hiphil may simply provide an available stem for representing a new meaning.

4.3.4 The Hithpael

The final Biblical Hebrew verbal stem to consider is the Hithpael. Hebrew grammars commonly characterize this stem as reflexive.[65] However, the Hithpael can express the passive voice and can also have a frequentative meaning. An important question once again, then, is how this stem's different functions may be connected, if at all. Naturally, scholars have offered a variety of frameworks for answering this question.

Below I survey important studies on the Hithpael, focusing especially on scholars' understandings of the relationship between this stem's various functions. I discuss the different views in terms of five categories: reflexive, intensive, resultative, inversative, and middle.

4.3.4.1 The Hithpael as Reflexive
4.3.4.1.1 PAUL MAZARS

One of the first systematic studies on the Hithpael was conducted by Paul Mazars.[66] He argues that the Hithpael is primarily reflexive. However, he also notes the frequent use of the Hithpael with simple transitive meanings, similar to the Qal stem. According to Mazars, these and other non-reflexive usages of the Hithpael are due to stylistic concerns (especially when found in the books of Kings and Psalms) and to a lexical shortage of certain stems. Mazars thus does not think that the Hithpael's non-reflexive functions have a grammatical explanation.

Overall, Mazar's analysis is not guided by sound linguistic methodology. Furthermore, some of Mazars's conclusions regarding stylistic use of the Hithpael seem subjective, especially because other scholars looking at the same data have reached different conclusions.[67] Yet Mazars's study is important because it shows that sometimes the Hithpael occurs with non-reflexive meanings.

4.3.4.1.2 E. A. SPEISER

E. A. Speiser considers the Hithpael to be primarily reflexive.[68] However, he concerns himself with non-reflexive usages of the Hithpael, especially the

---

65. GKC §54e; Joüon §53i; *IBHS* §26.2.a.

66. Mazars, "Sens et usage de l'hitpael," 351–64. The earliest modern study on the Hithpael was Stein, *Stamm des Hithpael*. However, Stein unfortunately died before completing his work. The first volume is a list of all Hithpaels that occur in the Hebrew Bible, sorted by root but with little discussion because analysis was intended for the second volume.

67. E.g., Bean, "Hithpaʿel Verbal Stem," 169–70.

68. Speiser, "Durative Hitpaʿel," 118–21.

frequentative use for certain roots (e.g., הלך means "to walk" in the Qal but "to walk about" in the Hithpael). He explains this frequentative function as a remnant of a Hebrew *tan*-infix stem, parallel to the frequentative *tan* stem found in Akkadian. According to Speiser, this hypothetical *tan*-infix form merged with the Hithpael in Hebrew, resulting in a frequentative use of the Hithpael alongside its reflexive function.

Unfortunately, there is no evidence for the existence of a *tan*-infix stem in West Semitic. Only Akkadian possesses the conditions that would have brought about the existence of *tan* stems, namely a present tense with doubled middle radical and consistent assimilation of *n*.[69] Speiser's hypothesis cannot adequately explain the loss of intervocalic *a* between the first root letter and the *tan*-infix, nor can it account for its assumed metathesis of the first radical and the *t*. Yet Speiser is right to draw attention to the frequentative use of the Hithpael, and he is correct to note the parallels between the frequentative *tan* stem in Akkadian and the frequentative Hithpael.

4.3.4.1.3 ALBERT FREDRICK BEAN

Albert Frederick Bean offers an important study on the Hithpael in his 1976 PhD dissertation completed at Southern Baptist Theological Seminary.[70] He contends that the Hithpael is often, but not solely, reflexive. He thinks the primary function of the Hithpael is to indicate simple action even though it can also express reflexive, passive, desiderative, and reciprocal meanings. He concludes that the Hithpael is not restricted to a particular syntactic function, nor can its usage be attributed purely to genre, geographical location, or diachrony.

The main strength of Bean's study is his attention to Hithpaels that are not easily classified as reflexive. However, Bean excludes nearly one-third of the occurrences of the Hithpael by labeling their meaning as ambiguous, and this ignores a significant body of data. Bean's analysis, furthermore, does not interact significantly with insights from modern linguistics and comparative Semitics. As a result, his analysis is rather uninformed linguistically.

4.3.4.2 The Hithpael as Intensive

In another PhD dissertation on the Hithpael, Milton L. Boyle, Jr. rejects the primary classification of the Hithpael as reflexive.[71] He surveys *t*-infix forms in the Semitic languages. He then concludes that the function of the Hithpael in Hebrew is to express intensification, which he defines as strong emotion,

---

69. Cf. Kouwenberg, *Gemination in the Akkadian Verb*, 79.
70. Bean, "Hithpaʿel Verbal Stem."
71. Boyle, "Infix-*t* Forms in Biblical Hebrew."

a profound sense of urgency, repetition of the action, or duration of the verbal activity. According to Boyle, the reflexive usage of the Hithpael is not primary. Rather, its reflexive use is a byproduct of its intensive function, developed from the subject's deep personal interest and involvement in the verbal action.

Boyle's primary contribution is his investigation of the Hithpael within the broader context of comparative Semitics. However, the *t*-infix stems in the Semitic languages do not have the function of intensification as Boyle claims. Furthermore, Boyle does not adequately define the term "intensive" and assumes without proof that intensification can appear as the reflexive voice.

4.3.4.3 The Hithpael as Resultative
4.3.4.3.1 Richard C. Benton

Another scholar who tries to find a unified but non-reflexive function for the Hithpael stem is Richard C. Benton, whose work on the Niphal was mentioned above.[72] Benton contends that the Hithpael has a resultative meaning in that it relates to a state resulting from an action. As noted above, he argues that the primary difference between the Hithpael and Niphal is one of situation aspect. The Hithpael focuses on the process behind a resultative state whereas the Niphal focuses on the resultative state itself. The category of situation aspect, according to Benton, best explains the many different translation possibilities for the Hithpael.

The strengths and weaknesses of Benton's perspective on the Hithpael are similar to those of his view on the Niphal. He correctly recognizes the important role that situation aspect has for the Hebrew verbal stems. Nevertheless, he overemphasizes this feature at the expense of grammatical voice. He also does not discuss the role that the *t*-infix plays in the different Semitic languages.

4.3.4.3.2 Klaus-Peter Adams

Klaus-Peter Adams also argues that the Hithpael is resultative.[73] He rejects a reflexive function for the Hithpael, arguing that scholars have understood the Hithpael as reflexive only because of translation possibilities in modern Indo-European languages. For Adams, the Hithpael instead expresses a status that results from an action, without focusing on that action. Adams furthermore suggests that a good number of Hithpael verbs specifically highlight one's social status. Thus, for example, the Hithpael of נבא means "to act as a prophet" rather than "to be a prophet" as the Niphal of the same root indicates.

---

72. Benton, "Aspect and the Biblical Hebrew Niphal and Hitpael"; idem, "Verbal and Contextual Information," 385–99.

73. Adam, "(Socio-)Demonstrative Meaning of the Hithpael," 1–23.

Adams rightly notes that the Hithpael frequently describes social status. Like Benton, he is right to draw attention to the important role that situation aspect has in understanding the Hebrew verbal stems. But, also like Benton, Adams overlooks grammatical voice at the expense of situation aspect. Another weakness of Adam's socio-demonstrative understanding of the Hithpael is that it can only explain a portion of Hithpael verbs, rather than accounting for all Hithpael forms.

4.3.4.4 The Hithpael as Inversative

Bruno W. W. Dombrowski uniquely argues that the *t*-infix of the Hithpael is primarily inversative.[74] By this he means that the Hithpael indicates a change of direction in the verb with respect to the subject, a function that often appears as the reflexive and reciprocal voices (e.g., the Hithpael of ראה means "to look at one another").[75] To support this conclusion, Dombrowski points to the *t*-element found in Akkadian's second-person personal pronouns and verbal affixes, as well as the final *t* found on feminine nouns. He suggests that both of these elements represent the "other." Similar to Speiser, Dombrowski attributes the Hithpael's frequentative use to the merging of the Hithpael with another stem. However, he thinks that stem is the Gt stem rather than a *tan*-infix form.

Although by no means comprehensive, Dombrowski's study rightly attempts to understand the function of the Hithpael within the broader context of comparative Semitics. His hypothesis has great merit because it is likely that the *t*-element of verbal affixes is pronominal in origin.[76] However, Dombrowski's analysis lacks careful definition of the term "inversative." He also does not explore in detail the inversative's possible connections with the reflexive and reciprocal voices.

4.3.4.5 The Hithpael as Middle
4.3.4.5.1 MARK A. ARNOLD

In his 2005 dissertation completed at Harvard University, Mark A. Arnold argues that the Hithpael's primary function is to express the middle voice.[77] Relying on the work of Suzanne Kemmer,[78] he contends that many of the atypical Hithpael functions (e.g., verbs describing changes in body posture, emotional states, and thinking) can be classified cross-linguistically under the

---

74. Dombrowski, "Remarks on the Hebrew Hithpaʿel and Inversative -*t*-," 220–23.
75. Cf. Streck, *Akkadischen Verbalstämme mit ta-Infix*, 106–10.
76. Cf. Lieberman, "Afro-Asiatic Background of the Semitic N-Stem," 610–19. It is unlikely, however, that feminine *t* represents this same morpheme representing the "other."
77. Arnold, "Categorization of the Hitpaʿēl of Classical Hebrew."
78. Kemmer, *Middle Voice*.

category of the middle voice. This unifies the various functions of the Hithpael into a single meaning because, according to Arnold, the middle voice includes the reflexive.[79] Arnold accounts for exceptions by assuming that the Hithpael took on the functions of the Gt and Št stems once they were lost in Hebrew.

The primary contribution of Arnold's study is its provision of a cogent linguistic framework for understanding the Hithpael. Arnold recognizes that the Hithpael's many different usages may not be so disparate when classified as middle. What needs refinement, however, is interaction with other scholars' definitions of both the middle and reflexive voices. Additionally, Arnold's work needs to be supplemented by a more thorough analysis of the *t*-infix stems in the Semitic languages.

4.3.4.5.2 Ernst Jenni

Like Arnold, Ernst Jenni argues that the Hithpael is predominantly middle.[80] But, unlike Arnold, Jenni distinguishes sharply between the middle and reflexive voices and does not subsume reflexivity under the middle voice. Jenni argues that the exact way the Hithpael expresses the middle voice depends purely on the context of the verb's usage, and that it may not always be easy to express that nuance in modern target languages. Furthermore, according to Jenni, the difference between the Hithpael and the Niphal exists primarily at the pragmatic level: the Niphal expresses information that has already been given wheras the Hithpael introduces entirely new information.

Jenni is right to draw attention to the middle nature of the Hithpael. He also rightly distinguishes between the sense of the Hithpael in Hebrew and translation possibilities in modern languages. However, Jenni struggles to incorporate occurrences of the Hithpael that seemingly express the reflexive voice. Jenni's limitation of the Niphal-Hithpael distinction to the pragmatic level is also problematic because Hebrew verbal forms always communicate meaning at the semantic level.

4.3.4.6 Evaluation

Dombrowski's work provides a solid starting point for understanding the Hithpael. His hypothesis is supported by morphological connections between the *t*-infix and second-person personal pronouns. Furthermore, it is easy to see how an inversative function could encompass the reflexive, reciprocal, and middle senses of the Hithpael. However, more work is needed to explore how

---

79. Rainer Maria Voigt similarly argues that a *t*-infix expresses the middle voice when found in Afro-Asiatic, but he does not focus specifically on the Hithpael ("Derivatives und flektives ṯ," 85–107).
80. Jenni, "Nif'al und Hitpa'el," 131–303.

these different grammatical voices fit together, particularly in light of Arnold's study. Exploration of how the inversative developed differently in the Semitic languages would be beneficial.[81]

Along these lines, another fruitful topic of research is the relationship of the Hithpael to other *t*-infix stems. The Hithpael is often considered in opposition to the Piel, but this is not always evident from the Hithpael's actual usage. The possibility that the Hithpael has merged with other *t*-infix stems needs to be explored, and the reasons for the Hithpael's frequentative usage should also be investigated.

A final area for research is the difference between the Niphal and Hithpael. As medio-passive and inversative stems, there understandably is a good deal of functional overlap. However, these two stems are morphologically distinct in Hebrew and are even used alongside each other (e.g., Gen 3:8, 10; Lev 11:43–44). This suggests that, despite occasional overlap, each stem may communicate a specific nuance. Appeals to situation aspect are helpful but ultimately unsatisfying, and more work needs to be done.[82]

4.4 THE VERBAL STEMS IN BIBLICAL ARAMAIC

Having addressed the Biblical Hebrew verbal stems, I turn lastly to the verbal stems in Biblical Aramaic. Unlike the Biblical Hebrew verbal stems, which have occupied significant attention in scholarship, nothing substantial has been written on the verbal stems in Biblical Aramaic. The few discussions that exist are limited to those found in grammars and grammatical surveys of Aramaic. Such neglect of the verbal stems in Biblical Aramaic results from the relatively small size of the Biblical Aramaic corpus and the tendency of Aramaicists to focus on the diverse features of later Aramaic dialects at the expense of Biblical Aramaic. All this has left little room for controversy and disagreement regarding the Biblical Aramaic verbal stems.

Nevertheless, there is value in surveying what scholarship exists on this topic, especially because what does exist in modern scholarship frequently agrees with recent advances in our understanding of the Biblical Hebrew verbal stems. Accordingly, in this section I survey what grammars and grammatical surveys of Aramaic have to say about the primary derived stems in Biblical Aramaic: the Pael, the Haphel, and the *t*-infixed Hithpeel and Hithpaal.

---

81. Note, for example, how the Hithpael is commonly reflexive in Hebrew whereas Aramaic's *t*-infix stems are often passive in addition to reflexive.

82. A good, but brief, exploration of this topic is found in Boyd, "Medio-Passive-Reflexive in Biblical Hebrew," 239–72.

Referenced in my discussion are the grammars of Hans Bauer and Pontus Leander, Karl Marti, and Franz Rosenthal, as well as the recent grammatical surveys by Stephen A. Kaufman and Holger Gzella.

4.4.1 The Pael

Biblical Aramaic's Pael stem generally corresponds to the Piel stem in Biblical Hebrew. Marti labels the Pael the *Steigerungsstämme*, or "increasing stem," and states that its causative, iterative, declarative, and denominative uses can all be subsumed under its intensive function.[83] Rosenthal similarly labels the Pael as "intensive or causative."[84] Bauer and Leander, however, exhibit a more nuanced understanding. They state that the Pael of active verbs has both an "intensive" and "extensive" sense: "intensive" refers to thoroughness of the action (e.g., the Pael of קצץ means "to cut off thoroughly" rather than "to cut off"), and "extensive" denotes pluraction (e.g., the Pael of הלך means "to walk in a group" rather than "to walk"). For stative verbs, Bauer and Leander note that the Pael instead tends to be factitive.[85]

The recent grammatical surveys of Kaufman and Gzella largely agree with Bauer and Leander. But, importantly, they omit any reference to the Pael being "intensive." They instead say that the Pael is pluralitive for active verbs and factitive for stative verbs.[86] By distinguishing between active and stative verbs, by rejecting the misleading label "intensive" for the Pael, and by instead highlighting the pluralitive function of the Pael, Kaufman and Gzella are in line with important advances that have taken place in our understanding of the Biblical Hebrew Piel stem.

4.4.2 The Haphel

The Haphel in Biblical Aramaic essentially parallels the Hiphil in Biblical Hebrew.[87] Marti and Rosenthal give a relatively simple presentation in their discussions of the Haphel stem. They state that the Haphel is causative, without much explanation.[88] Bauer and Leander, however, once again pay attention to a given root's active-stative classification as it relates to the Haphel's mean-

---

83. Marti, *Kurzgefasste Grammatik*, 27–28 (§31a).

84. Rosenthal, *Grammar of Biblical Aramaic*, 46 (§99).

85. Bauer and Leander, *Grammatik des biblisch-Aramäischen*, 272–73 (§§276d–h).

86. Kaufman, "Aramaic," 125; Gzella, "Language and Script," 99.

87. Biblical Aramaic also possesses the variant Aphel and Shaphel stems, with prefixed *aleph* and *shin*, respectively, instead of *he*. Both, however, are rarer than the Haphel. The Aphel represents a weakening of the initial *he* (as is typical in later Aramaic), and the Shaphel results primarily from the influence of Akkadian (whose causative stem is the Š stem).

88. Marti, *Kurzgefasste Grammatik*, 28 (§31b); Rosenthal, *Grammar of Biblical Aramaic*, 46 (§99).

ing. The Haphel expresses causativity for active roots, whether transitive or intransitive, in a way that sometimes overlaps with the Pael's factitive function. Otherwise, for stative roots, the Haphel is intransitive.[89]

Both Kaufman and Gzella label the Haphel as a causative stem.[90] They therefore do not distinguish between the function of the Haphel for active versus stative roots, at least not in their published presentations of the verbal stems. However, as indicated by the terminology they use, they differentiate between the factitive function of the Pael and the causative function of the Haphel. On this point they differ from their predecessors and incorporate the same distinction between factitiveness and causativity that many modern Hebraists have applied to the Biblical Hebrew Piel and Hiphil.

4.4.3 The Hithpeel and Hithpaal

The two primary *t*-infixed stems in Biblical Aramaic are the Hithpeel (the *t*-infixed form of the Peal) and the Hithpaal (the *t*-infixed form of the Pael). According to Marti and Rosenthal, the Hithpeel and Hithpaal express the reflexive or passive of the Peal and Paal.[91] Bauer and Leander argue similarly. They contend that the *t*-infixed stems can express the true reflexive, in which the verb's Agent and Patient are identical, as well as the passive. But they also add that the *t*-infix can sometimes function like the dative case (i.e., the action is done on behalf of the subject) or express reciprocal action.[92]

Kaufman and Gzella understand the *t*-infix as a marker of the reflexive, middle, or passive voices. It originally indicated the reflexive and middle voice, but the gradual loss of the passive (marked by internal vowel modification) in Aramaic brought about the need for the *t*-infix forms to fulfill also the role of the passive voice.[93] In their presentations of the *t*-infixed forms as reflexive-middles, Kaufman and Gzella are once again in line with developments in our understanding of the Hithpael (the closest correspondent to Biblical Aramaic's *t*-infixed stems) in Biblical Hebrew.

4.4.4 Evaluation

Whereas there is significant dispute regarding the functions of the Biblical Hebrew verbal stems, much less controversy exists for the verbal stems in Biblical Aramaic. The way the Biblical Aramaic verbal stems were understood a century

---

89. Bauer and Leander, *Grammatik des biblisch-Aramäischen*, 273–74 (§§276i–m).
90. Kaufman, "Aramaic," 125; Gzella, "Language and Script," 99.
91. Marti, *Kurzgefasste Grammatik*, 28 (§31c); Rosenthal, *Grammar of Biblical Aramaic*, 46 (§99).
92. Bauer and Leander, *Grammatik des biblisch-Aramäischen*, 275–76 (§§276o–x).
93. Kaufman, "Aramaic," 125; Gzella, "Language and Script," 99–100.

ago is largely the same as the way we understand them now. Nevertheless, progress has been made in that our understanding of the Biblical Aramaic stems is now more nuanced. Two important advances are differentiating between the functions of active and stative roots and rejection of the label "intensive" for the Pael.

At the same time, much work remains to be done. The most significant gap to be filled is a comprehensive study of the verbal stems in Biblical Aramaic. Such a study would examine all the occurrences of each verbal stem and then synthesize the data into a coherent picture. Ideally this investigation would be informed by modern linguistic discussions of grammatical voice, valency, and semantic roles, and would also consider Biblical Aramaic's verbal system within the development of the verbal system in Aramaic more generally.

4.5 THE WAYS FORWARD

The above survey of the verbal stems in Biblical Hebrew and Biblical Aramaic reflects ongoing disagreement over their precise functions, especially when it comes to Biblical Hebrew. Yet, at the same time, our understanding of what the verbal stems mean has certainly advanced over the past century. I am hopeful that, as further research and discussion take place, our methodology for approaching the verbal stems will be refined, and even greater clarity regarding their functions will be achieved. With these hopes in mind, I now make a few general suggestions on how to move forward.

First, students and scholars need to familiarize themselves with modern linguistic concepts relevant to the verbal stems. Particularly important here are the notions of grammatical voice and *Aktionsart*, two of the most important concepts for understanding the verbal stems. This may sound intimidating, especially because most students and scholars of Hebrew are not trained as linguists. But, familiarity with these topics is necessary if we are to avoid many of the errors of the past and continue to advance our understanding of the verbal stems. Boyd's general discussion of the verbal stems provides an accessible starting point and should serve as the basis for all future explorations of the verbal stems.

Second, following the important insight of Kaufman, any overarching paradigm for the verbal stems should be limited to the active-stative dichotomy. The history of scholarship shows how misconceptions arise when scholars assume that each verbal stem has a single function in opposition to the others. Accordingly, future scholarly discussion should avoid forcing the verbal stems into a neat and tidy framework. Each stem has typical functions, but exceptions certainly exist. Because the verbal stems exist to create new meaning, sometimes a stem was used simply because it was the only one available.

Finally, there is need to develop ways to teach and learn the verbal stems in an accessible but accurate way. Many teaching grammars of Biblical Hebrew hold to outdated understandings of the verbal stems by classifying the Niphal as reflexive and the Piel as intensive. Thankfully, at least one exception to this trend exists. Brian L. Webster's *Reading Biblical Hebrew: Introduction to Grammar* contains a short, but linguistically informed, discussion of the Piel stem.[94] His analysis reveals a more nuanced, and accurate, understanding of the verbal stems than found in most grammars. Hopefully, future teaching grammars will follow suit.

4.6 FURTHER READING

Bjøru, Øyvind. "Diathesis in the Semitic Languages: Exploring the *Binyan* System." MA thesis, University of Oslo, 2012.

Boyd, Steven W. "The *Binyanim* (Verbal Stems)." Pages 85–125 in *"Where Shall Wisdom Be Found?" A Grammatical Tribute to Professor Stephen A. Kaufman*. Edited by Hélène M. Dallaire, Benjamin J. Noonan, and Jennifer E. Noonan. Winona Lake, IN: Eisenbrauns, 2017.

Cook, John A. "Actionality (*Aktionsart*): Pre-Modern Hebrew." *EHLL* 1:25–28.

———. "Verbal Valency: The Intersection of Syntax and Semantics." Pages 53–86 in *Contemporary Examinations of Classical Languages (Hebrew, Aramaic, Syriac, and Greek): Valency, Lexicography, Grammar, and Manuscripts*. Edited by Timothy Martin Lewis, Alison G. Salvesen, and Beryl Turner. Perspectives on Linguistics and Ancient Languages 8. Piscataway, NJ: Gorgias, 2017.

Creason, Stuart Alan. "Semantic Classes of Hebrew Verbs: A Study of *Aktionsart* in the Hebrew Verbal System." PhD diss., University of Chicago, 1995.

Dan, Barak. "*Binyanim*: Biblical Hebrew." *EHLL* 1:354–62.

Gzella, Holger. "Voice in Classical Hebrew against Its Semitic Background." *Or* 78 (2009): 292–325.

Sinclair, Cameron. "The Valence of the Hebrew Verb." *JANES* 20 (1991): 63–81.

Verheij, Arian J. C. *Bits, Bytes, and Binyanim: A Quantitative Study of Verbal Lexeme Formations in the Hebrew Bible*. OLA 93. Leuven: Peeters, 2000.

———. "Stems and Roots: Some Statistics Concerning the Verbal Stems in the Hebrew Bible." *ZAH* 5 (1990): 64–71.

---

94. Webster, *Reading Biblical Hebrew*, 160–61. Webster's analysis is more extensive—and also better—in the earlier edition of his grammar, which contains a whole chapter on issues related to the Piel (*Cambridge Introduction to Biblical Hebrew*, 247–52). There he also offers some wise, more general, advice regarding the Hebrew verbal stems: "Speakers try one of a limited number of forms for a meaning, and if the community accepts it, then that is what it means. Something does suggest to the speaker to try one stem or another. But, simply asking the question, What does this stem mean? can make the matter sound far more rigid and static than language really can be as if it has always done the same things in the same way without other influences" (252).

CHAPTER 5

TENSE, ASPECT, *and* MOOD

The ancient Israelite farmer certainly knew when to milk his cow and his language was adequate to explain the routine to his son.

—ANSON F. RAINEY[1]

5.1 INTRODUCTION

In the last chapter I surveyed the verbal stems of Biblical Hebrew and Biblical Aramaic. Related to that discussion—and just as important for understanding the verbal systems of Hebrew and Aramaic—are the concepts of tense, aspect, and mood. These three concepts represent fundamental properties of verbs cross-linguistically, and they are therefore worthy of our attention. This is especially the case when it comes to exegesis, because how we translate the tense, aspect, and mood of a verb directly affects how we understand it.

Similar to the ongoing debate over tense and aspect in Biblical Greek, recent years have seen significant discussion on tense, aspect, and mood in Biblical Hebrew and Biblical Aramaic. Several problems make this topic complex, but one significant difficulty is the usage of both *qatal* and *yiqtol* to express a wide variety of tenses, aspects, and even moods. Further muddying the waters is the use of *weqatal* and *wayyiqtol* in seemingly opposite ways than *qatal* and *yiqtol*.[2] The complexity of tense, aspect, and mood in the biblical languages is reflected in Wendy Widder's recent assessment that "one of the most vexing issues in biblical Hebrew linguistics is the way the verbal system encodes tense, aspect, and modality."[3]

---

1. Rainey, "Ancient Hebrew Prefix Conjugation," 7.
2. Widder, "Linguistic Issues in Biblical Hebrew," 145–46.
3. Widder, "Linguistic Issues in Biblical Hebrew," 144.

In this chapter I explore the intricacies of this difficult but relevant topic. I first sketch the modern linguistic framework for understanding tense, aspect, and mood. I then discuss how scholars have attempted to explain the verbal systems of Biblical Hebrew and Biblical Aramaic, especially with respect to which of these three categories is most prominent. I reserve presentation of scholarship concerned with the pragmatic discourse function of verbal forms—in other words, views of the verbal system that see discourse as more prominent than tense, aspect, or mood—for the next chapter.

5.2 THE MODERN LINGUISTIC FRAMEWORK FOR TENSE, ASPECT, AND MOOD

Linguists have done much to enhance our understanding of the concepts of tense, aspect, and mood over the past one hundred years. They have sought to define these important notions in light of a cross-linguistic framework. In addition, linguists have examined the relationship between tense, aspect, and mood and the criteria for distinguishing which of these three categories, if any, is most prominent in a given language. I now examine each of these topics in turn.

5.2.1 Tense

Tense refers to the location of a situation within time. It does so by locating the time of the situation—the event time—with respect to a point of reference.[4] In many instances that point of reference is the same as the time of speech, and tense refers to the location of a situation with respect to the time of speech. Thus, the past tense expresses a situation prior to the time of speech (e.g., *I wrote this book*), the present tense communicates a situation contemporaneous with the time of speech (e.g., *I am writing this book*), and the future tense denotes a situation after the time of speech (e.g., *I will write this book*).[5]

Sometimes, however, the point of reference is different than the time of speech. In these cases, the tense of the verb is known as a *relative tense*.[6] The addition of a third, abstract reference point is necessary to explain tenses that relate temporally to another clause. Examples of relative tenses in English include the perfect (e.g., *I had written this chapter by Christmas*) and the future perfect (e.g., *By next year I will have finished writing this book*). Hans Riechenbach was

---

4. Comrie, *Tense*, 2–13.
5. Comrie, *Tense*, 36–55.
6. Comrie, *Tense*, 56–82.

the first to develop a coherent theory (sometimes called the "R-Point Theory") of relative tenses.[7] Linguists have subsequently refined his theory in various ways, but its essence and major contribution of a third reference point to understanding tense remain unchanged.

Traditionally, tense has taken primary place in understanding the Biblical Hebrew verbal system. However, both *qatal* and *yiqtol* can express a variety of tenses even if they often communicate the past and future tense, respectively. There is also the question of whether *wayyiqtol* and *weqatal* function as tenses. In light of these difficulties, most modern scholarship on tense and Biblical Hebrew verbs attempts to connect tense with both aspect and modality, especially the latter. Recent scholars have also turned to relative rather than absolute tense to explain any anomalies. I highlight these and other trends in my summary of scholarship below.

5.2.2 Aspect

The term *aspect* can refer to several different things in linguistics. However, when it comes to discussions of tense, aspect, and mood, aspect refers specifically to *viewpoint aspect* (also called grammatical aspect). It describes the temporal structure of a situation from the speaker's viewpoint, either from outside the situation or inside it, and whether or not the temporal endpoints of that situation are in view.[8] On the one hand, a situation viewed from the outside, and therefore seen as completed from the perspective of the speaker (i.e., the temporal endpoints are in view), is known as *perfective aspect*. On the other hand, a situation viewed from the inside, and therefore seen as incomplete from the perspective of the speaker (i.e., the temporal endpoints are not in view), is known as *imperfective aspect*.[9] The sentence *I wrote this book* represents perfective aspect whereas the sentence *I was writing this book* represents imperfective aspect.

In addition to these examples of English sentences, it may be helpful to consider a classic example of viewpoint aspect. The example, introduced by the Austrian-Russian linguist Alexander V. Isačenko and popularized within biblical studies by New Testament Greek scholars, entails two different individuals and a parade.[10] Perfective aspect is illustrated by a person watching

---

7. Reichenbach, *Elements of Symbolic Logic*, 287–98.

8. Comrie, *Aspect*, 1–6.

9. Comrie, *Aspect*, 16–40.

10. Isačenko, Грамматический строй русского языка [*Grammatical Structure of the Russian Language*], 2:132–33. Stanley E. Porter has popularized a different version of Isačenko's illustration in which aspect is divorced from time (*Verbal Aspect*, 91). This, however, is misleading because modern linguists do not separate the two (cf. Thomson, "What Is Aspect?" 24).

the parade from the stand: she stands outside the parade and sees the entire parade, from the beginning to the end. Imperfective aspect is illustrated by a participant marching in the parade: she walks within the parade and does not experience the entire parade because she does not see its beginning or end. Despite the spatial nature of this illustration, it is important to remember that aspect directly relates to time because it refers to the temporal phase(s) that the speaker has in mind.[11]

Interest in aspect is a relatively recent phenomenon in Biblical Hebrew studies. Many modern scholars have claimed that *qatal* and *yiqtol* express perfective and imperfective aspect, respectively, because they do not exclusively denote one tense over another. This raises the question of how to derive non-aspectual usages from the "core" aspectual meaning of *qatal* and *yiqtol*, and many scholars have done so via grammaticalization. There is also the question of whether or not other verbal conjugations in Hebrew (e.g., *wayyiqtol* and *weqatal*) also express aspect, and, if so, how they can be related to the perfective-imperfective opposition of *qatal* and *yiqtol*. I treat these and other questions in my presentation of scholarship below.

5.2.3 Mood

Mood may be defined as the speaker's attitude toward the factual status of a situation.[12] Situations can have one of two moods: *realis* or *irrealis*. The *realis* mood portrays a situation as having occurred or actually occurring, whereas the *irrealis* mood portrays situations as possible but not yet actualized.[13] Consider the two sentences *I wrote this book for Zondervan* and *I want to write another book for Zondervan*. The first sentence, *I wrote this book for Zondervan*, expresses the *realis* mood because it describes something that actually took place in real space and real time. However, the second sentence, *I want to write another book for Zondervan*, expresses the *irrealis* mood because it has not yet happened—writing another book for Zondervan is a situation that, at least at this point, exists purely in my imagination.

When it comes to Biblical Hebrew and Biblical Aramaic, most scholars use the terms *mood* and *modality* exclusively with reference to the *irrealis* mood. Such an expression of *irrealis* can be thought of in terms of two different categories: deontic modality and epistemic modality.[14] First, *epistemic modality* (also known as *propositional modality*) expresses the speaker's view of the reality

---

11. Johnson, "Unified Temporal Theory," 145–75; Klein, *Time in Language*, 99–119.
12. Palmer, *Mood and Modality*, 24.
13. Palmer, *Mood and Modality*, 1.
14. Palmer, *Mood and Modality*, 7–8.

of a situation. It includes statements of possibility (e.g., *Ben may be writing a book now*) or speculation (e.g., *Ben could be writing a book now*).[15] Second, *deontic modality* (also known as *event modality*) expresses a speaker's judgment toward a situation, asserting what the speaker wants or thinks should happen. Deontic modality includes commands (e.g., *Write the book!*) as well as indirect statements of obligation (e.g., *You should write the book*) or permission (e.g., *You may write the book*).[16]

The cohortative, imperative, and jussive conjugations are used to express deontic modality in the Hebrew Bible. However, scholars disagree on the extent to which the *qatal*, *yiqtol*, *weqatal*, and even *wayyiqtol* conjugations can also communicate modality, whether epistemic or deontic. Some argue that these forms are primarily modal whereas others argue that they take on modal functions in certain syntactical constructions. A related topic is the possible connection between modality and word order. Once again, I discuss these and other issues in my presentation of scholarship below.

5.2.4 Prominence of Tense, Aspect, and Mood

As discussed especially by D. N. Shankara Bhat, many languages attribute prominence to either tense, aspect, or mood over the other two.[17] Use of the term *prominence* here does not mean that either tense, aspect, or mood excludes the other two categories, nor does it mean that the other two categories are less important than the prominent one. Instead, prominence simply refers to the centrality of one category for understanding a language's verbal system. The most prominent category in a language will serve as a "center" of sorts around which the other categories can be organized.

The prominence a category receives in language is determined by its degree of grammaticalization, paradigmatization, obligatoriness, and pervasiveness.[18] A category is grammaticalized when affixes—a grammatical element—are used to mark that category. Both obligatoriness and paradigmatization directly relate to grammaticalization. The more grammaticalization of a category there is, the more necessary (i.e., obligatory) that category becomes for use in the language, and the more it shows up in verbal paradigms (i.e., it is paradigmatized). This naturally leads to pervasiveness, or the degree to which the category appears across all major verb types. One good way of measuring a category's pervasiveness is the extent to which it appears in the non-indicative moods.

---

15. Palmer, *Mood and Modality*, 24–69.
16. Palmer, *Mood and Modality*, 70–106.
17. Shankara Bhat, *Prominence of Tense, Aspect, and Mood*.
18. Shankara Bhat, *Prominence of Tense, Aspect, and Mood*, 95–97.

In light of this framework, we can consider modern English a tense-prominent language.[19] On the one hand, English uses endings like -s and -ed to mark the present and past tense, respectively. On the other hand, English requires the use of non-affixing helping verbs to express both aspect (e.g., perfective *I wrote* versus imperfective *I was writing*) and mood (e.g., realis *I write* versus irrealis *I could be writing*). Thus, a paradigm of the English verb is primarily marked for tense rather than aspect or mood. This is true even in English's non-indicative moods, which generally utilize the same inflectional paradigm as the indicative paradigm with the addition of helping verbs.

5.3 TENSE, ASPECT, AND MOOD IN BIBLICAL HEBREW

Having laid a foundation for understanding tense, aspect, and mood cross-linguistically, I turn now to Biblical Hebrew scholarship on these concepts. Prior to the nineteenth century, little debate existed over the Biblical Hebrew verbal system.[20] Medieval Jewish grammarians like Saadiah Gaon, David Kimḥi, and Elias Levita all believed that the verbal system was tense-prominent. Christian Hebraists of the Renaissance and Enlightenment eras, such as Johann Reuchlin and N. W. Schroeder, likewise based their understanding of the Biblical Hebrew verbal system on tense. Thus, *qatal* was thought to express the past tense and *yiqtol* the future tense. For the Jewish grammarians, at least, *weqatal* and *wayyiqtol* were also thought to be "converted" forms of *qatal* and *yiqtol* in which the addition of *waw* converted the tense.

This picture changed significantly during the nineteenth century, largely due to the efforts of Heinrich Ewald and S. R. Driver.[21] Both Ewald and Driver argued that the Biblical Hebrew verbal system was based on aspect, not tense. They referred to *qatal* with the Latin term *perfectum* and *yiqtol* with the term *imperfectum*, claiming that *qatal* expressed completed action and *yiqtol* incomplete action. They used the term *consecutive* for *weqatal* and *wayyiqtol* because they thought that these two forms expressed sequential action in the future and past, respectively.

Ewald's and Driver's view of the Biblical Hebrew verbal system remained highly influential into the twentieth century, but the discovery and decipherment of Akkadian and Ugaritic led to comparison of Biblical Hebrew's verbal system

---

19. Shankara Bhat, *Prominence of Tense, Aspect, and Mood*, 120.
20. Cook, *Time and the Biblical Hebrew Verb*, 83–86; McFall, *Enigma of the Hebrew Verbal System*, 26.
21. Cook, *Time and the Biblical Hebrew Verb*, 86–93; McFall, *Enigma of the Hebrew Verbal System*, 43–57, 60–77.

with verbal systems in these and other Semitic languages.[22] The historical-comparative approach made possible various connections between the Biblical Hebrew verbal conjugations and other Semitic forms: *qatal* represents the West Semitic adjective-turned-verb **qatala*, *yiqtol* comes from West Semitic **yaqtulu*, and *wayyiqtol* contains the remnants of a West Semitic preterite **yaqtul*.

Scholars responded to this comparative Semitic data in different ways. Some incorporated it into Ewald's and Driver's aspectual theory whereas others turned to tense or even mood to explain the Biblical Hebrew verbal system.[23] Below I sketch the variety of perspectives according to four major categories: tense-prominent, aspect-prominent, mood-prominent, and functional. Because the literature is so vast, I focus on scholarship from the 1980s onward.

5.3.1 Tense-Prominent Theories

The comparative Semitic data introduced during the late nineteenth and early twentieth centuries led to a revival of interest in Biblical Hebrew as tense-prominent. Some of these studies include the work of scholars like Frank R. Blake[24] and James A. Hughes.[25] In the modern era, a number of scholars—especially ones associated with the University of Toronto—have proposed tense-prominent theories of the Biblical Hebrew verbal system.

5.3.1.1 E. J. Revell

E. J. Revell's theory of the Biblical Hebrew verbal system has been relatively influential, especially upon his University of Toronto students who have developed his ideas further in their own studies of the verb.[26] Contrary to the modern interest in aspect, Revell instead argues for the prominence of tense. For Revell, the prominence of tense naturally follows from the observation that Hebrew expressed tense both prior to Biblical Hebrew (e.g., as the preterite *yiqtol*) and in post-biblical Rabbinic Hebrew: if the Hebrew language marked tense both prior to and after Biblical Hebrew, it must also have done so in between. Revell claims that any exceptions to the prominence of tense are only apparent, just as they are in tense-based English.

Revell contends that *qatal* communicates the past tense whereas *yiqtol* expresses both the present and future tenses. He also argues that the time reference of

22. Cook, *Time and the Biblical Hebrew Verb*, 93–120.

23. Cook, *Time and the Biblical Hebrew Verb*, 120–49.

24. Blake, *Resurvey of Hebrew Tenses*; idem, "Hebrew Waw Conversive," 271–95; idem, "Form of Verbs after *Waw*," 51–57.

25. Hughes, "Problems of the Hebrew Verbal System"; idem, "Imperfect with *Waw* Conjunctive and Perfect with *Waw* Consecutive"; idem, "Another Look at the Hebrew Tenses," 12–24.

26. Revell, "System of the Verb," 1–37.

both *qatal* and *yiqtol* is conditioned by the time reference of the context in which they are used: in other words, he formulates a relative tense theory of the verbal system. Thus, according to Revell, *qatal* presents an event in the past from the perspective of the speaker, and *yiqtol* presents an event in the present or future from the viewpoint of the speaker. Furthermore, secondary elements such as modality are marked by word order: *weqatal* expresses modality because it occurs in clause-initial position, unlike *qatal* that instead occurs in non-initial position; and clause-initial *yiqtol* has modal value, whereas non-initial *yiqtol* does not.

5.3.1.2 J. Brian Peckham

J. Brian Peckham, who like Revell taught at the University of Toronto, also considers the role that word order has in marking tense, aspect, and mood.[27] However, unlike Revell, he proposes that word order primarily serves to mark tense rather than mood, although he does admit that word order can sometimes mark mood. Peckham also incorporates aspect to a greater degree than Revell does. Peckham focuses on *qatal* and *yiqtol*, examining how clauses with these two verbal forms express different tenses depending on the clause's word order and whether or not a clause is linked with *waw* to what precedes it.

The result is a very complicated system of relative tenses. When *qatal* occurs in initial position without the conjunction, it communicates the present perfect tense (e.g., *I have written*), but in non-initial position it expresses the simple past (e.g., *I wrote*) or past perfect (e.g., *I had written*). When *yiqtol* occurs in initial position without the conjunction, it expresses the present (e.g., *I am writing*), but in non-initial position it communicates the past habitual (e.g., *I would write*) or durative (e.g., *I was writing*). Furthermore, the consecutive forms *wayyiqtol* and *weqatal* continue the tense of the verb in the clause that precedes them. Thus, *wayyiqtol* typically expresses past action (e.g., *I wrote*) when it follows *qatal*, and *weqatal* typically communicates the past habitual (e.g., *I would write*) when it follows *yiqtol*.

5.3.1.3 Vincent DeCaen

In his 1995 University of Toronto dissertation, Vincent DeCaen offers a tense-prominent understanding of the verbal system.[28] Naturally, he builds upon the work of his mentors Revell and Peckham to do so, but he also approaches the question of the Biblical Hebrew verbal system from the perspective of

---

27. Peckham, "Tense and Mood in Biblical Hebrew," 139–68.
28. DeCaen, "Verb in Standard Biblical Hebrew Prose"; cf. idem, "Ewald and Driver on Biblical Hebrew 'Aspect,'" 129–51.

Generative Grammar, specifically Noam Chomsky's Government-Binding Theory. As pointed out by DeCaen, it is difficult to incorporate a purely tenseless language into such a generative framework. This, in turn, motivates DeCaen to argue that tense—and, to a lesser degree, mood—provide the key component of the Biblical Hebrew verbal system.

DeCaen contends that nearly all verb forms in Biblical Hebrew possess perfective aspect; according to him, only the participle expresses imperfective aspect. Biblical Hebrew verbs are instead otherwise inflected for tense, and then each form is associated with a particular mood, subsumed under tense. The suffixed *qatal* marks the past tense and belongs to the *realis* mood, whereas all prefixed forms express the non-past tense and can be either *realis* or *irrealis*. Only the "long" *yiqtol* expresses the *realis* mood, whereas both the jussive and cohortative express the *irrealis* mood along with the imperative and, most notably, *wayyiqtol*. According to DeCaen, modality directly correlates with word order in that verb-initial clauses tend to express the *irrealis* rather than *realis* mood.

5.3.1.4 Tal Goldfajn

Tal Goldfajn is not directly influenced by the Toronto school of thinking, but she also holds to a tense-prominent theory of the Biblical Hebrew verbal system.[29] Her basic argument is that the major role of the verbal forms in Biblical Hebrew is to indicate the temporal relationship between the events in the text. Goldfajn does not deny the existence of aspect in various verbal forms, but she does not follow Heinrich Ewald, S. R. Driver, and others in arguing that aspect is more prominent than tense

Goldfajn analyzes four verb forms in detail: *qatal, yiqtol, wayyiqtol,* and *weqatal*. She distinguishes between active (i.e., fientive) and stative verbs for *qatal*, arguing that *qatal* expresses anterior action for active verbs but contemporaneous action for stative verbs. The form *yiqtol*, however, expresses posterior action. Goldfajn also argues that *wayyiqtol* and *weqatal* represent the sequential counterparts of *qatal* and *yiqtol*. Thus, the past tense *wayyiqtol* and the future tense *weqatal* both move the reference time of the narrative forward. Thus, similar to the Toronto school, Goldfajn contends that word order plays an important role in expressing tense.

5.3.1.5 Ziony Zevit

Ziony Zevit also holds to a tense-prominent theory of the Biblical Hebrew verbal system, although his presentation is slightly different than any of the

---

29. Goldfajn, *Word Order and Time.*

above scholars.[30] He argues that the two most basic verbal forms, *qatal* and *yiqtol*, are each marked for tense: *qatal* the past tense and *yiqtol* the present-future tense. According to Zevit, both *qatal* and *yiqtol* can express aspect, but they do so only under tense and are not actually marked for aspect. In support of this contention, Zevit appeals to modern living languages, arguing that languages expressing aspect always do so within the framework of a tense system.

One of Zevit's most noteworthy contributions is his additional claim that both *qatal* and *wayyiqtol* express anteriority in certain constructions. He argues that Biblical Hebrew had no morphological means of indicating that an action took place prior to another action (i.e., anterior action). So, to express the relative past tense Biblical Hebrew relies on syntax and word order. An anterior clause, according to Zevit, is any clause beginning with a noun or pronoun and followed by *qatal*. In these instances, *qatal* communicates either the perfect (e.g., *I have written*) or the pluperfect (e.g., *I had written*). The form *wayyiqtol* can also express the perfect or pluperfect, but only when it follows a *qatal* functioning as such.

5.3.1.6 Frank Matheus

Lastly, Frank Matheus puts forth a new understanding of time and the Biblical Hebrew verb.[31] For Matheus, the tense of a verbal form locates a proposition in a text, not a time. Because tense is dependent on text, he distinguishes between two types of texts that reflect two different communication situations: active (e.g., speech) and passive (e.g., narrative). Within these two categories, Matheus further distinguishes between topic time (i.e., the time established by a keyword in the utterance, like *yesterday*) and situation time (i.e., the time-frame in which the event actually occurs). In this he largely follows the work of the German linguist Wolfgang Klein.[32]

According to Matheus, the way a given verbal form should be understood depends on whether or not the situation time overlaps with the topic time. Specifically, Biblical Hebrew verbs express tense when the situation time falls within the topic time. On the one hand, *qatal*, *yiqtol*, *wayyiqtol*, and *weqatal* all express the past (narrative) tense in passive communication. On the other hand, in active communication *qatal* expresses the past or present tense, *yiqtol* expresses the present or future tense, and *weqatal* expresses the future tense.

---

30. Zevit, *Anterior Construction in Classical Hebrew*; idem, "Talking Funny in Biblical Henglish," 25–33.

31. Matheus, *Jegliches hat seine Zeit*.

32. E.g., Klein, *Time in Language*; idem, "How Time Is Encoded," 39–82.

Aspect, according to Matheus, primarily comes into play only when the situation time falls outside of the topic time.

5.3.1.7 Evaluation

Modern scholars who believe the Biblical Hebrew verbal system primarily expresses tense are in good company with the individuals who held to such a view throughout most of history. These scholars have done a decent job of reviving the traditional perspective while simultaneously improving upon it. In particular, recent tense-prominent theories rightly give significant attention to the way that word order correlates with tense, aspect, and mood. This is a significant advance because, even though the Hebrew Bible exhibits a clear connection between verb usage and word order, that connection has thus far received little attention in the conversation on tense, aspect, and mood.

Yet it remains unclear to what extent word order determines the tense, aspect, or mood of a given verbal form. It seems unlikely that word order alone can account for these categories, otherwise there would be no need to use different morphological forms. In addition, the above tense-prominent theories give little attention to comparative Semitics and tend to force a perspective on Biblical Hebrew that does not fit with what is known of the Semitic languages. Perhaps the main reason why tense-prominent theories dominated historically is that Biblical Hebrew was interpreted in light of post-Biblical Hebrew, where tense is much more important. However, post-Biblical Hebrew's expression of tense seems to be a late development given what we know of the development of the Semitic verbal system.

5.3.2 Aspect-Prominent Theories

The most common view of the Biblical Hebrew verbal system today is that aspect, not tense, best explains the usage of all forms. This theory was popularized by individuals like Heinrich Ewald and S. R. Driver during the heyday of Comparative Philology. The work of Carl Brockelmann[33] subsequently led to the incorporation of aspect into the Semitic verbal system as a whole, and his ideas were further developed in the mid-twentieth century by scholars like Frithiof Rundgren.[34] In modern times, John A. Cook has been the most vocal advocate of aspect-prominence, although others have contributed to the discussion and even departed significantly from the original arguments of Ewald and Driver.

---

33. Brockelmann, "'Tempora' des Semitischen," 133–54.
34. Rundgren, *Althebräische Verbum.*

5.3.2.1 John A. Cook

As just noted, the most significant—and prolific—modern proponent of aspect for the Biblical Hebrew verbal system is John A. Cook.[35] Like Ewald and Driver, he argues that the fundamental opposition in Biblical Hebrew is between perfective and imperfective action, but he gives this viewpoint a solid foundation in modern linguistic notions of tense, aspect, and mood. In addition, Cook draws significantly from linguistic typology and grammaticalization to validate his theory of the Biblical Hebrew verbal system. Thus, for Cook, any viable model of the verbal system must not depart significantly from trends and patterns observed across the world's languages. This approach, according to Cook, counteracts potentially subjective analysis of any given verbal form.

Within this framework, Cook defines *qatal* as perfective and *yiqtol* as imperfective. Regarding *qatal*, he argues that it was originally resultative. This function gradually developed into a perfective or simple past, a common grammaticalization path across the world's languages. Regarding *yiqtol*, Cook contends that it was originally progressive but developed into an imperfective as it was displaced by the participle, which also communicates progressive action. Both *qatal* and *yiqtol*—as well as *weqatal*—are modal when they occur in clause-initial position. Thus, according to Cook, modality is marked syntactically rather than morphologically. This differs from *wayyiqtol*, which, although it always occurs in clause-initial position, serves as a preterite and the only genuine tense in the Biblical Hebrew verbal system.

5.3.2.2 Jill E. Zwyghuizen

Jill E. Zwyghuizen applies Cook's grammaticalization model to the verbal system of Biblical Hebrew poetry.[36] Like Cook, she holds to an aspectual model: *qatal* (< West Semitic **qatala*) is perfective, *yiqtol* (< West Semitic **yaqtulu*) is imperfective, and *wayyiqtol* and its bare form *yiqtol* (< West Semitic **yaqtul*) are both simple past-tense preterites. She further contends that the loss of final short vowels in Biblical Hebrew has caused morphological ambiguity between *yiqtol* imperfectives, *yiqtol* jussives, and *yiqtol* preterites. However, unlike Cook, Zwyghuizen gives greater attention to the interplay between aspect and situation aspect and the role that this interplay has in establishing time reference. She also focuses exclusively on poetry rather than narrative.

---

35. Cook, *Time and the Biblical Hebrew Verb*; idem, "Finite Verbal Forms in Biblical Hebrew," 21–35; idem, "Hebrew Verb," 117–43. Cook's *Time and the Biblical Hebrew Verb* originated as his PhD dissertation completed at the University of Wisconsin–Madison in 2002.

36. Zwyghuizen, "Time Reference of Verbs."

Zwyghuizen draws a basic distinction between active (i.e., fientive) and stative verbs, which can be distinguished morphologically by their vowel patterns. The time reference of each verb in poetic texts is determined by a combination of aspect and situation aspect. On the one hand, the perfective *qatal* has past time reference for active verbs but either past or present time reference for stative verbs. On the other hand, the imperfective *yiqtol* has present or future time reference for active verbs but future time reference for stative verbs. According to Zwyghuizen this framework helps to distinguish between long (imperfective) and short (preterite) prefix forms morphologically: a genuine preterite form (< West Semitic **yaqtul*) tends to occur near a fientive perfective or *wayyiqtol*, both of which express the past tense, whereas imperfective *yiqtol* (< West Semitic **yaqtulu*) does not.

5.3.2.3 T. David Andersen

T. David Andersen's aspect-based model of the Biblical Hebrew verbal system relies significantly on comparative Semitics.[37] He considers the aspectual nature of Biblical Hebrew verbs within the broader context of the development of the Semitic verbal system. Building on I. M. Diakonoff's reconstruction of the Proto-Semitic verbal system,[38] Andersen focuses on three different verbal conjugations: **qatala/*qatila*, **yaqtulu*, and **yaqtul*. From these he explains the different origins and functions of Biblical Hebrew *qatal*, *yiqtol*, *wayyiqtol*, and *weqatal*. Along the way he invokes grammaticalization to explain change in usage.

Andersen takes Proto-Semitic **qatala/*qatila* as the origin of Biblical Hebrew *qatal*. He argues that this form was originally progressive but subsequently acquired two different uses. On the one hand, it developed into a perfective, hence the use of Biblical Hebrew *qatal* as a past tense; on the other hand, it also developed into an imperfective, which lies behind the use of Biblical Hebrew *weqatal* to express repeated and future action. Andersen also reconstructs a Proto-Semitic imperfective **yaqtulu* that gradually came to be restricted to subordinate clauses when another imperfective form, **yaqattal*, emerged. The original imperfective, **yaqtulu*, lies behind Biblical Hebrew *yiqtol*, which according to Andersen is imperfective. Finally, Andersen sees the Proto-Semitic preterite **yaqtul*, separate from Proto-Semitic **yaqtulu*, as the origin of Biblical Hebrew *wayyiqtol*. As a preterite, *wayyiqtol* expresses past perfective action.

---

37. Andersen, "Evolution of the Hebrew Verbal System," 1–66.
38. Diakonoff, *Afrasian Languages*, 85–104.

5.3.2.4 Ulf Bergström

Ulf Bergström also uses comparative Semitics and grammaticalization to explain the Biblical Hebrew verbal system.[39] Like Andersen, he devotes significant attention to *qatal*, long *yiqtol* (< West Semitic **yaqtulu*), and short *yiqtol* (< West Semitic **yaqtul*). However, he also substantially integrates the Biblical Hebrew participle into his analysis. The result is a quadripartite model of the verbal system: *qatal*, long *yiqtol*, short *yiqtol*, and the participle. According to Bergström, these four forms can be classified in terms of two different original functions: both *qatal* and short *yiqtol* were originally resultative, and both long *yiqtol* and the participle were originally progressive.

Bergström connects each aspect with a specific tense. He develops a theory of aspect and tense, a process he calls "temporalization," in which tense comes about through reanalysis of aspect. Thus, Hebrew speakers reanalyzed the resultatives *qatal* and short *yiqtol* as expressing the past tense, and progressives were reanalyzed as communicating future action. Bergström further claims that the difference between forms that share an aspect-tense is one of "appeal function": *qatal* and the participle prompt the listener to take immediate action, whereas short *yiqtol* and long *yiqtol* do not do so. This distinction, according to Bergström, explains why there are two different conjugations for each aspect-tense.

5.3.2.5 Axel van de Sande

Axel van de Sande bases his study of the Biblical Hebrew verbal system in analysis of three key forms: *qatal*, short *yiqtol* (< West Semitic **yaqtul*), and long *yiqtol* (< West Semitic **yaqtulu*).[40] In this point he overlaps much with Andersen and Bergström. But, unlike them as well as most modern scholarship, he does not give significant attention to either *wayyiqtol* or *weqatal*. This is because he thinks that *wayyiqtol* and *weqatal* are artificial Masoretic creations. He rejects, therefore, the notion that *wayyiqtol* derives from West Semitic **yaqtul* or that *weqatal* originated from *qatal*'s use in conditional clauses, instead claiming that *wayyiqtol* and *weqatal* are simply *yiqtol* and *qatal* with the conjunction.

Within this tripartite framework, Sande argues that aspect is the primary component of *qatal*, short *yiqtol*, and long *yiqtol*. He contends that *qatal* can express both perfective and imperfective aspect. Following the common use of suffixed conjugations in West Semitic, *qatal* can express punctual action, but it

---

39. Bergström, "Temporality and the Semantics of the Biblical Hebrew Verbal System."
40. Sande, *Système verbal de l'hébreu ancien*. This work originated as Sande's PhD dissertation completed at L'Institut orientaliste de Louvain in 2006.

also can express the volitive or optative moods (for active verbs) or the permansive (for stative verbs). Furthermore, following Josef Tropper,[41] Sande argues that short *yiqtol* and long *yiqtol* have different functions stemming from a binary opposition between perfective and imperfective aspect. In the indicative, short *yiqtol* expresses past, punctual action, whereas long *yiqtol* expresses durative action (in both the present and the past), future action, and gnomic statements.

5.3.2.6 Rolf Furuli

Rolf Furuli's aspectual model of the Biblical Hebrew verbal system is unique.[42] He defines aspect differently than it has traditionally been defined, following Mari Broman Olsen[43] in arguing that aspect refers to the intersection between reference time (the part of the event that is visible) and event time (the whole event). The result is a redefinition of aspect in terms of progressive action: for Furuli, perfective action is a view of an event in which the progressive action is not visible, whereas imperfective action is a view of an event in which the progressive action is visible. This leads Furuli to connect components traditionally associated with *Aktionsart* with aspect.

Within this framework, Furuli classifies both *qatal* and *weqatal* as perfective and both *yiqtol* and *wayyiqtol* as imperfective. This differs significantly from the traditional viewpoint, which sees *wayyiqtol* as perfective and *weqatal* as imperfective. Another significant departure from most modern scholarship is that Furuli does not think that *wayyiqtol* and *weqatal* differ semantically from their non-consecutive counterparts. Rather, similar to Sande, he sees *wayyiqtol* and *weqatal* as artificial Masoretic creations. The only reason for using one form over the other, according to Furuli, is whether or not a biblical author wanted to place a word before the verb: *wayyiqtol* and *weqatal* are used when the verb occurs at the beginning of a clause, whereas *qatal* and *yiqtol* appear when the verb occurs in non-initial position.

5.3.2.7 David O. Moomo

Finally, David O. Moomo argues that the Biblical Hebrew verbal system is aspectually prominent, but he does so in a very different way from everyone else.[44] He rejects comparative Semitics and grammaticalization as reliable tools for understanding the Biblical Hebrew verbal system. Rather, he seeks a

---

41. Tropper, "Althebräisches und semitisches Aspektsystem," 164–81.

42. Furuli, *New Understanding of the Verbal System*. This work originated as Furuli's PhD dissertation completed at the University of Oslo in 2005.

43. Olsen, *Lexical and Grammatical Aspect*.

44. Moomo, "Meaning of the Biblical Hebrew Verbal Conjugation."

universal, cross-linguistic parameter that can establish typological categories for tense, aspect, and mood. Accordingly, Moomo turns to psycholinguistics as well as Shankara Bhat's parameters for categorizing languages as tense-, aspect-, or mood-prominent, referred to earlier.[45]

Moomo then contends that Biblical Hebrew verbs are inflected to mark the ways events and states are viewed aspectually. For Moomo, *qatal* is perfective, *yiqtol* and *weqatal* are imperfective, and the participle expresses progressive action. He rejects the notion that Biblical Hebrew does not always consistently distinguish aspect. Moomo instead claims that verbs alleged to "break the rules" can be explained entirely in terms of aspect, giving cross-linguistic examples to support his contention.

5.3.2.8 Evaluation

The above survey reflects the many advances in our understanding of aspect's role within the Biblical Hebrew verbal system. Many of those who hold to aspect-prominence situate the different verbal forms within their broader linguistic context, both in terms of comparative Semitics and modern linguistic theory. Particularly noteworthy is Cook's use of grammaticalization and linguistic typology. Attention to these two topics is necessary to provide external confirmation of what otherwise might be philological judgments of an individual scholar. Accordingly, Cook's work has especially helped to establish aspect-prominence as the most plausible theory of the Biblical Hebrew verbal system.

At the same time, a significant issue facing proponents of aspect-prominence is their lack of agreement on how to define aspect and how to understand the Semitic verbal system. Bergström and especially Furuli create more problems than they solve because their theories rely on non-standard definitions of aspect. Regarding comparative Semitics, Andersen, Sande, and Furuli each rely upon hypothetical and even flawed reconstructions of the Semitic verbal system. Particularly troubling are Sande's and Furuli's arguments that *weqatal* and *wayyiqtol* are really no different from *qatal* and *yiqtol* in terms of function and origin. Such a conclusion betrays a significant lack of awareness of the many ways that comparative Semitics has contributed to our understanding of the Semitic verbal system over the past century.

5.3.3 Mood-Prominent Theories

Although less common than the tense-prominent and aspect-prominent theories, there is a small handful of scholars who propose that mood best

---

45. Shankara Bhat, *Prominence of Tense, Aspect, and Mood.*

explains the Biblical Hebrew verbal system. Those who hold to this perspective disagree on how to relate mood to tense and aspect. Some connect mood closely with tense, whereas others instead subsume aspect under mood. Jan Joosten, who holds the prestigious Regius Professorship of Hebrew at the University of Oxford, is the most significant advocate of mood-prominence today.

5.3.3.1 Jan Joosten

Joosten's[46] understanding builds on the relative-tense theory of Jerzy Kuryłowicz, which argues that the primary dichotomy in the Semitic verbal system is between action contemporaneous to the moment of speaking and action prior to the moment of speaking.[47] Joosten argues that tense and especially mood account for the Biblical Hebrew verbal system, but not aspect. For Joosten, there are too many anomalies for aspect to serve as a primary component of the Biblical Hebrew verbal system (e.g., the predominant use of *yiqtol* is to express the future or *irrealis* mood, not imperfective action). Joosten also thinks that it is less necessary for a language to express aspect than mood and tense, which leads him to reject aspect as a significant component of the verbal system.

According to Joosten, all Biblical Hebrew verbs can be categorized as *realis* (indicative) or *irrealis* (modal). On the one hand, the conjugations *qatal*, *wayyiqtol*, and the participle belong to the *realis* mood. Of these, only *wayyiqtol* expresses tense, namely the past tense. Both *qatal* and the participle are tenseless, with *qatal* expressing anterior action and the participle expressing contemporaneous action. On the other hand, the conjugations *yiqtol*, *weqatal*, and the volitives belong to the *irrealis* mood. Both *yiqtol* and *weqatal* communicate what has not actually happened but might happen, and thus are modal. However, they differ from the volitives, which are also modal but instead communicate wish, desire, or intention, not merely what might happen.

5.3.3.2 Beat Zuber

Beat Zuber also argues that mood serves as the basis for the Biblical Hebrew verbal system, but his analysis differs from Joosten's.[48] Zuber considers *qatal*, *yiqtol*, *wayyiqtol*, and *weqatal*, grouping them into two different categories based on mood. On the one hand, both *qatal* and *wayyiqtol* belong to the

---

46. Joosten, *Verbal System of Biblical Hebrew*; idem, "Indicative System of the Hebrew Verb," 51–71; idem, "Finite Verbal Forms in Biblical Hebrew," 49–70.

47. Kuryłowicz, "Verbal Aspect in Semitic," 114–20.

48. Zuber, *Tempussystem des biblischen Hebräisch*.

category of *realis* and express the indicative mood; on the other hand, both *yiqtol* and *weqatal* belong to the category of *irrealis* and express modality. Furthermore, according to Zuber, there is no semantic difference within each category because the consecutive forms serve as tense stylistic variants of *qatal* and *yiqtol*. Thus, the *realis* forms both communicate the past tense whereas the *irrealis* forms both communicate the future.

Zuber supports his understanding of the Biblical Hebrew verbal system with the Septuagint and Vulgate. He finds a high correlation—more than 90 percent—between these translations and modality. The Septuagint and Vulgate use non-future indicative forms to translate *qatal* and consecutive *wayyiqtol* but utilize the future, subjective, or optative to translate *yiqtol* and consecutive *weqatal*. For Zuber, these ancient translations provide important insight into the Biblical Hebrew verbal system because they date closer to the time Biblical Hebrew was actually spoken than we do. Not only are they more contemporaneous, they are also a more reliable guide than our potentially subjective understanding of the verbal system today.

5.3.3.3 Susan Rattray

Finally, Susan Rattray argues that modality serves as the primary category for understanding the Biblical Hebrew verbal system.[49] Similar to Joosten, but unlike Zuber, she subsumes aspect rather than tense as secondary. For Rattray, the primary opposition in Biblical Hebrew is between "immediate reality" (the *realis* mood) and "non-immediate reality/irreality" (the *irrealis* mood). Each of these moods can be expressed, according to Rattray, with either progressive or non-progressive aspect. Furthermore, because Biblical Hebrew verbs are not marked for tense, context rather than morphology determines whether a given form is past, present, or future.

Rattray contends that three verbal forms fall within the category of the *realis* mood: *qatal*, *weqatal*, and the participle. Of these, *qatal* and *weqatal* communicate non-progressive aspect whereas the participle expresses progressive aspect. This leaves the three remaining verbal forms as belonging to the *irrealis* mood: *yiqtol*, the volitives, and *wayyiqtol*. Rattray considers the volitives to be progressive but takes *yiqtol* and *wayyiqtol* as non-progressive. According to Rattray, furthermore, both *qatal* and *yiqtol* have each acquired their own special uses, such as portraying action within a background setting. This means that *weqatal* and *wayyiqtol* are not merely interchangeable with *qatal* and *wayyiqtol*.

---

49. Rattray, "Tense-Mood-Aspect System of Biblical Hebrew."

5.3.3.4 Evaluation

Mood-prominent theories rightly draw attention to the important role that modality plays in the Biblical Hebrew verbal system. As such, they contribute to a growing interest in mood and modality within Biblical Hebrew scholarship.[50] Those who hold to mood-prominence are also to be thanked for their careful analysis of the Hebrew Bible's data. They have formulated their theories of the Biblical Hebrew verbal system "from the ground up," through analysis of actual verb usage rather than through imposition of an outside framework that may or may not accurately explain all the data.

At the same time, those who promote mood-prominence have largely failed to support their theories with evidence from modern linguistics and comparative Semitics. Our understanding of the Biblical Hebrew verbal system is limited in that, without any native speakers, scholars inevitably rely on their own philological judgments to determine the function of individual verb forms. Ancient versions like the Septuagint can be helpful in that they show how different conjugations were understood in antiquity, but there is no guarantee that they preserve the correct understanding of every Biblical Hebrew verb. So, modern linguistics and comparative Semitics are needed as an external control. Unfortunately, those who promote mood-prominence have yet to significantly incorporate either modern linguistics or comparative Semitics into their theories of the Biblical Hebrew verbal system.

5.3.4 Functional Theories

Finally, some theories of the Biblical Hebrew verbal system do not argue for the prominence of tense, aspect, or mood. Rather, they simply observe that tense, aspect, and mood are each present—to one degree or another—in Biblical Hebrew. These theories can be called *functional* theories because they highlight the various meanings that a given verb can have in light of tense, aspect, and mood without claiming prominence of one over the other. The primary advocates of this approach in recent years are Alexander Andrason, Christopher Jero, and Ronald S. Hendel.

5.3.4.1 Alexander Andrason

Alexander Andrason is the most prolific advocate for a functional view of the Biblical Hebrew verbal system.[51] He labels his own approach as a "pan-

---

50. E.g., Dallaire, *Syntax of Volitives*.

51. Andrason, *Sistema verbal hebreo*; idem, "Biblical Hebrew Verbal System," 19–51; idem, "Performative *qatal* and Its Explanation," 1–58; idem, "Gnomic *qatal*," 5–53; idem, "Future Values of the *qatal*," 7–38; idem, "Cognitive-Typological Approach to the Precative *qatal*," 1–41; idem, "Panchronic

chronic" perspective. It is similar to Cook's model in that he uses grammaticalization to explain the development of different forms. However, unlike Cook, Andrason is not as concerned with establishing a single core meaning for each verbal form. Rather, Andrason seeks to explain synchrony in diachronic terms. He therefore describes the meaning of a given verbal form as an amalgam of different meanings that reflect various stages along a grammaticalization path. The result is a wide variety of proposed functions for each verbal form.

For Andrason, *qatal* is a resultative that has taken three different grammaticalization paths leading to three different usages: the anterior, which leads to the past/perfective; the simultaneous, which leads to the stative/present; and the inferential, which leads to the evidential. Andrason also argues that *weqatal* and *wayyiqtol* originated as resultatives: *weqatal* exhibits modal contamination, and *wayyiqtol* (unlike *qatal*) took only the anterior and simultaneous grammaticalization paths. Regarding *yiqtol*, Andrason distinguishes between indicative and modal uses. Indicative *yiqtol* exhibits grammaticalization from imperfective action to the present-future tense except when in past contexts, where it remains restricted to habitual and durative usage. Modal *yiqtol*, grammaticalized from ability to possibility and finally to the volitional moods, has a different origin than indicative *yiqtol* and therefore exhibits no contamination from it as others have contended. Finally, the participle reflects partial grammaticalization of the imperfective aspect.

5.3.4.2 Christopher Jero

Christopher Jero argues that any presentation of the Biblical Hebrew verbal system must describe each form according to its diachronic development.[52] This aligns him with Andrason over scholars such as Cook in that he does not focus on finding a single core meaning for each verbal form. However, Jero is more careful to explain the particular contexts in which a given meaning will occur. This is largely because Jero recognizes that Biblical Hebrew exhibits different historical and geographical dialects. Accordingly, Jero traces the use of each verbal form in both Archaic Biblical Hebrew (most common in poetry) and Standard Biblical Hebrew (most common in prose). Another important feature of Jero's work that distinguishes it from Andrason's is that, similar to Zwyghuizen, Jero highlights the relationship between a verbal root's situation aspect and its expression of tense and aspect.

---

yiqtol," 1–63; idem, "Biblical Hebrew *wayyiqtol*," 1–58; idem, "BH *weqatal* (Part 1)," 1–26; idem, "BH *weqatal* (Part 2)," 1–30. Andrason's *Sistema verbal hebreo* originated as his PhD dissertation completed at the Universidad Complutense in 2011.

52. Jero, "Tense, Mood, and Aspect," 65–84; idem, "Verbal System of Biblical Hebrew Poetry."

Jero derives Biblical Hebrew *qatal* from the West Semitic verbal adjective **qatala*. According to Jero, *qatal* retains much of its original adjectival·sense in Archaic Biblical Hebrew but elsewhere expresses anteriority. For the prefix conjugations, Jero distinguishes between long *yiqtol* (< West Semitic **yaqtulu*) and short *yiqtol* (< West Semitic **yaqtul*). He argues that long *yiqtol* originally expressed the imperfective aspect, a function still evident in Archaic Biblical Hebrew, but came to indicate the future tense (through grammaticalization) and modality (through grammaticalization as well as confusion with West Semitic **yaqtula*). He attributes the loss of long *yiqtol*'s imperfective aspect to the increasing use of the progressive participle. Finally, short *yiqtol*, the origin of the preterite past tense *wayyiqtol*, belongs to the volitives. Along with the imperative and cohortative, it expresses deontic modality, which communicates a speaker's will regarding a situation.

5.3.4.3 Ronald S. Hendel

Finally, Ronald S. Hendel also holds to a functional view of the Biblical Hebrew verbal system. He argues that linguistic categories of tense, aspect, and mood are present to varying degrees in the verbal system.[53] He also contends that theoretical models giving priority to tense or aspect or mood work well overall, but they downplay exceptions. Therefore, according to Hendel, attention to all three categories—tense, aspect, and mood—is necessary to fully understand the Biblical Hebrew verbal system. The end result is that Hendel describes the verbal system similarly to scholars like Cook, but he does not attempt to synthesize that description and explain how tense, aspect, and mood relate to one another.

Regarding tense, Hendel follows modern linguistic theory by considering tense in light of three variables: the speaker, the event itself, and the reference point. According to Hendel, this plays out differently depending on whether a verb is stative or active: *qatal* expresses either the non-future (i.e., present or past) for stative verbs but the past for active verbs, and *yiqtol* expresses the future for stative verbs but the non-past (i.e., present or future) for active verbs. Regarding aspect, Hendel sees a basic opposition between perfective and imperfective aspect. This opposition corresponds to the difference between *qatal* and *yiqtol*, respectively, regardless of the tense associated with them in any given context. Lastly, regarding mood, Hendel categorizes all verbs as indicative or modal. According to Hendel, only the volitives are explicitly marked for mood; both *qatal* and *yiqtol* can be used modally, but only as indicated by the context.

---

53. Hendel, "Margins of the Hebrew Verbal System," 152–81.

5.3.4.4 Evaluation

The primary strength of the functional view is its recognition that tense, aspect, and mood all play varying roles in the Biblical Hebrew verbal system. Supposing that the verbal system must be dominant in one of these three categories—tense, aspect, or mood—can potentially lead to oversimplifications and forcing data into a framework they were not meant to fit. It must be remembered that languages, including Biblical Hebrew, reflect ongoing change. The types of changes that take place in the Biblical Hebrew verbal system undoubtedly follow certain grammaticalization paths. But the expression of tense, aspect, and mood will naturally depend on where in the history of the language the verb used falls. Furthermore, it is always possible that a given form is in-between stages of development.

Only Jero's approach navigates these challenges well. The problem with Hendel's work is that interpreters are left with very little guidance on how to determine what a verbal form means in its specific context. Although it can explain how all a verbal form's different meanings relate to one another, Andrason's perspective causes a similar dilemma. It is because Jero gives attention to the particular contexts in which specific meanings are intended—as well as the correlation between situation aspect and verb forms—that his approach is much more useful than Hendel's or Andrason's. Hopefully, future studies adopting a functional perspective on the Biblical Hebrew verbal system will follow Jero's lead.

5.4 TENSE, ASPECT, AND MOOD IN BIBLICAL ARAMAIC

Although the Biblical Hebrew verbal system has been the subject of a lively debate, there have been few studies of the verbal system of Biblical Aramaic. In 1927, Hans Bauer and Pontus Leander addressed this issue in their Biblical Aramaic grammar,[54] but by its very nature their analysis was far from comprehensive. Since that time only two major studies on the Biblical Aramaic verbal system have appeared: one by Haaim B. Rosén (1961) and one by Tarsee Li (2008). I now summarize both of their contributions before evaluating the state of scholarship on the Biblical Aramaic verbal system.

5.4.1 Haaim B. Rosén

In an article published in the *Journal of Semitics*, Haaim B. Rosén comprehensively analyzes the Biblical Aramaic verbal system.[55] Rosén's study represents

---

54. Bauer and Leander, *Grammatik des biblisch-Aramäischen*, 276–300 (§§277–84).
55. Rosén, "Tenses in the Aramaic of Daniel," 183–203.

a major breakthrough in Biblical Aramaic studies, especially because it was the first of its kind—the Aramaicist E. Y. Kutscher labeled it as a "brilliant revolutionary article."[56] Rosén takes the work of Bauer and Leander as his starting point but provides a much more nuanced presentation of the verbal system in Biblical Aramaic than they do.

One of Rosén's most significant contributions is his consideration of the different functions of the Biblical Aramaic verb in light of the verb's situation aspect. He distinguishes between two types of verbs. On the one hand, "point aspect" verbs, known more commonly today as active or fientive verbs, express an action. Rosén provides the root נפל ("to fall") as an example of a point aspect verb. On the other hand, "linear aspect" verbs, known more commonly today as stative verbs, express an ongoing state or characteristic. Rosén gives the root דור ("to dwell") as an example of this type of verb. According to Rosén, point aspect verbs and linear aspect verbs have different functions depending on the conjugation and type of discourse in which they occur.

Point aspect verbs like נפל ("to fall") can have one of four functions: narrative, future-volitive, present, or subordinate. The default form used for past-tense narrative is the active participle, which expresses past ongoing action (e.g., וְכָתְבָן "and they were writing" in Dan 5:5). When the participle occurs with אִיתַי, it indicates the present tense (e.g., אִיתַיְנָא פָלְחִן "we are serving" in Dan 3:18), and *yqtl* expresses the future tense or modality (e.g., יִפֵּל "he should fall" in Dan 3:10). Finally, *qtl* is used as the default verb in subordinate clauses (e.g., יְהַבְתְּ "you gave" in Dan 2:23).

According to Rosén, linear aspect verbs like דור ("to dwell") have these same four functions but express them with different constructions. The past-tense narrative form is instead *yqtl*, which communicates past habitual or past durative action (e.g., יְתוּב "it was returning" in Dan 4:33 [4:36]). The simple active participle communicates the present tense (e.g., דָּאְרִין "are dwelling" in Dan 3:31), and the *yqtl* conjugation of הוה + participle expresses the future tense or modality (e.g., לֶהֱוֹן דָּבְקִין "they will be united" in Dan 2:43). Lastly, the *qtl* conjugation of הוה + participle is used as the default verbal form in subordinate clauses (e.g., הֲוָא מִתְנַצַּח "he was distinguishing himself" in Dan 6:4).

5.4.2 Tarsee Li

The sole work on the Biblical Aramaic verbal system to appear in recent years is that of Tarsee Li.[57] He seeks to analyze the verbal system in terms of grammaticalization, focusing primarily on the book of Daniel because it

---

56. Kutscher, "Aramaic," 379.
57. Li, *Verbal System of the Aramaic of Daniel*.

presents the most extended corpus of Biblical Aramaic. Li's basic premise is that languages are always in a process of change in that grammatical forms take on new functions and lose old ones. This means that Biblical Aramaic presents a snapshot of both old and new usages of the verb. Thus, Li's study takes a similar approach to Cook's *Time and the Biblical Hebrew Verb*.

Regarding the conjugation *qtl*, Li says it originated as a verbal adjective, just like Biblical Hebrew *qatal* (< West Semitic **qatala*). Following a common grammaticalization path attested throughout the world's languages, *qtl* developed a resultative function and eventually became the simple past tense. Biblical Aramaic preserves some instances of *qtl*'s older resultative function (e.g., עֲדָת "it has departed" in Dan 4:28), but it also preserves this last development (e.g., דָּקוּ "they were shattered" in Dan 2:35). Li notes that the passive participle, which also originally functioned as a verbal adjective, shows evidence of a resultative function in Biblical Aramaic (e.g., מְכַפְּתִין "bound" in Dan 3:23).

Regarding the conjugation *yqtl*, Li argues that it originally expressed imperfective action, just like Biblical Hebrew *yiqtol* (< West Semitic **yaqtulu*). The form *yqtl* gradually came to express the future tense and eventually modality, following a common grammaticalization path—imperfective action to the future tense to modality—attested across the world's languages. Biblical Aramaic contains some uses of *yqtl* functioning as a true imperfect (e.g., יְקוּמוּן "they were standing" in Dan 7:10). But most instances of *yqtl* instead reflect its other functions, either the future tense (e.g., תִּשְׁנֵא "it will be different" in Dan 7:23) or modality (e.g., תְּקִים "you should establish" in Dan 6:9). According to Li, this happened because the active participle, which expresses progressive action, gradually displaced *yqtl* as the default form used to express imperfective action.

Li concludes that Biblical Aramaic shows signs of transitioning from aspect-prominence to tense-prominence. In an earlier stage of the language, still preserved in occasional uses of *qtl* as a resultative and *yqtl* as a true imperfect, aspect was more prominent than tense. However, the use of *qtl* as a past tense and *yqtl* as a future tense demonstrate a shift toward tense. This shift, according to Li, is especially evident in the active participle's use: the *qtl* conjugation of הוה + participle expresses imperfective action in past time (e.g., הֲוָא עָבֵד "he would do" in Dan 6:11), whereas the *yqtl* conjugation of הוה + participle communicates imperfective action or modality in non-past time (e.g., לֶהֱוֵא נָזִק "he might suffer loss" in Dan 6:3).

5.4.3 Evaluation

The studies of Rosén and Li make different contributions to our understanding of the Biblical Aramaic verbal system. Rosén's primary contribution is his distinction between point aspect and linear aspect verbs. This is an especially important distinction because the Semitic languages exhibit a fundamental dichotomy between active and stative verbs. Yet, he does not explore the diachronic development of the Biblical Aramaic verbal system in much detail. Li's analysis, which does so, is particularly helpful in this regard. Naturally, Li's grammaticalization approach possesses many of the same strengths as Cook's approach to the Biblical Hebrew verbal system: attention to common language behaviors and linguistic typology.

Yet, the fact that only two major studies on the Biblical Aramaic verbal system have appeared over the past one hundred years indicates that much more remains to be done. The role that tense, aspect, and mood have for Biblical Aramaic verbs could be further explored in light of advances in our understanding of the same in contemporary (i.e., Imperial) Aramaic.[58] It would be beneficial to explore the development of the Biblical Aramaic verbal system within its broader Semitic context, with greater attention to how the active versus stative opposition and *Aktionsart* correlate with the use of specific verbal forms.

5.5 THE WAYS FORWARD

As the above survey demonstrates, there is a plethora of different perspectives on the Biblical Hebrew and Biblical Aramaic verbal systems. On the one hand this is good, because it shows that scholars are engaging this important topic. On the other hand, the diversity of options can make it difficult to know where to go from here. In what follows I would like to summarize several important points made by Cook regarding what is needed to advance the discussion,[59] adding some thoughts of my own along the way.

First, scholars explaining the Biblical Hebrew and Biblical Aramaic verbal systems need to utilize current linguistic definitions for tense, aspect, and mood. While many of the works discussed in this chapter are based in a modern linguistic understanding of these categories, a surprising number are not. Some even come up with their own definitions of tense, aspect, and mood or adopt perspectives not commonly held within the linguistic guild. For the conversation to move forward, it is crucial that scholars of Biblical Hebrew and Biblical Aramaic adopt common definitions that are supported by modern linguistics.

Second, as pointed out by Cook, there is also the need for situating theories

---

58. Cf. Gzella, *Tempus, Aspekt und Modalität*.
59. Cook, "Current Issues," 79–108.

of the verbal systems within their broader linguistic context. This requires attention to linguistic typology and grammaticalization, for any proposed theory of the Biblical Hebrew or Biblical Aramaic verbal systems should not depart significantly from the way that the world's languages typically behave. Evaluating verbal system theories in this way provides an external control for how particular verbal forms are interpreted, which is important because we are not native speakers. Cook's work with Biblical Hebrew and Li's work with Biblical Aramaic offer especially excellent models to adopt in future research on the verbal systems.

Third, although not discussed much by Cook, I would emphasize that situating theories of the verbal system within their broader linguistic context requires attention to comparative Semitics. In other words, any theory of the Biblical Hebrew or Biblical Aramaic verbal systems must ultimately fit with what we know of the development of the Semitic languages. Uncertainties in their development exist, but enough is known of the basic picture to prevent the formulation of theories that do not fit within this framework, and knowledge of this basic picture would have saved some of the above scholars from unfortunate errors. Comparative Semitics also offers a way forward for future research because it attests to a dichotomy between active and stative verbs and to the importance of situation aspect. Hopefully, future studies of the verbal systems will follow the lead of Zwyghuizen and Jero in this regard.

This leads, finally, to another desideratum if our understanding of the Biblical Hebrew and Biblical Aramaic verbal systems is to advance further. Scholars must recognize that Biblical Hebrew and Biblical Aramaic are real languages that change over time. This makes it difficult to label them with tense, aspect, or mood as the prominent category. Rather, each of the three come into play in varying degrees depending on the stage of the language, as argued by some functionalists like Jero. It is therefore encouraging that several recent studies have focused on particular stages in the development of the verbal system.[60] If this trend continues, we can expect further advances in our understanding of the verbal systems in the years ahead.

5.6 FURTHER READING

Buth, Randall. "The Hebrew Verb in Current Discussions." *JOTT* 5 (1992): 91–105.
Callaham, Scott N. "Mood and Modality: Biblical Hebrew." *EHLL* 2:687–90.
Cook, John A. "Aspect: Pre-Modern Hebrew." *EHLL* 1:201–5.

---

60. Notarius, *Verb in Archaic Biblical Poetry*; Cohen, *Verbal Tense System*.

———. "Current Issues in the Study of the Biblical Hebrew Verbal System." *Kleine Untersuchungen zur Sprache des Alten Testaments und seiner Umwelt* 17 (2014): 79–108.

———. *Time and the Biblical Hebrew Verb: The Expression of Tense, Aspect, and Modality in Biblical Hebrew.* LSAWS 7. Winona Lake, IN: Eisenbrauns, 2012.

Gzella, Holger. "Some General Remarks on Interactions between Aspect, Modality, and Evidentiality in Biblical Hebrew." *FO* 49 (2012): 225–32.

Hatav, Galia. "Tense: Biblical Hebrew." *EHLL* 3:736–40.

Jero, Christopher. "Tense, Mood, and Aspect in the Biblical Hebrew Verbal System." Pages 65–84 in *"Where Shall Wisdom Be Found?" A Grammatical Tribute to Professor Stephen A. Kaufman.* Edited by Hélène M. Dallaire, Benjamin J. Noonan, and Jennifer E. Noonan. Winona Lake, IN: Eisenbrauns, 2017.

———. "The Verbal System of Biblical Hebrew Poetry: The Morphosyntactic Role of Internal Aspect (*Aktionsart*)." PhD diss., Hebrew Union College–Jewish Institute of Religion, 2008.

Joosten, Jan. "Verbal System: Biblical Hebrew." *EHLL* 3:921–25.

Li, Tarsee. *The Verbal System of the Aramaic of Daniel: An Explanation in the Context of Grammaticalization.* Studies in the Aramaic Interpretation of Scripture 8. Leiden: Brill, 2009.

Zwyghuizen, Jill E. "Time Reference of Verbs in Biblical Hebrew Poetry." PhD diss., Dallas Theological Seminary, 2012.

CHAPTER 6

DISCOURSE ANALYSIS

Discourse analysis emerges not as an option or as a luxury for the serious student of a language but as a necessity.

—ROBERT E. LONGACRE[1]

6.1 INTRODUCTION

The previous three chapters dealt primarily with semantics, or the inherent meaning a construction has outside of a particular context. In this chapter I move from semantics to pragmatics, or the meaning a construction has within a specific context. The idea here is that a construction can take on additional meaning when it occurs within a particular context. For example, the basic meaning (i.e., the semantics) of the statement *Today is Monday* is fairly clear. However, its connotation is highly dependent on the nature of the conversation. If you know I have a faculty meeting that Monday, *Today is Monday* probably expresses disappointment; the same statement probably communicates excitement if you know that Monday is the first day of a new semester.

Discourse analysis falls within the realm of pragmatics because it looks at language in use rather than language as an abstraction. Yet the term *discourse analysis* itself can mean different things depending on who uses it. For some scholars it is has a strong sociolinguistic bent in that it deals with how specific sociocultural groups of people communicate.[2] However, for many linguists discourse analysis refers more broadly to how people use and structure language in order to communicate.[3] The term *text linguistics* is sometimes used instead of

---

1. Longacre, *Discourse Grammar*, 1:2.
2. Cf. Paltridge, *Discourse Analysis*, 6–12.
3. Brown and Yule, *Discourse Analysis*, vii–ix.

discourse analysis when the form of communication is a written text, although not everyone makes such a hard and fast distinction between discourse analysis and text linguistics.[4]

Discourse analysis is a relatively new field within linguistics. Its modern roots are often traced back to Zellig S. Harris, a Semiticist turned linguist, who popularized the term in 1952.[5] Given the newness of discourse analysis, it is not surprising that Hebraists and Aramaicists have only recently begun to apply it to the Hebrew Bible. Nevertheless, the past few decades have seen some exciting developments in the application of discourse analysis to the Hebrew Bible. So, after presenting a modern linguistic framework for discourse analysis, in this chapter I explore those developments by surveying different approaches to, as well as resources for, discourse analysis of the Hebrew Bible. I leave discussion of the closely related topic of word order for the next chapter.

6.2 THE MODERN LINGUISTIC FRAMEWORK FOR DISCOURSE ANALYSIS

The modern linguistic framework for discourse analysis entails three foundational concepts: coherence and cohesion, discourse units and relations, and information structure. I discuss each of these three concepts as the background for my examination of works on discourse analysis and the Hebrew Bible.

6.2.1 Coherence and Cohesion
6.2.1.1 Coherence

The term *coherence* describes whether or not the different elements of a text fit into a single overall mental representation.[6] Everyone has knowledge of the world—a mental representation—that informs their knowledge of the text and even shapes their expectations of what the text means to say. Coherent texts can be fit into one's mental representation, whereas incoherent texts cannot. Consider the following two units of text:

Yesterday I saw a car driving down the street with a canoe strapped to its top. Noticing the car, a dog came out of his doghouse and started barking at it. The driver of the car did not pay any attention to the dog and simply drove on, passing one of my favorite restaurants that happens to serve pancakes.

---

4. Cf. Georgakopoulou and Goutsos, *Discourse Analysis*, 3–4.
5. Harris, "Discourse Analysis," 1–30.
6. Dooley and Levinsohn, *Analyzing Discourse*, 21–25; cf. De Beaugrande and Dressler, *Text Linguistics*, 84–112; Brown and Yule, *Discourse Analysis*, 223–71.

If you saw a canoe coming down the street with four flat tires, how many pancakes would it take to cover a doghouse? The same amount, because there are no bones in ice cream, and he doesn't like tomatoes anyhow.

Both of these textual units are correct grammatically. But only the first one is coherent because it fits within a single mental representation, whereas the second does not!

6.2.1.2 Cohesion

Whereas coherence deals with whether a text makes sense conceptually, *cohesion* is the use of linguistic means to give a text coherence.[7] This concept can be traced back to the work of the functionalists M. A. K. Halliday and Ruqaiya Hasan, who originally applied it to English.[8] Nevertheless, cohesion applies cross-linguistically because all languages have ways of signaling how part of a text links up conceptually with some other part. These links are called *cohesive ties*.[9] There are many different types of cohesive ties in written texts, including discourse markers, participant reference, lexical patterning, and morphosyntactic patterning.[10]

First, *discourse markers* signal relationships between textual units. Conjunctions and other similar linguistic markers serve this purpose. Typically, narrative and non-narrative texts use different types of discourse markers. On the one hand, in narrative discourse markers tend to focus on time or cause and effect (e.g., English *meanwhile, then,* and *afterward*). On the other hand, in non-narrative discourse markers tend to focus on logical sequence (e.g., English *but, so,* and *now*).[11] Examples of discourse markers from Biblical Hebrew include אַף ("also"), עַתָּה ("now"), כִּי ("because, for"), and עַל־כֵּן ("therefore"), as well as the deictic particle הִנֵּה. The conjunction *waw* also commonly serves to link clauses of a text together in Biblical Hebrew.[12]

Second, *participant reference* relates to how elements of a text are identified and re-identified. The same participant, whether a person or a thing, can be referred to in different ways. Typically, the most explicit reference to a

---

7. Dooley and Levinsohn, *Analyzing Discourse*, 27–34.

8. Halliday and Hasan, *Cohesion in English*; Halliday, *Halliday's Introduction to Functional Grammar*, 593–658.

9. Dooley and Levinsohn, *Analyzing Discourse*, 27.

10. Cf. Dooley and Levinsohn, *Analyzing Discourse*, 27–34; Georgakopoulou and Goutsos, *Discourse Analysis*, 90–128; De Beaugrande and Dressler, *Text Linguistics*, 48–83; Brown and Yule, *Discourse Analysis*, 191–204.

11. Georgakopoulou and Goutsos, *Discourse Analysis*, 95–98.

12. Di Giulio, "Discourse Marker: Biblical Hebrew," 1:757–58.

participant is found at the beginning of the text or at major textual boundaries, whereas less explicit references occur later in the text.[13] Thus, for example, the character *Frodo Baggins* is introduced by his full name early on in *The Lord of the Rings* but afterward is most often simply referenced as *Frodo* or *he*. In Biblical Hebrew, the personal (e.g., הוּא "he" and הִיא "she"), demonstrative (e.g., זֶה "this"), and relative (אֲשֶׁר "who, which") pronouns as well as various titles (e.g., הָאִשָּׁה "the woman" and הַמֶּלֶךְ "the king") are used to re-identify a text's participants.[14]

Third, *lexical patterning* denotes the use of similar lexical items to create cohesion. Lexical patterning can be accomplished through repetition of the exact same lexical item. However, synonyms (words with similar meanings) and hyponyms (words that represent a subset or subclass of another word) also establish cohesion. For example, in the sentences *I gave the flower to my wife* and *She liked the rose*, the hyponymous relationship between *flower* and *rose* (a specific type of flower) creates a lexical link between the two sentences. An example of lexical patterning in Biblical Hebrew can be found in Lev 11:13–19, which refers to birds in general (הָעוֹף) before listing specific types of birds (e.g., נֶשֶׁר "vulture") that are not to be eaten.

Fourth, *morphosyntactic patterning* refers to the use of similar syntactical constructions to create cohesion. Included here are verbs of the same tense or aspect, noun phrases with a similar syntactical structure, and repeated prepositional phrases. For example, the use of the two past tense verbs *hiked* and *reached* in the sentence *I hiked up the mountain and reached the top* creates cohesion because the reader naturally links the similar verbs together. A good, and very common, example of morphosyntactic patterning in Biblical Hebrew is the use of *wayyiqtol* to express past action in narrative. The repeated use of *wayyiqtol* in a narrative connects the different events for the reader.

6.2.2 Discourse Units and Relations

People eat meals bite by bite because it is easier (and healthier!) to swallow small chunks of our food than to eat the entire meal all at once. Similarly, people take in information in chunks, which can be processed more easily by the brain than all the information at one time. Accordingly, written texts consist of distinct units or "chunks" of thought.[15] The process of dividing a text into its distinct, meaningful units is known as *segmentation*.

The most basic chunk of thought is the *thematic grouping*. A thematic

---

13. Georgakopoulou and Goutsos, *Discourse Analysis*, 99.
14. Regt, "Disjoining in Discourse," 3:30–33.
15. Dooley and Levinsohn, *Analyzing Discourse*, 35–37.

grouping exhibits internal cohesion in that it deals with a single, unified theme: presentation of a single topic (for non-narrative) or a single set of characters in one location at a particular time (for narrative). Thus, a shift in theme indicates a new thematic grouping. A thematic grouping's boundaries are often also marked by linguistic signals, such as preposed expressions (e.g., *in conclusion*), special connectors (e.g., *then, now,* and *so*) or the absence of normal connectors, and summary statements (e.g., *this demonstrates that*).[16] Common boundary markers in Biblical Hebrew include asyndeton as well as וַיְהִי ("and it happened . . .") or וְהָיָה ("and it will happen").

A thematic grouping itself contains even smaller chunks of thought. The most basic unit at this level is the *idea unit*, which often corresponds to a clause.[17] A clause contains a subject and predicate and can be one of two types: main (i.e., grammatically independent, as in *I went for a run*) or subordinate (i.e., grammatically dependent, as in *before I went for a run*). Examples of subordinate clauses in Biblical Hebrew include temporal clauses introduced by an adverb (e.g., אַחַר "after") or infinitive construct, relative clauses introduced by אֲשֶׁר ("who, which"), and causal clauses introduced by כִּי ("because, for"). Semantically, a clause typically corresponds to a *proposition*, or a single unit of thought.[18]

Adjacent idea units, as well as adjacent paragraphs, can be linked to one another in a variety of ways. The interrelationship of textual units is expressed by *discourse relations*, a concept informed by both Semantic and Structural Analysis (developed by SIL's John Beekman) and Rhetorical Structure Theory (developed by William C. Mann and Sandra Thompson).[19] Discourse relations can describe any number of relationships between units, including sequentiality, contrast, elaboration, and result.[20] Linguistic signals help the reader to determine the syntactic relationship between units. This, in turn, enables the reader to deduce their semantic relationships and thereby trace the text's flow of thought.[21] Discourse relations has been applied to Scripture by biblical scholars and Bible translators in several different ways. Within the context of

---

16. Dooley and Levinsohn, *Analyzing Discourse*, 38–40; Georgakopoulou and Goutsos, *Discourse Analysis*, 66–68.

17. Georgakopoulou and Goutsos, *Discourse Analysis*, 66–68.

18. Dooley and Levinsohn, *Analyzing Discourse*, 87.

19. Beekman, Callow, and Koposec, *Semantic Structure of Written Communication*, 77–113; Mann and Thompson, "Relational Propositions in Discourse," 57–90; idem, "Rhetorical Structure Theory," 243–81.

20. Cf. Georgakopoulou and Goutsos, *Discourse Analysis*, 80–81.

21. Dooley and Levinsohn, *Analyzing Discourse*, 87–89; Beekman, Callow, and Koposec, *Semantic Structure of Written Communication*, 77–113; Georgakopoulou and Goutsos, *Discourse Analysis*, 80–84.

biblical exegesis, this specific application is often the focus of what is meant by "discourse analysis."[22]

Another important way in which a discourse's individual components relate together is through their location in the foreground or background of the text. Certain elements of a text stand out as prominent in the reader's mental representation whereas others do not. On the one hand, the *foreground* represents the parts of a text that establish the text's basic outline and create structural coherence. On the other hand, the *background* fills in the text's basic outline with details.[23] Consider the two sentences *Katy ran around singing* and *Katy is a seven-year-old girl with lots of energy*. When joined together in discourse, the first sentence represents the foreground because it moves our understanding forward whereas the second sentence represents the background because it provides information necessary to understand the foreground.

6.2.3 Information Structure

The final level of discourse analysis, at the sentence level, involves investigation of what is called *information structure*, a concept first popularized by M. A. K. Halliday and subsequently developed by Knud Lambrecht and Simon C. Dik.[24] Information structure relates to the way that information is "packaged" or arranged in a sentence, in light of what the reader already knows and what the author wants the reader to know.[25] As such, information structure entails several different concepts. These include topic and comment, focus, and other forms of discourse-pragmatic structuring.

The concepts of topic and comment have been understood in several different ways. However, generally speaking, *topic* is what a sentence talks about and *comment* is what the sentence says about the topic.[26] Normally, the topic of the sentence is the subject, and the comment is the predicate. For example, in the sentence *Moses went up the mountain*, *Moses* is the topic and *went up the*

---

22. E.g., Beekman and Callow, *Translating the Word of God*, 287–342; Nida and Taber, *Theory and Practice of Translation*, 39–55; cf. Cotterell and Turner, *Linguistics and Biblical Interpretation*, 188–229.

23. Dooley and Levinsohn, *Analyzing Discourse*, 79.

24. Halliday, "Notes on Transitivty and Theme: Part 2," 199–244; Lambrecht, *Information Structure and Sentence Form*; Dik, *Theory of Functional Grammar*.

25. Cf. Chafe, "Givenness, Contrastiveness, Definiteness, Subjects, Topics and Point of View," 27–55.

26. Dooley and Levinsohn, *Analyzing Discourse*, 63; cf. Erteschik-Shir, *Information Structure*, 7–27; Lambrecht, *Information Structure and Sentence Form*, 117–31. Sometimes the Prague School's terms *theme* and *rheme* are used in place of topic and comment, respectively (e.g., Firbas, "Theme in Functional Sentence Perspective," 267–80; Beneš, "Verbstellung im Deutschen," 6–19). Notably, Halliday's definition of theme differs slightly in that he sees theme as the first element in the sentence ("Notes on Transitivty and Theme: Part 2," 199–244).

mountain is the comment that tells us about the topic (i.e., Moses). In written languages, topic and comment can be marked either morphologically (e.g., through use of a particular grammatical form or an affix) or syntactically (e.g., through word order and placement in the sentence).[27]

There are also several different understandings of the concept of focus. However, in general, *focus* refers to information provided in order to produce a change in the reader's mental representation.[28] So, the focus of a sentence depends on what the reader already knows. Returning to the sentence *Moses went up the mountain*, the entire sentence would be the focus if the reader knows nothing about Moses or what he did. However, if the reader has already been introduced to Moses but knows nothing of what he did, then *went up the mountain* would be the focus. Material in focus typically adds new or contrastive information, although this need not always be the case.[29]

Many sentences contain additional elements that provide information. Adding an *adjunct*, or a word or phrase that is not necessary for the sentence to make sense, can accomplish this. But there are also other specific ways of packaging information in a sentence. A *frame of reference* and *left-dislocation* (i.e., *casus pendens*) both provide an information "anchor" for the reader prior to the main clause.[30] They do so by helping the reader understand what follows (e.g., as *when I got home* does in the sentence *When I got home, my daughter was waiting by the door*) or drawing attention to something that follows (e.g., as *those books* does in the sentence *Those books, they are my favorite*). An element that occurs after the main clause is called a *tail* or *extraposition* and is said to be *right-dislocated*.[31] Typically, this type of element provides clarification, as *my wife* does in the sentence *I gave the flowers to Jenn, my wife*.

6.3 Approaches to Discourse Analysis and the Hebrew Bible

With this linguistic framework for discourse analysis in mind, I now turn to applications of discourse analysis to the Hebrew Bible. Some scholars apply

---

27. Erteschik-Shir, *Information Structure*, 40–42. Intonation is frequently used to mark topic and comment in spoken languages, but the precise intonation of the text of the Hebrew Bible is now lost to us.

28. Dooley and Levinsohn, *Analyzing Discourse*, 62. Some scholars contend that focus refers to new information (e.g., Lambrecht, *Information Structure and Sentence Form*, 206–18). Others hold that focus refers only to the most important or salient information in a clause (e.g., Erteschik-Shir, *Information Structure*, 42–55; Dik, *Theory of Functional Grammar*, 1:326–28).

29. Dooley and Levinsohn, *Analyzing Discourse*, 62.

30. Dooley and Levinsohn, *Analyzing Discourse*, 68–70.

31. Dooley and Levinsohn, *Analyzing Discourse*, 70–71.

a sociocultural form of discourse analysis to the Hebrew Bible.[32] However, many studies applying discourse analysis to the Hebrew Bible do so in the more general, linguistic sense of the term. These studies examine the role that the concepts of coherence and cohesion, discourse units and relations, and information structure have in understanding the Hebrew Bible.

Scholars who apply discourse analysis to the Hebrew Bible like this do so by means of four basic approaches: the tagmemic approach, the distributional approach, the information structure approach, and the inter-clausal approach. I explore these different approaches now, paying particular attention to the unique contribution that each offers for discourse analysis of the Hebrew Bible.

6.3.1 Tagmemic Approaches

One popular approach to discourse analysis of the Hebrew Bible is the tagmemic approach. Tagmemics originated in American Structuralism and was especially popularized by the descriptivist Kenneth Lee Pike, the first president of the Summer Institute of Linguistics.[33] In essence, tagmemics looks for patterns in discourse that can be arranged hierarchically. Robert E. Longacre is the most well-known proponent of applying tagmemics to discourse analysis of the Hebrew Bible, but several other scholars also adopt this approach.

6.3.1.1 Robert E. Longacre

Robert E. Longacre wrote his doctoral dissertation under the supervision of Zellig S. Harris. Then, through his work with Pike as a Bible translator for the Summer Institute of Linguistics, Longacre was significantly influenced by tagmemics. In addition to several works on general discourse analysis,[34] Longacre eventually published several books on tagmemics' application to Biblical Hebrew. His first book-length work on this topic was *Joseph: A Story of Divine Providence*, but his later *Understanding Biblical Hebrew Verb Forms: Distribution and Function across Genres* is much more comprehensive.[35]

Longacre identifies several different types of discourse in Biblical Hebrew, including narrative (discourse that reports a past event), predictive (discourse that speaks of a future event), procedural (discourse that tells how to do something), expository (discourse that explains or describes a situation), and hortatory (discourse that tries to elicit a particular response). Each type of discourse has its own array of verbal forms with a unique hierarchical arrangement.

---

32. E.g., Matthews, *More than Meets the Ear*.
33. Pike, *Language in Relation to a Unified Theory*.
34. E.g., Longacre, *Grammar of Discourse*.
35. Cf. Longacre, "Discourse Perspective on the Hebrew Verb," 177–89.

The verbal form at the top of the hierarchy expresses action in the foreground, whereas those below it express increasingly backgrounded information. For example, according to Longacre the default verbal form for expressing main-line, sequential action in narrative discourse is *wayyiqtol*. Other constructions express background information, with nominal clauses at the bottom of the hierarchy and therefore the furthest in the background.

6.3.1.2 David Alan Dawson

David Alan Dawson expands Longacre's original focus on narrative in *Joseph: A Story of Divine Providence* to include both narrative and non-narrative discourse types.[36] He examines narrative discourse (Judg 2), hortatory discourse (Lev 6:1–7:37; 14:1–32), and parallel pericopes from Exodus that express both the instructions for building the tabernacle (Exod 25–31) and the account of its construction (Exod 35–40). Dawson also investigates direct and non-direct speech as embedded in the story of Jephthah (Judg 10:6–12:7) and the book of Ruth.

Like Longacre, Dawson argues that each text type utilizes a specific type of clause to express foregrounded action; clauses that do not belong to that type express backgrounded information. Dawson also contends, similar to Longacre, that *wayyiqtol* is the main clause type for narrative, *weqatal* is the main clause type for predictive discourse, volitive forms are the main clause type for hortatory discourse, and the verbless clause is the main clause type for expository discourse. Dawson further argues that there is no difference in terms of clause type between reported speech and non-reported speech.

6.3.1.3 Brian G. Toews

In his 1993 University of California, Los Angeles dissertation, Brian G. Toews applies Longacre's tagmemic analysis to Biblical Aramaic, focusing especially on the book of Daniel.[37] Accordingly, he adopts a top-down approach to discourse analysis and focuses especially on identifying the default verbal forms for the foreground and background. At the same time, Toews expands Longacre's model to include other concerns. Among other things, he seeks to move beyond word order and explain discourse patterns at the level of the noun phrase and the sentence.

Toews identifies אֱדַיִן/בֵּאדַיִן as the major discourse marker that introduces clause clusters. Clause type then serves to mark foregrounded and backgrounded action. In narrative, *qtl* marks perfective action and therefore

---

36. Dawson, *Text-Linguistics and Biblical Hebrew.*
37. Toews, "Aramaic in the Book of Daniel."

expresses the foreground, whereas *yqtl* and the participle are imperfective and therefore mark the background. The situation is different in prophetic discourse, however, in which *yqtl* forms the mainline whereas the participle forms the background. Toews also contends that the construct chain is used for routine, backgrounded noun phrases whereas יִדּ appears in foregrounded noun phrases; thus, the choice between these two constructions is not stylistic but determined by discourse factors.

6.3.1.4 Other Voices

Other scholars adopt a tagmemic approach to discourse analysis but apply it in more specific ways. Many of these scholars follow Longacre's basic approach. Bryan M. Rocine has written an introductory Biblical Hebrew grammar based largely on Longacre's approach to discourse analysis.[38] Both Roy L. Heller and Javier del Barco del Barco have applied Longacre's theory of discourse genre types to different portions of the Hebrew Bible. On the one hand, Heller analyzes the Joseph Cycle (Gen 37–50) and the Succession Narrative (2 Sam 9–1 Kgs 2), concluding with Longacre that *wayyiqtol* is the main sequential verb in biblical narrative.[39] On the other hand, del Barco del Barco applies Longacre's approach to the preexilic Minor Prophets and concludes that *weqatal* is the primary verbal form of the predicative discourse type that dominates prophetic material.[40]

Not all scholars adopting a tagmemic approach follow Longacre so closely, however. Kirk E. Lowery instead investigates the organizing structures of Biblical Hebrew narrative within a tagmemic framework that incorporates the case roles of participants.[41] Likewise, Mats Eskhult adopts a tagmemic approach without relying extensively on Longacre. He characterizes the verbal system in narrative as a binary opposition between stativity (expressed by *wayyiqtol*) and action (expressed by *qatal*), which respectively correspond to the foreground and background.[42]

6.3.1.5 Evaluation

The tagmemic approach to discourse analysis has several advantages. Its close attention to discourse types rightly recognizes that language use frequently varies depending on the genre. Longacre and his followers are also to be commended for examining how transitions and climaxes could potentially be

---

38. Rocine, *Learning Biblical Hebrew*.

39. Heller, *Narrative Structure and Discourse Constellations*.

40. del Barco del Barco, *Profecía y sintaxis*. This work originated as del Barco del Barco's PhD dissertation completed at Universidad Complutense in 2001.

41. Lowery, "Toward a Discourse Grammar of Biblical Hebrew"; idem, "Theoretical Foundations of Hebrew Discourse Grammar," 103–30.

42. Eskhult, *Studies in Verbal Aspect and Narrative Technique*.

marked by specific verbal forms. But, Longacre's focus on clause type inevitably leads to neglect of other important discourse features, such as discourse relations and information structure. Another significant problem with Longacre's approach is that the foreground does not always correspond with temporal succession, nor do departures from temporal succession always indicate the background.[43] Finally, and most problematically, the tagmemic approach assumes that pragmatics overrules semantics to the extent that a verbal form has no primary semantic meaning or function because a verb's meaning is determined by its use in discourse.

Nevertheless, Longacre's tagmemic approach provides some helpful perspectives on the macro-structure of discourse. His theory has a basis in the broader linguistic analysis of discourse, not merely in discourse analysis of the Hebrew Bible. It is especially with respect to cross-linguistic study of different text types that the tagmemic approach makes a significant contribution.

6.3.2 Distributional Approaches

The distributional approach to discourse analysis of the Hebrew Bible first emerged in the 1970s, around the same time that the tagmemic approach was popularized by Longacre. It is based in the premise that, because there are no native speakers of Biblical Hebrew and Biblical Aramaic today, the statistical distribution of a particular form determines its function and pragmatic effect. Thus, similar to Longacre, the distributional approach seeks to uncover linguistic patterns. However, unlike the tagmemic approach, the distributional approach moves from form to function rather than vice versa. Most scholars adopting this approach follow, to some degree, the work of Wolfgang Schneider.

6.3.2.1 Wolfgang Schneider

Wolfgang Schneider was the first scholar to substantially apply a bottom-up, distributional approach to discourse analysis of the Hebrew Bible.[44] His approach seeks to go beyond clause boundaries by interpreting the constitution and demarcation of the biblical text. To accomplish this goal, Schneider directly applies to Biblical Hebrew the text linguistic theory of the structuralist Harald Weinrich, who sees syntax as grammatical signals that arrange the world by situation of communication.[45]

Schneider classifies the Hebrew Bible's verbal forms into two categories:

---

43. Cook, "Semantics of Verbal Pragmatics," 247–73; cf. Robar, "Grounding: Biblical Hebrew," 2:152–53.

44. Schneider, *Grammatik des biblischen Hebräisch*.

45. Weinrich, *Tempus*.

narrative and speech. On the one hand, in narrative *wayyiqtol* marks the foreground and *qatal* marks the background. On the other hand, in speech *yiqtol* marks the foreground and *qatal* or *weqatal* marks the background. Thus, a biblical text can be categorized as narrative or speech depending on the verbal form it uses; shifts between *wayyiqtol* and *yiqtol* signal a shift in discourse type. According to Schneider, *wayyiqtol* and *yiqtol* fit this basic pattern even when they occur in other discourse types. Thus, *wayyiqtol* can represent a short narrative within direct speech, and *yiqtol* can express speech within narrative when the reader and writer share the same situation of communication.

6.3.2.2 Alviero Niccacci

Alviero Niccacci builds upon the work of Schneider and therefore also adopts a bottom-up, distributional approach to discourse analysis.[46] Like Schneider, Niccacci categorizes the Hebrew Bible's verbal forms into narrative or speech, but he further subdivides narrative into either historical narrative or oral narrative and speech into either direct speech or indirect speech. He recognizes that a given verbal form may not be limited to a single genre, but he contends that if a verbal form occurs in more than one genre it will have different functions in each genre.

Niccacci distinguishes between clauses that begin with a verb (verbal clauses) and those that do not (nominal clauses). According to him, nominal clauses sometimes mark new information (i.e., focus), but they can also indicate subordination or topicalization. Niccacci also allows for more flexibility than Schneider regarding the use of verbal forms and foregrounding. In Niccacci's perspective, *wayyiqtol* can simply continue the tense and aspect of a non-*wayyiqtol* form; furthermore, *qatal* can mark foregrounded action in speech when in clause-initial position within speech, and *weqatal* can represent foregrounded, anticipated action within speech.

6.3.2.3 Eep Talstra

Eep Talstra also builds on the work of Schneider.[47] He holds to a distributional approach and argues strongly for a movement from linguistic form to communicative function, rather than vice versa. What makes Talstra's approach particularly distinctive is his reliance on computational analysis to identify the syntactical functions of specific grammatical forms. His research with the

---

46. Niccacci, *Syntax of the Verb in Classical Hebrew Prose*; idem, "On the Hebrew Verbal System," 117–37. The original Italian edition of *Syntax of the Verb in Classical Hebrew Prose* was published as *Sintassi del verbo ebraico nella prosa biblica classica*.

47. Talstra, "Elements of a Theory," 168–74; idem, "Syntax and Semantics," 26–38; idem, "Clause Types and Clause Hierarchy," 180–93.

Werkgroep Informatica Vrije Universiteit (now the Eep Talstra Centre for Bible and Computer) and the creation of a syntactically tagged Hebrew text made this form of analysis possible.

Talstra's computer analysis reflects a bottom-up approach in that it starts with morphology and parts of speech, next constructs phrases from those individual words, then determines how those phrases make up clauses, and finally establishes the boundaries between major textual units. Talstra argues that it is crucial to distinguish between these different hierarchical levels when determining the meaning of a given form. Following Schneider, Talstra further argues that tense and aspect are not intrinsic to any particular form but derive from the writer's orientation.

6.3.2.4 Michael B. Shepherd

Whereas most scholars utilizing a distributional approach focus on Biblical Hebrew, Michael B. Shepherd instead applies it to Biblical Aramaic.[48] He contends that the opposition between *qtl* and *yqtl* in Biblical Aramaic cannot be explained in terms of tense, aspect, mood, or *Aktionsart*. To explain Biblical Aramaic's opposition between *qtl* and *yqtl*, he instead turns to a distributional approach based on the work of Schneider. The result is an approach very similar to Schneider's and Talstra's but applied to the Biblical Aramaic corpus.

Shepherd uses an electronic database of all the clauses in Biblical Aramaic, tagged according to category, to carry out his distributional analysis. Shepherd argues that *qtl* is the primary verbal form for narration whereas *yqtl* is the primary verbal form for discourse. He further contends that a nominal clause, with or without a participle, serves as a secondary form for both narrative and discourse. According to Shepherd, a similar distribution of *qtl* and *yqtl* is evident in Egyptian Aramaic as well as the Targums.

6.3.2.5 Other Voices

The distributional approach to discourse analysis appears in the work of several other scholars. Nicolai Winther-Nielsen integrates functionalist Role and Reference Grammar with Talstra's computational analysis to determine the relationship between clauses and narrative units within the entire book of Joshua.[49] A. F. den Exter Blokland, who completed his dissertation under Talstra's supervision, uses computational analysis to segment 1 Kings 1–2 into its different discourse units while tracking participant reference.[50] Finally,

---

48. Shepherd, *Verbal System of Biblical Aramaic*.
49. Winther-Nielsen, *Functional Discourse Grammar of Joshua*.
50. Exter Blokland, *In Search of Text Syntax*.

Lénart J. de Regt identifies a number of macro-structure paradigmatic features, including verbal sequence, in Deuteronomy 1–30.[51]

6.3.2.6 Evaluation

The distributional approach offers a helpful way of understanding discourse analysis. It uncovers some noteworthy patterns through statistical analysis of grammatical constructions. At the same time, the distributional approach can only find patterns in a given discourse type, not explain why certain forms are used instead of others. This is problematic because there is not always a clear correlation between discourse type and grammatical form. Furthermore, many of the above distributional approaches tend to focus on the distribution of verbal forms at the expense of other important discourse features, especially information analysis and discourse relations. Finally, as was the case with the tagmemic approach, distributionists assume that each verb's meaning is determined by pragmatics to the exclusion of semantics.

Despite these shortcomings, distributional analysis provides a useful way of uncovering linguistic patterns in the Hebrew Bible. It also offers an interesting application of computer analysis to the study of both Biblical Hebrew and Biblical Aramaic. Hopefully, future discourse studies adopting a distributional approach will incorporate attention to key components of discourse analysis in addition to the mere distribution of verbal forms.

6.3.3 Information Structure Approaches

Information structure approaches to discourse analysis of the Hebrew Bible are based in modern theories of information structure—in other words, how information is packaged in a sentence—especially as formulated by Lambrecht and Dik. These and other theories of information structure have largely grown out of Functionalism. Unlike the distributional and tagmemic approaches, an information structure approach tends to operate at the level of the sentence. Despite being relatively new, having emerged only since the 1990s after the publications of Lambrecht's and Dik's studies, information structure has occupied the attention of a number of works on discourse analysis and the Hebrew Bible.

6.3.3.1 Katsuomi Shimasaki

One application of information structure to discourse analysis of the Hebrew Bible is found in the work of Katsuomi Shimasaki.[52] Shimasaki's primary

---

51. Regt, *Parametric Model for Syntactic Studies.*
52. Shimasaki, *Focus Structure in Biblical Hebrew*; cf. idem, "Information Structure: Biblical Hebrew," 2:279–83.

interest is in focus, which he defines slightly differently than either Lambrecht or Dik do. He instead defines focus as the marking of information as informationally prominent. In this, focus can include both old and new information, depending on what the writer wishes to convey. Thus, for Shimasaki, focus may overlap with—but is not to be equated with—emphasis (i.e., intensification of prominent elements) or contrast (i.e., contextually implied opposition).

According to Shimasaki, Biblical Hebrew utilizes word order and pitch prominence to express focus. Any information in clause-initial position therefore represents focused information. Shimasaki furthermore defines three types of focus, each with different structures and functions. Both predicate focus and argument focus structures mark information as sequential: the former provides comment on a clause's subject, and the latter identifies by relating the clause's argument to the predicate. Clause focus structures, however, serve other (typically non-sequential) pragmatic functions at each level of discourse. They can introduce new referents or activate old ones, anchor information within a clause, or provide key pieces of information for understanding an entire textual unit.

6.3.3.2 Jean-Marc Heimerdinger

Jean-Marc Heimerdinger applies information structure to Biblical Hebrew narrative. His approach to discourse analysis finds as its basis Lambrecht's formulation of information structure.[53] Furthermore, Heimerdinger offers his approach to discourse analysis as an alternative to that of Longacre's grounding approach. He rejects Longacre's simple equation between *wayyiqtol* and foregrounding and argues that Longacre's criteria for determining the foreground and background of a text are circular. Rather, for Heimerdinger foregrounding is related to topic and focus.

According to Heimerdinger, foregrounding occurs when a biblical author chooses to make specific elements of the text salient for the purposes of communication. A biblical author clues his readers in to the topic of a text by repeatedly mentioning that entity or making it the subject of verbs. Provision of new information (i.e., focus) within the discourse also serves to foreground material. For Heimerdinger, an entity's activation within the text, as well as the type of focus structure utilized, determines whether an author uses verb-initial *wayyiqtol*, non-verb-initial *qatal*, or another construction.

6.3.3.3 Nicholas P. Lunn

Nicholas P. Lunn, who completed his PhD dissertation under Heimerdinger, investigates how information structure applies to Biblical Hebrew

---

53. Heimerdinger, *Topic, Focus, and Foreground.*

poetry.[54] Like Heimerdinger, Lunn adopts Lambrecht's theory of information structure, including Lambrecht's understandings of focus and topic. One of the major conclusions that emerges from Lunn's study is that Biblical Hebrew poetry exhibits the same varieties of pragmatic word order that are found in Biblical Hebrew narrative.

Lunn explains departures from Verb-Subject-Object word order in Biblical Hebrew poetry by means of two different mechanisms. Topic and focus account for many instances of variant word order, just as they do in narrative. However, according to Lunn, this cannot explain all the word order variation, especially because Biblical Hebrew poetry contains twice as many departures from standard word order than narrative. Lunn argues that "poetic defamiliarization" (i.e., use of stylistic or rhetorical devices) accounts for the remaining instances of word order variation. Poetic defamiliarization tends to occur in certain situations, such as the second of two synonymously parallel poetic lines or when the biblical poet wishes to set apart a unit as performing a higher-level function (i.e., aperture, closure, or climax).

6.3.3.4 Walter Gross

In a number of different publications, Walter Gross puts forth an information structure model for analyzing Biblical Hebrew discourse.[55] Gross's analysis centers on three main conceptual pairs: theme and rheme, topic and comment, and focus and background. Of these three pairs, focus and background occupies most of his attention. Gross relies largely on the work of Dik in that he distinguishes elements that come before the verb (*Vorfeld*) from elements that come after the verb (*Hauptfeld*). Thus, Gross's approach to discourse analysis depends directly on word order. For Gross, the default order in Biblical Hebrew is Verb-Subject-Object.

Although Gross does deal with constituents that come after the verb, most of his work is devoted to what comes before the verb. According to Gross, a constituent is fronted when placed prior to a clause's verb. Fronting indicates focus or serves any number of pragmatic functions, such as providing background information, commenting on the narrative, or marking a text boundary. Notably, Gross distinguishes fronting from left-dislocation, or *casus pendens*. Left-dislocation serves to focus on the preposed element, to add an additional focus to a sentence, or to denote a topic other than the sentence's subject.

54. Lunn, *Word-Order Variation in Biblical Poetry.*

55. Gross, *Satzteilfolge im Verbalsatz alttestamentlicher Prosa*; idem, *Doppelt besetztes Vorfeld*; idem, *Pendenskonstruktion im biblischen Hebräisch*; idem, "Compound Nominal Clause in Biblical Hebrew?" 19–49; idem, "Position des Subjekts im hebräischen Verbalsatz," 170–87; idem, "Vorfeld als strukturell eigenständiger Bereich," 1–24; idem, "Syntaktischen Struktur des Vorfelds," 203–14.

6.3.3.5 Robert D. Holmstedt

Whereas the preceding scholars all apply information structure to discourse analysis as functionalists, Robert D. Holmstedt does so from the perspective of Generative Grammar.[56] His concern lies primarily at the sentence level. As such, he examines the role that a sentence's different constituents have in the packaging of information. He finds two basic layers of information—theme and rheme in the first layer, and topic and focus in the second layer—packaged in a sentence.

Holmstedt takes theme as existing (i.e., old or already known) information and rheme as information that is added or reinvoked. He defines topic as information that either orients the reader or sets the scene, and he defines focus as information contrasted with possible alternatives. In doing so, Holmstedt draws from both Halliday's Systemic Functional Linguistics and the Prague School, even though these approaches are methodologically distinct. Holmstedt's model of information structure also gives significant attention to constituents outside the main clause. He thus discusses phenomena such as fronting, left-dislocation, extraposition, and right-dislocation.

6.3.3.6 Adina Moshavi

Another significant contribution to the application of information structure to Biblical Hebrew is that of Adina Moshavi.[57] She assumes the traditional classification of Biblical Hebrew as a Verb-Subject-Object language. However, unlike any of the studies mentioned above, she justifies her classification of Biblical Hebrew word order as Verb-Subject-Object in light of this order's statistical dominance over Subject-Verb-Object. Moshavi's typological classification of Biblical Hebrew as Verb-Subject-Object is important because her analysis focuses on non-verbal constituents placed prior to (i.e., preposed) the main verb.

Moshavi's primary contribution is her findings on focusing and topicalization. Focusing signals a relation between the clause and the context of the reader's attention state, in which the constituent is activated but not necessarily presupposed. Topicalization signals a relation between the clause and the linguistic context that accompanies it, similar to the way that discourse markers function. Moshavi notes that her conclusions primarily apply to narrative because speech contains a significantly higher proportion of preposed

---

56. Holmstedt, "Word Order and Information Structure," 111–39; idem, "Constituents at the Edge in Biblical Hebrew," 110–58.

57. Moshavi, *Word Order*.

clauses and because, according to her, the pragmatic function of many of them is unclear.

6.3.3.7 Ilya S. Yakubovich

Ilya S. Yakubovich offers one of the few applications of discourse analysis to the Aramaic portions of the Hebrew Bible, and the only substantial application utilizing information structure.[58] Focusing on the book of Daniel, Yakubovich argues that there is no syntactic pattern that can account for the diverse word order attested in the book. According to Yakubovich, pragmatic factors instead account for this variation.

Yakubovich turns to Lambrecht's theory of information structure to establish his framework for discourse analysis. Following Lambrecht, Yakubovich adopts the categories of predicate focus, sentence focus, and argument focus to explain the ordering of elements in the book of Daniel's clauses. Yakubovich also investigates topicalization in the book of Daniel, noting how left-dislocation can be used to mark a topic that needs to be reactivated in the mind of the reader.

6.3.3.8 Christo H. J. van der Merwe

An especially important voice regarding information structure and Biblical Hebrew is Christo H. J. van der Merwe.[59] He relies primarily upon the information structure model of Lambrecht, as opposed to Dik, and therefore approaches this issue from a cognitive-oriented perspective. Furthermore, Merwe argues that word order represents one of the primary ways that information is structured in Biblical Hebrew. He contends that the default order is Verb-Subject-Object for verbal clauses but Subject-Verb-Object for nominal and participial clauses.

Merwe defines focus as the element that turns a presupposed proposition into a piece of information and topic as the element that advances the reader's knowledge. Following Lambrecht, he identifies three types of focus—argument focus, predicate focus, and sentence focus—that can be expressed through fronting, or the placement of a constituent at the beginning of the sentence. Fronting can signal either argument focus or sentence focus in verbal clauses, indicating a new topic, but fronting only signals argument focus in nominal and participial clauses. According to Merwe, *casus pendens* constructions function differently in that they move non-active entities to a state of discourse activeness.

---

58. Yakubovich, "Information Structure and Word Order," 373–96.

59. Merwe, "Explaining Fronting in Biblical Hebrew," 173–86; idem, "Better Understanding of Biblical Hebrew Word Order," 277–300; cf. Merwe and Talstra, "Biblical Hebrew Word Order," 68–107.

6.3.3.9 Sebastiaan Jonathan Floor

Finally, Sebastiaan Jonathan Floor's doctoral thesis, supervised by Merwe, represents the most comprehensive application of information structure to Hebrew discourse analysis.[60] Like Heimerdinger, Floor largely follows Lambrecht in his definitions of topic and focus. However, unlike Heimerdinger, Floor more substantially integrates different types of topic (i.e., topics within the main clause and dislocated topics) and focus structures (i.e., predicate, sentence, and argument) into his discourse approach.

Another distinctive element of Floor's work is its linking of topic and focus with discourse theme. He puts forth a methodology for identifying the theme of a discourse in light of its elements. These elements include the topics and foci of a thematic grouping's individual sentences as well as other features that establish cohesion. According to Floor, attention to these details enables the reader to trace the various themes of a discourse, observe shifts in themes through topic promotion and topic shift, and establish boundaries in the discourse. By integrating topic and focus with discourse theme, Floor offers a holistic approach to discourse analysis that encompasses both the intra-clausal and inter-clausal levels.

6.3.3.10 Other Voices

Many other voices are present in the application of information structure to discourse analysis of the Hebrew Bible. A notable trend is incorporation of information structure into two Biblical Hebrew grammars, one introductory and the other advanced: John A. Cook and Robert D. Holmstedt's *Beginning Biblical Hebrew* and Christo H. J. van der Merwe, Jackie A. Naudé, and Jan H. Kroeze's *A Biblical Hebrew Reference Grammar*.[61] Naturally, *Beginning Biblical Hebrew* follows Holmstedt's generative approach to discourse analysis, and *A Biblical Hebrew Reference Grammar* follows Merwe's cognitive approach.

Other scholars discuss information structure in a more limited way or with reference to a more limited corpus. The vast majority investigate preverbal elements as they relate to topic and focus.[62] However, at least a few studies examine postverbal constituents in Biblical Hebrew.[63] In addition, building

---

60. Floor, "From Information Structure, Topic, and Focus"; cf. idem, "From Word Order to Theme in Biblical Hebrew Narrative," 197–236.

61. Cook and Holmstedt, *Beginning Biblical Hebrew*, 114–15, 127–28; *BHRG* §§46–48.

62. E.g., Muraoka, *Emphatic Words and Structures*; Payne, "Functional Sentence Perspective," 62–82; Naudé, "Syntactic Analysis of Dislocations," 115–30; Revell, "Conditioning of Word Order in Verbless Clauses," 1–24; idem, "Thematic Continuity and the Conditioning of Word Order," 297–319; Bailey and Levinsohn, "Function of Preverbal Elements," 179–207; Longacre, "Analysis of Preverbal Nouns," 208–24; Bandstra, "Word Order and Emphasis in Biblical Hebrew Narrative," 109–23.

63. E.g., Lode, "Postverbal Word Order in Biblical Hebrew," 113–64; idem, "Postverbal Word Order in Biblical Hebrew, Part Two," 24–38.

on the work of Heimerdinger, several scholars have examined the role that information structure has in foregrounding and backgrounding for both narrative and poetry.[64] Rather than linking foregrounding to a hierarchy of clause types as Longacre does, these scholars see foregrounding as a function of evaluative devices (e.g., *yiqtol* and the participle as historical presents) or word order variation.

6.3.3.11 Evaluation

Information structure approaches are of great value for interpretation. This is because they investigate what each clause is about and how the biblical authors have arranged their words to make it say what they want it to say. This strength is also a weakness in that information structure approaches are largely limited to the level of the clause; this is especially true of generative approaches to information structure like Holmstedt's. Also problematic is the fact that nearly all the scholars discussed above presume a default word order for Biblical Hebrew without justification. This is an issue because, as discussed in the next chapter, there is no clear consensus on Biblical Hebrew's default word order.

Yet, information structure offers a fruitful methodological approach to discourse analysis of the Hebrew Bible. The work of Floor, who ably links information structure at the sentence level to the broader discourse, presents a particularly profitable model. Hopefully, future scholarship taking an information structure approach will build on the work of Floor while engaging with the important question of Biblical Hebrew's default word order.

6.3.4 Inter-Clausal Approaches

The tagmemic and distributional approaches tend to operate at the macro-structure level of discourse, whereas information structure approaches tend to focus on the sentence level. The inter-clausal approach to discourse analysis serves as a hybrid of sorts in that it connects the macro-structure of the text with the level of the sentence. This approach first emerged in the 1970s with the work of Francis I. Andersen, who focused especially on the relationships between clauses. Then, during the 1990s, renewed interest in the Biblical Hebrew verbal system shifted this approach's focus to issues of sequentiality, as is evident from the work of Douglas M. Gropp, Randall Buth, and Peter J. Gentry. Most recently, scholars such as Elizabeth Robar and Jason S. DeRouchie have demonstrated an interest in both sequentiality and discourse relations.

---

64. E.g., Cotrozzi, *Expect the Unexpected*; Rosenbaum, *Word-Order Variation in Isaiah 40–55*.

6.3.4.1 Francis I. Andersen

Francis I. Andersen offers an inter-clausal approach to discourse analysis largely focused on discourse relations and the logical relationship between clauses.[65] He arranges discourse into different hierarchical levels, including the clause, sentence, and paragraph. In this, his primary interest is the interrelationship between clauses within a discourse. Andersen is especially concerned with the relationship between independent (i.e., clauses that are not subordinate) clauses within a sentence, which he defines as a construction of at least two main clauses.

Andersen proposes a number of different possible relationships between clauses. According to him, these relationships—which include apposition, conjunction, circumstance, disjunction, and contrast, among others—may or may not be explicitly marked grammatically. Context determines the nature of the discourse relation when there are no explicit grammatical clues. Furthermore, he contends that the surface-level relationships between clauses in Biblical Hebrew reveal the deep structures of the language itself.

6.3.4.2 Douglas M. Gropp

About fifteen years later Douglas M. Gropp shifted the focus of the inter-clausal approach away from logical discourse relations, the main subject of Andersen's work, to the use of particular verbal forms to express sequentiality.[66] Gropp argues for a tense-aspect opposition between *qatal* and *yiqtol*, and *wayyiqtol* and *weqatal*. The distinction between each pair is one of relative tense, with *qatal* and *wayyiqtol* expressing action anterior to the moment of speaking and *yiqtol* and *weqatal* communicating action afterward.

Furthermore, and most importantly for understanding his contribution to inter-clausal discourse analysis, Gropp argues that the primary distinction between the forms in each pair—between *qatal* and *wayyiqtol*, and between *yiqtol* and *weqatal*—is sequentiality. He follows Longacre in understanding sequentiality as contingent temporal succession. Thus, for Gropp, both *wayyiqtol* and *weqatal* move biblical narrative forward by describing successive events, whereas *qatal* and *yiqtol* do not. He also distinguishes between sequentiality and non-sequentiality in non-indicative verbal forms. Simple *yiqtol* along with the plain imperative, jussive, and cohortative are non-sequential, whereas *weqatal* or the imperative, jussive, and cohortative with *waw* are sequential.

---

65. Andersen, *Sentence in Biblical Hebrew.*
66. Gropp, "Function of the Finite Verb," 45–62.

6.3.4.3 Randall Buth

Randall Buth presents an approach to inter-clausal discourse analysis that focuses primarily on thematic continuity between clauses, resulting in an approach very similar to Gropp's.[67] According to Buth, the verbal system in both Biblical Hebrew and Biblical Aramaic operates as a binary system that expresses either continuity or discontinuity. Past, perfective action is expressed either by *wayyiqtol* (continuity) or *x + qatal* (discontinuity) whereas non-past, imperfective action is expressed either by *weqatal* (continuity) or *x + yiqtol* (discontinuity).

To avoid the problems that result from equating specific verbal forms with foregrounding, Buth sees foregrounding and backgrounding as pragmatic (rather than semantic) functions. Thus, according to Buth, sequentiality often indicates foregrounding, but there is not a one to one correspondence between the two. His approach is also unique in that it incorporates inter-clausal analysis with information structure, especially as informed by Functional Grammar. Buth contends that, although discontinuity can sometimes mark a clause's topic, it need not always do so. Rather, discontinuity can also mark new thematic units and dramatic peaks in narrative.

6.3.4.4 Peter J. Gentry

Similar to Gropp and Buth, Peter J. Gentry puts forth a theory of the Biblical Hebrew verbal system that incorporates tense, aspect, and mood with discourse considerations.[68] Gentry argues for a basic opposition between perfective and imperfective action, with tense flowing out of this basic opposition as well as discourse considerations. Thus, the perfectives *qatal* and *wayyiqtol* normally express the past tense and the imperfectives *yiqtol* and *weqatal* typically express non-past action.

Gentry's understanding of the Hebrew verbal system incorporates discourse considerations with respect to both word order and sequentiality. Following his teacher E. J. Revell as well as the work of Niccacci, Gentry argues that mood is primarily marked by word order. For Gentry, Biblical Hebrew places a verb in initial position to mark it as modal because morphology does not mark modality, with the exception of the imperative. Furthermore, Gentry largely follows Buth's model of continuity and discontinuity. For Gentry, *qatal* and *yiqtol* express discontinuity (i.e., non-sequentiality) whereas *wayyiqtol* and *weqatal* communicate continuity (i.e., sequentiality).

---

67. Buth, "Functional Grammar, Hebrew and Aramaic," 77–102; idem, "Word Order in the Verbless Clause," 89–108.

68. Gentry, "System of the Finite Verb," 7–41.

6.3.4.5 Galia Hatav

Another proponent of sequentiality is Galia Hatav.[69] She argues that Biblical Hebrew is a tenseless language in that its verbs do not encode any distinction between past, present, and future. This leaves sequentiality as the central factor in determining the choice of verb forms in Biblical Hebrew. However, she does not follow the traditional definition of sequentiality as an event following the event reported in the preceding clause. Rather, following Hans Kamp and Uwe Reyle,[70] she defines sequentiality as time movement, where a sequential verb moves the reference time forward.

Despite this different definition of sequentiality, similar to many others Hatav takes *wayyiqtol* and *weqatal* as the two verbal forms in Biblical Hebrew that express sequentiality. According to Hatav, the primary difference between *wayyiqtol* and *weqatal* is modality in that *wayyiqtol* is non-modal and *weqatal* is modal. This leaves *qatal*, *yiqtol*, and the participle as non-sequential. The function of these verbal forms within discourse is to express perfective aspect (*qatal*), modality (*yiqtol*), or progressive aspect (the participle).

6.3.4.6 Elizabeth Robar

Elizabeth Robar also examines thematic continuity between clauses, especially with respect to larger units of discourse.[71] However, unlike all the previous scholars mentioned, Robar explicitly grounds her analysis in Cognitive Linguistics. She takes as her starting point the observation that discourse is presented in manageable chunks, the most basic chunk being the paragraph. Doing so allows Robar to examine how Biblical Hebrew organizes discourse information via the schema, or the structuring of a paragraph.

According to Robar, Biblical Hebrew narrative structures its paragraphs primarily in terms of continuity and discontinuity. She identifies three key verbal forms that she contends mark continuity: *wayyiqtol* (continuity for simple past action), *weqatal* (continuity for habitual past action), and *weyiqtol* (continuity for present action and volitives). She also points to two different ways that Biblical Hebrew narrative creates discontinuity: first, atypical usage of a standard verbal form (e.g., using *weqatal* in narrative sequence), and second, using non-standard verbal forms (e.g., verbs with paragogic *nun* or *he* and long *wayyiqtol* forms) in the discourse.

---

69. Hatav, *Semantics of Aspect and Modality*; idem, "Anchoring World and Time," 491–526.
70. Kamp and Reyle, *From Discourse to Logic*.
71. Robar, *Verb and the Paragraph in Biblical Hebrew*.

6.3.4.7 Jason S. DeRouchie

The work of Jason S. DeRouchie, particularly his *How to Understand and Apply the Old Testament*, reflects a return to Andersen's focus on discourse relations.[72] According to DeRouchie, the most basic building block of discourse is the clause. He distinguishes between two types of clauses, each of which provides structure for the discourse in its own way. Syndetic clauses, or clauses joined to one another with *waw*, go together because they operate on the same hierarchical level; asyndetic clauses, or clauses without *waw*, often begin a new textual unit. Thus, new units are marked for the reader by asyndeton. Changes in discourse genre, morphosyntactic patterning, participant reference, and the presence of markers like וַיְהִי or וְהָיָה also help to establish boundaries between literary units.

For DeRouchie, determining a discourse's structure like this is the necessary prerequisite to understanding the text's flow of thought. He provides a list of possible discourse relations that can be used to describe the relationship between clauses for both coordinate (e.g., series and both-and) and subordinate (e.g., action-manner, ground, and situation-response) clauses. In this, DeRouchie largely adopts the discourse relations popularized by Daniel P. Fuller of Fuller Theological Seminary[73] and those of the website BibleArc.[74] Determining the discourse relations between clauses enables the reader to create a logical outline of the discourse and thereby discover the main idea and purpose of each major thematic unit.

6.3.4.8 Other Voices

A few other scholars seek to bridge the gap between traditional grammar and discourse analysis through an inter-clausal approach. On the one hand, similar to Buth, Yoshinobu Endo finds three basic oppositions that describe the interrelationship between clauses: *wayyiqtol* (sequential) versus *qatal* (non-sequential) in past contexts, *weqatal* (sequential) versus *yiqtol* (non-sequential) in non-past contexts, and *weqatal* (sequential) versus imperative, jussive, or cohortative (non-sequential) in volitive contexts.[75] On the other hand, similar to DeRouchie, Stephen G. Dempster uses syndeton and asyndeton, participant reference, and lexical patterning to determine the interrelationship between clauses in the Joseph Cycle (Gen 37–50), the Succession Narrative (2 Sam 9–1 Kgs 2), and the Synchronistic History (1 Kgs 12–2 Kgs 18:12).[76]

---

72. DeRouchie, *How to Understand and Apply the Old Testament*, 98–127, 181–268. DeRouchie applies his approach in a more limited way to part of Deuteronomy in his *Call to Covenant Love*.

73. Cf. Fuller, "Hermeneutics: A Syllabus for NT 500."

74. http://biblearc.com.

75. Endo, *Verbal System of Classical Hebrew*.

76. Dempster, "Linguistic Features of Hebrew Narrative."

6.3.4.9 Evaluation

The inter-clausal approach to discourse analysis is very profitable because it facilitates the tracing of the biblical text's flow of thought, one of the primary goals of exegesis. It accomplishes this goal by giving significant attention to the cohesion and coherence of a discourse, as well as the relations between discourse units. However, one significant weakness is that the analysis of a text's inter-clausal relationships can be somewhat subjective. This is because few clear criteria exist for evaluating the accuracy of a discourse unit's proposed flow of thought. Another major weakness of the inter-clausal approach is that it tends to neglect information structure. Its analysis takes place primarily at the macro-level at the expense of the intra-clausal level. Finally, there is significant need to integrate inter-clausal analysis with a coherent (and plausible) model of the Biblical Hebrew verbal system. Buth's approach provides an especially good step in the right direction, but more work is needed here to ensure that pragmatics is better connected to the semantics of the verbal system.

Despite any weaknesses, the inter-clausal approach remains quite promising for exegesis. Scholars of the Hebrew Bible have yet to apply this approach to the extent that New Testament scholars have applied it. So, we look forward to continued refinement and application of this approach to discourse analysis of the Hebrew Bible. Such developments are sure to enhance both our exegesis and exposition of the Old Testament.

6.4 Hebrew Bible Discourse Grammars and Commentaries

Having surveyed Hebraists' and Aramaicists' various approaches to discourse analysis, I turn now to helpful resources on discourse analysis and the Hebrew Bible. Included here is the discourse grammar *Basics of Hebrew Discourse*, which aims to present the building blocks of discourse and how discourse works in Biblical Hebrew. Also included are several works that apply the principles of discourse analysis to the Hebrew Bible: the *Lexham Discourse Hebrew Bible*, the Zondervan Exegetical Commentary on the Old Testament, and the Baylor Handbook on the Hebrew Text series.

6.4.1 Basics of Hebrew Discourse

A very helpful resource for learning to do discourse analysis of the Hebrew Bible is Zondervan's *Basics of Hebrew Discourse: A Guide to Working with Hebrew Prose and Poetry*, by Matthew H. Patton and Frederic Clarke Putnam. This book consists of two main sections, one dealing with narrative (authored by Patton) and one dealing with poetry (authored by Putnam). Miles V. Van Pelt serves as the book's editor.

Patton's section on narrative examines both narrative proper as well as direct speech embedded in narrative. The introductory chapter presents the need for discourse analysis and surveys key scholarship on this topic. Then, he examines the different types of relationships that can exist between clauses in narrative (e.g., sequential action, simultaneous action, result, and circumstances) and direct speech (e.g., reason, answer, and comparison). The next several chapters present key elements necessary for discourse analysis of Biblical Hebrew narrative. Included here are discourse markers (i.e., conjunctions, relatives, interrogatives, adverbs, interjections, and special markers like לֵאמֹר or הִנֵּה), verbal sequences that communicate discourse relationships (e.g., *wayyiqtol* and *weqatal*), preposing (i.e., placing of any non-verbal element prior to the verb), and verbless clauses. The final chapters of this section present a process for conducting discourse analysis on narrative as well as examples of that process carried out on several different passages.

Putnam's section on poetry begins by highlighting the need for a distinct approach to discourse analysis of biblical poetry in light of poetry's unique features. Putnam discusses the role that line length plays in determining a poem's structure. Then, he explores how verbal forms (both conjugation and stem) and clause type (e.g., verbal and nominal) can structure a poem through morphosyntactic patterning. He also discusses word order in poetry, which he argues most often relates a line to its immediately adjacent lines. The final chapters of this section explore cohesion of biblical poetry in terms of both semantics (e.g., ellipsis and participant reference) and logic (e.g., relationships between lines).

Basics of Hebrew Discourse is designed for intermediate students of Biblical Hebrew, but scholars and even pastors will benefit much from this work too. It fills a significant gap in scholarship in that it presents a broad, multifaceted approach by synthesizing many of the strengths of the various approaches to discourse analysis of the Hebrew Bible. In addition, especially helpful is the fact that narrative and poetry are discussed separately. Treating these two genres separately enables the reader to grasp the unique discourse features of both narrative and poetry, and to conduct discourse analysis in a way appropriate to each.

One weakness of *Basics of Hebrew Discourse* is its primary focus on discourse analysis at the inter-clausal level. It does deal with issues of word order within clauses, especially with respect to preposing and the use of word order to structure a text. However, its analysis of these topics assumes a default word order (Verb-Subject-Object) for Biblical Hebrew prose without much justification. Furthermore, on the whole *Basics of Hebrew Discourse* neglects important issues related to information structure, including topic, focus, and constituents located outside the main clause of a sentence.

Nevertheless, there is no question that *Basics of Hebrew Discourse* represents a noteworthy advancement in applying discourse analysis to the Hebrew Bible. Patton and Putnam offer helpful guidance on how to conduct discourse analysis on the Hebrew Bible that is relatively well informed by broader linguistic scholarship on discourse analysis. As a handbook, *Basics of Hebrew Discourse* also presents a helpful synthesis of scholarship on discourse analysis and the Hebrew Bible. The result is a practical, useful tool for understanding discourse analysis that provides a solid foundation for exegesis of the Hebrew Bible.

6.4.2 The Lexham Discourse Hebrew Bible

The *Lexham Discourse Hebrew Bible*, edited by Steven E. Runge and Joshua R. Westbury, is part of a suite of discourse analysis resources developed by Logos Bible Software.[77] Similar to Logos Bible Software's *Lexham Discourse Greek New Testament* (edited by Runge), this resource comprehensively presents the discourse features of the entire Hebrew Bible. As such, it represents a valuable resource for those wanting to see how a particular passage could be analyzed in terms of discourse analysis.

In the introduction, Runge and Westbury outline the key presuppositions that shape their approach to discourse analysis. Fundamental to the *Lexham Discourse Hebrew Bible* is the functionalist notion that choice implies meaning. A biblical author's use of a specific form communicates the specific meaning that he intends it to have, and that particular meaning is different than the meaning that another form would express. The choice to use a particular form over another is especially relevant, according to Runge and Westbury, when that form is considered within its specific context. Every form has its own inherent meaning, but a form's pragmatic effect will vary depending on the context. Runge and Westbury's approach, therefore, makes a clear distinction between semantics and pragmatics.

The introduction to the *Lexham Discourse Hebrew Bible* also provides detailed definitions and examples of all the specific discourse features that Runge and Westbury identify in the Hebrew Bible. These features are divided into several different categories. Forward-pointing devices (e.g., explicit metacomments and

---

77. This resource is available in a modified form in English as the *Lexham High Definition Old Testament*, also edited by Runge and Westbury.

attention getters like הִנֵּה) draw attention to what follows. Thematic highlighting (e.g., right-dislocation and changes in participant reference) provides additional information that prompts the reader to think about something in a specific way. Emphasis places part of a clause in a special position (e.g., fronted position) in order to attract extra attention to it. Frames of reference (e.g., temporal clauses and left-dislocation) anchor what follows into the context. Additional discourse features discussed include reported speech, verbless clauses, and outline annotations (e.g., principle, support, subpoint, and elaboration).

The *Lexham Discourse Hebrew Bible* proper, a dataset for the Masoretic Text in Logos, presents Runge and Westbury's discourse analysis of the entire Hebrew Bible. They divide the Hebrew Bible into distinct textual units. They also label these units according to their discourse function and arrange them hierarchically, with subordinate units indented. The result is an outline of sorts that enables the reader to follow the biblical authors' flow of thought. Furthermore, each specific discourse feature is marked with a custom-made symbol and linked via hypertext to a definition of the specific feature it represents. Each definition is taken from the work's glossary, which is in turn based on the definitions discussed in the introduction.

Here is the *Lexham Discourse Hebrew Bible*'s analysis of Ruth 1:1–5. A key, created from the definitions found in the work's glossary, appears directly following the excerpt.

[TM] וַיְהִי בִּימֵי שְׁפֹט הַשֹּׁפְטִים [TM] וַיְהִי רָעָב בָּאָרֶץ 1	SENTENCE
וַיֵּלֶךְ אִישׁ מִבֵּית לֶחֶם יְהוּדָה לָגוּר בִּשְׂדֵי מוֹאָב	SENTENCE
‹▲ הוּא וְאִשְׁתּוֹ וּשְׁנֵי בָנָיו ▲›:	
[T] וְשֵׁם הָאִישׁ [T] אֱלִימֶלֶךְ 2	SENTENCE
וְשֵׁם אִשְׁתּוֹ [T] נָעֳמִי	SENTENCE
וְשֵׁם שְׁנֵי־בָנָיו	[T] מַחְלוֹן וְכִלְיוֹן	SENTENCE
אֶפְרָתִים מִבֵּית לֶחֶם יְהוּדָה	ELABORATION
וַיָּבֹאוּ שְׂדֵי־מוֹאָב	SENTENCE
וַיִּהְיוּ־שָׁם:	SENTENCE
וַיָּמָת אֱלִימֶלֶךְ ‹▲ אִישׁ נָעֳמִי ▲› 3	SENTENCE
וַתִּשָּׁאֵר הִיא וּשְׁנֵי ‹▲△ בָנֶיהָ ▲△›:	SENTENCE
וַיִּשְׂאוּ לָהֶם נָשִׁים מֹאֲבִיּוֹת 4	SENTENCE
שֵׁם הָאַחַת [T] עָרְפָּה	SENTENCE
וְשֵׁם הַשֵּׁנִית [T] רוּת	SENTENCE
וַיֵּשְׁבוּ שָׁם כְּעֶשֶׂר שָׁנִים:	SENTENCE
וַיָּמוּתוּ ‹+גַם־▲ שְׁנֵיהֶם ▲› מַחְלוֹן וְכִלְיוֹן +‹ 5	SENTENCE
וַתִּשָּׁאֵר ‹▲△ הָאִשָּׁה ▲△› ‹▲ מִשְּׁנֵי יְלָדֶיהָ וּמֵאִישָׁהּ ▲›:	SENTENCE

KEY

SENTENCE: One or more clauses that have a coordinate relationship to the preceding discourse. Sentences that begin a speech reported within the discourse are labeled as "sentences" but are indented one level in the outline to reflect that they are technically dependent on (i.e., subordinate to) the verb of speaking that introduces them. Sentences are most often coordinated to the preceding discourse using וֹ or the absence of a conjunction.

ELABORATION: A clause or a phrase usually consisting of a participle or an infinitive that expands on the action of the main verb on which it depends. Elaboration is also used to mark utterances that are grammatically incomplete due to an omission of some phrase which is to be inferred from the previous clause (i.e., elision). Elaboration always follows the clause it modifies.

[TM **TEMPORAL FRAMES** TM]: Fronting of time-related information to establish a specific time frame for the clause that follows. Temporal frames accomplish two functions:

- to establish a new point in time for the clause or discourse that follows and
- to draw extra attention to changes in time within the discourse, effectively sharpening comparisons or contrasts.

‹▲ **RIGHT-DISLOCATION** ▲›: Information that is added at the end of a clause to further describe something previously mentioned in the clause. While the information is separated, it agrees in case and number with the previous mention.

[T **TOPIC** T]: A label to identify the topic or subject of a clause where no finite verb form is present.

‹▲ **OVERSPECIFICATION** ▲›: A description of individuals or ideas that is more specific than required to identify the intended referent. This extra information is often thematically loaded—connected to the theme of the context in some way. The overspecification prompts the reader to conceptualize the referent in a specific way.

‹♟ **CHANGED REFERENCE** ♟›: The use of a different expression to refer to an established participant to recharacterize the participant or highlight some thematically important information, or to explicitly indicate the current center of attention by switching from a proper name to a more generic reference that connects one participant to another (e.g., "his mother" instead of "Hannah" in 1 Sam 2:19).

‹+ **THEMATIC ADDITION** +›: Various means of creating a connection between two things, essentially adding a parallel element. The most common means for accomplishing this is the use of גַּם (i.e., also, even). Compare BHRG §41.4.5.

The *Lexham Discourse Hebrew Bible*'s main advantage is its comprehensive scope. It applies Runge and Westbury's discourse methodology to the entire Hebrew Bible, not simply portions of it, and works with all the Hebrew Bible's different genres. To develop their approach as laid out in the introduction, Runge and Westbury had to work through—and therefore ultimately account for—the whole Old Testament. Thus, Runge and Westbury's approach is not mere theory. Rather, their methodology has a practical application and can be applied to the entirety of the Hebrew Bible.

The *Lexham Discourse Hebrew Bible*'s primary weakness is its near-exclusive focus on discourse at the level of the clause. The outline annotations do give attention to the larger flow of discourse. Moreover, its identification of discourse features such as forward-pointing devices and frames of reference implicitly acknowledges that clauses have a relationship with those immediately surrounding them. Nevertheless, for the most part the *Lexham Discourse Hebrew Bible* does not deal much with discourse relations, discourse and boundary markers, and elements that provide textual cohesion.

Despite this drawback, the *Lexham Discourse Hebrew Bible* remains an extremely helpful resource for discourse analysis of the Old Testament. It offers an accessible application of discourse analysis to the entire Hebrew Bible and is well informed by general linguistic scholarship on discourse analysis. When read in light of the methodological approach Runge and Westbury lay out in the introduction, the result is a robust application of discourse analysis to the Hebrew Bible. As such, the *Lexham Discourse Hebrew Bible* deserves to be a standard reference work on this topic for years to come.

6.4.3 The Zondervan Exegetical Commentary on the Old Testament (ZECOT)

A significant commentary series for analyzing discourse is the Zondervan Exegetical Commentary on the Old Testament (ZECOT) series.[78] ZECOT takes a bottom-up approach to discourse analysis and determination of a passage's structure and message. As such, it emphasizes formal signals in the text—like discourse markers and conjunctions—that help the reader follow the text's flow of thought. ZECOT also devotes significant attention to the text's literary context and form.

ZECOT does not adopt a single approach to discourse analysis. So, each commentary author is free to employ his or her own method of discourse analysis.

---

78. https://www.zondervancommentaries.com/zecot/. I am grateful to Daniel I. Block and Jason S. DeRouchie for discussing the ZECOT series with me (email message to author, January 19, 2018).

Ruth 1:1 – 5

A. Setting the Stage for Naomi's Emptying

1a — Now it happened, — וַיְהִ֗י

1b — in the days when the chieftains governed, — בִּימֵי֙ שְׁפֹ֣ט הַשֹּׁפְטִ֔ים
    1. The Time of the Crisis

1c — that famine stalked the land. — וַיְהִ֥י רָעָ֖ב בָּאָ֑רֶץ
    2. The Precipitant of the Crisis

1d — Then a certain man from Bethlehem of Judah moved — וַיֵּ֜לֶךְ אִ֣ישׁ מִבֵּ֧ית לֶ֣חֶם יְהוּדָ֗ה
    3. The Target of the Crisis

1e — to reside temporarily in the territory of Moab — לָגוּר֙ בִּשְׂדֵ֣י מוֹאָ֔ב
      a. His Home

1f — he and his wife and his two sons. — ה֥וּא וְאִשְׁתּ֖וֹ וּשְׁנֵ֥י בָנָֽיו׃
      b. His Move

2a — Now the name of the man was Elimelech, — וְשֵׁ֣ם הָאִ֣ישׁ אֱ‍ֽלִימֶ֡לֶךְ
      c. His Family

2b — and the name of his wife was Naomi, — וְשֵׁם֩ אִשְׁתּ֨וֹ נָעֳמִ֜י

2c — and the names of his two sons Mahlon and Chilion. — וְשֵׁ֥ם שְׁנֵֽי־בָנָ֣יו ׀ מַחְל֤וֹן וְכִלְיוֹן֙
      d. His Clan

2d — [They were] Ephrathites from Bethlehem of Judah. — אֶפְרָתִ֔ים מִבֵּ֥ית לֶ֖חֶם יְהוּדָ֑ה

2e — And they entered the territory of Moab, — וַיָּבֹ֥אוּ שְׂדֵי־מוֹאָ֖ב
    4. The Location of the Crisis

2f — and they lived there. — וַיִּ‍ֽהְיוּ־שָֽׁם׃

B. The Nature of Naomi's Emptying

    1. Phase 1 of the Crisis

3a — But Elimelech, the husband of Naomi, died, — וַיָּ֥מָת אֱלִימֶ֖לֶךְ אִ֣ישׁ נָעֳמִ֑י
      a. The Event

3b — and she was left, along with her two sons. — וַתִּשָּׁאֵ֥ר הִ֖יא וּשְׁנֵ֥י בָנֶֽיהָ׃
      b. The Effect

4a — And they both married Moabite women. — וַיִּשְׂא֣וּ לָהֶ֗ם נָשִׁים֙ מֹֽאֲבִיּ֔וֹת
    2. The Ray of Hope in the Midst of Crisis

4b — The name of the first was Orpah, — שֵׁ֤ם הָֽאַחַת֙ עָרְפָּ֔ה
      a. The Sons' Marriages

4c — and the name of the second was Ruth. — וְשֵׁ֥ם הַשֵּׁנִ֖ית ר֑וּת

4d — And they lived there about ten years. — וַיֵּ֥שְׁבוּ שָׁ֖ם כְּעֶ֥שֶׂר שָׁנִֽים׃
      b. The Sons' Tenure in Moab

    3. Phase 2 of the Crisis

5a — Then the two of them, Mahlon and Chilion, also died, — וַיָּמֻ֥תוּ גַם־שְׁנֵיהֶ֖ם מַחְל֣וֹן וְכִלְי֑וֹן
      a. The Event

5b — and the woman was deprived of both her sons and her husband. — וַתִּשָּׁאֵר֙ הָֽאִשָּׁ֔ה מִשְּׁנֵ֥י יְלָדֶ֖יהָ וּמֵאִישָֽׁהּ׃
      b. The Effect

Nevertheless, there is some uniformity of presentation as determined by ZECOT's editors. The analysis of each major text unit presents the flow of thought as an exegetical outline, in both Hebrew and English. The outline drives the commentary proper, which is guided by textual thoughts growing out of the main headings of the exegetical outline. The outline also provides the basis for a single-sentence main idea statement for each unit.

To better see ZECOT in action, see its exegetical outline of Ruth 1:1–5 on the preceding page.[79]

ZECOT is a helpful resource for discourse analysis. Perhaps its greatest strength is its treatment of how each clause fits within its textual unit and how each textual unit fits within its whole book. This focus enables ZECOT to do an excellent job of tracing the biblical author's flow of thought, even if the relationships between clauses are not expressed in terms of specific discourse relations. Unfortunately, ZECOT's emphasis on inter-clausal relationships comes at the expense of other levels of discourse, especially information structure. This means that overall topic, focus, and the various constituents of the clause are neglected. Nevertheless, ZECOT fills a significant need by incorporating discourse analysis into the commentary genre. All students and scholars of the Hebrew Bible will profit greatly from this series, but ZECOT is particularly helpful for pastors and Bible teachers who need to present the main ideas of the biblical text to a lay audience.

6.4.4 The Baylor Handbook on the Hebrew Bible Series

A second series that touches on discourse analysis is the Baylor Handbook on the Hebrew Bible series.[80] The purpose of this series is to serve as a "prequel" to the theological and exegetical comments found in most commentaries. To accomplish this purpose, the series focuses on the Hebrew text, specifically the linguistic character of the text.

The Baylor Handbook on the Hebrew Bible series presents detailed analysis of the Hebrew text at the word and clausal level. Discussion often focuses on syntactical issues, but special attention is also given to discourse analysis, so each author comments on relevant discourse features. Similar to ZECOT, the Baylor Handbook on the Hebrew Bible series does not adopt a uniform approach to discourse analysis. The series' earlier volumes tend to adopt a top-down approach that emphasizes foregrounding and backgrounding in

---

79. Block, *Ruth*, 62, 70.

80. http://www.baylorpress.com/en/Series/5/Baylor%20Handbook%20on%20the%20Hebrew%20 Bible. I would like to thank W. Dennis Tucker, Jr. for discussing the Baylor Handbook on the Hebrew Bible series with me (email message to author, February 7, 2018).

discourse, similar to Longacre. However, recent volumes adopt more of a generative approach, characterized by the approach of Holmstedt, and the intent is for future volumes to follow in this trend.

The following excerpts, which consist of selected commentary on discourse-related features of Ruth 1:1–5 from the Baylor Handbook on the Hebrew Bible, provide an example of what this series has to offer in terms of discourse analysis.[81]

וַיְהִי בִּימֵי שְׁפֹט הַשֹּׁפְטִים [Ruth 1:1]. ויהי followed by a temporal phrase (often with an inf constr, as we have here בִּימֵי שְׁפֹט הַשֹּׁפְטִים) is a typical construction for establishing the time and/or place of a new narrative section (see Josh 1:1; Judg 1:1; 2 Sam 1:1; Ezek 1:1). Moreover, the *wayyiqtol* in general (not just ויהי) begins the books of Leviticus, Numbers, Joshua, Judges, 1 Samuel, 2 Samuel, 2 Kings, Ezekiel, Jonah, and 2 Chronicles, and many lower level narrative units (e.g., Gen 6:1; 11:1; 14:1; 17:1; 22:1; 26:1; 27:1; 38:1, among many more, at various narrative levels).

וַיְהִי רָעָב בָּאָרֶץ [Ruth 1:1]. *Wayyiqtol*—Subject NP—oblique PP complement. This is the most common word order in BH narrative (indeed, a slight variation, *wayyiqtol*—Subject NP—PP/inf constr, occurs in the very next clause). However, the V-S order itself is derived from a basic S-V order because whatever the gemination in the *wayyiqtol* used to be (it is now unrecoverable), it triggered the S-V-to-V-S inversion.

וְשֵׁם הָאִישׁ אֱלִימֶלֶךְ וְשֵׁם אִשְׁתּוֹ נָעֳמִי וְשֵׁם שְׁנֵי־בָנָיו׀ מַחְלוֹן וְכִלְיוֹן אֶפְרָתִים מִבֵּית לֶחֶם יְהוּדָה [Ruth 1:2]. Departure from the use of the *wayyiqtol*, in this case by the use of a null-copula clause, is a marked linguistic strategy within Hebrew narrative and it may convey any number of discourse signals. In this case, the departure signals the addition of background information: the audience is finally given the names and clan association of the characters introduced in v. 1. Note that the constituent order is Subject NP—Predicate NP (so too in each of the two subsequent null-copula clauses), which is the expected order in pragmatically netural null-copula clauses.

וַיָּבֹאוּ שְׂדֵי־מוֹאָב [Ruth 1:2]. *Wayyiqtol* 3mpl Qal √בוא with complement NP. This clause resumes the narrative from v. 1 and succinctly provides the conslusion of their trip to Moab: they arrived. The use of a *wayyiqtol* clause shifts from the narrative background to the narrative foreground by resuming the narrative progression and plot development. The NP שְׂדֵי מוֹאָב functions as the complement of the verb ויבאו, which mostly takes oblique PP complements specifying either the destination (often with אֶל or בְּ) or origin (mostly with מִן) of movement. In Ruth the verb בוא is used with the preposition אֶל four times: 3:16, 17; 4:11, 13. However, this verb also takes the accusative complement (explicit or implicit) for the destination of movement thirteen times: Ruth 1:2, 19 (2×), 22; 2:3, 7, 12, 18; 3:4, 7 (2×), 14, 15.

שֵׁם הָאַחַת עָרְפָּה וְשֵׁם הַשֵּׁנִית רוּת [Ruth 1:4]. In this verse we are finally introduced to the heroine of the story, Ruth, as well as her foil, Orpah. As with the first set of names provided in v. 2, we have here the departure from the use of a *wayyiqtol* clause by the use of a null-copula clause in order to provide background information.

וַתִּשָּׁאֵר הָאִשָּׁה מִשְּׁנֵי יְלָדֶיהָ וּמֵאִישָׁהּ [Ruth 1:5]. This clause mirrors the statement made in v. 3 after the report of Elimelek's death. The similarity of the two statements serves to reinforce No'omi's isolation and contributes to the tension of the unfolding plot.

The Baylor Handbook on the Hebrew Bible is extremely helpful when it comes to syntactical analysis. Its parsings and explanation of the meanings of different forms are especially useful to both students and scholars who are interested in the syntactical nuances of the Hebrew text. However, overall the Baylor Handbook on the Hebrew Bible is not so helpful when it comes to discourse analysis. The series' lack of a uniform methodology results in a lack of consistency—and sometimes even contradictory approaches—between volumes. Hopefully, the methodological standardization of more recent volumes in the series will provide a helpful corrective to this shortcoming. As new volumes emerge alongside revisions of previously published ones, the Baylor Handbook on the Hebrew Bible is bound to become a standard, go-to resource for discourse analysis of the Old Testament.

6.5 THE WAYS FORWARD

The abundance of works on discourse analysis and the Hebrew Bible reflects an ever-growing interest in this important topic. There is a rich diversity in the four different approaches these works embody: the tagmemic, distributional, information structure, and inter-clausal approaches. Each approach makes its own unique contribution to the discussion. The tagmemic and distributional approaches are helpful in that they emphasize the need to look for patterns in discourse, especially patterns tied to text type. Even more useful are the information structure and inter-clausal approaches, which have a solid foundation in current linguistic methodology and can be applied consistently to the Hebrew Bible. Yet, adoption of either the information-structure approach or the inter-clausal approach as a sole methodology inevitably leads to a limited focus either on discourse within the sentence or beyond the level of the sentence. What is needed is a holistic, integrated approach that fully takes into account both levels of discourse, similar to those put forward by Floor and Buth. As scholars continue to explore the application of discourse analysis to the Hebrew Bible, we look forward to more studies in this vein.

Especially encouraging is the emergence of resources that seek to help students, professors, and pastors apply discourse analysis to the Hebrew Bible. *Basics of Hebrew Discourse* offers a particularly helpful guide on how to conduct discourse analysis on the Hebrew Bible, both narrative and poetry. The *Lexham Discourse Hebrew Bible* is also a very useful tool because it shows what a linguistically robust application of discourse analysis to the Hebrew Bible might look like. These two resources approach discourse analysis in two different ways: *Basics of Hebrew Discourse* from a primarily inter-clausal approach, and the *Lexham Discourse Hebrew Bible* primarily from an information-structure approach. Ideally, both of these resources would hold to a broader methodology that fully integrates micro-level and macro-level approaches to discourse analysis. Perhaps revised editions of these works will accomplish such integration better. In the meantime, *Basics of Hebrew Discourse* and the *Lexham Discourse Hebrew Bible* complement each other quite nicely and can be used with great profit.

Finally, the appearance of discourse-focused commentary series like ZECOT and the Baylor Handbook on the Hebrew Bible is also encouraging. Although limited in terms of its inter-clausal approach, ZECOT offers a discourse analysis of individual books that should be especially helpful to those preaching or teaching the biblical text. The Baylor Handbook on the Hebrew Bible series is less valuable at present due to its lack of consistency, but it has the potential to be a very useful series for engaging discourse features. Unfortunately, there are not yet as many discourse-focused commentary series on the Hebrew Bible as there are for the New Testament.[82] However, the publication of both ZECOT and the Baylor Handbook on the Hebrew Bible suggests that discourse analysis of the Hebrew Bible has a bright future.

---

82. In addition to the New Testament correspondents of ZECOT and the Baylor Handbook on the Hebrew Bible, namely the Zondervan Exegetical Commentary on the New Testament and the Baylor Handbook on the Greek New Testament, discourse analysis of the Greek New Testament also offers the High Definition Commentary (published by Lexham Press) and the Semantic and Structural Analysis Series (published by the Summer Institute of Linguistics).

6.6 FURTHER READING

Bergen, Robert D., ed. *Biblical Hebrew and Discourse Linguistics.* Dallas: Summer Institute of Linguistics, 1994.

———. "Discourse Analysis: Biblical Hebrew." *EHLL* 1:746–49.

———. "Text as a Guide to Authorial Intention: An Introduction to Discourse. Criticism." *JETS* 30 (1987): 327–36.

Bodine, Walter R., ed. *Discourse Analysis of Biblical Literature: What It Is and What It Offers.* SemeiaSt. Atlanta: Scholars Press, 1995.

Callow, Kathleen. *Discourse Considerations in Translating the Word of God.* Grand Rapids: Zondervan, 1974.

Floor, Sebastiaan Jonathan. "From Information Structure, Topic, and Focus, to Theme in Biblical Hebrew Narrative." DLitt thesis, University of Stellenbosch, 2004.

MacDonald, Peter J. "Discourse Analysis and Biblical Interpretation." Pages 153–75 in *Linguistics and Biblical Hebrew.* Edited by Walter R. Bodine. Winona Lake, IN: Eisenbrauns, 1992.

O'Connor, Michael. "Discourse Linguistics and the Study of Biblical Hebrew." Pages 17–42 in *Congress Volume: Basel, 2001.* Edited by André Lemaire. VTSup 92. Leiden: Brill, 2002.

Patton, Matthew H. and Frederic Clarke Putnam. *Basics of Hebrew Discourse: A Guide to Working with Hebrew Prose and Poetry.* Edited by Miles Van Pelt. Grand Rapids: Zondervan, 2019.

Runge, Steven E. and Joshua R. Westbury, eds. *Lexham Discourse Hebrew Bible.* Bellingham, WA: Lexham, 2012.

Talstra, Eep. "Text Linguistics: Biblical Hebrew." *EHLL* 1:755–60.

Wendland, Ernst R. "The Discourse Analysis of Hebrew Poetry: A Procedural Outline." Pages 1–27 in *Discourse Perspectives on Hebrew Poetry in the Scriptures.* Edited by Ernst R. Wendland. United Bible Society Monograph Series 7. New York: United Bible Societies, 1994.

CHAPTER 7

WORD ORDER

A debate ensues concerning the identity of basic word order in B[iblical] H[ebrew]. . . . This debate has made it essential for students to be able to interact with the ramifications of the differing proposals.

—JEREMIAH XIUFU ZUO[1]

7.1 INTRODUCTION

Recent years have seen a rise in the application of discourse analysis to the Hebrew Bible, including information structure and the way that constituents are packaged together in a clause. This naturally brings up the issue of word order, or the ordering of a clause's constituents. The recent interest in discourse analysis has therefore led to exploration of word order in the Hebrew Bible.

Traditionally, Biblical Hebrew has been characterized as a verb-initial language and Biblical Aramaic has been thought to have a free word order. Recent investigation of word order in the Hebrew Bible has sought not only to confirm but also to challenge the traditional perspective. Given the growing number of scholars who argue for non-traditional positions on word order, it is important that we are aware of this change. Furthermore, because one's view of word order directly relates to exegesis, we need to be familiar with the different positions on word order, the basic arguments for each position, and the implications that adopting one school of thought over another might have.

To this end, in this chapter I explore recent scholarship on word order in Biblical Hebrew and Biblical Aramaic. I begin by presenting a modern linguistic framework for understanding word order. Then I examine key works on word order in Biblical Hebrew and word order in Biblical Aramaic separately.

---

1. Zuo, *Biblical Hebrew Word Order Debate*, 3.

Finally, I offer some suggestions for the way forward in anticipation of continued discussion of this exciting topic.

7.2 The Modern Linguistic Framework for Word Order

Two key concepts provide the linguistic framework for discussing word order. The first is the concept of markedness, and the second is the notion of basic word order itself, particularly as it relates to linguistic typology. I examine these two topics now before exploring analyses of word order in the Hebrew Bible.

7.2.1 Markedness

Although the concepts behind it were recognized much earlier, the structuralist-functionalist Prague School largely popularized markedness theory in the earlier part of the twentieth century.[2] The terminology of *marked* and *unmarked* (in German, *merkmalhaltig* and *merkmallos*) first appeared in discussions between Nikolai Trubetzkoy and Roman Jakobson in 1930.[3] Trubetzkoy primarily applied these terms to phonology and phonetic opposition.[4] Jakobson, however, expanded the study of markedness to include grammar and lexical semantics.[5]

At the most basic level, markedness entails an opposition between two different features in a language, unmarked and marked. An unmarked feature is the "default" or normal feature, whereas a marked feature is any feature that differs from the default, standard one.[6] On the one hand, the English word *book* is unmarked because it represents the most basic form; on the other hand, *books* is marked because it is plural and not the default form. Similarly, in Hebrew סֵפֶר ("book") would be the unmarked form whereas סְפָרִים ("books") would be the marked form.

Naturally, the concept of markedness is foundational for determining word order. This is because exploration of word order requires knowledge of the way a language normally orders a sentence's elements. Departures from the unmarked word order commonly have pragmatic functions, such as topicalization or focus. With this in mind, I turn now to the subject of basic word order.

---

2. Andersen, "Markedness Theory," 21–27; Battistella, *Logic of Markedness*, 19–34; Andrews, *Markedness Theory*, 13–15.

3. Trubetskoĭ, *N.S. Trubetzkoy's Letters and Notes*, 162–64; cf. Andersen, "Markedness Theory," 21–23.

4. Trubetskoĭ, "Phonologischen Systeme," 96–116; idem, "Phonologie actuelle," 219–46.

5. Jakobson, "Zur Struktur des russichen Verbums," 74–84; idem, "Signe zéro," 143–52.

6. Battistella, *Markedness*, 2; Gvozdanović, "Defining Markedness," 59–64.

7.2.2 Word Order Typology

The modern study of word order has its foundations in linguistic typology. Generally speaking, *linguistic typology* may be defined as the classification of structural types across languages.[7] Each language has its own unique features when compared with other languages, but that language will also share similarities with other languages. Languages can therefore be grouped together and classified by their relative similarities and differences, similar to how we classify animals and plants by phylum, class, order, and so on. The modern study of linguistic typology can be traced back to the work of the functionalist Joseph H. Greenberg.[8]

Typological research shows that most of the world's languages can be classified according to their basic, or unmarked, word order. Most significant here is the relative order of the subject (S), verb (V), and object (O). Using these categories, the world's languages can be categorized according to the six logically possible orders: SOV, SVO, VSO, VOS, OVS, and OSV.[9] Interestingly, Greenberg discovered that there is often a correlation between a language's basic word order and certain syntactical elements. For example, languages like English, in which the verb comes prior to the object (i.e., SVO, VSO, and VOS languages), tend to use prepositions whereas languages in which the verb comes after the object (i.e., SOV, OVS, and OSV languages) tend to use postpositions.[10]

Most languages exhibit a variety of different word orders. For example, in English the word order is SVO for declarative statements (e.g., *You want to go outside*) but VSO for questions (e.g., *Do you want to go outside?*). This raises the issue of how to determine the basic word order of a given language. Linguists do not agree entirely on how to address this issue. However, generally speaking, linguists utilize several different criteria to determine the basic word order of a language: frequency, distribution, simplicity, and pragmatics.[11]

First, the criterion of frequency means that the most dominant order in a language represents its basic word order.[12] For many languages it is easy to determine what order is statistically dominant. For other languages, however,

---

7. Croft, *Typology and Universals*, 1; Mallinson and Blake, *Language Typology*, 3–6.

8. E.g., Greenberg, *Language Typology*; idem, *Language Universals*.

9. Fried, "Word Order," 289–90. The orders SOV (≈45 percent) and SVO (≈42 percent) are the most common across the world's languages, the order VSO (≈9 percent) is less common but still attested, and the orders VOS (≈3 percent), OVS (≈1 percent), and OSV (≈0 percent) are extremely rare cross-linguistically. See Tomlin, *Basic Word Order*, 21–22.

10. Greenberg, "Some Universals of Grammar," 73–113; cf. Dryer, "Greenbergian Word Order Correlations," 81–138; Hawkins, *Word Order Universals*.

11. Dryer, "Word Order," 73–78; cf. Siewierska, *Word Order Rules*, 8–13.

12. Dryer, "Word Order," 73–74.

it can be more difficult. This is especially true if only a limited sample of the language is preserved. For example, the dominant word order in English is SVO, but this would not be obvious if most of the sentences in our text sample were interrogative sentences, which use VSO order. Thus, for frequency to serve as a viable criterion, it is important to consider large enough samples of text that accurately represent the language as a whole.

Second, distribution serves as a criterion for determining basic word order.[13] If one order appears in more types of constructions than another order, then the former should be considered more basic whereas the latter should be considered non-basic. This is because the more limited order is probably connected with the specific environments in which it occurs. To return to the example of interrogative sentences, VSO word order occurs in English primarily only in interrogative sentences whereas SVO word order occurs in most other environments. Based on the criterion of distribution, therefore, SVO and not VSO is the basic word order in English.

Third, the criterion of simplicity can help to determine a language's basic word order.[14] The basic principle is that, when there are at least two different ways to express an idea in terms of word order, the simplest one is likely to be the most basic. Consider the phrases *the smarter teacher*, with the word order adjective-noun, and *the teacher smarter than him*, with the word order noun-adjective. Both are acceptable phrases in English, but the simplest phrase *the smarter teacher* is the most basic.

Fourth, pragmatics can help determine basic word order.[15] Most languages can vary word order to express pragmatic effect. On the one hand, if the word order of a sentence does not communicate anything special, as in the sentence *I talked to Jenn*, the word order should be considered unmarked or basic. On the other hand, if the word order of a sentence communicates something beyond the expression itself, as in the sentence *Jenn I talked to*, that word order is considered marked and therefore non-basic. The main problem with this criterion is that it is not always easy to tell if a given word order has a pragmatic function, especially for non-native speakers.

In most cases, these criteria—frequency, distribution, simplicity, and pragmatics—can identify a language's basic word order. However, some languages exhibit a relatively flexible, or free, word order.[16] Yet, even for these

---

13. Dryer, "Word Order," 74–75.

14. Dryer, "Word Order," 75–76.

15. Dryer, "Word Order," 76.

16. Some linguists argue for the existence of pragmatically based languages, in which word order exclusively reflects pragmatic considerations (e.g., Mithun, "Is Basic Word Order Universal?" 15–61).

languages, word order typology remains relevant because these languages are themselves a linguistic type. Furthermore, although free-word-order languages may show flexibility in the position of the subject, verb, and object at one level, these languages tend to be fairly rigid in the ordering of elements at other levels.[17]

7.3 Biblical Hebrew Word Order

Having sketched a modern framework for understanding word order, I move on to how scholars have applied these concepts to the study of the Hebrew Bible. I look first at Biblical Hebrew.

Statistically speaking, the most frequent word order in Biblical Hebrew is VSO. This results from the extremely common usage of *wayyiqtol* in verbal clauses. Therefore, the vast majority of the standard reference grammars argue that Biblical Hebrew exhibits a basic VSO word order.[18] The vast majority of first-year Biblical Hebrew grammars also advocate a VSO word order.[19] For these grammars, departure from the basic VSO word order has a pragmatic function, such as contrast or "emphasis."

Yet, this position has not gone unchallenged. In the first half of the twentieth century the Hebrew grammarian Paul Joüon argued that Biblical Hebrew exhibits a SVO rather than VSO word order.[20] More recently, a small minority of scholars[21] and some introductory grammars[22] have taken exception to classifying Biblical Hebrew as a VSO language. The emergence of such a perspective has challenged the traditional view on basic word order in Biblical Hebrew, which was assumed more than it was demonstrated. Naturally, the appearance of scholarship arguing for a basic SVO word order has encouraged those holding to VSO to refine and defend their position.

The primary advocate for the SVO position is Robert D. Holmstedt. The major voices in recent years to offer support for the VSO position are Adina

---

17. Dryer, "Word Order," 113–14.

18. E.g., GKC §§141l, 142f; *IBHS* §§8.3b, 8.4a; *BHRG* §46; Williams, *Hebrew Syntax*, 201–8 (§§570–82).

19. E.g., Futato, *Beginning Biblical Hebrew*, 371; Kelley, *Biblical Hebrew*, 110–11; Lambdin, *Biblical Hebrew*, 39–40, 162–65; Pratico and Van Pelt, *Basics of Biblical Hebrew Grammar*, 251–60; Ross, *Biblical Hebrew*, 416–17; Seow, *Grammar for Biblical Hebrew*, 149–51.

20. Joüon, *Grammaire de l'hébreu biblique*, 474 (§155k). In his revised translation of Joüon's grammar, Takamitsu Muraoka departs from Joüon's original perspective and inserts his own view that Biblical Hebrew exhibits a VSO word order (§155k).

21. E.g., Schlesinger, "Zur Wortfolge im hebräischen Verbalsatz," 381–90; DeCaen, "Verb in Standard Biblical Hebrew Prose," 136–37; idem, "Unified Analysis of Verbal and Verbless Clauses," 117–18; Cook, *Time and the Biblical Hebrew Verb*, 235–37; Doron, "Word Order in Hebrew," 41–56.

22. E.g., Cook and Holmstedt, *Beginning Biblical Hebrew*, 60; Bornemann, *Grammar of Biblical Hebrew*, 217–18.

Moshavi, Aaron D. Hornkohl, and Karel Jongeling. Because Moshavi and Hornkohl both spend some time attempting to refute Holmstedt, I present Holmstedt's argumentation first for the SVO view. Then, after examining the SVO position as represented by Holmstedt, I explore the VSO position as represented by Moshavi, Hornkohl, and Jongeling.

7.3.1 Robert D. Holmstedt

Robert D. Holmstedt takes a generative approach to the question of word order in Biblical Hebrew. Adherents of Generative Grammar often believe that all VSO languages have an underlying, "deep structure" SVO word order, and Holmstedt is no exception. His arguments for Biblical Hebrew having an underlying SVO language appear in a number of his publications.[23] To arrive at his conclusion that Biblical Hebrew is a SVO language, Holmstedt applies to Biblical Hebrew the four basic criteria for identifying a language's word order. He also offers some arguments against the viability of a VSO order.

Regarding frequency,[24] Holmstedt does not deny that VSO is statistically the most dominant word order in the Hebrew Bible. However, Holmstedt argues that VSO's dominance does not necessarily mean that VSO represents the basic word order of Biblical Hebrew. He contends that VSO is marked, rather than unmarked, and therefore not basic in light of his remaining three criteria.

Regarding distribution,[25] Holmstedt observes that *wayyiqtol* occurs in a significantly more restricted environment than the verbal forms *qatal* and *yiqtol* do. He notes that with *wayyiqtol* the subject always comes after the verb, the verb cannot be negated, constituents cannot be fronted before the verb, and it cannot follow subordinators like אֲשֶׁר or כִּי. In contrast, *qatal* and *yiqtol* occur with a variety of word order patterns in both main and subordinate clauses. For Holmstedt, this means that *wayyiqtol* clauses must be excluded from any consideration of word order.

Regarding clause type,[26] Holmstedt largely follows Anna Siewierska in arguing that basic word order is found in independent, indicative clauses with

23. Holmstedt, "Typological Classification of the Hebrew of Genesis," 1–39; idem, "Possible Verb-Subject to Subject-Verb Shift," 3–31; idem, "Word Order and Information Structure," 111–39; idem, "Word Order in the Book of Proverbs," 135–54; idem, "Relative Clause in Biblical Hebrew," 126–59.

24. Holmstedt, "Typological Classification of the Hebrew of Genesis," 7–9; idem, "Word Order and Information Structure," 116–17.

25. Holmstedt, "Typological Classification of the Hebrew of Genesis," 9–13; idem, "Word Order and Information Structure," 117–19.

26. Holmstedt, "Typological Classification of the Hebrew of Genesis," 13–20; idem, "Word Order and Information Structure," 119.

an explicit human, agentive subject and object and with an active rather than stative verb.[27] Holmstedt therefore excludes clauses without an overt subject, which results in a slight predominance of SVO over VSO. He further omits VSO narrative clauses with *wayyiqtol*, identifying the SVO order that tends to be found in speech as more basic. Also excluded are VSO modal clauses, which following Siewierska's definition are less basic because they are non-indicative.

Regarding pragmatics,[28] Holmstedt argues that many instances of SVO order reflect fronting of the topic or marking a subject for focus. Thus, Holmstedt acknowledges that most SVO clauses are pragmatically marked. However, he points to a number of SVO examples that he contends cannot be explained pragmatically. According to Holmstedt, pragmatically neutral SVO clauses in Genesis outnumber the book's pragmatically neutral VSO clauses. For Holmstedt, this presents a challenge to the classification of Hebrew as a VSO language.

Finally, in addition to application of these criteria, Holmstedt contends that a VSO word order faces two significant challenges with respect to Biblical Hebrew.[29] He argues that VSO cannot explain why there are so few VSO simple clauses (i.e., main indicative clauses with no fronted phrases preceding the verb) in the Hebrew Bible. He also contends that the VSO position creates an asymmetry in that all adherents to this position acknowledge the SVO order of verbless and participial clauses.

On the basis of these considerations, Holmstedt concludes that Biblical Hebrew should be considered a SVO rather than VSO language. He argues that, far from representing the norm, all instances of VSO order reflect the generative concept of triggered inversion. VSO order is triggered by one of several different factors: a fronted constituent, a negative particle, modality, an interrogative, or a subordinating particle such as כִּי or אֲשֶׁר.[30] Without one of these triggers, Hebrew preserves its SVO order.

Yet, Holmstedt also recognizes that the Semitic languages in general are VSO rather than SVO. He suggests that an original VSO order may be preserved in subordinate clauses, which cross-linguistically tend to preserve basic word order more than independent clauses.[31] Holmstedt argues, therefore, that the original word order was VSO but that this word order changed, over time,

---

27. Siewierska, *Word Order Rules*, 8.

28. Holmstedt, "Typological Classification of the Hebrew of Genesis," 20–25; idem, "Word Order and Information Structure," 119–20.

29. Holmstedt, "Typological Classification of the Hebrew of Genesis," 28–29.

30. Holmstedt, "Word Order and Information Structure," 124–26; idem, "Relative Clause in Biblical Hebrew," 148–50.

31. Holmstedt, "Typological Classification of the Hebrew of Genesis," 16–18. Holmstedt refers

to SVO. According to Holmstedt, this happened through reanalysis of fronted subjects as "normal" word order by child learners of Hebrew.[32] In doing so, he builds upon the work of Talmy Givón, who also argues for a shift from VSO to SVO in Hebrew.[33]

Holmstedt supports his conclusion that Hebrew shifted from VSO to SVO by investigating representative samples of the Hebrew Bible.[34] According to Holmstedt, these representative samples evidence three trends when arranged chronologically. First, there is an increase in the overall use of SVO order, especially in contexts where the subject does not carry topic- or focus-fronting. Second, there is an increase in SVO order in subordinate and negated clauses, both of which tend to be conservative and preserve older word orders cross linguistically. Third, there is a slight increase in use of left-dislocation (i.e., casus pendens) that serves as an alternative to fronting once the SVO pattern becomes dominant.

7.3.2 Adina Moshavi

Unlike Holmstedt, but like the traditional perspective, Adina Moshavi argues that Biblical Hebrew is a VSO language. She does so primarily in her book *Word Order in the Biblical Hebrew Finite Clause.*[35] Moshavi recognizes the difficulties with identifying word order purely based on statistical dominance. To get around those difficulties, she defines basic word order as the word order that is pragmatically neutral. Removing marked expressions provides a filter on the raw statistical data, and the remaining data can then be analyzed in terms of the criterion of frequency.[36]

Moshavi characterizes Hebrew as a VSO language on the basis of her own analysis of main (i.e., non-subordinate) clauses in Genesis through Kings, although most of her discussion focuses on the book of Genesis.[37] She finds that 84 percent of these clauses are VSO rather than SVO. To get this number, Moshavi includes all independent *wayyiqtol*, *weqatal*, and modal clauses.

to the so-called Penthouse Principle to support this point, on which see Ross, "Penthouse Principle," 397–422.

32. Holmstedt, "Possible Verb-Subject to Subject-Verb Shift," 19–20; idem, "Typological Classification of the Hebrew of Genesis," 26–27.

33. Givón, "Drift from VSO to SVO in Biblical Hebrew," 181–254; cf. Cryer, "Problem of Dating Biblical Hebrew," 190.

34. Holmstedt, "Possible Verb-Subject to Subject-Verb Shift," 19–24. Holmstedt draws his data from the books of Genesis, Joel, Amos, Obadiah, Jonah, Nahum, Habakkuk, Ruth, Ecclesiastes, Esther, Daniel, and Ezra.

35. This work originated as Moshavi's PhD dissertation completed at Yeshiva University in 2000.

36. Moshavi, *Word Order*, 7–9.

37. Moshavi, *Word Order*, 7–9.

She even includes clauses that lack an explicit subject. For Moshavi, clauses with and without an explicit subject can be considered as one because Biblical Hebrew typically drops pronominal subjects unless they precede the verb. Notably, Moshavi does not consider verbless or participial clauses in her analysis.

Thus, Moshavi does not exclude the same types of clauses that Holmstedt does in his analysis of word order in Biblical Hebrew. She argues that omitting *wayyiqtol* and *weqatal* clauses necessarily skews the data because such clauses are simply positional variants of their corresponding simple forms (*qatal* and *yiqtol*), used whenever the verb immediately follows a conjunction.[38] She also contends that modal clauses should not be excluded because modality is a semantic—rather than pragmatic—feature.[39]

Moshavi furthermore takes issue with Holmstedt's application of Siewierska's basic word order definition to Biblical Hebrew.[40] She contends that this definition requires the exclusion of sentences that are marked, but to exclude marked sentences one must already have some idea of which order is marked. This, according to Moshavi, is circular. Moshavi also objects to excluding thousands of clauses from consideration as Holmstedt's approach requires. She contends that determining word order on such a small sample seems precarious, especially because Holmstedt's exclusions result in a language that looks very little like the Hebrew of the Bible.

Finally, Moshavi objects to Holmstedt's use of triggered inversion to account for VSO clauses, including *wayyiqtol* clauses, in Hebrew.[41] She argues that triggered inversion does not count as evidence for Hebrew's characterization as a SVO language. Rather, it is merely a way of explaining the existence of VSO clauses in Hebrew. Moshavi argues that it is just as easy, if not better supported by the evidence, to argue that VSO is the basic word order of Hebrew and that SVO order is the result of pragmatic marking.

7.3.3 Aaron D. Hornkohl

Aaron D. Hornkohl's arguments for Biblical Hebrew as a VSO language are found primarily in his MA thesis, completed at Hebrew University, but also appear in at least one other of his publications.[42] Hornkohl uses several criteria

---

38. Moshavi, *Word Order*, 12–13.
39. Moshavi, *Word Order*, 14.
40. Moshavi, *Word Order*, 14–15.
41. Moshavi, *Word Order*, 16.
42. Hornkohl, "Pragmatics of the X+Verb Structure"; idem, "Tense-Aspect-Mood, Word Order and Pragmatics," 27–56.

to identify word order in Biblical Hebrew: statistical dominance, statistical dominance with preceding particles, the markedness of non-VSO word order with preceding function words, and descriptive simplicity. For Hornkohl, the book of Genesis serves as a representative sample of the Hebrew Bible upon which he applies his criteria.

Hornkohl first points to the statistical dominance of relative VSO word order.[43] He finds, similar to Moshavi, that approximately 83 percent of clauses in Genesis exhibit a VSO order. But Hornkohl recognizes that there is more to the picture. He observes that the dominance of VSO is much more marked in narrative than direct speech. He also observes that the exclusion of *wayyiqtol* and modal forms results in a nearly even distribution between VSO and SVO word order in Genesis. These observations lead Hornkohl to turn to his other criteria for a more accurate picture of word order in Biblical Hebrew.

Recognizing that the exclusion of *wayyiqtol* results in some ambiguity, Hornkohl examines word order for clause types in which *wayyiqtol* cannot occur.[44] These include both main and subordinate clauses headed by particles like אֲשֶׁר, לֹא, and כִּי. Hornkohl finds that VSO word order is much more common than SVO word order. He emphasizes that the statistical dominance of VSO word order therefore holds true even in syntactic environments where it cannot be claimed that *wayyiqtol* forms require VSO word order.

Hornkohl further observes that most of the SVO clauses with particles are best explained by pragmatic marking.[45] This is particularly true of narrative but also evident in direct speech. According to Hornkohl, the observation that SVO clauses with particles exhibit pragmatic marking is highly significant because it provides an explanation for why SVO word order occurs if VSO is the default, basic order for Biblical Hebrew.[46]

Finally, Hornkohl utilizes the criterion of descriptive simplicity.[47] He argues that VSO word order explains the data more simply than SVO. This is especially true of clauses where a constituent X other than the verb or subject is fronted. In such cases, the overwhelming order attested in the Hebrew Bible is XVS. If Hebrew is VSO, then such a clause needs only a one-step process: the fronting of a single element before the verb. But, if Hebrew is SVO, then such a clause requires a two-step process: first, the fronting of X, and second, the fronting of the verb before the subject. According to Hornkohl, the fact that

---

43. Hornkohl, "Pragmatics of the X+Verb Structure," 12–13.

44. Hornkohl, "Pragmatics of the X+Verb Structure," 14–16.

45. Hornkohl, "Pragmatics of the X+Verb Structure," 16–17.

46. Cf. Hornkohl, "Tense-Aspect-Mood, Word Order and Pragmatics," 40–41.

47. Hornkohl, "Pragmatics of the X+Verb Structure," 18–20.

Holmstedt needs to appeal to triggered inversion for SVO word order to work only shows the superiority of the VSO position.[48]

Overall, Hornkohl agrees with Holmstedt's methodological approach regarding the need to filter raw frequency data to determine basic word order, but Hornkohl argues that if Holmstedt were to apply his methodology strictly, the results would support VSO rather than SVO word order.[49] Siewierska states that for basic word order the verb must be active and the subject must be human and agentive. Yet, according to Hornkohl, the majority of Holmstedt's pragmatically neutral SVO cases contain a non-active verb and a non-human or non-agentive subject. Omitting these clauses results in VSO as the statistically dominant order for pragmatically neutral clauses.

7.3.4 Karel Jongeling

The final scholar to argue substantially for a VSO basic word order is Karel Jongeling.[50] His research predates that of Holmstedt, so naturally he does not have opportunity to interact with Holmstedt's work. Nevertheless, he recognizes that a VSO basic word order is assumed more so than proven in the traditional grammars and seeks to remedy this deficiency. Furthermore, Jongeling contributes uniquely to the conversation of Biblical Hebrew's basic word order by integrating typological considerations with frequency analysis.

Jongeling's defense of a VSO basic word order begins with an argument from statistical dominance.[51] He takes the book of Ruth as a test case and observes that the verb comes first in most instances, without excluding *wayyiqtol* clauses. Filtering the raw data by ignoring all clauses without an explicit subject, he argues that approximately 75 percent of the clauses in the book of Ruth have the verb in initial position. For Jongeling, this constitutes good evidence for classifying Biblical Hebrew as a VSO language.

Jongeling's argumentation also entails typological comparison of Biblical Hebrew with Welsh, which is known to be a VSO language.[52] He observes that both Biblical Hebrew and Welsh make common use of nominal sentences, construct compound nominal sentences similarly, reinforce a suffixed pronoun by means of a separate pronoun, and create relative clauses comparably. Jongeling does not think there is a genetic relationship between Biblical Hebrew and

---

48. Hornkohl, "Pragmatics of the X+Verb Structure," 19–20.

49. Hornkohl, "Tense-Aspect-Mood, Word Order and Pragmatics," 38–44.

50. Jongeling, "VSO Character of Hebrew," 103–11.

51. Jongeling, "VSO Character of Hebrew," 104–6.

52. Jongeling, "VSO Character of Hebrew," 106–11. Similarly, some other scholars suggest that Biblical Hebrew exhibits various typological features characteristic of VSO languages (e.g., Longacre, "Left Shifts in Strongly VSO Languages," 332).

Welsh, but he contends that Biblical Hebrew's typological similarities with Welsh reinforce its classification as a VSO language.

7.3.5 Evaluation

Recent attention to the question of word order in Biblical Hebrew represents a significant advance in the field. Especially due to Holmstedt's work, scholars can no longer simply assume without proof—as was done for many years—that Biblical Hebrew exhibits a basic VSO order. Regardless of whether or not one accepts his conclusions, Holmstedt is to be thanked for challenging the status quo. Reconsideration of the question of Biblical Hebrew's word order can only lead to a better understanding of the issue, as it already has done.

In terms of defining basic word order, the works of Holmstedt and Hornkohl are especially helpful. Both Holmstedt and Hornkohl discuss basic word order in light of the modern linguistic understanding of the term, which is a significant contribution. However, even they do not agree on how the Hebrew Bible's clauses should be filtered, if at all, to separate clauses exhibiting basic word order from non-basic word order. In fact, this is where the heart of the debate lies for Holmstedt, Moshavi, and Hornkohl. Moving forward, it is essential that Hebraists reexamine the definition of basic word order for Biblical Hebrew in light of broader linguistic definitions of basic word order. As they do, they will need to give greater attention to the specific factors that can impact word order.

Another question that needs further exploration is that of word order typology, which is becoming an increasingly important component of word order research, even for those who understand word order in light of non-typological frameworks (e.g., Generative Grammar).[53] Accordingly, Jongeling is right to focus on this issue even if the comparisons he raises between Biblical Hebrew and Welsh are somewhat misguided.[54] The issue is complicated by the fact that SVO languages and VSO languages tend to exhibit similar features,[55] and there is the question of what features—if any—are distinctive of verb-initial languages.[56] Nevertheless, Hebraists would do well to investigate further the topic of word order typology and Biblical Hebrew, especially within the context of the Semitic languages' standard VSO order.

---

53. Cf. Song, *Word Order*, 308.

54. Cf. DeCaen, "Unified Analysis of Verbal and Verbless Clauses," 118. Jongeling lists some word order characteristics that had been thought to correlate with typology (e.g., the order of adjectives and nouns) but are now known not to. He also does not distinguish between word order universals that are unidirectional and bidirectional. On these issues, see Dryer, "Word Order," 61–73, 89–110.

55. Dryer, "Word Order," 70–71.

56. Cf. Carnie, Dooley, and Harley, *Verb First*, 2.

Finally, Hebraists need to test the explanatory power of the SVO and VSO approaches. This is particularly true as theories of word order relate to exegesis. On the one hand, if Biblical Hebrew is a SVO language as theorized by Holmstedt, then SVO clauses can be either basic or marked, and only VSO order without a trigger reflects pragmatic marking of the verb; on the other hand, if Biblical Hebrew is a VSO language as postulated by Moshavi and Hornkohl, then all instances of SVO order must reflect pragmatic marking of the subject. Thus, whether one characterizes Hebrew as a SVO language or a VSO language can potentially have significant implications for interpretation. Jeremiah Xiufu Zuo presents an excellent analysis of some of these implications, using Gen 18–19 as a case study.[57] Nevertheless, there is a need for additional studies like Zuo's that focus on other portions of the Hebrew Bible.

7.4 Biblical Aramaic Word Order

Having investigated word order in Biblical Hebrew, I turn now to the topic of word order in Biblical Aramaic. Interestingly enough, the tradition in Biblical Aramaic grammar has been to characterize the language as having a free word order even if SVO is the statistically dominant order. This perspective is held by both the older grammars written during the late nineteenth and earlier twentieth centuries[58] as well as the modern standard reference grammar authored by Franz Rosenthal.[59] These and other scholars advocated a free word order in light of the fact that all six possible types of word orders (i.e., SVO, SOV, VSO, VOS, OSV, and OVS) are attested even in the small corpus of Biblical Aramaic.[60]

This position has been challenged in recent years. An interest in the application of discourse analysis, particularly information structure, to Biblical Aramaic is largely responsible for this trend. Scholars who fall into this camp make their arguments from different starting points and, as a result, have reached different conclusions. Most of the work done on this topic, furthermore, has used the book of Daniel as a starting point because Daniel's Aramaic makes up the majority of the Biblical Aramaic corpus.

---

57. Zuo, *Biblical Hebrew Word Order Debate*. This work originated as Zuo's PhD dissertation completed at Trinity Evangelical Divinity School in 2016.

58. E.g., Kautzsch, *Grammatik des Biblisch-Aramäischen*, 160–61 (§196); Bauer and Leander, *Grammatik des biblisch-aramäischen*, 339, 342–45 (§§ 100p, 101).

59. E.g., Rosenthal, *Grammar of Biblical Aramaic*, 60 (§183).

60. For earlier scholarship, the question of basic word order in Biblical Aramaic was important because it impacted the classification of Biblical Aramaic. E. Y. Kutscher in particular sought to identify Biblical Aramaic as having a free word order because this was thought to be characteristic of Imperial Aramaic in the east ("ארמית המקראית [Biblical Aramaic]," 123–27).

I now survey recent scholarship on Biblical Aramaic's basic word order. The two primary works I examine are the full monograph length treatments of Randall Buth and Adriaan Lamprecht. I also discuss several smaller-scale, but still noteworthy, studies. After exploring all these works on word order in Biblical Aramaic, I offer an evaluation of their contributions.

7.4.1 Randall Buth

A very thorough analysis of word order in Biblical Aramaic is found in Randall Buth's University of California, Los Angeles PhD dissertation.[61] His dissertation deals more broadly with word order in Aramaic ca. 850 BCE–250 CE, including Old Aramaic, Imperial Aramaic, and Middle Aramaic (as represented in the Dead Sea Scrolls, the Genesis Apocryphon, and the Antiochus Scroll). Despite this broad scope, Buth's dissertation devotes a significant amount of time to investigating the Aramaic of the books of Ezra and Daniel.[62]

Buth approaches the question of word order in Biblical Aramaic from the perspective of Simon C. Dik's Functional Grammar. As such, he argues that every sentence has several different "slots" for putting information and that those slots follow a standard order cross-linguistically. The core of the sentence contains the subject, verb, and object. Prior to the core are the frame of reference, as well as any fronted focus or topic, whereas the tail or any other additional elements (e.g., adverbs) appear after the core. Within Dik's framework, Buth argues that the basic functional order of Biblical Aramaic is VSO whereas the statistically dominant order is SVO. According to Buth, SVO dominates because topicalization and focus frequently require placement of the subject before the verb.

Buth's analysis of Biblical Aramaic begins with the book of Daniel. He categorizes all the main (i.e., non-subordinate) narrative clauses in the book according to their word order.[63] Then he rules out both SOV and SVO as the basic word order for the main narrative clauses in Daniel.[64] He invalidates the SOV word order by drawing attention to clauses with a constituent before the verb that cannot be explained as a marked topic. He also invalidates the SVO word order by noting clauses in which the placement of the subject after the verb cannot be accounted for pragmatically.

According to Buth, invalidation of both SOV and SVO leaves VSO as the only possible word order for Daniel's main narrative clauses. After demonstrat-

---

61. Buth, "Word Order in Aramaic."
62. Buth, "Word Order in Aramaic," 126–349.
63. Buth, "Word Order in Aramaic," 126–29.
64. Buth, "Word Order in Aramaic," 131–38.

ing this, Buth goes on to argue that placement of the subject prior to the verb in Daniel's main narrative clauses can be explained pragmatically. He appeals to foregrounding, topicalization, frame of reference, and focus as pragmatic factors.[65] After demonstrating that the book of Daniel exhibits a basic VSO word order, Buth checks this conclusion against the main narrative clauses in the book of Ezra. He argues that, like the book of Daniel, Ezra exhibits a basic VSO word order.[66]

Buth considers verbless clauses, clauses with the particle of existence אִיתַי, and infinitive clauses separately from main narrative clauses. He argues that each can be explained in terms of Functional Grammar without presenting any problems for Biblical Aramaic's basic VSO word order.[67] For Buth, verbless clauses place the subject before the predicate, existence clauses reflect ordering of information from least salient to more salient, and infinitive clauses can place a marked topic prior to the infinitive but rarely do so.

7.4.2 Adriaan Lamprecht

Like Buth, Adriaan Lamprecht concludes that the basic word order of Biblical Aramaic is VSO.[68] However, he arrives at this conclusion through a very different methodological approach than Buth. Lamprecht adopts a generative rather than functionalist approach, specifically the Minimalist Program put forward by Noam Chomsky.[69] Lamprecht rejects the notion of a free word order for several reasons.[70] First, he argues that the ability of the human mind to learn a language requires that certain linguistic structures, including word order, be innate to humanity. Second, Lamprecht contends that a lack of distinction between unmarked and marked word order would create great difficulty in conveying certain meanings in Biblical Aramaic. Lamprecht finally suggests that the need to express specific constructions with a fixed word order argues against a free word order for Biblical Aramaic.

Lamprecht's generative approach to Biblical Aramaic word order manifests itself in another important way. When Lamprecht says the basic word order of Biblical Aramaic is VSO, he means that VSO appears at the surface structure of the language. In contrast, according to Lamprecht, Biblical Aramaic's deep structure exhibits a SVO word order.[71] This differs significantly from Buth's

65. Buth, "Word Order in Aramaic," 138–237.
66. Buth, "Word Order in Aramaic," 327–49.
67. Buth, "Word Order in Aramaic," 238–327.
68. Lamprecht, *Verb Movement in Biblical Aramaic*.
69. E.g., Chomsky, *Minimalist Program*.
70. Lamprecht, *Verb Movement in Biblical Aramaic*, 6–8.
71. Cf. Lamprecht, *Verb Movement in Biblical Aramaic*, 11.

functionalist approach, which attempts to connect form—in this case, the word order used—with function.

Lamprecht accounts for Biblical Aramaic's surface VSO order through the phenomenon of verb movement.[72] Remember that, in Generative Grammar, sentences consist of phrases (e.g., the noun phrase and verb phrase) arranged in a particular order, and this order has a hierarchical structure. In verb movement, a transformational rule causes the verb to move up the hierarchy while the subject, represented by the noun, remains where it is. The result is that the verb is placed prior to the noun rather than after it, as would normally be the case.

After explaining his methodological approach, Lamprecht explores how verb movement takes place in Biblical Aramaic for intransitive and transitive (and even ditransitive) verbs.[73] Lamprecht highlights how both the aspect and subject-agreement encoded by *qtl*, *yqtl*, and the participle contribute to these verb forms' movement prior to the subject. The subject of both intransitive and transitive verbs, as well as the object of transitive verbs, does not move when the verb moves. The result is that the verb precedes the subject (and object) in terms of word order.

According to Lamprecht, whenever Biblical Aramaic wants to establish a given subject or object as the topic, that element is fronted.[74] Thus, Lamprecht attributes cases in which the subject or object precedes the verb, as well as cases in which the object precedes the subject, to topicalization. Instances in which both the subject and object precede the verb are also explained via topicalization. In sum, Lamprecht attributes all non-verb-initial clauses to pragmatic factors, enabling him to maintain a basic VSO order for Biblical Aramaic.

7.4.3 Edward M. Cook

A smaller-scale exploration of word order in Biblical Aramaic is that of Edward M. Cook.[75] He limits his study to clauses in the book of Daniel that have a finite verb, excluding the stereotyped phrase עָנֵה וְאָמַר ("he answered and said"). In terms of the raw statistical data, he observes that SVO is the most common order but that, nevertheless, all other possible combinations appear.[76] However, Cook argues that such raw data is unhelpful unless it is interpreted and one is able to give specific explanations for why certain word orders appear.

---

72. Lamprecht, *Verb Movement in Biblical Aramaic*, 13–26.
73. Lamprecht, *Verb Movement in Biblical Aramaic*, 27–155.
74. Lamprecht, *Verb Movement in Biblical Aramaic*, 47–55, 79–83, 94–130.
75. Cook, "Word Order in the Aramaic of Daniel," 1–16.
76. Cook, "Word Order in the Aramaic of Daniel," 3–4.

For this reason, Cook attempts to explain departures from the basic word order. He contends that usage of the independent pronoun הִמּוֹן ("them") as direct object and the relative particle דִּי with verbs of perception (e.g., יְדַע "to know," חֲזָה "to see," and שְׁמַע "to hear") both require placement of the verb before the object.[77] Cook also suggests that word order directly relates to the role of the verb.[78] For example, for the *qtl* conjugation, the verb appears before the object when expressing consecutive action, whereas the verb comes after the object when indicating the perfect or pluperfect.

7.4.4 Christine Elizabeth Hayes

Christine Elizabeth Hayes also examines word order in the book of Daniel, but with a different corpus than that of Cook.[79] She limits her analysis to narrative clauses in the book of Daniel, excluding clauses found in poetry, prophetic visions, and in the interpretation of those visions because they may reflect elevated speech.[80] Like Cook, Hayes concludes that the subject normally precedes the verb in Biblical Aramaic. Focusing her study on the order of the verb and the object, she also sees SOV and SVO as coexisting basic word orders.[81]

According to Hayes, SVO order can be explained through case marking and the complexity of the object.[82] Hayes notes a cross-linguistic correlation between the presence or absence of case markings and rigidity of word order, and she observes that the verb in Biblical Aramaic tends to occur before the object when the object is marked with -לְ or יָת. Referring to the cross-linguistic principle that shorter elements tend to precede longer elements, Hayes notes that simple objects nearly always precede the verb in Biblical Aramaic whereas more complex ones almost always follow the verb. Mood, style, and topicalization account for the remaining exceptions to these trends, according to Hayes.[83]

7.4.5 Sung-dal Kwon

Finally, the work of Sung-dal Kwon represents a return to the traditional understanding of free word order in Biblical Aramaic.[84] Kwon's study is more comprehensive than those of Cook and Hayes in that he examines every clause in the entire Biblical Aramaic corpus, not just a limited portion. He emphasizes

---

77. Cook, "Word Order in the Aramaic of Daniel," 5–6.
78. Cook, "Word Order in the Aramaic of Daniel," 7–14.
79. Hayes, "Word Order in Biblical Aramaic," 2–11.
80. Hayes, "Word Order in Biblical Aramaic," 4.
81. Hayes, "Word Order in Biblical Aramaic," 4–5.
82. Hayes, "Word Order in Biblical Aramaic," 5–6.
83. Hayes, "Word Order in Biblical Aramaic," 7–10.
84. Kwon, "성서 아람어의 어순에 관한 [Word Order in Biblical Aramaic]," 52–74.

that every possible word order (i.e., SVO, SOV, VSO, VOS, OSV, and OVS) is attested in this corpus. Furthermore, in terms of the distributional difference between VO and OV, Kwon finds little difference with respect to main versus subordinate clauses and therefore argues that there is no apparent correlation between verb type and word order. The only noticeable pattern, according to Kwon, is that the subject most often comes before the predicate in nominal (i.e., verbless) clauses.[85]

In light of these observations, Kwon argues it is not possible to determine a basic word order for Biblical Aramaic. He then explores possible explanations for Biblical Aramaic's free word order, especially because the Semitic languages in general exhibit a VSO order.[86] He rejects pragmatic explanations that attempt to account for Biblical Aramaic's word order through information structure. Rather, Kwon attributes the flexibility of word order to the influence of Akkadian, which has an SOV word order, upon Aramaic speakers in Mesopotamia. According to Kwon, verb-initial Aramaic's linguistic contact with verb-final Akkadian in Mesopotamia accounts for the relatively even distribution between VO and OV in Biblical Aramaic.[87]

7.4.6 Evaluation

These studies on word order in Biblical Aramaic represent a significant advancement in the field. This is because traditional scholarship on word order in Biblical Aramaic did not offer conclusive proof for any particular position. Until recently there were no substantial treatments of this topic, and basic word orders were assumed rather than proven. Thus, the fact that word order in Biblical Aramaic has lately been a topic for investigation is a very good thing.

Nevertheless, scholarship on word order in Biblical Aramaic is quite diverse. All the scholars discussed above approach this topic from different starting points and very different linguistic frameworks. It would be beneficial for future scholarship to analyze word order in Biblical Hebrew without being so tied to such specific linguistic theories, as is the case for both Buth (Functional Grammar) and Lamprecht (the Minimalist Program). There remains significant need for defining basic word order in broader linguistic terms. Particularly important here is the need to establish which clauses should be included and which should be excluded when determining basic word order.

Another important issue surfaced by the above scholarship is how to account for the diversity of word orders attested in Biblical Aramaic. On the one hand,

---

85. Kwon, "성서 아람어의 어순에 관한 [Word Order in Biblical Aramaic]," 57–65.
86. Kwon, "성서 아람어의 어순에 관한 [Word Order in Biblical Aramaic]," 66–67.
87. Kwon, "성서 아람어의 어순에 관한 [Word Order in Biblical Aramaic]," 68–70.

Buth, Cook, and Hayes are right to invoke pragmatics as well as the possibility that features like modality or foregrounding can result in departures from word order. On the other hand, Kwon correctly draws attention to the possibility of language contact, especially since the word orders of Akkadian and Old Persian likely influenced Biblical Aramaic. A full-orbed model that accounts for multiple factors like these is likely to have the most potential.

Finally, the above studies demonstrate the need for situating word order in Biblical Aramaic within broader discussions of word order in the wider Aramaic corpus. The first millennium BCE attests to a plentiful and diverse corpus of Aramaic texts. This opens the door for comparison between Biblical Aramaic word order and the word orders of Old and Imperial Aramaic, especially given the Aramaic language's general shift from VSO to SVO during the first millennium BCE.[88] Yet only Buth has attempted to connect his understanding of Biblical Aramaic word order with this broader picture. Hopefully, others will contribute to this important conversation and enhance our understanding of the factors at play in Biblical Aramaic word order.

7.5 THE WAYS FORWARD

The most significant advance with respect to word order in the Hebrew Bible is that it is discussed at all. Thankfully, gone are the days when scholars simply assumed without proof that Biblical Hebrew and Biblical Aramaic exhibit a particular word order. Nevertheless, the question of basic word order in the Hebrew Bible remains disputed. The scholarly literature attests to a lively debate on this important issue, and it is likely that it will remain an important topic of conversation in the years ahead. I am hopeful that continued discussion will only clarify the issues that are now disputed.

Moving forward, perhaps the most important task at hand is clearly defining the notion of basic word order without overreliance on a specific linguistic framework like the Minimalist Program or Functional Grammar. The definition for word order adopted necessarily determines which clauses are considered when establishing basic word order, so more consensus here is crucial. By necessity, investigation of word order in Biblical Hebrew and Biblical Aramaic along these lines will have to give attention to the specific factors (e.g., pragmatics, modality, and discourse type) that can impact word order in particular situations.

As scholars look at these issues, hopefully they will also give attention to

---

88. Cf. Kaufman, "Aramaic," 127.

linguistic typology. Particularly important here is discussion of how the word orders of Biblical Hebrew and Biblical Aramaic fit within the typological context of the Semitic language family. The form and function of word order in other Semitic languages could potentially clarify word order in Biblical Hebrew and Biblical Aramaic. Ideally, any typological consideration of word order in the Hebrew Bible should incorporate both synchronic and diachronic factors.

Finally, scholars need to explore the implications that word order can have for interpretation of the Hebrew Bible. The contemporary debate over word order is certainly fascinating in and of itself. However, as exegetes our goal should always be faithful interpretation of Scripture. Word-order analysis ultimately enables us to understand and teach the Hebrew Bible more accurately and more precisely than we would otherwise. It is for this reason that word order remains an important topic for students, teachers, and pastors.

7.6 FURTHER READING

Buth, Randall. "Word Order in Aramaic from the Perspectives of Functional Grammar and Discourse Analysis." PhD diss., University of California, Los Angeles, 1987.

Holmstedt, Robert D. "The Typological Classification of the Hebrew of Genesis: Subject-Verb or Verb-Subject." *JHebS* 11.14 (2011): 1–39. http://www.jhsonline.org.

Hornkohl, Aaron D. "Biblical Hebrew Tense-Aspect-Mood, Word Order and Pragmatics: Some Observations on Recent Approaches." Pages 27–56 in *Studies in Semitic Linguistics and Manuscripts: A Liber Discipulorum in Honour of Professor Geoffrey Khan*. Edited by Nadia Vidro, Ronny Vollandt, and Esther-Miriam Wagner. Acta Universitatis Upsaliensis: Studia Semitica Upsaliensia 30. Uppsala: Uppsala Universitet, 2018.

Moshavi, Adina. "Word Order: Biblical Hebrew." *EHLL* 3:991–98.

———. *Word Order in the Biblical Hebrew Finite Clause: A Syntactic and Pragmatic Analysis of Preposing*. LSAWS 4. Winona Lake, IN: Eisenbrauns, 2010.

Zuo, Jeremiah Xiufu. *The Biblical Hebrew Word Order Debate: A Testing of Two Language Typologies in the Sodom Account*. GlossaHouse Thesis Series 3. Wilmore, KY: GlossaHouse, 2017.

CHAPTER 8

REGISTER, DIALECT, STYLE-SHIFTING, *and* CODE-SWITCHING

The sociolinguistics of Ancient and Modern Hebrew remains a field of pioneering research.

—MARIA MADDALENA COLASUONNO[1]

8.1 INTRODUCTION

Our tendency may be to think of Biblical Hebrew and Biblical Aramaic as unified, homogenous languages. The titles of most grammars, which have names like *Introduction to Biblical Hebrew Syntax* or *Grammar of Biblical Hebrew*, only reinforce this perception. However, all languages contain variation. Among other things, this variation depends on who speaks, when and where they are speaking, and their intended audience.

Biblical Hebrew and Biblical Aramaic are no exception to this basic feature of language. It should not surprise us that Biblical Hebrew in particular contains variation because the portions of the Hebrew Bible it represents were written by many different individuals over the course of a long span of time. Despite any editing and standardization that has taken place, the Hebrew Bible preserves the diverse origin of its contents just as any other diverse literary composition would. The scribes who preserved the Hebrew Bible for us—the Masoretes—did not attempt to obliterate these changes. Rather, they

---

1. Colasuonno, "Sociolinguistics," 3:584.

simply transmitted the Hebrew and Aramaic text as they received it, variations and all.[2]

This chapter investigates linguistic variation within the Hebrew Bible, which like the previous two chapters falls within the realm of pragmatics because it deals with language use. I begin with a general discussion of sociolinguistics, the branch of linguistics that provides the framework for understanding language variation. Then I survey several topics relevant for applying sociolinguistics to the Hebrew Bible: register, dialect, style-shifting, and code-switching. The important issue of how Biblical Hebrew and Biblical Aramaic may have changed over time presents unique challenges and is discussed separately in the next chapter.

8.2 THE MODERN LINGUISTIC FRAMEWORK FOR REGISTER, DIALECT, STYLE-SHIFTING, AND CODE-SWITCHING

Sociolinguistics is the study of linguistic variation. All languages contain variation because all languages contain a variety of ways to express something. This variation can be attributed to any number of explanations. These include social status, gender, age, perceptions of what is offensive and acceptable, standards of formality, and geography. Thus, as argued by Joshua A. Fishman, sociolinguistics seeks to determine who speaks what language to whom and when.[3]

The discipline of sociolinguistics largely has its origins in the work of the linguist William Labov, who began presenting and publishing on sociolinguistic phenomenon during the early 1960s. Particularly significant was his analysis of the social stratification of English in New York City, published in 1966. Labov connected linguistic variation with different social contexts, including social class, age, and gender.[4] Labov's pioneering research led to a flurry of research on language variation in America, Central America, and Europe. Today, sociolinguistics enjoys a prominent place within linguistics.[5]

The value of sociolinguistics for Hebraists is clearly articulated in a 2004 publication by William M. Schniedewind.[6] In this article, Schniedewind emphasizes that Biblical Hebrew can serve as a social marker because language and linguistic forms can reflect social groups. Calling for the application of sociolinguistics to Biblical Hebrew, he argues that potential methodological

---

2. Rendsburg, "Strata of Biblical Hebrew," 81.
3. Fishman, "Who Speaks What Language," 67–88.
4. Labov, *Social Stratification of English*.
5. Chambers, "Studying Language Variation," 1–4.
6. Schniedewind, "Sociolinguistics of Classical Hebrew," 1–32.

issues—including a limited written corpus and the lack of native speakers today—can be overcome by identifying and assessing the social forces that contributed to linguistic change in ancient Israel.

Schniedewind's study is largely conceptual and concerned with how one might go about integrating sociolinguistics with Hebrew Bible scholarship, leaving the task of exploring the details of variation in the Hebrew Bible to others. Maria Maddalena Colasuonno offers an excellent analysis of the Hebrew Bible's sociolinguistic variation in her PhD dissertation.[7] Gary A. Rendsburg and Agustinus Gianto present similar but smaller-scale surveys of the types of language variation that occur in the Hebrew Bible.[8] Frank H. Polak has spent much of his career investigating sociolinguistics as it relates to style; because his publications relate directly to the dating of biblical texts, I will return to his work in the next chapter.[9]

In sum, scholars like Schniedewind, Colasuonno, Rendsburg, Gianto, and Polak have put the sociolinguistic analysis of the Hebrew Bible on solid footing. Their work covers several different types of variation in the Hebrew Bible, including register, dialect, style-shifting, and code-switching. With the above sociolinguistic framework and their studies in mind, I now discuss these concepts in more detail.

8.3 REGISTER IN THE HEBREW BIBLE

One important aspect of sociolinguistics is *register*, a concept largely popularized in the 1960s by the functionalist M. A. K. Halliday.[10] A linguistic register may be defined as a variety of a language used in a particular setting. Formal settings require a different register of language than informal settings, written language requires a different register than spoken language, and the style of language used depends on the audience. For example, the styles of language I use when writing a book such as this, reporting to my academic dean, lecturing to my Hebrew students, texting my wife, and talking with my daughter are each very different.

As indicated by these examples, register is closely connected with genre.[11] Each genre, or type of literature, is characterized by a particular "style" of language. Whenever an author writes in a particular genre, he or she is expected

---

7. Colasuonno, "Linguistic Variation in Ancient Hebrew."

8. Rendsburg, "Strata of Biblical Hebrew," 81–99; Gianto, "Variations in Biblical Hebrew," 494–508.

9. Polak, "Parler de la langue," 13–37; Polak, "Sociolinguistics," 115–62.

10. E.g., Halliday, McIntosh, and Strevens, *Linguistic Sciences and Language Teaching*, 111–34.

11. Trosborg, "Text Typology," 3–23; Biber and Conrad, *Register, Genre, and Style*, 19–21.

to conform generally to that particular style. Otherwise, his or her writing (and the purpose of the writing) may be misunderstood. Thus, genre largely explains the similar styles between different pieces of literature and can account for register. At the same time, register also depends on a variety of other factors.

Many of the registers discussed by sociolinguists have also been studied to varying extents by scholars of Biblical Hebrew. I turn now to these different registers, which I discuss according to several different categories: generational register, gender register, politeness, and diglossia.

8.3.1 Generational Register

Each generation has its own particular way of speaking. Typically, older generations tend to be more conservative and resist change, whereas the speech of younger generations is more susceptible to change and contains new colloquialisms.[12] For example, younger generations are more likely than older generations to pick up recent slang or SMS abbreviations like *LOL*.

To my knowledge, no one has conducted a detailed study of generational register in the Hebrew Bible. One of the few scholars to even raise the issue is Edward F. Campbell, Jr., whose discussion of this topic is quite brief and limited to the book of Ruth.[13] Campbell notes allegedly archaic forms in the speech of Naomi and Boaz and concludes that they speak differently because they are older than Ruth.[14] Unfortunately, Campbell's analysis is quite limited in scope, and the forms he alleges are archaic can be better explained as style-shifting.[15] Accordingly, more work on generational register in the Hebrew Bible remains to be done.

8.3.2 Gender Register

Sociolinguists have observed how the speech of men and women sometimes differs. Important differences can appear regarding politeness and domination of the conversation, and some languages even have gender-specific vocabulary. The modern study of gender register originated with Robin Lakoff,[16] and since then scholars such as Deborah Tannen, Kira Hall, and Mary Bucholtz have further developed this concept.[17]

---

12. Coulmas, *Sociolinguistics*, 64–74.

13. Campbell, *Ruth*, 17, 24–25.

14. Among other features, Campbell points to feminine plural pronouns with *mem* rather than *nun* (Ruth 1:8–9), second-person feminine singular *qatal* forms ending with יתִּ- rather than תְּ- (Ruth 3:3–4), and usage of paragogic *nun* (Ruth 2:8–9; 3:4, 18). Holmstedt rejects these as archaic with the exception of the paragogic *nun* (*Ruth*, 49).

15. Cf. Bompiani, "Style Switching in the Speech of Transjordanians," 68–69.

16. Lakoff, *Language and Woman's Place*.

17. Tannen, *Gender and Discourse*; Hall and Bucholtz, *Gender Articulated*.

Although some scholars have examined the grammatical representation of gender in Biblical Hebrew,[18] little work has been done on gender register in the Hebrew Bible. That which exists focuses on the book of Ruth, which contains a good amount of female dialogue. Robert M. Johnson, Jr. compares the speech of Boaz with Naomi and Ruth.[19] He concludes that Naomi and Ruth speak more politely and less frequently than Boaz. Thus, according to Johnson, the book of Ruth presents the speech of men and women differently. Another scholar to treat this topic is Elitzur Avraham Bar-Asher.[20] He argues that Naomi's use of masculine-looking forms with reference to women (Ruth 1:8–9) is a literary way of representing female speech.

Given the limited nature of these two studies, there is need for more comprehensive examination of gender register in the Hebrew Bible. Our data on this topic, however, are admittedly limited.

8.3.3 Politeness

Because we use language to communicate with other people, language is interpersonal and directly connected with social dynamics. When people speak, they choose their words to match the expectations of their social context. This requires attention to the relationship between the speaker and the audience, and whether or not they have the same social status (e.g., greater to lesser, lesser to greater, or equals). It also requires attention to how one communicates respect. In sociolinguistics these issues all fall within the concept of *politeness*.

Modern politeness theory begins with the observation that human society contains social inequality. Politeness enables people to navigate this inequality because it establishes and maintains courtesy within society. Perhaps the most influential formulation of politeness theory is that of Penelope Brown and Stephen C. Levinson. They argue that speakers attempt to "save face," or maintain rapport with their audiences, by showing appreciation (positive politeness) or by interacting with their audiences in a non-threatening way (negative politeness).[21]

There are many different ways to express politeness. A speaker can communicate politeness by using a particular form that marks the degree of formality and deference he needs to show to his audience. Various other politeness techniques include the addition of politeness particles (e.g., *please*), indirectness (e.g., *Take out the trash!* versus *Could you take out the trash?*), and terms of address that express honor (e.g., *your royal highness*) or deference (e.g., *your servant*).

---

18. E.g., Stein, "Grammar of Social Gender," 7–26.

19. Johnson, "Words in Their Mouths."

20. Bar-Asher, "סימוני לשון במגילת רות [Linguistic Markers in the Book of Ruth]," 25–42.

21. Brown and Levinson, *Politeness*.

Recent research on politeness in Biblical Hebrew has focused largely on syntactical structures, politeness particles, and terms of address.[22] I now discuss each of these topics and provide evaluation along the way.

8.3.3.1 Syntactical Structures

Politeness can be encoded through syntactical structures, or specific forms that mark politeness. This method is not common in English and other Indo-European languages, but it is especially common in Asian languages such as Korean and Japanese, which use various levels of speech depending on the speaker's relationship to the audience.

It has long been recognized that the Biblical Hebrew imperative expresses a direct command whereas the jussive and cohortative are typically more indirect and therefore polite. Recent scholarship, however, has expanded our understanding of syntactical structures and politeness regarding several forms. These include the long imperative, the infinitive absolute, the prohibition לֹא + *yiqtol*, and *weqatal*. I now survey each of these forms.

8.3.3.1.1 LONG IMPERATIVE

One syntactical structure that relates to social dynamics is the long imperative. It looks similar to the simple imperative (כְּתֹב) but with final *qameṣ-he* (כָּתְבָה). Scholars have argued that the long imperative is a stylistic variant of the simple imperative,[23] is emphatic,[24] directs the action to the speaker,[25] or expresses a softened, polite command.[26] The problem with the first three of these views is that they cannot adequately explain the frequent presence of the long imperative within polite contexts and its complete absence from legal material (for which softened commands would not be appropriate).[27]

These observations indicate that scholars like Hélène M. Dallaire are right to say the long imperative softens requests. However, as she and others also point out, the long imperative is not used only by a lesser to a greater (e.g., Num 10:35; Deut 26:15) but can also sometimes be used by a greater to a lesser (e.g., Exod 32:10; 1 Kgs 21:2, 6) or between equals (e.g., 1 Sam 17:44). Thus, its usage is not limited to any particular social group even though it is connected with social dynamics and politeness.

---

22. Cf. Morrison, "Courtesy Expressions," 1:633–35; Di Giulio, "Mitigating Devices," 33–62.

23. E.g., *IBHS* §34.4.a; Lambdin, *Biblical Hebrew*, 114.

24. E.g., GKC §§48i, k; Joüon §48d.

25. E.g., Shulman, "Use of Modal Verb Forms," 65–84; Fassberg, "Lengthened Imperative קָטְלָה," 7–13.

26. E.g., Dallaire, *Syntax of Volitives*, 63–72; Jenni, "Höfliche bitte im Alten Testament," 3–16; Kaufman, "Emphatic Plea," 195–98.

27. Cf. Dallaire, *Syntax of Volitives*, 71–72.

8.3.3.1.2 INFINITIVE ABSOLUTE

A second syntactical structure sometimes connected with social dynamics is the infinitive absolute. Sometimes the infinitive absolute expresses a command, and the question is whether this function differs from the imperative at all. Some scholars say that the two are equivalent,[28] whereas at least one other claims it expresses a softer command than the imperative.[29] Most recent scholarship, however, argues that the infinitive absolute represents a strong, enduring command.[30]

This last function is likely given the infinitive absolute's frequent expression of general rules—rather than immediate commands—in legal material (e.g., Gen 17:10; Exod 20:8). Furthermore, the infinitive absolute is never accompanied by the politeness marker נָא and is always used by a greater to a lesser. These observations suggest that recent scholarship is right to characterize the infinitive absolute as a strong, enduring command. It does not attempt to "save face" or be polite in any way but represents a very direct request from a greater to a lesser.

8.3.3.1.3 PROHIBITION לֹא + *YIQTOL*

A third syntactical structure marked for social dynamics is the prohibition לֹא + *yiqtol*. This structure occurs, for example, in each of the Decalogue's prohibitions (Exod 20:3–5, 7, 13–17). At least one scholar contends that it is the equivalent of the simple prohibition expressed by אַל + jussive.[31] However, the vast majority of recent scholarship on this topic argues that לֹא + *yiqtol* expresses a strong, enduring prohibition.[32]

This conclusion makes the best sense of the contexts in which לֹא + *yiqtol* occurs. Particularly helpful from a sociolinguistics perspective is the work of Hélène M. Dallaire, who notes that לֹא + *yiqtol* is almost always used when a greater—most commonly God or one of his messengers—gives a prohibition to a lesser. She contrasts this with the usage of אַל + jussive, which appears in other social dynamics.[33]

8.3.3.1.4 *WEQATAL*

A fourth and final syntactical structure sometimes connected with social dynamics is *weqatal* (often called the perfect consecutive). Unlike the structures

---

28. E.g., Joüon §123u; Goddard, "Origin of the Hebrew Infinitive Absolute," 59–61.

29. E.g., Watts, "Infinitive Absolute as Imperative," 141–45.

30. E.g., Wang, "Use of the Infinitive Absolute," 99–105; Dallaire, *Syntax of Volitives*, 150–59; Shulman, "Use of Modal Verb Forms," 131–38; Hospers, "Imperative Use of the Infinitive Absolute," 97–102.

31. E.g., Gerstenberger, *Wesen und Herkunft*, 50–54.

32. E.g., Dallaire, *Syntax of Volitives*, 74–76, 97–100; Shulman, "Use of Modal Verb Forms," 148–58; Bright, "Apodictic Prohibition," 185–204; Stabnow, "Syntax of Clauses Negated by לֹא," 11–14.

33. Dallaire, *Syntax of Volitives*, 99.

previously discussed, the possible connection of *weqatal* with social dynamics has largely been ignored in the secondary literature. This is because much work on *weqatal* tends to focus on its aspect or discourse function.

However, recent work by Hélène M. Dallaire, Ahouva Shulman, and E. J. Revell has noted that volitive *weqatal* (i.e., *weqatal* following an imperative or the infinitive absolute) appears when a greater gives commandments to a lesser.[34] These same scholars note that God is very frequently the one who gives these commands and that the politeness particle נָא never occurs with volitive *weqatal*. These observations indicate that volitive *weqatal* expresses a strong command from a greater to a lesser.

8.3.3.1.5 Evaluation

This brief survey demonstrates that some good work has been done recently on syntactical structures and politeness. It is encouraging that recent scholarship is paying attention to social dynamics in this way. Nevertheless, there is need for further study. Much of the scholarship mentioned above does not frame its discussion in light of modern politeness theory. It would also be useful to compare these syntactical structures with parallel ones in the other Semitic languages. Hopefully, others will join this important conversation and add to our understanding of syntactical structures and social dynamics.

8.3.3.2 Politeness Markers

Many of the world's languages add particles to an utterance to make it more polite or mitigated. A good example of this is English *please*, added to soften a request's directness (e.g., *Sit down!* versus *Please sit down*). The addition of a politeness particle helps the speaker to "save face" with the audience, especially when he or she belongs to a lower social status than the audience.

Biblical Hebrew's main candidate for marking politeness is the particle נָא.[35] Many scholars argue either that נָא is emphatic (i.e., it draws attention to speech)[36] or marks logical consequence (i.e., "then" or "therefore").[37] However, נָא frequently occurs with volitive forms in contexts that focus on the addressee, and it never appears within legislative material. Emphasis and logical conse-

---

34. Dallaire, *Syntax of Volitives*, 144–50; Shulman, "Imperative and Second Person Indicative Forms," 271–87; Revell, "System of the Verb," 21–25.

35. Other words used for mitigation include אַךְ ("only"), רַק ("only"), אוּלַי ("perhaps"), and מְעַט ("a little") (Di Giulio, "Mitigating Devices," 47–52).

36. Bar-Magen, "המלה 'נא' במקרא [The Word 'נָא' in the Bible]," 163–71; Juhás, *Biblisch-hebräische Partikel* נָא.

37. Lambdin, *Biblical Hebrew*, 170; Fassberg, סוגיות בתחביר המקרא [*Studies in Biblical Syntax*], 36–73; cf. *IBHS* §34.7.

quence should not be limited to such contexts. For this reason, much recent work adopts the ancient rabbinic understanding that נָא marks politeness (*Ber.* 9a; *Sanh.* 43b; 89b).[38] Particularly insightful from a sociolinguistic perspective is the work of Timothy Wilt. In accordance with modern politeness theory, he distinguishes between direct volitives (i.e., volitives without נָא) and volitives that "save face" and are marked for politeness (i.e., volitives with נָא).[39]

As these recent studies argue, understanding נָא as a politeness marker that softens requests makes good sense of the data. Nevertheless, there is room for further discussion. One issue especially needing clarification is the usage of נָא with the singular cohortative, which is not easily translated politely in certain contexts (e.g., soliloquies). To deal with this difficulty, Bent Christiansen argues that נָא indicates the propositive mood, which expresses proposals or suggestions.[40] However, such a function does not fit the usage of נָא everywhere. Worthy of further pursuit is Stephen A. Kaufman's argument that נָא softens a request and that the cohortative with נָא means "I think it may be a good idea to . . . . "[41]

8.3.3.3 Terms of Address

Terms of address express the social status of a conversation's participants. Many languages use a special form to address someone within a formal setting, especially when that person has a high social status. Honorific forms may appear as special titles (e.g., *Mr.*, *Mrs.*, *Dr.*, and *Rev.*) or distinct grammatical forms used for formal versus informal settings (e.g., formal *usted* versus informal *tú* in Spanish). A person of low social status may also use deferential forms when speaking (e.g., *your servant* instead of the normal *me* or *I*). Our modern understanding of terms of address can be traced to the work of Roger Brown, Albert Gilman, and Marguerite Ford, who first published on this topic around 1960.[42]

There are only a few studies on terms of address in the Hebrew Bible, none of which examines this important topic comprehensively. In a very brief discussion, Cynthia Miller-Naudé distinguishes between speaker-based deference (e.g., אֲדֹנִי "my lord") and addressee-based deference (e.g., עַבְדְּךָ "your servant"), as well as indirect address (e.g., עַבְדּוֹ "his servant" and הַמֶּלֶךְ "the king") in the books of Genesis through Kings.[43] E. J. Revell's treatment of this topic—which

---

38. Dallaire, *Syntax of Volitives*, 53–58; Kaufman, "Emphatic Plea," 195–98; Shulman, "Particle נָא," 57–82; Wilt, "Sociolinguistic Analysis of *nāʾ*," 237–55; Jenni, "Höfliche bitte im Alten Testament," 1–16.

39. Wilt, "Sociolinguistic Analysis of *nāʾ*," 237–55.

40. Christiansen, "Biblical Hebrew Particle *nāʾ*," 379–93.

41. Kaufman, "Emphatic Plea," 197–98; cf. Shulman, "Particle נָא," 77–79.

42. Gilman and Brown, "Who Says 'Tu' to Whom," 169–74; Brown and Gilman, "Pronouns of Power and Solidarity," 253–76; Brown and Ford, "Address in American English," 375–85.

43. Miller-Naudé, *Representation of Speech*, 269–81.

is limited to the books of Judges, Samuel, and Kings—examines how characters are addressed, the relationship of speaker and addressee, the attitude of the speaker toward the addressee, and the social context in which the term of address appears.[44] Other noteworthy studies include Bryan D. Estelle's works on deferential language in the Hebrew Bible (Esther, Daniel, and Ezra) and extrabiblical Aramaic (the Arsames Correspondence and Ahiqar)[45] and Edward J. Bridge's analysis of deferential slave terms in the Hebrew Bible.[46]

It is encouraging to see this attention to forms of address in the Hebrew Bible. Nevertheless, each of these studies is far from comprehensive in terms of corpus and scope. Furthermore, many of these studies have not clearly applied a modern understanding of terms of address to the Hebrew Bible. Accordingly, there is still significant room for work in this important area.

Thankfully, at least one scholar has recently taken on this task. Young Bok Kim is currently completing a dissertation at the University of Chicago on forms of address in the Hebrew Bible.[47] His study seeks to be comprehensive and will be well-informed by modern understandings of address terms and politeness theory. We look forward to his contribution.

8.3.4 Diglossia

The fourth and final topic of register is *diglossia*, or a language community's use of a "high" literary register and a "low" colloquial register. The literary register is more formal and used in "high" contexts such as literature, and the colloquial register is informal and used in everyday speech. It has long been recognized that many languages often contain these two registers (e.g., literary Arabic versus spoken Arabic, standard French versus Haitian Creole). However, the modern notion of diglossia can largely be attributed to the linguist Charles A. Ferguson, who defined the state of the field in a 1959 article.[48]

Like most religious texts, the Hebrew Bible represents a high literary register rather than a spoken, colloquial one.[49] Nevertheless, scholars have often wondered if traces of spoken Hebrew can be found. Accordingly, the existence of colloquial language in the Old Testament was the object of several studies during the twentieth century. G. R. Driver argued that unusual forms in the

---

44. Revell, *Designation of the Individual*.

45. Estelle, "Know Before Whom You Stand"; idem, "Deferential Language," 43–74; idem, "Esther's Strategies," 61–88.

46. Bridge, "Use of Slave Terms."

47. Kim, "Hebrew Forms of Address."

48. Ferguson, "Diglossia," 325–40; idem, "Diglossia Revisited," 214–34.

49. Ullendorff, "Is Biblical Hebrew a Language?" 241–55.

Old Testament may reflect colloquialisms,[50] and J. MacDonald tried to find colloquialisms in direct speech.[51] However, the modern study of diglossia in the Hebrew Bible is largely the work of Gary A. Rendsburg.

8.3.4.1 Gary A. Rendsburg

Rendsburg argues that the Hebrew Bible contains various colloquialisms that represent the spoken rather than literary dialect of ancient Hebrew.[52] He observes that the Hebrew of the Dead Sea Scrolls (i.e., Qumran Hebrew) and of the Mishnah (i.e., Mishnaic Hebrew) coexisted as literary and colloquial dialects, respectively. Rendsburg then argues that Mishnaic Hebrew is the descendant of earlier colloquial Hebrew, just as Qumran Hebrew grew out of the literary dialect of the Hebrew Bible. He identifies colloquialisms in the Hebrew Bible as features that resemble Mishnaic Hebrew, such as gender neutralization in pronouns (e.g., צֹאנָם with third-person feminine plural referent in Exod 2:17) and use of the anticipatory pronominal suffix (e.g., אֲנִי נֹתֵן לָהֶם לִבְנֵי יִשְׂרָאֵל "I give to them, to the children of Israel" in Josh 1:2). As noted by Rendsburg, many of these same types of colloquialisms are also characteristic of colloquial Arabic.

8.3.4.2 Ian Young

Ian Young also postulates the existence of diglossia in ancient Israel, although his reconstruction is slightly different than Rendsburg's.[53] Young argues that Biblical Hebrew represents a literary dialect that originated as a pre-Israelite, Canaanite prestige language. Behind this literary language are numerous colloquial registers—in other words, multiple diglossia—that reflect the social diversity of the Israelite tribes. These many different registers largely account for the Hebrew Bible's linguistic variation. According to Young, the exile brought about linguistic unity as well as a religious unity centered on Torah. The result was a single diglossia, the precursor of Mishnaic Hebrew. I will return to Young's work, which has important bearing on the possible diachronic development of Biblical Hebrew, in the next chapter.

8.3.4.3 Scobie Philip Smith

Scobie Philip Smith presents a completely different picture of diglossia.[54] He agrees that Mishnaic Hebrew and Qumran Hebrew represent colloquial and

---

50. Driver, "Colloquialisms in the Old Testament," 232–39.

51. MacDonald, "Distinctive Characteristics of Israelite Spoken Hebrew," 162–75.

52. Rendsburg, "Diglossia: Biblical Hebrew," 1:724–25; idem, *Diglossia in Ancient Hebrew*.

53. Young, *Pre-Exilic Hebrew*.

54. Smith, "Question of Diglossia," 37–52.

literary registers during the Second Temple period. However, he disagrees that diglossia is attested for the biblical period and critiques Rendsburg's approach. Specifically, he characterizes Rendsburg's identification of colloquialisms as *ad hoc*, disputes Rendsburg's use of cognates as methodologically problematic, and accuses Rendsburg of ignoring Hebrew inscriptions as a possible source of colloquialisms.

8.3.4.4 Maria Maddalena Colasuonno

Maria Maddalena Colasuonno also challenges Rendsburg's view of diglossia.[55] She argues that Rendsburg has not adequately addressed the different roles that spoken and written Hebrew would have in biblical times. She also disputes several of the features that Rendsburg identifies as diglossia, contending that they can be explained in other ways (e.g., contact with Aramaic and intentional literary devices). Colasuonno concludes that the sociolinguistic situation of ancient Israel is best understood as a mixture of dialects rather than diglossia as postulated by Rendsburg.

8.3.4.5 Other Voices

A number of other scholars have contributed to the conversation on diglossia. Among those accepting the existence of diglossia are Daniel C. Fredericks, who attributes some of Ezek 1's unusual language to colloquialisms, and Takamitsu Muraoka, who suggests that the alternation between אֲשֶׁר and -שֶׁ in the book of Jonah reflects literary and colloquial registers.[56] Others have been more skeptical. Sverrir Ólafsson suggests that alleged colloquialisms are either slips of later scribes influenced by Mishnaic Hebrew or dialectal variations.[57] Joshua Blau understands linguistic variation as reflecting different scribal traditions rather than genuine diglossia.[58]

8.3.4.6 Evaluation

As this brief survey demonstrates, the existence of diglossia in the Hebrew Bible is a lively topic of debate. Rendsburg's research provides a good foundation for the discussion, but much work remains to be done. The possible connection of colloquialisms with genre needs to be explored in more detail. Also to be investigated is the relationship of the Hebrew Bible's diglossia to

---

55. Colasuonno, "Problem of Diglossia in Biblical Hebrew," 124–45.

56. Fredericks, "Diglossia, Revelation, and Ezekiel's Inaugural Rite," 189–99; Muraoka, "Diglossia in the Book of Jonah?" 129–31.

57. Ólafsson, "On Diglossia in Ancient Hebrew," 193–205.

58. Blau, "שתלשלות עברית המקרא [Development of the Hebrew Bible]," 21–32.

formal and colloquial registers preserved in extrabiblical Hebrew inscriptions. As these and other questions are examined, there is the need for interaction with modern linguistic conceptions of diglossia and clearly established models of diglossia in other languages, especially Arabic.

8.4 DIALECT IN THE HEBREW BIBLE

A *dialect* may be defined as a variety of a language associated with a particular region or people group. The English language exists as many different dialects, each associated with a different part of the world. For example, American English uses different spellings and expressions than, say, British English (e.g., in American English *pants* refers to an outer garment worn on the legs whereas in British English *pants* refers to underwear). Dialect differs from register in that it reflects a relatively permanent pattern of language. Specifically, it represents what people speak regularly because it is determined by where one lives geographically.[59]

Linguists disagree on what makes something a dialect rather than a language—it is often said that "a language is a dialect with an army and a navy"—but one commonly suggested criterion is mutual intelligibility (i.e., a speaker proficient in one dialect must be able to understand enough of a related dialect).[60] The study of dialects goes back to the medieval period, but in its modern form dialectology can be traced to nineteenth- and twentieth-century European philologists who produced grammars of regional dialects.[61]

The famous "shibboleth" incident of Judg 12:5–6 attests to the existence of different dialects in ancient Israel. Taking this as a starting point, already during the early twentieth century C. F. Burney detected traces of different dialects in the Hebrew Bible.[62] Subsequent scholars postulated the existence of Israelian Hebrew, a dialect of Hebrew spoken in the northern portions of ancient Israel.[63] They argued that Israelian Hebrew differs lexically and grammatically from the standard Judahite dialect that makes up most of the Hebrew Bible.

Recently, scholars such as W. Randall Garr and Stephen A. Kaufman have provided a helpful framework for understanding the ancient Northwest Semitic dialects.[64] In accordance with modern dialectology they view these dialects

---

59. Halliday and Hasan, *Language, Context, and Text*, 43.

60. Chambers and Trudgill, *Dialectology*, 3–4.

61. Cf. Petyt, *Study of Dialect*, 37–57.

62. Burney, *Hebrew Text of the Books of Kings*, 208–9; Burney, *Book of Judges*, 171–76.

63. *Israelian* Hebrew is not to be confused with *Israeli* Hebrew, the form of Hebrew spoken in Israel today.

64. Garr, *Dialect Geography*; Kaufman, "Classification of the North West Semitic Dialects," 41–57.

along a dialect continuum, with Phoenician and Aramaic on opposite sides of the spectrum. However, as far as ancient Hebrew dialects go, the most prolific author is undoubtedly Gary A. Rendsburg. I begin with discussion of his work before turning to other scholars who have treated this topic.

8.4.1 Gary A. Rendsburg

Gary A. Rendsburg has surveyed Israelian Hebrew in numerous articles and monographs.[65] He argues that much of the Hebrew Bible—which was written about Jerusalem and Judah—represents a Judahite dialect of Hebrew. However, a significant portion can also be attributed to the north, such as portions of Judges that take place in the north (e.g., the narratives concerning Deborah, Gideon, and Jephthah) and material in the book of Kings devoted to the Northern Kingdom of Israel. In addition to geographical clues, Israelian Hebrew can be identified through vocabulary and grammar that is atypical to Judahite Hebrew but is attested in Semitic languages spoken to the north (e.g., Ugaritic, Phoenician, and Aramaic).

By Rendsburg's calculations, at least 15 percent of the Hebrew Bible represents Israelian Hebrew.[66] In addition to Judges and Kings, it can be found in blessings to the northern tribes (e.g., Gen 49; Deut 33), prophetic oracles that relate to the north (e.g., Hosea, Amos, and Micah), northern psalms (e.g., Pss 9–10, 29, 36, 45, 53, 132), and other compositions with northern connections (e.g., Proverbs, Song of Songs, and Ecclesiastes). Rendsburg also suggests that the Hebrew Bible contains a small amount of material written in the Samaritan and Benjaminite dialects, primarily in texts that concern these regions (e.g., the Benjaminite dialect is found in portions of Jeremiah and texts regarding the tribe of Benjamin).

8.4.2 Daniel C. Fredericks

Daniel C. Fredericks was the first scholar to offer a substantial critique of Rendsburg's approach to dialects and Israelian Hebrew.[67] He does not reject the existence of different dialects but thinks that we are not able to identify them reliably. Fredericks observes that many features said to be northern do not occur exclusively in Israelian Hebrew but also occur in southern Judahite texts. He also wonders why such features occur only sporadically in Israelian

---

65. E.g., Rendsburg, "Dialects and Linguistic Variation," 1:338–41; idem, "Northern Hebrew through Time," 339–59; idem, "Comprehensive Guide to Israelian Hebrew," 5–35.

66. Sometimes, according to Rendsburg, a Judahite author incorporates Israelian Hebrew into the speech of characters who live in the north (e.g., the wise woman of Tekoa in 2 Sam 14). When these texts are included, the corpus of Israelian Hebrew grows to nearly 25 percent of the Hebrew Bible.

67. Fredericks, "North Israelite Dialect in the Hebrew Bible," 7–20.

Hebrew, suggesting that more should be present if a text is genuinely northern. Fredericks concludes that many features attributed to Israelian Hebrew should instead be explained as colloquialisms.

8.4.3 Na'ama Pat-El

Na'ama Pat-El has offered another substantial critique of Rendsburg. Like Fredericks, Pat-El does not deny the existence of dialects in ancient Israel but questions whether or not we can reliably identify them.[68] She argues that just because a text takes place in the north does not mean that it represents the northern dialect. She critiques the identification of northern characteristics as features also found in Northwest Semitic languages north of ancient Israel because, being a Northwest Semitic language, Hebrew will naturally share features with other Northwest Semitic languages. Ultimately, Pat-El concludes that the Hebrew Bible reflects a standard scribal tradition, a learned, written form that obliterates dialectical differences.

8.4.4 Other Voices

Several other scholars have contributed to the conversation on dialect in the Hebrew Bible. Of these, some follow Rendsburg in identifying other dialects whereas others dispute his argumentation.

On the one hand, some scholars maintain that different dialects are observable in the Hebrew Bible. Most of these, but not all, are associated with Rendsburg in some way. Several of Rendsburg's students have completed dissertations on Israelian Hebrew (Chen Yiyi and Yoon Jong Yoo[69]) and the Benjaminite dialect (Collin J. Smith[70]). Richard M. Wright and Scott B. Noegel, two of Rendsburg's former students, have written on dialectical features since completing their doctorates.[71] The Japanese scholar Jun Ikeda has written several articles on dialects in the Hebrew Bible, focusing especially on Israelian Hebrew in the book of Kings.[72] William M. Schniedewind and Daniel Sivan accept the existence of Israelian Hebrew in Kings but argue that its identification requires a more robust methodology than Rendsburg's.[73]

---

68. Pat-El, "Israelian Hebrew," 227–63.

69. Yiyi, "Israelian Hebrew in the Book of Proverbs"; Yoo, "Israelian Hebrew in the Book of Hosea."

70. Smith, "With an Iron Pen and a Diamond Tip."

71. Wright, "North Israelite Contributions," 129–48; Noegel, "Dialect and Politics in Isaiah 24–27," 177–92.

72. Ikeda, "聖書ヘブライ語に見られる地域差について [Regional Dialects in Biblical Hebrew]," 1–16; idem, "Three Notes on Israelian Hebrew Syntax," 51–65; idem, "聖書ヘブライ語における言語変種 [Linguistic Varieties in Biblical Hebrew]," 179–204; idem, "ユダとイスラエル [Judah and Israel]," 1–21.

73. Schniedewind and Sivan, "Elijah-Elisha Narratives," 303–37.

On the other hand, other scholars dispute the existence of Israelian Hebrew, or at least argue for more caution in identifying its features. Ian Young questions Rendsburg's methodology and suggests that variant features are not "northern" but intentional literary representations of foreigners.[74] Similarly, David Talshir contends that some features commonly identified as northern reflect linguistic diversity—but not Israelian Hebrew—because they occur in non-northern texts.[75]

8.4.5 Evaluation

Once again, the work of Rendsburg provides an excellent starting point for the ongoing discussion of dialects in the Hebrew Bible. However, similar to the topic of diglossia, a more careful methodology is needed for identifying different dialects. Scholars should operate under a model in which geographical association suggests—but does not definitively prove—dialectal association with that region. In addition, more attention should be given to possible dialectal features as they fit within the dialect continuum of Northwest Semitic. Particularly helpful here will be the recognition that not all isoglosses (i.e., dialect features) are created equal—grammatical features of greater frequency in normal speech are more useful for classification than infrequent ones.[76] Such an approach may help determine whether a feature is authentically dialectal, especially given the fact that "northern" features are often found in non-northern texts.

Another possibility to be considered is that unusual features in the biblical text represent a literary dialect rather than a geographical dialect. In other words, perhaps some unusual features reflect an intentional literary device on the part of the biblical author to color the text in some way. This leads us to the final topic I discuss in this chapter, the phenomena of style-shifting and code-switching.

8.5 Style-Shifting and Code-Switching in the Hebrew Bible

Style-shifting, sometimes called *style-switching* by biblical scholars, refers to the intentional use of different language varieties (i.e., styles or dialects) within speech or writing; the similar phenomenon of *code-switching* refers to the

---

74. Young, "'Northernisms' of the Israelite Narratives in Kings," 63–70; cf. idem, "Evidence of Diversity," 7–20.

75. Talshir, "Habitat and History of Hebrew," 270–75.

76. Cf. Kaufman, "Classification of the North West Semitic Dialects," 47–48.

intentional use of two different languages, rather than language varieties.[77] Although scholars of literature began discussing these concepts in written texts during the mid-1900s,[78] for the most part linguists have focused on style-shifting and code-switching in speech rather than the literary kind. However, that situation is now changing as scholars have begun to address style-shifting and code-switching in ancient, medieval, and modern literature.[79]

In literature, style-shifting and code-switching can have several different functions. Most often, they mark out different parts of a text or portray characters in specific ways. They are commonly used in literature and are, in many ways, the mark of a good writer because they give the text an authentic feel and aid characterization. For example, in *The Lord of the Rings* J. R. R. Tolkien recounts the speech of his characters differently in order to portray them differently. This is particularly evident in the account of the Council of Elrond at Rivendell.[80] For example, the elf king Elrond uses archaic vocabulary and inverted word order whereas the dwarf Glóin uses short sentences and apposition:

[Glóin:] "Also we crave the advice of Elrond. For the Shadow grows and draws nearer. We discover that messengers have come also to King Brand in Dale, and that he is afraid. We fear that he may yield. Already war is gathering on his eastern borders . . . ."

[Elrond:] "You have done well to come . . . . You will hear today all that you need in order to understand the purposes of the Enemy. There is naught that you can do, other than to resist, with hope or without it. But you do not stand alone. You will learn that your trouble is but part of the trouble of all the western world. The Ring! What shall we do with the Ring, the least of rings, the trifle that Sauron fancies? That is the doom that we must deem. That is the purpose for which you are called hither."[81]

Scholars have long recognized the presence of stylistic and non-native elements in the Hebrew Bible, but it was not until recently that scholars began to

---

77. Despite this difference between them, the terms "style-shifting" and "code-switching" are often used interchangeably, especially in Hebrew and Aramaic studies.

78. E.g., Ives, "Theory of Literary Dialect," 137–82. This essay was reprinted in revised form in *A Various Language*, 144–77.

79. E.g., Gordon and Williams, "Raids on the Articulate," 75–96; Hess, "Code Switching and Style Shifting," 5–18; Gardner-Chloros and Weston, "Code-Switching and Multilingualism in Literature," 182–93.

80. Shippey, *J.R.R. Tolkien*, 68–77. Tolkien also uses foreign elements (i.e., code-switching) to aid in characterization; see Bütikofer, "Lord of the Languages."

81. Tolkien, *Fellowship of the Ring*, 255.

investigate these phenomena in detail. Chaim Rabin was the first in the modern era to identify a particular example of them,[82] and subsequent scholars such as Avi Hurvitz, Jonas C. Greenfield, and E. Y. Kutscher have suggested that the biblical authors color foreigners' speech with stylistic and non-native elements.[83] Since then, the primary scholars to discuss these concepts in detail are Stephen A. Kaufman, Gary A. Rendsburg, and Brian A. Bompiani. I now discuss their contributions along with several other more minor voices, focusing especially on style-shifting because that has occupied the most scholarly attention.

8.5.1 Stephen A. Kaufman

Stephen A. Kaufman was the first scholar to draw significant attention to the phenomenon of style-shifting in Biblical Hebrew.[84] He argues that Aramaisms (i.e., Aramaic-like features) need not reflect a postexilic text written under Aramaic influence or translation from Aramaic as is often argued. Rather, Aramaisms frequently serve as intentional, stylistic representations of Trans-Jordanian speech on the part of Hebrew authors. Kaufman points to several different examples of style-shifting, including the oracles of Balaam (Num 22–24), the words of Agur and Lemuel (Prov 30:1–31:9), the desert oracles of Isaiah (Isa 21:11–14), and the poetic speeches of the book of Job, especially those of Elihu (Job 32–37).

In addition, Kaufman also speaks very briefly to style-shifting in Biblical Aramaic within the broader context of Imperial Aramaic.[85] He notes that Imperial Aramaic, including Biblical Aramaic, evidences a tendency toward verb-final position in clauses. According to Kaufman, this tendency cannot reflect Aramaic's actual word order because verb-final word order is not attested in later Aramaic dialects. Rather, Kaufman argues that the use of verbs in final position reflects a literary artifice, specifically an attempt to mimic the Aramaic of native Persian speakers.

8.5.2 Gary A. Rendsburg

Gary Rendsburg's work on dialects and diglossia in the Hebrew Bible naturally entails discussion of style-shifting.[86] He builds significantly on the work

---

82. Rabin, "Arabic Phrase in Isaiah," 303–9.

83. Hurvitz, "Aramaisms in Biblical Hebrew," 236–37; Greenfield, "Aramaic Studies and the Bible," 129; Kutscher, *History of the Hebrew Language*, 72–73.

84. Kaufman, "Classification of the North West Semitic Dialects," 54–56.

85. Kaufman, "Aramaic," 127; idem, "Aramaic," 4:177.

86. Rendsburg, "Style-Switching," 3:633–36; idem, "Style-Switching in Biblical Hebrew," 65–85; idem, "Linguistic Variation and the 'Foreign' Factor," 178–84; idem, "Kabbîr in Biblical Hebrew," 649–51.

of Kaufman by discussing this topic in more detail and providing additional examples of style-shifting, such as the narratives about finding a wife for Isaac (Gen 24), Jacob's sojourn in Aram (Gen 29–31), the Gibeonite deception (Josh 9), and the Aramean Naaman (2 Kgs 5–6). According to Rendsburg, style-shifting is most often employed when the scene shifts to a foreign land or a foreigner is present in the land of Israel.

Rendsburg also discusses what he calls "addressee-switching," or the use of non-Hebrew elements in prophetic oracles to the foreign nations.[87] He finds evidence of addressee-switching in the books of Isaiah (Isa 17:10, 12; 18:12–13; 33:12), Jeremiah (Jer 48:36; 49:25), and Ezekiel (Ezek 26:11; 32:19), as well as the Minor Prophets (Joel 4:5; Zech 9:3). Addressee-switching, according to Rendsburg, helps us to better appreciate the rhetorical devices employed by the biblical prophets.

8.5.3 Brian A. Bompiani

Brian A. Bompiani, one of Kaufman's students, contributes significantly to our understanding of style-shifting in the Hebrew Bible.[88] He finds additional examples of style-shifting not specifically discussed by Kaufman and Rendsburg (e.g., the speech of Esau in Gen 25:30). He also formulates a clear methodology for identifying style-shifting, based largely on Avi Hurvitz's methodology for identifying diachronic change in Biblical Hebrew.[89] According to Bompiani, the use of rare forms that take the place of everyday vocabulary or grammar are likely to represent style-shifting. This is especially the case when the rare form is found at key junctures in a narrative (especially the first time a foreign character speaks), is juxtaposed with a synonymous form used by a Hebrew speaker, or is accompanied by other unusual forms. Thus, for example, the use of the otherwise-unattested הַלְעִיטֵנִי ("give me to eat") in Esau's first recorded words (Gen 25:30), rather than the expected Hiphil of אכל, reflects Esau's characterization as a foreigner.

Bompiani argues that style-shifting helps us to appreciate the literary genius of the Hebrew Bible's authors. Style-shifting encourages us to pay attention to the details of biblical narrative so that we can better understand and interpret it. Bompiani also notes how style-shifting provides an alternative explanation

---

87. Rendsburg, "Addressee-Switching," 1:34–35; idem, "Linguistic Variation and the 'Foreign' Factor," 184–88; idem, "Kabbîr in Biblical Hebrew," 649–51; idem, "False Leads in the Identification of Late Biblical Hebrew Texts," 23–46.

88. Bompiani, "Style-Switching"; idem, "Style Switching in the Jacob and Laban Narratives," 43–57; idem, "Style Switching in the Speech of Transjordanians," 51–71; idem, "Is Genesis 24 a Problem for Source Criticism?" 403–15.

89. Cf. Hurvitz, בין לשון ללשון [Between Languages], 67–69.

for the presence of Aramaisms and synonymous word-pairs. Rather than indicating a late text or different authors, these features can simply reflect the literary artistry of the biblical writers.

8.5.4 Other Voices

A number of other scholars, many of them students of Kaufman and Rendsburg, have joined the fray and also written on style-shifting in the Hebrew Bible. Aside from Bompiani, Kaufman has supervised theses on style-shifting by Laura S. Lieber (on the book of Judges) and Elaine A. Bernius (on the book of Job).[90] Rendsburg has supervised a dissertation by Clinton J. Moyer that includes discussion of style-shifting in the oracles of Balaam (Num 22–24).[91] Other contributions include a brief survey of style-shifting in the book of Ruth by Robert D. Holmstedt and Ian Young's identification of features in the book of Kings as style-shifting rather than Israelian Hebrew.[92]

In addition to style-shifting, several scholars have also explored code-switching. A few studies investigate code-switching within Biblical Hebrew.[93] However, most discussion of code-switching has focused on the bilingual nature of the books of Daniel and Ezra, which contain both Hebrew and Aramaic. For scholars like Bill T. Arnold and Joshua A. Berman, switching between Hebrew and Aramaic reflects a shift in perspective: the use of Hebrew represents the perspective of the Judean exiles, whereas the use of Aramaic represents an external, international perspective.[94] Timothy Hogue further labels the Aramaic of Ezra's narratives as local, like the Hebrew of the book, and the Aramaic of Ezra's letters as internationalist.[95] Arnaud Sérandour instead attributes the language used to the difference between profane and sacred subject matter.[96] These and other studies offer interesting sociolinguistic—rather than diachronic or structural—explanations of the bilingualism in the books of Daniel and Ezra.

8.5.5 Evaluation

Style-shifting and code-switching offer many powerful explanations for linguistic variation in the Hebrew Bible. Kaufman and Rendsburg are to be

---

90. Lieber, "Regional Dialect in the Book of Judges"; Bernius, "When Foreigners Speak."

91. Moyer, "Literary and Linguistic Studies in *Sefer Bilʿam*."

92. Holmstedt, *Ruth*, 41–49; Young, "'Northernisms' of the Israelite Narratives in Kings," 63–70.

93. E.g., Holmstedt and Kirk, "Subversive Boundary Drawing in Jonah," 542–55.

94. Arnold, "Use of Aramaic in the Hebrew Bible," 1–16; Berman, "Narratological Purpose of Aramaic," 165–91.

95. Hogue, "Return from Exile," 54–68.

96. Sérandour, "Bilinguisme dans le livre d'Esdras," 131–44.

thanked for drawing attention to these phenomena. The work of Bompiani especially offers a solid approach for identifying and understanding style-shifting in the Hebrew Bible. I trust that scholars will adopt his methodology and discover additional examples of style-shifting as well as code-switching.

One area that needs special attention is addressee-switching. Although Rendsburg has drawn attention to this phenomenon, there are still no comprehensive studies on this important topic. Examination of addressee-switching will undoubtedly enhance our understanding of the prophets' various oracles against the nations and increase our appreciation for their literary artistry.

Another area that requires investigation is code-switching with languages that are not Northwest Semitic. Nearly all analyses of code-switching focus on the literary use of Northwest Semitic languages, especially Aramaic. However, scholars need to explore possible literary usage of Akkadianisms in contexts associated with the Assyrians or the Babylonians. Furthermore, the Hebrew Bible also uses non-Semitic words within the speech of foreigners (e.g., the Egyptian exclamation אַבְרֵךְ "pay attention!" in Gen 41:43) or within oracles against the nations (e.g., the Egyptian loans יְאֹר "Nile," סוּף "reed, rush," and עָרָה "reed" in Isa 19, an oracle against Egypt). I have investigated examples of non-Semitic code-switching in some detail in my own research on the Hebrew Bible's non-Semitic terminology,[97] but there is still work to be done.

8.6 THE WAYS FORWARD

The above survey demonstrates that sociolinguistic analysis of the Hebrew Bible's variation is a fruitful field of study. A number of different scholars—especially Gary A. Rendsburg and Stephen A. Kaufman—have clearly shown the benefits of applying sociolinguistics to Biblical Hebrew and Biblical Aramaic. Their attention to register, dialect, style-shifting, and code-switching offers a powerful explanation for much of the Hebrew Bible's linguistic variation.

Yet, as stated by Maria Maddalena Colasuonno, the sociolinguistics of the Hebrew Bible "remains a field of pioneering research" and "further investigation may shed light on general sociolinguistic phenomena in the history of the language."[98] As Hebrew Bible scholars respond to this challenge, they will need to interact more explicitly with current research on sociolinguistics. Scholars will also need to develop a cogent methodology for determining which of the available explanations applies to a given instance of variation, giving special

---

97. Noonan, *Non-Semitic Loanwords in the Hebrew Bible*.
98. Colasuonno, "Sociolinguistics," 3:584.

attention to the likelihood of style-shifting or code-switching. In addition to register, dialect, style-shifting, and code-switching, another possible explanation is the diachronic development of Biblical Hebrew and Biblical Aramaic. This is the topic of the next chapter.

8.7 Further Reading

Colasuonno, Maria Maddalena. "Linguistic Variation in Ancient Hebrew (1000 BCE–200 CE)." PhD diss., University of Naples, 2015.

———. "Sociolinguistics." *EHLL* 3:581–84.

Gianto, Agustinus. "Variations in Biblical Hebrew." *Bib* 77 (1996): 494–508.

Kaufman, Stephen A. "The Classification of the North West Semitic Dialects of the Biblical Period and Some Implications Thereof." Pages 41–57 in *Proceedings of the Ninth World Congress of Jewish Studies, Jerusalem, 4–12 August, 1985: Division D: Panel Sessions, Hebrew and Aramaic Languages*. Jerusalem: Magnes, 1988.

Kawashima, Robert S. "Stylistics: Biblical Hebrew." *EHLL* 3:643–50.

Person, Raymond F., Jr. "Linguistic Variation Emphasized, Linguistic Variation Denied." Pages 119–25 in *The Archaeology of Difference: Gender, Ethnicity, Class, and the "Other" in Antiquity: Studies in Honor of Eric M. Meyers*. Edited by Douglas R. Edwards and C. Thomas McCoullough. AASOR 60-61. Boston: American Schools of Oriental Research, 2007.

Polak, Frank H. "Parler de la langue: Labov, Fishman et l'histoire de l'hébreu biblique." Pages 13–37 in *Le Proche-Orient ancien à la lumière des sciences sociales*. Edited by Madalina Vârtejanu-Joubert. Yod 18. Paris: Publications langues O', 2013.

———. "Sociolinguistics: A Key to the Typology and the Social Background of Biblical Hebrew." *HS* 47 (2006): 115–62.

Rendsburg, Gary A. *How the Bible Is Written*. Peabody, MA: Hendrickson, 2019.

———. "The Strata of Biblical Hebrew." *JNSL* 17 (1991): 81–99.

Schniedewind, William M. "Prolegomena for the Sociolinguistics of Classical Hebrew." *JHebS* 5.6 (2004): 1–32.

———. *Social History of Hebrew: Its Origins through the Rabbinic Period*. ABRL. New Haven: Yale University Press, 2013.

CHAPTER 9

DATING BIBLICAL HEBREW *and* BIBLICAL ARAMAIC TEXTS

There is advancement in our understanding of the diachrony of Biblical Hebrew. . . . There is progress in the debate in that misunderstandings have been clarified and claims have become more nuanced.

—JACOBUS A. NAUDÉ AND CYNTHIA L. MILLER-NAUDÉ[1]

9.1 INTRODUCTION

In the last chapter I introduced the concept of sociolinguistic variation within the Hebrew Bible. The forms of variation I considered were primarily synchronic in that they related to the coexistence of different linguistic features—features that exist at the same point in time but are spoken by different groups of people in different places. Another important aspect of linguistic variation is diachronic variation, or the change of a language over time. We should expect to find this kind of variation in the Hebrew Bible, which describes events that span approximately 1500 years and therefore was probably written over a long period of time.

So, it should come as no surprise that many interpreters have also looked to chronology to explain some of the Hebrew Bible's variation. They identified early features in books believed to be earlier and late features in books describing events from late in Israel's history. Identification of these chronological markers then helped scholars to date the Hebrew Bible's many anonymous portions. This, in turn, enabled them to establish the historical contexts for those parts of the Hebrew Bible, providing a solid foundation for exegesis. Linguistic dating thus has very practical application for biblical interpretation.

---

1. Naudé and Miller-Naudé, "Historical Linguistics, Editorial Theory, and Biblical Hebrew," 834.

However, in recent years an increasing number of scholars have questioned whether Biblical Hebrew and Biblical Aramaic exhibit diachronic change. So, in this chapter I survey the present debate over diachrony in the Hebrew Bible. I first examine the notions of language change and linguistic dating within the context of historical linguistics. Then I summarize and evaluate the debates over dating Biblical Hebrew texts and Biblical Aramaic texts. I conclude with a summary of the resulting advances and then suggest some possible ways forward, focusing especially on how this debate is relevant for exegeting the Hebrew Bible.

9.2 THE MODERN LINGUISTIC FRAMEWORK FOR DATING ANCIENT TEXTS

In this section I examine the modern linguistic framework for dating ancient texts as a background to discussing diachrony in the Hebrew Bible. Two concepts are especially important: language change, which falls under the realm of historical linguistics, and linguistic dating, which falls under the realm of philology. I now explore both language change and linguistic dating in some detail.

9.2.1 Language Change

All languages change over time. To help appreciate the reality of this fact, consider the following English translations of John 3:16. Each represents a different stage in the development of the English language, beginning with Old English and continuing until our time.

Old English	God lufode middan-eard swa þæt he seale his áncennedan Sunu þæt nán ne forweorðe þe on hine gelyfð ac hæbbe þæt ece líf. (*The West-Saxon Gospels*, ca. 1050)
Middle English	For God louede so the world, that he ȝaf his oon bigetun sone, that ech man that bileueth in him perische not, but haue euerlastynge lijf. (*Wycliffe Bible*, fourteenth century)
Early Modern English	For God so loued þe world, that he gaue his only begotten Sonne: that whosoeuer beleeueth in him, should not perish, but haue eternall life. (*King James Version*, 1611)
Modern English	For God so loved the world that he gave his one and only Son, that whoever believes in him shall not perish but have eternal life. (*New International Version*, 2011)

Comparison of the above translations reveals changes regarding phonology and orthography, grammar, and the lexicon. Earlier stages of English use some consonants unfamiliar to us today (þ, ð, and ჳ), and some words are spelled differently (e.g., *hæbbe* and *haue* for modern English *have*). Grammatically, earlier English dialects use *eth* for modern English *(e)s*, as is evident in earlier forms of the word *believes* (i.e., *bileueth* and *beleeueth*). Even the words used are different: for example, the *West-Saxon Gospels* uses words that are now obsolete like *middan-eard* ("world") and *forweorðan* ("to perish"). Changes like these are the object of study of historical linguistics, which explores the change of language over time.[2]

Historical linguists typically distinguish between *internal* and *external* causes of language change.[3] Internal change occurs within the language itself, due to physical and psychological factors. One important type of internal change is *sound change*, which tends to take place in certain linguistic situations.[4] An example of this from Biblical Hebrew is the Canaanite shift, in which *ā* became *o* when accented, as is evident in Hebrew שָׁלוֹם ("peace"; cf. Arabic *salām*, pronounced with the original *a*-vowel). Another important type of internal change is *analogy*.[5] Through analogy, a feature of a language that applies in one situation is extended to a different situation. In Hebrew, the so-called pseudo-cohortative is a good example of this. Based on the similarity between *wayyiqtol* and *waw* + volitive forms, a *wayyiqtol* form was created from the cohortative, complete with final *he* (וָאֶכְתְּבָה).

External change is motivated by factors outside the language. The most frequent form of external change is *borrowing*, or the adoption of a particular feature from another language.[6] Languages borrow from other languages for many reasons, but the two most common are necessity (i.e., lack of a native way to express something) and prestige (i.e., because a foreign linguistic feature is highly esteemed).[7] Borrowings often appear as *loanwords*, or words adopted from another language.[8] Loanwords in Biblical Hebrew come from other Semitic languages (e.g., סֶגֶן "governor, prefect" < Akkadian *šaknu*) or non-Semitic languages (e.g., פַּרְעֹה "Pharaoh" < Egyptian *pr-ʿ³* and פַּרְדֵּס "garden" < Old Iranian *pardēza-*). However, phonological, morphological, and syntactical features can also be borrowed.

---

2. Campbell, *Historical Linguistics*, 3–5.

3. Campbell, *Historical Linguistics*, 325–26.

4. Campbell, *Historical Linguistics*, 14–46; Hock and Joseph, *Language History, Language Change, and Language Relationship*, 8–9.

5. Campbell, *Historical Linguistics*, 91–105; Hock and Joseph, *Language History, Language Change, and Language Relationship*, 9–10.

6. Campbell, *Historical Linguistics*, 56–75; Hock and Joseph, *Language History, Language Change, and Language Relationship*, 13–14.

7. Campbell, *Historical Linguistics*, 58–59.

8. Campbell, *Historical Linguistics*, 56–57.

Internal and external changes operate at different levels, as demonstrated best by William Labov.[9] Internal change occurs within a language from below. In other words, internal changes happen naturally—and relatively regularly—with little, if any, awareness of the language speakers. This is because internal changes simply come about as language is transmitted from one generation to the next. Nevertheless, external change also plays a significant role. External change is change from above, or change that takes place when language speakers consciously adopt a non-native linguistic feature. It takes place through diffusion, which is naturally less predictable than transmitted change.

9.2.2 Linguistic Dating of Written Texts

Languages themselves cannot be dated because they are always changing, but linguistic features found in a language can, in theory, be dated.[10] Philologists attempt to date texts linguistically in light of what they know of the language's development. They determine how that language changed by applying principles of historical linguistics and by comparing related (i.e., cognate) languages. This allows them to identify early and late features in the language, in at least relative but often absolute terms. In this way, specific linguistic features can be linked with a particular stage of the language.

With a knowledge of these features, philologists can date texts that do not possess any extra-linguistic evidence—such as colophons or discovery of the manuscript *in situ*—for their date. The most common application of linguistic dating takes place with medieval European texts, whose existing manuscripts are either undated or are copies of earlier, now lost manuscripts. Examples of texts that fall into this category include Old English poetry like *Beowulf*, Old French literature like the *Chanson de Roland*, Middle French plays (e.g., *Le Mystère de la Passion Nostre Seigneur*), undated medieval charters written in Latin, and Old Norse poetry attested in the *Poetic Edda*.[11] Although European literature has seen the most use of linguistic criteria to date texts, a similar approach has been applied to other texts, including ancient Near Eastern literature.[12]

---

9. Labov, *Principles of Linguistic Change*, 1:421–543, 3:305–66; cf. Campbell, *Historical Linguistics*, 185–97; Hock, *Principles of Historical Linguistics*, 627–61.

10. Alinei, "Problem of Dating in Linguistics," 212–13.

11. E.g., Fulk, "*Beowulf* and Language History," 19–36; idem, "Archaisms and Neologisms," 267–88; idem, *History of Old English Meter*; Russom, "Dating Criteria for Old English Poems," 245–65; Amos, *Dates of Old English Literary Texts*; Farrier, "Linguistic Dating of the Oxford *Chanson de Roland*"; Runnalls, "Linguistic Dating of Middle French Texts," 757–61; Gervers, *Dating Undated Medieval Charters*; Tilahun, Feuerverger, and Gervers, "Dating Medieval English Charters," 1615–40; Fidjestøl, *Dating of Eddic Poetry*.

12. E.g., Stauder, *Linguistic Dating of Middle Egyptian Literary Texts*; Moers, Widmaier, and Giewekemeyer, *Dating Egyptian Literary Texts*; Phua, "Dating the Chapters in *Guanzi*."

To date texts like these, scholars turn to a variety of linguistic criteria, including phonological, morphological, syntactical, and lexical features. As an example, consider some of the evidence for dating *Beowulf*. Considerations of phonology and meter are especially helpful here.[13] *Beowulf* contains words that must date early because the poem treats them metrically as if they are early, prior to certain changes in the English language. For example, *Beowulf*'s meter indicates that the word *hleahtor* ("laughter") was treated as the monosyllabic **hleahtr* before parasiting (i.e., the addition of a vowel before *r*) took place during the seventh century CE. *Beowulf* also contains other archaisms that point to an early date. For example, regarding morphology, the poem uses the old genitive plural *ia* (for later *a*) with the words *Dene* ("Dane") and *wine* ("friend"). As another example, regarding syntax, *Beowulf* uses the dative case to mark the direct object for verbs beginning with the prefix *for* (e.g., *forgrindan* "crush"). *Beowulf* shows signs of scribal updating, but there is otherwise no clear evidence of linguistic innovation. This observation, contrasted with the poem's archaic features, points to an early (i.e., eighth century CE) composition for *Beowulf*.[14]

Linguistic dating is not foolproof. In absence of a clear chronological anchor, linguistic features like phonology can only provide a relative chronology. Because of limitations like these, lexical evidence is often the most useful criterion for linguistic dating.[15] Furthermore, it is always possible that a text was updated or that the text's author tried to make his language look older than it really was. Nevertheless, linguistic criteria are held to be a generally reliable form of dating texts. They cannot provide definitive proof of a text's date in the scientific sense, but they can indicate probable dates.[16]

9.3 THE DATING OF BIBLICAL HEBREW TEXTS

With the above linguistic framework in mind, I explore the application of linguistic dating to Biblical Hebrew. Traditionally, scholars have argued that the Hebrew Bible evidences three distinct phases in the stage of the Hebrew language: Archaic Biblical Hebrew (ABH) from the late second millennium BCE, a classical form of Hebrew called Standard Biblical Hebrew (SBH) from the period of the monarchy, and an exilic-postexilic form of Hebrew called Late Biblical Hebrew (LBH). Extrabiblical Hebrew inscriptions from

---

13. Cf. Fulk, *History of Old English Meter*, 66–268.
14. Fulk, "*Beowulf* and Language History," 19–36; idem, "Archaisms and Neologisms," 267–88.
15. Cf. Alinei, "Problem of Dating in Linguistics," 213–16, 222–31.
16. Cf. Fulk, "On Argumentation in Old English Philology," 1–26.

the preexilic period are also attested. During the Second Temple period, Hebrew further developed into the Hebrew attested in the Dead Sea Scrolls, other non-canonical writings (e.g., Ben Sira), and eventually Rabbinic Hebrew.[17]

Phase of Hebrew	Date	Texts
Archaic Biblical Hebrew	1200–1000 BCE	Blessing of Jacob (Gen 49:1–27), Song of the Sea (Exod 15:1–18), Balaam's Oracles (Num 23–24), Song of Moses (Deut 32:1–43), Blessing of Moses (Deut 33:2–29), Song of Deborah (Judg 5:2–31), Song of Hannah (1 Sam 2:1–10), Song of David (2 Sam 22:2–51)
Standard Biblical Hebrew	1000–600 BCE	Genesis–Numbers (except for the P source), Deuteronomy, Joshua, Judges, 1–2 Samuel, 1 Kings 1–2 Kings 23, Isaiah 1–39, Hosea, Amos, Obadiah, Micah–Zephaniah
Late Biblical Hebrew	600–200 BCE	the P source, 2 Kings 24–25, Ezra–Esther, Ecclesiastes, Isaiah 40–66, Jeremiah, Lamentations, Ezekiel, Daniel, Haggai–Malachi
Post-Biblical Hebrew	200 BCE– 100 CE	Ben Sira Masada Fragments Dead Sea Scrolls Samaritan Pentateuch
Rabbinic Hebrew	100–400 CE	Bar Kokhba Letters Mishnah Tosefta

However, this consensus has been challenged in recent years. Within the past few decades a handful of scholars—particularly Ian Young, Robert Rezetko, and Martin Ehrensvärd—have argued that ABH, SBH, and LBH should be explained as different but coexisting scribal styles rather than distinct chronological phases of the Hebrew language. Not surprisingly, these ideas have been met with significant opposition by those holding to traditional diachronic typology. The resulting conversation has led to a better understanding of dating biblical texts and of Biblical Hebrew as a language.

---

17. Cf. Kutscher, *History of the Hebrew Language*, 77–85; Sáenz-Badillos, *History of the Hebrew Language*, 50–75, 112–29; Young, Rezetko, and Ehrensvärd, *Linguistic Dating of Biblical Texts*, 1:10–11.

9.3.1 Establishment of a Diachronic Typology for Biblical Hebrew

The earliest studies on diachronic typology were those of William F. Albright and two of his students, Frank Moore Cross and David Noel Freedman. These early studies focused exclusively on ABH as it appears in poetry. The 1970s saw further exploration of ABH through the work of David A. Robertson. It was also during the 1970s that serious investigation of LBH began under Robert Polzin, Paul D. Hanson, and Avi Hurvitz. In this section I survey the work of each of these scholars, focusing especially on Hurvitz because he has contributed most significantly to establishing a methodology for diachronic analysis of the Hebrew Bible.

9.3.1.1 William F. Albright, Frank Moore Cross, and David Noel Freedman

Initial exploration of chronological typology began under William F. Albright. Although certainly gifted in many areas, Albright's primary field was archaeology. His familiarity with ceramic typology, which proposes a relative chronology for pottery in light of various features, led him to propose a similar relative chronology for Biblical Hebrew poetry.[18] Albright relies on stylistic features like repetitive parallelism (e.g., עוּרִי עוּרִי דְּבוֹרָה עוּרִי עוּרִי דַּבְּרִי־שִׁיר, "Awake, awake, Deborah! Awake, awake, sing a song!" [Judg 5:12]), typical of Ugaritic poetry, as well as themes attested in Ugaritic literature (e.g., victory over the sea) to establish his typology. However, he also points to linguistic features like the remnants of case endings and defective orthography as characteristic of ABH.

Two of Albright's most influential students were Frank Moore Cross and David Noel Freedman, who co-wrote one of their PhD dissertations on archaic biblical poetry and subsequently published it as *Studies in Ancient Yahwistic Poetry*.[19] Following their mentor, Cross and Freedman argue that it is possible to establish a typology of Biblical Hebrew poetry analogous to ceramic typology.[20] Like Albright they point to archaic stylistic and thematic features to support the antiquity of certain poems. Included among the archaic features they discuss are metrical structure, the preservation of case endings, and the use of *yiqtol* as a preterite or true imperfect. But, unlike Albright, they rely more significantly on defective orthography as a marker of archaic poetry.[21]

---

18. E.g., Albright, "Catalogue of Early Hebrew Lyric Poems," 1–39; idem, "Earliest Forms of Hebrew Verse," 69–86; idem, "Oracles of Balaam," 207–33; idem, "Remarks on the Song of Moses," 339–46; idem, "Additional Notes on the Song of Deborah," 284–85.

19. Their dissertation was completed in 1950 at Johns Hopkins University, and the original edition of *Studies in Yahwistic Poetry* was published in 1975.

20. E.g., Cross and Freedman, "Blessing of Moses," 191–210; idem, "Song of Miriam," 237–50; idem, "Royal Song of Thanksgiving," 15–34.

21. Cf. Cross and Freedman, *Studies in Ancient Yahwistic Poetry*, 21–25.

The ABH corpus as defined by Albright, Cross, and Freedman spans several centuries.[22] The oldest poems, which date to the thirteenth through tenth centuries BCE, are the Song of the Sea (Exod 15), the Song of Deborah (Judg 5), the Oracles of Balaam (Num 23–24), the Song of Moses (Deut 32), and the Blessing of Moses (Deut 33). Dating to the tenth century BCE are David's Lament (2 Sam 1:19–27) and Jacob's Last Blessing (Gen 49). Finally, David's Thanksgiving Hymn (2 Sam 22 // Ps 18) and Habakkuk's Psalm (Hab 3) date to the ninth through eighth centuries BCE.

9.3.1.2 David A. Robertson

The early study of ABH found its fullest expression in David A. Robertson's *Linguistic Evidence in Dating Early Hebrew Poetry.*[23] Robertson's reliance upon linguistic evidence—rather than stylistic, orthographical, and historical concerns—sets his work apart from that of his predecessors. Robertson takes as his starting point the typology of the classical prophets, whose writings reflect "standard" poetic Hebrew. According to Robertson, ABH's features can be reconstructed by correlating rare grammatical features of Biblical Hebrew poetry with Ugaritic poetry and the language of the Amarna Letters.[24]

Robertson identifies six key features of ABH that he connects with Ugaritic and Amarna Akkadian: use of the *yiqtol* prefix-form as a preterite and true imperfect, preservation of the *yod/waw* in final *yod/waw* roots, use of זֶה/זֹה/זוּ as relative pronouns, the third-person masculine singular pronominal suffix -ֹהוּ, the third-person masculine plural suffix -מוֹ, use of *yod* and *waw* as affixes, and use of enclitic *mem.*[25] According to Robertson, only the use of *yiqtol* and the pronominal suffix -מוֹ occur frequently enough to be significant for dating.

To demonstrate that these features are genuine archaic features, Robertson shows that hymnic poetry did not significantly differ from prophetic poetry during the eighth century BCE or afterward.[26] This enables Robertson to establish an ABH corpus. He dates Exod 15 and Judg 5 to the twelfth century BCE and Deut 32, 2 Sam 22 // Ps 18, Hab 3, and the poetic portions of Job to the eleventh–tenth centuries BCE. He also dates Ps 78 early, to the late tenth or early ninth century BCE.[27]

---

22. Cf. Vern, *Dating Archaic Biblical Hebrew Poetry*, 11.

23. This work originated as Robertson's PhD dissertation completed at Yale University in 1966.

24. Robertson, *Linguistic Evidence in Dating Early Hebrew Poetry*, 2–5.

25. Robertson, *Linguistic Evidence in Dating Early Hebrew Poetry*, 7–146.

26. Robertson, *Linguistic Evidence in Dating Early Hebrew Poetry*, 147–53.

27. Robertson, *Linguistic Evidence in Dating Early Hebrew Poetry*, 153–56.

9.3.1.3 Paul D. Hanson

Paul D. Hanson similarly adopts Cross's and Freedman's typological approach.[28] Like Cross and Freedman, and Albright before them, he believes that it is possible to establish a typology of Biblical Hebrew poetry, analogous to ceramic typology.[29] But, rather than focusing on ABH, Hanson applies the typological approach to LBH as it appears in the poetic material of Third Isaiah and Second Zechariah. His approach to typology examines prosodic structure and poetic meter as markers of these texts' late date.

First, regarding prosodic structure, Hanson pays particular attention to the length of poetic cola.[30] He claims, like Cross and Freedman, that ABH poetry is characterized by relatively short bi- or tri-cola. According to Hanson, classical Hebrew poetry largely adopted this poetic structure. But later poetry—specifically that of Third Isaiah and Second Zechariah—instead tends to contain longer, embellished cola. Hanson supports this development in Biblical Hebrew by comparing a similar development in Akkadian poetry.

Second, regarding poetic meter, Hanson argues that LBH's increase in colon length produces a more erratic metrical pattern.[31] He adopts a syllable-counting approach, rather than an accent-counting method, to determine poetic meter. He therefore labels each colon as long (*longum*) or short (*breve*) based on the number of syllables it contains. Hanson finds that the poetic meter of Third Isaiah and Second Zechariah contrasts with the meter of classical Hebrew poetry. According to Hanson, LBH poetry as found in Third Isaiah and Second Zechariah tends to be less stable and exhibits more variety than that of classical Hebrew poetry.

9.3.1.4 Robert Polzin

Robert Polzin compares the language of Chronicles and the P source.[32] Like Hanson, Polzin also focuses on the distinction between SBH and LBH. On the whole, his approach differs significantly from that of Hanson. Polzin analyzes LBH with the goal of establishing its primary features and characteristics. The book of Chronicles forms the basis for Polzin's analysis of LBH because he considers the non-synoptic portions of Chronicles the most representative example of LBH.[33]

---

28. Hanson, *Dawn of Apocalyptic*. This work originated as Hanson's PhD dissertation completed at Harvard University in 1969.

29. Hanson, *Dawn of Apocalyptic*, 47.

30. Hanson, *Dawn of Apocalyptic*, 46–47.

31. Hanson, *Dawn of Apocalyptic*, 47–48.

32. Polzin, *Late Biblical Hebrew*. This work originated as Polzin's PhD dissertation completed at Harvard University in 1971.

33. Polzin, *Late Biblical Hebrew*, 1–2.

Polzin identifies LBH's characteristics as found in Chronicles. He finds both grammatical and lexical characteristics of LBH in this corpus, but he considers grammatical features to be more reliable than lexical features and therefore settles on nineteen grammatical—not lexical—characteristics of LBH.[34] He divides these features into those that developed within Hebrew independently (e.g., increased use of שֶׁל to express possession) and those that developed under Aramaic influence (e.g., use of לְ- to mark direct objects).

Polzin contrasts these features with those of other portions of the Hebrew Bible. He compares the LBH of Chronicles with samples from the J and E sources (exemplified by the books of Exodus and Numbers), the Succession Narrative (2 Sam 13–20; 1 Kgs 1), Deuteronomy, and the P source.[35] Of particular note is Polzin's conclusion that P serves as a transition between SBH and LBH, and should be dated to the exilic period.[36] In this he differs from other scholars like Avi Hurvitz, who instead argues that the book of Ezekiel serves as the transition between SBH and LBH.

Polzin's approach to diachronic typology serves as the basis for several other studies on LBH. Andrew E. Hill uses Polzin's LBH features to determine whether Malachi and Second Zechariah are closer to SBH or LBH. Based on the number of SBH versus LBH features they contain, he concludes that they typologically match early exilic material.[37] Allen R. Guenther compares the syntax of Jer 37–45 and Esth 1–10, isolating various features that represent diachronic syntactic change between the two corpora.[38] Similar to Hill, Guenther then places Jer 37–45 and Esth 1–10 typologically within Polzin's framework.

9.3.1.5 Avi Hurvitz

Avi Hurvitz is perhaps the most influential scholar working on diachronic typology. Since the completion of his dissertation on the diachronic typology of post-exilic psalms,[39] Hurvitz has devoted most of his research to diachronic typology.[40] Hurvitz argues that the Hebrew Bible attests to two

---

34. Polzin, *Late Biblical Hebrew*, 27–84, 123–58.

35. Polzin, *Late Biblical Hebrew*, 85–115.

36. Polzin, *Late Biblical Hebrew*, 111–12.

37. Hill, "Book of Malachi"; idem, "Dating the Book of Malachi," 77–89; idem, "Dating Second Zechariah," 105–34.

38. Guenther, "Diachronic Study of Biblical Hebrew Prose Syntax."

39. Hurvitz, "בחנים לשנויים לזהוי מזמורים מאוחרים [Linguistic Investigations into the Identification of Late Psalms]." Hurvitz's dissertation was later published as בין לשון ללשון [*Between Languages*].

40. E.g., Hurvitz, "Linguistic Criteria," 74–79; idem, *Relationship between the Priestly Source and the Book of Ezekiel*; idem, "Language of the Priestly Source," 83–94; idem, "Aramaisms in Biblical Hebrew," 234–40; idem, "Usage of שש and בוץ in the Bible," 117–21. Many of these articles have been republished in מבראשית לדברי הימים [*From Genesis to Chronicles*].

major typologies, each linked to a particular time in history: preexilic SBH as attested in the Pentateuch and Deuteronomistic History, and postexilic LBH as found in Esther, Daniel, Ezra–Nehemiah, and Chronicles.[41] For Hurvitz, the upheaval of the exile and resulting contact with Aramaic significantly changed the Hebrew language so that it became LBH. The exile had such an impact, furthermore, that it became impossible for postexilic Hebrew speakers to speak or even perfectly mimic SBH.[42]

Hurvitz uses three criteria to identify LBH features in Biblical Hebrew: linguistic distribution, linguistic opposition, and extrabiblical sources.[43] First, regarding the criterion of linguistic distribution, any LBH feature must occur exclusively or primarily in undisputed postexilic books (i.e., Esther, Daniel, Ezra–Nehemiah, and Chronicles). Second, the criterion of linguistic opposition requires that any LBH feature be used in place of a clear SBH counterpart of similar meaning. This ensures that the proposed feature is actually a new one and not simply a feature that was unattested in SBH. Third, the criterion of extrabiblical sources requires that any LBH feature also appear in extrabiblical texts like the Dead Sea Scrolls or Mishnaic Hebrew. According to Hurvitz, a book or text can be identified as LBH only if it contains a significant accumulation of LBH features.[44]

For Hurvitz, the most reliable features are lexical rather than grammatical.[45] Of special note here are Aramaisms (words borrowed or influenced by Aramaic) and Persian and Greek loanwords (words borrowed into Hebrew from Persian and Greek). One of his classic examples along these lines entails the words מַמְלָכָה and מַלְכוּת, both of which mean "kingdom."[46] The form מַלְכוּת occurs frequently in Esther–Chronicles, but only rarely elsewhere, where מַמְלָכָה is instead more common. Given this distribution, and because מַמְלָכָה and מַלְכוּת have the same meaning, Hurvitz argues that in LBH מַלְכוּת replaces SBH's מַמְלָכָה. This was prompted by emergence of Aramaic as an ancient Near Eastern *lingua franca* as indicated by the fact that מלכות is the typical Aramaic word for "kingdom." מַלְכוּת's identification as an LBH feature is then confirmed by its common usage in the Dead Sea Scrolls and Rabbinic Hebrew.

As noted earlier, Hurvitz has had significant influence on studies of

---

41. Hurvitz, "Linguistic Criteria," 76; idem, "Language of the Priestly Source," 84–85; idem, *Relationship between the Priestly Source and the Book of Ezekiel*, 157–58.

42. Hurvitz, "Linguistic Criteria," 76; idem, "Language of the Priestly Source," 84–85; idem, "Aramaisms in Biblical Hebrew," 234.

43. Hurvitz, "Linguistic Criteria," 74–79.

44. Hurvitz, "Linguistic Criteria," 76–77.

45. Cf. Hurvitz et al., *Concise Lexicon of Late Biblical Hebrew*.

46. Hurvitz, בין לשון ללשון [*Between Languages*], 79–88, 110–13.

diachronic typology. William James Adams, Jr. does not adopt Hurvtiz's methodology but does share his concern for extrabiblical sources; he uses diachronic variation in Hebrew inscriptions (dating from the tenth century BCE through the first century CE) as an external control to determine the date of biblical texts.[47] Many other scholars have applied Hurvitz's methodological approach directly to specific corpora of the Hebrew Bible. Ronald L. Bergey applies Hurvitz's methodology to the book of Esther, arguing that Esther is a postexilic composition.[48] Mark F. Rooker similarly analyzes the book of Ezekiel, concluding from the book's ratio of SBH to LBH features that Ezekiel reflects a transitional stage between SBH and LBH.[49] Richard M. Wright argues that the J source is preexilic in light of its features, which contrast with those of LBH.[50] Finally, using Hurvitz's methodology Aaron D. Hornkohl dates the book of Jeremiah to the sixth century BCE.[51]

9.3.2 Challenges to Diachronic Typology

Hurvitz's primary contribution to our understanding of diachronic typology is his formulation of a methodology for distinguishing between SBH and LBH—he made it possible to date biblical texts purely by linguistic means. As already noted, Hurvitz's methodology was applied to specific portions of the Hebrew Bible by his own students and others. Even Hebraists who did not directly engage in diachronic typology considered Hurvitz's approach and results reliable. The outcome was that, by the turn of the twenty-first century, the vast majority of the scholarly community believed that Biblical Hebrew texts could be dated linguistically.[52]

This all changed drastically, however, early in the new millennium. In 2003 *Biblical Hebrew: Studies in Chronology and Typology* (edited by Ian Young) appeared. Although many of the essays in this volume championed diachronic typology, several of them challenged it. In response, the National Association of Professors of Hebrew arranged special sessions to explore dating biblical texts at the 2004 and 2005 annual meetings of the Society of Biblical Literature.[53]

---

47. Adams, "Diachronic Distribution of Morphological Forms and Semantic Features"; idem, "Dating of Biblical Passages," 160–64.

48. Bergey, "Book of Esther"; idem, "Late Linguistic Features in Esther," 66–78; idem, "Linguistic Developments in Esther," 161–68.

49. Rooker, *Biblical Hebrew in Transition.*

50. Wright, *Pre-Exilic Date of the Yahwistic Source.*

51. Hornkohl, *Language of the Book of Jeremiah.*

52. Cf. Kim, *Early Biblical Hebrew, Late Biblical Hebrew, and Linguistic Variability*, 1–2.

53. "Historical Linguistics and the Dating of Biblical Texts," San Antonio, TX, November 22, 2004 and "Historical Linguistics and the Dating of Biblical Hebrew Texts: A Second Round of Presentations," Philadelphia, PA, November 21, 2005.

The contributions to these sessions were published in two issues of the journal *Hebrew Studies*, volumes 46 (2005) and 47 (2006).[54] As in *Biblical Hebrew: Studies in Chronology and Typology*, the contributors included advocates of diachronic typology as well as those opposed to it.

The most significant challenge to Hurvitz's approach appeared a few years afterward with the 2008 publication of *Linguistic Dating of Biblical Texts* by Ian Young, Robert Rezetko, and Martin Ehrensvärd. This was the first comprehensive work to directly challenge Hurvitz's method, and with a unified voice, too. In light of its importance, most of my survey of challenges to diachronic typology in this section focuses on the contribution of this work, although I consider some other key challengers as well.

9.3.2.1 *Linguistic Dating of Biblical Texts* (*LDBT*)

In *Linguistic Dating of Biblical Texts* (*LDBT*), Ian Young, Robert Rezetko, and Martin Ehrensvärd argue that the scholarly use of language in dating biblical texts—and even the traditional standpoint on the chronological development of Biblical Hebrew—require thorough reevaluation.[55] Their criticism of traditional diachronic typology focuses on four key issues: methodology, the use of Aramaisms and loanwords, textual fluidity, and non-diachronic variation in the Hebrew Bible.

First, *LDBT* criticizes Hurvitz's methodology.[56] Young, Rezetko, and Ehrensvärd observe that SBH features occur in LBH and that LBH features occur in SBH. The primary difference between SBH and LBH, in their opinion, is the accumulation of specific features. They acknowledge that SBH tends to have a higher accumulation of SBH features than LBH and that LBH tends to have a higher accumulation of LBH features than SBH. But, Young, Rezetko, and Ehrensvärd also point out that very few features said to belong to a particular time period are characteristic of every book in that corpus. For them the lack of limitation of SBH and LBH features to their respective corpora means that there is no clear linguistic distribution as Hurvitz argues. It also means, according to Young, Rezetko, and Ehrensvärd, that SBH and LBH features do not exhibit linguistic opposition as Hurvitz contends.

Second, Young, Rezetko, and Ehrensvärd dispute the use of Aramaisms and loanwords to date biblical texts. Regarding Aramaisms, they note that Aramaic influence can be found in texts other than LBH, including wisdom literature, texts of northern provenance, and texts relating to Aramaic speakers

---

54. *HS* 46 (2005): 321–76; *HS* 47 (2006): 83–210.
55. Young, Rezetko, and Ehrensvärd, *Linguistic Dating of Biblical Texts*, 1:4.
56. Young, Rezetko, and Ehrensvärd, *Linguistic Dating of Biblical Texts*, 1:83–142.

in some way. This means, according to *LDBT*, that Aramaisms cannot be seen as an LBH marker.[57] Regarding loanwords, Young, Rezetko, and Ehrensvärd argue that Old Persian and Greek loanwords could have been borrowed prior to the exile because there was opportunity for contact with Persians and Greeks before then. Thus, Old Persian and Greek loanwords cannot be correlated with LBH either.[58]

Third, *LDBT* argues that biblical texts cannot be dated because of textual fluidity.[59] According to Young, Rezetko, and Ehrensvärd, the text of the Hebrew Bible was fluid and existed in multiple forms until the first century CE. They find evidence for this view in several forms: differences in synoptic passages in the Hebrew Bible, the existence of multiple copies of biblical passages at Qumran, and differences between the ancient versions and the Masoretic Text. They argue that editors and scribes regularly altered texts, hence these variations. For Young, Rezetko, and Ehrensvärd, this textual fluidity undermines the stability of biblical texts required for the diachronic view.

Fourth, *LDBT* highlights the existence of non-diachronic variation in the Hebrew Bible. For Young, Rezetko, and Ehrensvärd, there is no need to resort to diachronic explanations for different features because variation can instead be explained in terms of register, dialect, style-shifting, and code-switching. *LDBT* supports this conclusion by pointing to extrabiblical Hebrew inscriptions, Mishnaic Hebrew, and Qumran Hebrew and Ben Sira.[60] Following recent scholarship on these corpora, *LDBT* argues that each corpus represents a unique dialect of Hebrew. They attest to the diversity of Hebrew and cannot be seen as earlier or later stages of Biblical Hebrew.

According to Young, Rezetko, and Ehrensvärd, all these points demonstrate that the distinction between SBH and LBH should not be viewed in diachronic terms. Rather, the best explanation for the Hebrew Bible's use of SBH and LBH features throughout is different scribal styles.[61] On the one hand, SBH represents a conservative style in which the scribes stuck to a limited number of linguistic forms. On the other hand, LBH reflects a non-conservative style in which the scribes were open to using a greater variety of linguistic forms. As argued by *LDBT*, these two styles coexisted and were used for different purposes.

---

57. Young, Rezetko, and Ehrensvärd, *Linguistic Dating of Biblical Texts*, 1:201–22.
58. Young, Rezetko, and Ehrensvärd, *Linguistic Dating of Biblical Texts*, 1:280–311.
59. Young, Rezetko, and Ehrensvärd, *Linguistic Dating of Biblical Texts*, 1:341–60.
60. Young, Rezetko, and Ehrensvärd, *Linguistic Dating of Biblical Texts*, 1:143–200, 223–79.
61. Young, Rezetko, and Ehrensvärd, *Linguistic Dating of Biblical Texts*, 2:96–99.

9.3.2.2 Philip R. Davies

While the arguments found in *LDBT* are largely limited to its authors, Philip R. Davies similarly holds that SBH and LBH were coexisting dialects during the postexilic period.[62] According to Davies, SBH represents the literary language of the returned exiles, and LBH represents the language they spoke in postexilic Judea. Davies argues that it is unlikely that scribes would have lost the ability to write flawless SBH given their role in copying and editing manuscripts.[63] Davies points to literary languages like Standard Babylonian Akkadian and Standard Literary Arabic, which coexisted with the common vernacular long after people stopped speaking them, to support the plausibility of his view.[64] Davies's understanding of SBH and LBH as coexisting styles naturally stems from his belief that the entire Hebrew Bible originated in Palestine during the Persian period.

9.3.2.3 Frederick H. Cryer

Finally, Frederick H. Cryer offers a unique perspective on dating biblical texts, different from *LDBT* and Davies.[65] Unlike nearly every other scholar, Cryer argues that Biblical Hebrew is homogeneous without any significant variation. Cryer contrasts the Hebrew Bible's alleged homogeneity with significant changes that have taken place in the English and German languages, changes that make works nearly 1000 years old like *Beowulf* (eighth century CE) and the *Nibelungenlied* (thirteenth century CE) unreadable today.[66] The Hebrew Bible's lack of linguistic variation, according to Cryer, demonstrates that the Old Testament was written over a relatively short period of time, if not more or less at a single point in time.[67]

9.3.3 Response and Refinement

These challenges to diachronic typology—particularly those of *LDBT*—have produced two different responses among scholars. A noteworthy minority have advanced the basic argumentation of *LDBT*, focusing on specific portions of the Hebrew Bible or particular issues related to the linguistic dating of biblical texts.[68]

---

62. Davies, "Biblical Hebrew and the History of Ancient Judah," 150–63; idem, *In Search of "Ancient Israel"*, 97–101.

63. Davies, "Biblical Hebrew and the History of Ancient Judah," 154–55.

64. Davies, "Biblical Hebrew and the History of Ancient Judah," 156–59.

65. Cryer, "Problem of Dating Biblical Hebrew," 185–98.

66. Cryer, "Problem of Dating Biblical Hebrew," 186–87.

67. Cryer, "Problem of Dating Biblical Hebrew," 192.

68. E.g., Römer, "How to Date Pentateuchal Texts," 357–70; Vern, *Dating Archaic Biblical Hebrew Poetry*; Person, *Deuteronomic History and the Book of Chronicles*, 23–40.

Others, especially Hurvitz himself, have reaffirmed the possibility of dating Biblical Hebrew linguistically.[69] In response to these reaffirmations, the authors of *LDBT*—particularly Young and Rezetko—have offered counter-arguments and continued to develop their approach. This is especially evident in their publishing of *Historical Linguistics and Biblical Hebrew: Steps Toward an Integrated Approach*.[70]

In addition to these, the linguistic dating of Biblical Hebrew has continued to occupy the attention of colloquia and academic journals. The Sixteenth World Congress of Jewish Studies held a special five-part session on historical linguistics in 2013. Diachronic typology occupied a significant portion of this session, and those papers were subsequently published.[71] Similarly, in 2015 the National Association of Professors of Hebrew held a session devoted to the topic of historical linguistics and dating Biblical Hebrew texts, and the papers were published the next year—along with many other articles on the same topic—in the *Journal for Semitics*.[72] Finally, in 2017 the journal *Hebrew Studies* presented a symposium entitled "Does Archaic Biblical Hebrew Exist?"[73]

In the midst of these discussions, an important development has taken place. As I noted in the previous chapter, in recent years Hebraists have become increasingly aware of sociolinguistic explanations for linguistic variation. This awareness, further encouraged by the publication of *LDBT*, has prompted scholars to explore new approaches to the study of diachronic typology. Having sketched both the establishment of and challenges to traditional diachronic typology, I now investigate the most recent responses to the challenges along with emerging sociolinguistic approaches to the study of diachronic typology.

9.3.3.1 *Diachrony in Biblical Hebrew* (*DBH*)

The publication of *LDBT* prompted the National Association of Professors of Hebrew to host five sessions titled "Diachrony in Biblical Hebrew" in 2009

---

69. E.g., Hurvitz, "'Linguistic Dating of Biblical Texts,'" 265–79; idem, "Recent Debate on Late Biblical Hebrew," 191–220; idem, "Can Biblical Texts Be Dated Linguistically?" 143–60; idem, "Historical Quest for 'Ancient Israel,'" 301–15; idem, "ויכוח ארכאולוגי-היסטורי [Archaeological-Historical Debate]," 34–46; Forbes, "Diachrony Debate," 7–42; Joosten, "Diachronic Linguistics and the Date of the Pentateuch," 327–44; Fassberg, "What Is Late Biblical Hebrew?" 1–15.

70. Cf. Young, "What Do We Actually Know?" 11–31; idem, "Ancient Hebrew without Authors," 972–1003; Rezetko, "Spelling of 'Damascus,'" 110–28; Rezetko and Naaijer, "Alternative Approach to the Lexicon of Late Biblical Hebrew," 1–39.

71. "Biblical Hebrew in the Light of Theoretical and Historical Linguistics," Jerusalem, July 28–August 13, 2013. The papers on diachronic typology were published in Moshavi and Notarius, *Advances in Biblical Hebrew Linguistics*, 1–149.

72. "Editing the Hebrew Bible and Historical Linguistics," Atlanta, GA, November 23, 2015; *JSem* 25 (2016): 833–1103.

73. *HS* 58 (2017): 47–118.

and 2010.[74] Invited to present at these sessions were both those who hold to diachronic typology and those who reject it. Most of these sessions' papers were subsequently published in 2012 as *Diachrony in Biblical Hebrew* (*DBH*), edited by Cynthia L. Miller-Naudé and Ziony Zevit. Of those who reject diachronic typology, only Martin Ehrensvärd agreed to publish his paper in this book, so *DBH* is essentially a defense of diachrony in Biblical Hebrew. In addition, the contributors represent some of the top-scholars in the field, including Hurvitz himself. As such, *DBH* serves as the most unified rejoinder to *LDBT* to date.

As noted by Miller-Naudé and Zevit in the preface, this book seeks to investigate key questions that *LDBT* raises: whether or not there is linguistic evidence for diachronic change in Biblical Hebrew, the possibility of using linguistic methods to date the Hebrew Bible's features to particular time periods, and the interrelation of language variation and language change.[75] To answer these questions, the first and second parts of the book establish a theoretical and methodological framework for diachronic study of the Hebrew Bible. They address issues like language change, language contact, stylistics, and sociolinguistics and together argue that written texts can be dated linguistically on the basis of historical linguistics.[76]

The bulk of *DBH*, represented by its third section, provides specific examples of diachronic change in the Hebrew Bible. The contributors to this section investigate orthography (e.g., defective versus full spelling), morphology (e.g., the third-person masculine plural pronoun מֹ-), syntax (e.g., Aramaic influence on Hebrew syntax), the lexicon (e.g., pseudo-classicisms that demonstrate a shift in semantic field), dialect (e.g., Northern Israelite Hebrew), and textual criticism.[77] For the most part, these explorations focus on diachronic development between SBH and LBH, although a few treat issues related to ABH. Furthermore, with the exception of the examples given, the argumentation in this section essentially only rehashes old arguments.[78] The fourth section of the book examines similar issues in other Semitic languages, namely Aramaic, Ugaritic, and Akkadian.[79]

DBH's afterword, written by Ziony Zevit, serves as a review of *LDBT*.[80] Zevit critiques several aspects of the book, focusing especially on *LDBT*'s

---

74. The first two of these sessions were presented in New Orleans, LA, on November 22, 2009, and the second three were presented in Atlanta, GA, on November 21–22, 2010.

75. Miller-Naudé and Zevit, *Diachrony in Biblical Hebrew*, xi.

76. Miller-Naudé and Zevit, *Diachrony in Biblical Hebrew*, 1–124.

77. Miller-Naudé and Zevit, *Diachrony in Biblical Hebrew*, 125–375.

78. Cf. Kaufman, review of *Diachrony in Biblical Hebrew*.

79. Miller-Naudé and Zevit, *Diachrony in Biblical Hebrew*, 377–451.

80. Miller-Naudé and Zevit, *Diachrony in Biblical Hebrew*, 453–89.

approach. These include an eclectic methodology and lack of engagement with studies that address the question of dating undated non-Semitic texts. Zevit also discusses at length the question of textual fluidity raised by *LDBT*. He contends that *LDBT* never proves that scribes actually erased evidence of diachrony to any significant degree. Rather, Zevit argues, scribal activity was limited to certain centers and that those centers' scribes were tasked with accurate transmission of the biblical text.

9.3.3.2 Ronald S. Hendel and Jan Joosten

Another book, published partially in response to *LDBT*, is Ronald S. Hendel and Jan Joosten's *How Old Is the Hebrew Bible? A Linguistic, Textual, and Historical Study*. Hendel and Joosten acknowledge potential difficulties in dating biblical texts, but they contend that trying to do so is important because the Hebrew Bible's narrative is shaped by its history and set within history. In response to works like *LDBT*, Hendel and Joosten state: "Contrary to recent claims, dating Hebrew texts on the basis of their language is not impossible."[81]

Hendel and Joosten open their study with several chapters that lay the context for the rest of the book. They examine the reality of language change, arguing that historical linguistics is a reliable tool even if it cannot definitively establish the date of a text.[82] Then they discuss various types of language change (e.g., grammaticalization and language contact). They set this diachronic change alongside synchronic variation stemming from dialect, style-shifting, and other factors.[83]

According to Hendel and Joosten, it is possible to distinguish diachronic variation from synchronic variation. Variation is diachronic rather than synchronic when the features are typologically earlier or later and have a relatively consistent distribution.[84] Hendel and Joosten also address *LDBT*'s claim that textual fluidity makes it impossible to distinguish diachronic development. According to them, textual variation does not alter the big picture; the criterion of accumulation permits the distinction between earlier and later texts.[85]

Finally, Hendel and Joosten lay out their diachronic model of Biblical Hebrew.[86] SBH is identified by early typological features and its similarities to preexilic Hebrew inscriptions. LBH is identified by its late typological

---

81. Hendel and Joosten, *How Old Is the Hebrew Bible?*, x.
82. Hendel and Joosten, *How Old Is the Hebrew Bible?*, 1–10.
83. Hendel and Joosten, *How Old Is the Hebrew Bible?*, 11–30.
84. Hendel and Joosten, *How Old Is the Hebrew Bible?*, 31–46.
85. Hendel and Joosten, *How Old Is the Hebrew Bible?*, 47–59.
86. Hendel and Joosten, *How Old Is the Hebrew Bible?*, 60–97.

features and the use of pseudoclassicisms, or imperfect imitations of SBH features. Transitional Biblical Hebrew—found in books like Jeremiah, Ezekiel, Lamentations, and Haggai—is more similar to SBH than LBH but is still a distinctive chronolect. According to Hendel and Joosten, this diachronic model matches well with what is known of the Hebrew Bible on historical-critical grounds.[87]

9.3.3.3 Frank H. Polak

A different, but refreshing, perspective on diachrony in Biblical Hebrew is found in the work of Frank H. Polak.[88] His approach is unique because it represents the most substantial effort to integrate sociolinguistics with diachronic differences between SBH and LBH. Specifically, Polak gives attention to the styles associated with oral culture and with literate writing culture.[89] For Polak, SBH tends to preserve an older, oral style whereas LBH represents a literate, written style.

One of Polak's methods for distinguishing between the SBH and LBH styles is statistics.[90] He determines two different ratios in the Hebrew Bible: noun to verb, and nominal verb (i.e., participles and infinitives construct) to finite verb (i.e., *qatal, yiqtol,* and volitives). Polak argues from these data that SBH tends to use more verbs than LBH, which instead tends to use complex nominal clauses. According to Polak, this shift from verbs to nominal clauses reflects a shift to a literate, writing culture.

Polak also contends that SBH and LBH can be distinguished lexically. On the one hand, epic formulas (e.g., וַיַּעַן וַיֹּאמֶר "he answered and said") typical of oral culture occur much more commonly in SBH than in LBH.[91] On the other hand, LBH tends to be marked by references to writing as well as Aramaisms and Persian loanwords. These differences again reflect a shift from an oral to a literate, writing culture, especially as brought on by the scribal chancellery of the Persian Empire.[92]

---

87. Hendel and Joosten, *How Old Is the Hebrew Bible?*, 98–125.

88. E.g., Polak, "Language Variation," 301–38; idem, "Style Is More Than the Person," 38–103; idem, "Oral and the Written," 59–105; idem, "Sociolinguistics," 115–62; idem, "Sociolinguistics and the Judean Speech Community," 589–628; idem, "Linguistic and Stylistic Aspects," 285–304; idem, "Style of the Dialogue," 53–95; idem, "תמורות ותקופות בלשון הסיפורת במקרא [Development and Periodization of Biblical Prose Narrative]," 30–52, 142–60; idem, "מעמד הדוברים ומבנה הדו-שיח [On Dialogue and Speaker Status]," 1–18, 97–119.

89. Polak, "Oral and the Written," 59–105; idem, "Style Is More Than the Person," 38–103.

90. Polak, "Oral and the Written," 69–71; idem, "Sociolinguistics," 135, 145, 147–48, 151.

91. Polak, "Linguistic and Stylistic Aspects," 285–304.

92. Polak, "Sociolinguistics and the Judean Speech Community," 596–606; idem, "Sociolinguistics," 119–27; idem, "Style Is More Than the Person," 89–98.

According to Polak, these data enable the distinction between three main styles that correspond chronologically to Israel's history.[93] The Classical Style (e.g., the Samuel-Saul-David narratives in Samuel, the Elijah-Elisha narratives in Kings, and other narratives in the Pentateuch and Joshua–Judges) is relatively "plain" and roughly corresponds to SBH. The Late Preexilic/Exilic Style (e.g., Deuteronomy and most of Kings) and Postexilic Style (e.g., Ezra–Nehemiah and non-synoptic Chronicles) have more rhetorical flourish and roughly correspond to LBH.

9.3.3.4 Dong-Hyuk Kim

Similar to Polak, Dong-Hyuk Kim puts forth a model for understanding the Hebrew Bible's variation that integrates sociolinguistics with diachronic typology.[94] Kim analyzes and attempts to correlate two types of variables commonly used in historical sociolinguistics: dependent and independent. Dependent variables are the Hebrew Bible's actual linguistic features, whether grammatical, lexical, or phraseological. Independent variables are factors that can influence the use of variant linguistic forms, such as age, gender, social status, genre, and time. For Kim, genre—specifically narrative versus direct speech—and time are the two independent variables relevant for analyzing the Hebrew Bible.[95]

Then, largely following the work of sociolinguist William Labov, Kim discusses both internal and external linguistic change.[96] He defines internal change as change from below that takes place with little awareness of the speakers; he defines external change as change from above that occurs when lower social classes consciously adopt the speech of the dominant social class. Kim assumes that, in the Hebrew Bible, internal change is more common in direct speech whereas external change is more frequent in narrative. Kim then argues that only change from below can serve as a reliable indicator of chronology when correlated with the independent variable of time.[97]

With this framework in mind, Kim evaluates eight grammatical (e.g., temporal infinitive construct clauses introduced with and without וַיְהִי/וְהָיָה) and lexical (e.g., מַמְלָכָה versus מַלְכוּת) features thought to be relevant for distinguishing SBH from LBH.[98] Through variationist analysis he concludes that seven of these features represent authentic linguistic change over time

---

93. Polak, "Sociolinguistics," 119, 127–52; idem, "Oral and the Written," 78–100.

94. Kim, *Early Biblical Hebrew, Late Biblical Hebrew, and Linguistic Variability*. This work originated as Kim's PhD dissertation completed at Yale University in 2011.

95. Kim, *Early Biblical Hebrew, Late Biblical Hebrew, and Linguistic Variability*, 72–84.

96. Kim, *Early Biblical Hebrew, Late Biblical Hebrew, and Linguistic Variability*, 89–94.

97. Kim, *Early Biblical Hebrew, Late Biblical Hebrew, and Linguistic Variability*, 94–96.

98. Kim, *Early Biblical Hebrew, Late Biblical Hebrew, and Linguistic Variability*, 97–150.

rather than idiolect (i.e., the linguistic "style" of an author). According to Kim, furthermore, three of these changes are internal and three are external; the direction of change for the seventh cannot be reliably determined.

Kim therefore concludes that the differences between SBH and LBH cannot be explained purely in terms of style as *LDBT* argues. Rather, there is a correlation between diachrony and the linguistic features he examines.[99] At the same time, because nearly half of these features are external rather than internal, Kim argues that various features were used with conscious knowledge of the biblical author—in other words, a stylistic choice. Thus, Kim agrees with *LDBT* that these features are not reliable guides for distinguishing between SBH and LBH.[100]

9.3.4 Evaluation

The above survey demonstrates the ongoing debate regarding diachrony and Biblical Hebrew. Challenge of the status quo has led to fruitful reexamination of the presuppositions and methodology behind traditional dating of biblical texts. Young, Rezetko, and Ehrensvärd are especially to be thanked for prompting such an important conversation. We can be thankful to their ongoing work as well as the thoughtful responses of those who maintain the possibility of diachronic typology.

Significant advances have taken place regarding our understanding of linguistic change. The possibility that variation may be explained non-diachronically has forced Hebrew Bible scholars to define more clearly what language variation in the Hebrew Bible signifies and how Biblical Hebrew may have changed over time. This has provoked the development of theories of language change that are more nuanced than before and that incorporate sociolinguistics to one degree or another. The creative, innovative work of Polak and Kim represents a welcome contribution here. In addition, Jacobus Naudé has contributed importantly through his theory of language change and diffusion, put forth in *DBH*.[101]

Another advance concerns models for analyzing the Hebrew Bible's variation. In the wake of *LDBT*, scholars have sought to develop methodologies for quantitative analysis. Rezetko and Young have contributed meaningfully here through their application of cross-textual variable analysis and variationist analysis to the Hebrew Bible. Another noteworthy scholar is A. Dean Forbes,

---

99. Kim, *Early Biblical Hebrew, Late Biblical Hebrew, and Linguistic Variability*, 154–55.

100. Kim, *Early Biblical Hebrew, Late Biblical Hebrew, and Linguistic Variability*, 155–56.

101. Naudé, "Diachrony in Biblical Hebrew," 61–82; cf. idem, "Transitions of Biblical Hebrew," 189–214; idem, "Complexity of Language Change," 395–411; idem, "Linguistic Dating of Biblical Hebrew Texts," 1–22.

well known for his statistical work with the Hebrew Bible. His contribution to the 2015 NAPH colloquium, published in the *Journal for Semitics*, lays forth a statistical approach that incorporates diachronic criteria while accounting for other textual parameters.[102]

Nevertheless, in another sense the diachrony debate remains largely unresolved. One key issue—in fact, the primary question raised by *LDBT*—that remains to be addressed is whether or not biblical authors could actually write in both SBH and LBH during the exilic and postexilic periods. On this point, Hebraists would benefit greatly from comparison with Arabic. This is because Arabic attests to a standardized, written form (Modern Standard Arabic) alongside its spoken, colloquial dialects. Analysis of this phenomenon would likely provide answers to this important question, in addition to enhancing our understanding of the relationship between written and spoken Hebrew in ancient Israel.[103]

Finally, Hebraists could enhance and refine their own understanding of linguistic dating by learning from other disciplines' approaches to linguistic dating.[104] The issues involved in dating *Beowulf*'s linguistic features, for example, closely parallel that of the Hebrew Bible—in both cases our textual evidence consists of manuscript copies rather than the original manuscripts themselves. Hebraists might also learn some fresh approaches to linguistic dating from ancient texts like *Beowulf*. The existence of meter in Biblical Hebrew is debated, but assuming it exists in some form—as is plausible—the meters of some poems may reflect dateable linguistic features, just as is the case in *Beowulf*. The connection between meter and diachronic typology was explored early in the development of diachronic typology but largely faded into the background with the work of Hurvitz. Some scholars have recently taken interest in meter and diachronic typology once again,[105] but more remains to be done.

9.4 THE DATING OF BIBLICAL ARAMAIC TEXTS

Even though Biblical Aramaic makes up only a small portion of the Hebrew Bible, significant debate has taken place over its origin. Much of this debate has centered on the dating of the book of Daniel. As far back as the third century CE, the Neo-Platonist and anti-Christian philosopher Porphyry argued along these lines. He stated that the book of Daniel could not have been composed in the sixth century BCE, when the character Daniel is purported to have written it

---

102. Forbes, "Diachrony Debate," 881–926.
103. Kaufman, review of *Diachrony in Biblical Hebrew.*
104. Cf. Kofoed, "Using Linguistic Difference in Relative Text Dating," 93–114.
105. E.g., Park, *Typology in Biblical Hebrew Poetic Meter.*

(cf. Jerome, *Expl. Dan.* Prologue).[106] However, his argumentation was primarily theological in that he did not believe in the possibility of predicative prophecy.

In modern times, the focus has shifted from theological arguments like this to linguistic arguments for dating Biblical Aramaic. Scholars have analyzed the relationship of Biblical Aramaic to other Aramaic dialects: Old Aramaic, Imperial Aramaic (also known as Official Aramaic), Middle Aramaic, and Late Aramaic.[107] The general consensus is that Ezra fits within Imperial Aramaic, but scholars disagree on whether Daniel falls within Imperial Aramaic (ca. 600–200 BCE) or Middle Aramaic (ca. 200 BCE–250 CE).[108]

Phase of Aramaic	Date	Dialects and Texts
Old Aramaic	850–600 BCE	Standard Syrian (e.g., Sefire) Samalian (e.g., Zinçirli) Tel Fakariyah Mesopotamian (e.g., Uruk) Deir Alla
Imperial Aramaic (Official Aramaic)	600–200 BCE	Egyptian (e.g., Elephantine) Mesopotamian (e.g., Murashu) Persia and Bactria (e.g., Persepolis) Asia Minor (e.g., Xanthos) Samaritan (e.g., Wadi Daliyeh)
Middle Aramaic	200 BCE–250 CE	Palmyrene Nabatean Hatran Jewish Literary Aramaic (e.g., Dead Sea Scrolls)
Late Aramaic	200–1200 CE	*Palestinian* Jewish Palestinian (e.g., the Palestinian Targum) Christian Palestinian Samaritan *Syrian* Syrian (e.g., Syriac) Late Jewish Literary Aramaic (e.g., Targum Pseudo-Jonathan) *Babylonian* Jewish Babylonian (e.g., Babylonian Talmud) Mandaic

---

106. Berchman, *Porphyry Against the Christians*, 157.

107. Kaufman, "Aramaic," 114–19; Fitzmyer, "Phases of the Aramaic Language," 60–63; Kutscher, "Aramaic," 347–48.

108. Fitzmyer, "Phases of the Aramaic Language," 61; Kutscher, "Aramaic," 347–48.

With this general picture of Aramaic's dialects in mind, I now sketch the history of scholarship on dating Biblical Aramaic. I begin with S. R. Driver, who launched the modern debate over dating Biblical Aramaic in the late nineteenth century when he contended that Daniel's Aramaic must date to the Hellenistic period. I survey Driver's arguments and the work of those who responded to him, then H. H. Rowley's defense of Driver and the scholars who responded to Rowley, and finally several other studies that take the debate in different directions. Throughout I give special attention to the Aramaic of Daniel in light of its importance for the conversation.

9.4.1 The Challenge of S. R. Driver

Some of the first discussions on dating Biblical Aramaic began to take place as critical scholarship became popular during the Enlightenment. Early investigations of Biblical Aramaic centered on the relationship between the Aramaic of Ezra and the Aramaic of Daniel, as well as how to account for the Greek loanwords found in the third chapter of the book of Daniel (קִיתְרֹוס, שַׂבְּכָא, פְּסַנְטֵרִין, and סוּמְפֹּנְיָה).[109] However, it was not until the late nineteenth century, when modern knowledge of Aramaic came to fruition, that S. R. Driver compared Daniel's Aramaic with other Aramaic dialects. In this section I present Driver's conclusions and the responses it prompted.

9.4.1.1 S. R. Driver

In his *An Introduction to the Literature of the Old Testament*, first published in 1891, S. R. Driver discussed the authorship and date of the book of Daniel, including the issue of the book's language.[110] Driver's conclusion on the matter is now infamous: "The verdict of the language of Daniel is thus clear. The *Persian* words presuppose a period after the Persian empire had been well established: the Greek words *demand*, the Hebrew *supports*, and the Aramaic *permits*, a date *after the conquest of Palestine by Alexander the Great* (B.C. 332)."[111]

Driver's first argument for Daniel's late date centers on the non-Semitic loanwords in the book.[112] Driver contends that the number of Persian loanwords in Daniel's Aramaic requires a late date. This is because he assumes that words can be borrowed only after lengthy periods of linguistic contact.

---

109. E.g., Bertholdt, *Historisch kritische Einleitung*, 1533–36; Hengstenberg, *Authentie des Daniel und die Integrität des Sacharja*, 10–18, 303–11; Hävernick, *Buch Daniel*, 95–104; Lengerke, *Buch Daniel*, 120–26.

110. Driver, *Literature of the Old Testament*, 469–76; cf. idem, *Daniel*, lvi–lxiii.

111. Driver, *Literature of the Old Testament*, 476. The emphasis is original.

112. Driver, *Literature of the Old Testament*, 469–71.

Furthermore, Driver argues that Jewish contact with Greeks could not have taken place prior to Alexander's conquest. Thus, for Driver, no Greek words could have been borrowed before then.

Driver's second argument relates to the grammatical features of Daniel's Aramaic.[113] He contends that Daniel's (and Ezra's) Aramaic is a western Aramaic dialect, of the type spoken in or near Palestine. He arrives at this conclusion by comparing Daniel's Aramaic with Palmyrene and Nabatean Aramaic as well as Targumic Aramaic. Driver points to several similarities between them, including the use of final *he* for originally final *aleph* roots, retention of *nun* in the *yqtl* conjugation of initial *nun* roots, use of later *dalet* for earlier *zayin* in the relative pronoun דִּי, and use of *ayin* for earlier *qoph* in the word אֲרַע "earth."

9.4.1.2 Robert Dick Wilson, William St. Clair Tisdall, and Charles Boutflower

Driver's statement regarding the date of Biblical Aramaic met mixed responses. Many critical scholars accepted Driver's conclusions on the Aramaic of Daniel.[114] However, several scholars holding to the traditional sixth-century BCE date individually published critiques of Driver. The most substantial of these responses was produced by Robert Dick Wilson, who taught at Princeton Theological Seminary before leaving to help start Westminster Theological Seminary.[115] Two other important responders were William St. Clair Tisdall and Charles Boutflower, who offered similar arguments to those of Wilson.[116]

Like Driver, Wilson, Tisdall, and Boutflower give significant attention to Daniel's vocabulary.[117] They argue that the number and nature of Daniel's Persian loans match that of the Elephantine Papyri. They also note the existence of Greek loanwords in the Elephantine Papyri, disproving Driver's contention that Greek words could not enter Aramaic prior to Alexander's conquest. Finally, they point to the book's many Akkadian words, which suggest a Mesopotamian rather than Palestinian setting for Daniel's Aramaic.

Regarding Driver's grammatical arguments, Wilson, Tisdall, and Boutflower offer several counterpoints.[118] They contend that Daniel's Aramaic and Ezra's

---

113. Driver, *Literature of the Old Testament*, 471–73.

114. E.g., Montgomery, *Daniel*, 15–23; Torrey, "Aramaic Portions of Ezra," 232–37.

115. Wilson, "Aramaic of Daniel," 261–306.

116. Tisdall, "Book of Daniel," 206–55; idem, "Egypt and the Book of Daniel," 340–57; Boutflower, *In and Around the Book of Daniel*, 226–67.

117. Wilson, "Aramaic of Daniel," 294–302; Tisdall, "Book of Daniel," 208–37; idem, "Egypt and the Book of Daniel," 346–54; Boutflower, *In and Around the Book of Daniel*, 241–67.

118. Wilson, "Aramaic of Daniel," 273–94; Tisdall, "Book of Daniel," 237–43; idem, "Egypt and the Book of Daniel," 354–56; Boutflower, *In and Around the Book of Daniel*, 226–40.

Aramaic share more similarities with the Elephantine Papyri—which were not available to Driver in 1891—than later Aramaic. They also argue for the relative uniformity of early Aramaic, contending that Driver's distinction between eastern and western Aramaic does not apply until later. Thus, Driver is wrong to locate Biblical Aramaic specifically in Palestine rather than Mesopotamia. Finally, to explain the existence of later forms (e.g., the relative דִּי for earlier זִי), they suggest that later scribes have updated the text to reflect newer spellings and forms of words.

9.4.2 H. H. Rowley's Aramaic of the Old Testament *and Response*

Together Wilson, Tisdall, and Boutflower offered a forceful critique of Driver's position on the Aramaic of Daniel. But, as thorough as their studies were, a comprehensive comparison of Biblical Aramaic with other Aramaic dialects was still lacking. This challenge was met by H. H. Rowley, who also sought to defend Driver against Wilson, Tisdall, and Boutflower. But, like Driver before him, Rowley's argumentation was challenged on several fronts.

9.4.2.1 H. H. Rowley

In 1929 H. H. Rowley published *Aramaic of the Old Testament*, a full monograph-length treatment of Biblical Aramaic and its relationship with other Aramaic dialects.[119] Rowley's general conclusion is that the Aramaic of both Ezra and Daniel exhibit features later than those of the Elephantine Papyri but earlier than the Targums and Palmyrene and Nabatean Aramaic. But Daniel's Aramaic is more similar to these later dialects than Ezra's and therefore dates later than Ezra's. For Rowley, furthermore, the similarities of Biblical Aramaic with Palmyrene, Nabatean, and Targumic Aramaic indicates a Palestinian rather than Mesopotamian origin.[120] To arrive at this conclusion, Rowley focuses on four key areas: phonology, morphology, syntax, and vocabulary.

First, Rowley argues that Biblical Aramaic's consonants clearly reflect a later stage of Aramaic than the Elephantine Papyri.[121] Aramaic underwent a phonological shift in which the consonants *zayin, shin, qoph, tsade,* and *samek* were later replaced by *dalet, tav, ayin, tet,* and *sin*, respectively, in the spelling of certain words. The Elephantine Papyri use the earlier set of consonants whereas Biblical Aramaic uses the latter set (e.g., the word "gold" appears as זהב at

---

119. Around this same time, two very similar but less-substantial studies emerged: Baumgartner, "Aramäische im Buche Daniel," 81–133; Driver, "Aramaic of the Book of Daniel," 110–19.

120. Rowley, *Aramaic of the Old Testament*, 153–56.

121. Rowley, *Aramaic of the Old Testament*, 16–50; cf. Baumgartner, "Aramäische im Buche Daniel," 90–104; Driver, "Aramaic of the Book of Daniel," 112–15, 117.

Elephantine but as דְּהַב in Biblical Aramaic). Rowley also examines alternation between final *aleph* and *he*, observing that the Elephantine Papyri tend to have *he* whereas later Aramaic tends to have *aleph*. According to Rowley, all these observations place Biblical Aramaic chronologically later than the Elephantine Papyri and geographically in the west.

Second, Rowley contends that Biblical Aramaic morphology reflects a stage between the Elephantine Papyri and the Targums.[122] To do so he examines the morphology of Biblical Aramaic's pronouns, nouns, adverbs, prepositions, particles, and verbs. He observes that, at least for some morphological features, Ezra tends to contain earlier ones whereas Daniel tends to have later ones. For example, in Biblical Aramaic the third-person masculine plural pronoun "they" is הִמּוֹ in Ezra (as in the Elephantine Papyri) but הִמּוֹן in Daniel (as in later Aramaic). For Rowley, this indicates that both Ezra and Daniel postdate the Elephantine Papyri but that Daniel dates later than Ezra.

Third, Rowley maintains that Biblical Aramaic syntax also seems to contain developments later than the Elephantine Papyri.[123] A number of his points here relate to the use of the preposition -לְ. For example, Rowley notes how the preposition -לְ marks the direct object only sporadically in the Elephantine Papyri but commonly in Biblical and later Aramaic. As another example, he points out that Biblical Aramaic and later Aramaic tend to use -לְ with the infinitive construct to express modality or purpose whereas the Elephantine Papyri tend to use *yqtl*. Rowley highlights how these features are more common in Daniel than Ezra, suggesting that Daniel therefore dates later than Ezra.

Fourth, Rowley argues that Biblical Aramaic's vocabulary places it later than the Elephantine Papyri.[124] For Rowley, there are few significant differences in terms of actual Aramaic vocabulary. Rather, the differences in vocabulary appear primarily with loanwords. Rowley contends that, despite also being common in the Elephantine Papyri, Biblical Aramaic's Akkadian loanwords only demonstrate the widespread persistence of these words at a later period. Rowley further argues that the Persian loanwords in Biblical Aramaic more closely match those of the Targums than of the Elephantine Papyri. Finally, Rowley says that Daniel's Greek loanwords reflect a late date because Greek words are rarely attested at Elephantine but are common in the Targums as well as Nabatean and Palmyrene Aramaic.

---

122. Rowley, *Aramaic of the Old Testament*, 50–98; cf. Baumgartner, "Aramäische im Buche Daniel," 104–16; Driver, "Aramaic of the Book of Daniel," 115–17.

123. Rowley, *Aramaic of the Old Testament*, 98–108.

124. Rowley, *Aramaic of the Old Testament*, 108–53; cf. Driver, "Aramaic of the Book of Daniel," 118–19.

9.4.2.2 Kenneth A. Kitchen

Rowley's (and Driver's) argument that Biblical Aramaic originated in Palestine was decisively refuted in 1930 by Hans Heinrich Schaeder, who demonstrated that Aramaic cannot clearly be divided into eastern and western branches until ca. 200 CE onward.[125] But many of Rowley's linguistic arguments remained unanswered. Kenneth A. Kitchen took up this very challenge in what was originally part of the Tyndale Fellowship Old Testament Study Group meeting at Tyndale House, Cambridge in 1964.[126] His study seeks to defend an early date for the book of Daniel on linguistic grounds. In doing so he addresses three key issues: vocabulary, orthography and phonology, and morphology and syntax.

First, Kitchen analyzes the vocabulary of Daniel's Aramaic.[127] He focuses primarily on the significance of Daniel's Persian and Greek loanwords. Regarding the Persian loans, Kitchen notes that many of them also occur in Imperial Aramaic and Elamite and that they are specifically Old Persian in form (i.e., originating prior to 300 BCE). In doing so Kitchen discredits Rowley's argument that Daniel's Persian words overlap more with the Targums than the Elephantine Papyri. Regarding the Greek loanwords in Dan 3, Kitchen argues that there was plenty of opportunity in Mesopotamia for contact with Greeks prior to Alexander the Great, but he notes how few the Greek loans are compared with the Persian ones. The higher frequency of Persian loanwords in the book, along with the fact that they are primarily related to administration, suggests an earlier date for Daniel's Aramaic. This is because a late writer would have used Greek, not Persian, administrative terms.

Second, Kitchen explores the orthography and phonology of Daniel's Aramaic.[128] With Rowley, Kitchen recognizes that Daniel's consonants seem to reflect a later stage of Aramaic than Old and Imperial Aramaic. Kitchen also notes that orthography does not always strictly reflect phonology. This is clear because earlier orthographical conventions are found even in later Middle Aramaic. According to Kitchen, it also is likely that copyists updated the spelling of words, especially since this was a common practice throughout the ancient Near East. For similar reasons, Kitchen does not attach chronological significance to alternations between final *aleph* and *he* and full versus defective spellings.

---

125. Schaeder, *Iranische Beiträge I*, 225–54; cf. Linder, "Aramäische im Buche Daniel," 503–45.

126. Kitchen, "Aramaic of Daniel," 31–79.

127. Kitchen, "Aramaic of Daniel," 32–50.

128. Kitchen, "Aramaic of Daniel," 50–67.

Third, Kitchen examines the morphology and syntax of Daniel's Aramaic.[129] He claims that, because early morphological forms like הִמּוֹ continue to appear alongside late morphological forms like הִמּוֹן throughout Aramaic, they are of little chronological value. Kitchen further cautions against arguing for a form's lateness based on a lack of evidence for early attestation. As an example, he points out that the accusative particle יָת—attested only in late Nabatean and Palmyrene Aramaic when Rowley published *Aramaic of the Old Testament*—was subsequently discovered in Papyrus Brooklyn 3, which dates to the fifth century BCE.

9.4.2.3 E. Y. Kutscher

The Aramaicist E. Y. Kutscher discusses the dating of Biblical Aramaic in his detailed analysis of the Aramaic dialects.[130] He addresses Driver's and Rowley's contention that Daniel's Aramaic is western (i.e., Palestinian).[131] He agrees with Schaeder that the relative uniformity of Imperial Aramaic prevents reading the eastern-western distinction of Late Aramaic back into earlier periods. Nevertheless, he thinks that Biblical Aramaic exhibits "eastern" (i.e., "Mesopotamian") features not as prevalent in the Dead Sea Scrolls, written in Palestine. According to Kutscher, this is particularly true of word order, which is relatively free in Biblical Aramaic because of influence from the word orders of Akkadian and Old Persian.

Furthermore, Kutscher largely affirms Kitchen's refutation of Rowley. Kutscher criticizes Rowley for rejecting, without rationale, the possibility of scribal updating.[132] He notes how orthography cannot be a definite clue of a text's date because exceptions occur: for example, the Hermopolis Papyri use final *he* when all other inscriptions of the fifth century BCE use *aleph*, and Nabatean inscriptions of the first century BCE preserve archaic *zayin*. Kutscher also addresses Daniel's Greek loanwords.[133] He observes how these words are limited to the semantic domain of music. He therefore suggests that the linguistic influence of Greeks in the east was limited to certain domains, like music, prior to Alexander's conquest. Although some of the Greek words borrowed by Daniel do not actually occur in Greek texts until the late period, Kutscher argues that we should not expect them to— the Greeks in the east prior to Alexander's conquest were predominantly

---

129. Kitchen, "Aramaic of Daniel," 68–75.
130. Kutscher, "Aramaic," 399–403; cf. idem, "ארמית המקראית [Biblical Aramaic]," 123–27.
131. Kutscher, "Aramaic," 402–3; cf. idem, "ארמית המקראית [Biblical Aramaic]," 123–27.
132. Kutscher, "Aramaic," 401.
133. Kutscher, "Aramaic," 401–2.

non-Attic Greeks, and we have less extant textual material for non-Attic Greek than we do Attic Greek.[134]

9.4.2.4 Peter W. Coxon

Another significant response to Rowley is found in the work of Peter W. Coxon, who in a series of articles addresses the linguistic dating of Daniel's Aramaic.[135] Coxon supports the need for reanalysis of Rowley's conclusions given the discovery of many new Aramaic texts (e.g., the Dead Sea Scrolls) since 1929, when Rowley published his study. Like Kitchen, Coxon also finds Rowley's methodology lacking. Yet, unlike Kitchen, Coxon does not aim to offer a response to Rowley or a defense of the traditional sixth-century BCE date of Daniel.

Coxon acknowledges, along with Rowley and Kitchen, that the best potential evidence for Biblical Aramaic's lateness is its orthography: its use of later *dalet, tav, ayin, tet,* and *sin* for earlier *zayin, shin, qoph, tsade,* and *samek*. But, like Kitchen, Coxon reiterates that late orthography does not necessarily indicate a late date. His argument for this consists of two points. First, older orthographical conventions appear in late texts such as the Nisa Ostraca (second century BCE), so there is not always a one-to-one correspondence between orthography and date. Second, it is likely that Jewish scribes updated the orthography of Biblical Aramaic in order to standardize it, similar to the way that the Masoretes standardized the orthography of the Hebrew text.

Coxon also reexamines the morphology and syntax of Daniel's Aramaic. For morphology, he looks at the use of the Haphel versus Aphel for the causative stem.[136] Coxon observes that Biblical Aramaic aligns most closely with the Elephantine Papyri in its preference for the Haphel. For syntax, Coxon looks at the seven points of difference that Rowley observed between Biblical Aramaic and other dialects.[137] He observes that most of the syntactical features are either more common in Imperial Aramaic than Rowley knew or have no relevance for dating. In contrast, Daniel's flexible word order aligns with Imperial Aramaic, which often departs from standard Semitic word order due to Akkadian and Persian influence.

Finally, Coxon addresses the question of whether Daniel's vocabulary indicates a late date. Here he addresses two specific issues: native vocabulary and Greek loanwords. Coxon's treatment of native vocabulary is especially

---

134. In my own work I have developed Kutscher's argumentation here further. See Noonan, "Daniel's Greek Loanwords," 575–603.

135. Coxon, "Distribution of Synonyms," 497–512; idem, "Greek Loan-Words and Alleged Greek Loan Translations," 24–40; idem, "Morphological Study," 416–19; idem, "Problem of Consonantal Mutations," 8–22; idem, "Syntax of the Aramaic of *Daniel*," 107–22.

136. Coxon, "Morphological Study," 416–19.

137. Coxon, "Syntax of the Aramaic of *Daniel*," 107–22.

important because this issue is largely ignored by Kitchen.[138] Coxon examines seven pairs of early/late synonyms. He finds that two pairs (שׂים/שׂוה "to set, make" and בעה/בקר "to ask, seek") align with Imperial Aramaic, one pair (אֱנָשׁ/אִישׁ "man") aligns with later Aramaic, and the rest have no clear alignment. Thus, according to Coxon, Daniel's native vocabulary has little bearing on its date. Coxon's conclusion regarding the Greek words in Daniel is similar.[139] Like Kitchen, he disputes Rowley's claim that Greek words could only be borrowed late, given evidence for Greeks in the east prior to Alexander the Great. Thus, according to Coxon, Greek words could have been borrowed at any time and are irrelevant for dating purposes.

9.4.3 Redirection and Refinement

The decades following Rowley's *Aramaic of the Old Testament* saw the discovery of many Aramaic texts. While many of the texts discovered in this period belonged to Imperial Aramaic, a notable number belonged to earlier and later dialects. Particularly ground breaking was the discovery of the Dead Sea Scrolls, which—although primarily written in Hebrew—contained a number of Aramaic texts. The result was several studies that sought to compare Biblical Aramaic with these newly discovered texts rather than to respond solely to Rowley. In this section, I examine contributions that fall within this category and conclude by exploring the most comprehensive analysis of Biblical Aramaic to date, that of Jongtae Choi.

9.4.3.1 Robert I. Vasholz and Gleason L. Archer, Jr.

Two studies that represent a focus on dialects other than Imperial Aramaic are those of Robert I. Vasholz and Gleason L. Archer, Jr. Rather than asking whether or not Biblical Aramaic aligns with Imperial Aramaic—therefore determining the plausibility of a sixth century BCE date for Daniel's Aramaic— Vasholz and Archer seek to exclude a second century BCE date for Daniel.[140] They do so by comparing Daniel's Aramaic with the Aramaic of the Dead Sea Scrolls, specifically the *Targum of Job* (11Q10) and *Genesis Apocryphon* (1Qap Gen^ar).[141] This enables them to date Daniel's Aramaic, in relative terms, prior to both the *Targum of Job* and the *Genesis Apocryphon*.

---

138. Coxon, "Distribution of Synonyms," 497–512.

139. Coxon, "Greek Loan-Words and Alleged Greek Loan Translations," 24–40.

140. Vasholz, "Philological Comparison of the Qumran Job Targum"; idem, "Qumran and the Dating of Daniel," 315–21; Archer, "Aramaic of the 'Genesis Apocryphon,'" 160–69.

141. Vasholz, "Philological Comparison of the Qumran Job Targum," 23–84; Archer, "Aramaic of the 'Genesis Apocryphon,'" 161–69.

Vasholz and Archer date the *Genesis Apocryphon* to the first century BCE. This date is suggested by the manuscript's paleography, its similarity with *Jubilees* (ca. 100 BCE), its grammar, and finally its vocabulary, which includes many words characteristic of Targumic and Talmudic Aramaic.[142] Archer contends that the linguistic differences between the *Genesis Apocryphon* and Daniel indicate that Daniel must be dated prior to the second century BCE.[143] Vasholz takes this line of argumentation a step further by dating the *Targum of Job* earlier than *Genesis Apocryphon*—to the third or second century BCE—in light of its orthography, morphology, and vocabulary.[144] According to Vasholz, the even older linguistic features of Daniel's Aramaic require a date for Daniel prior to the *Targum of Job*, in other words, prior to the third or second centuries BCE.[145]

9.4.3.2 Zdravko Stefanovic

Zdravko Stefanovic's comparison of Old Aramaic and Daniel represents another attempt to situate Daniel's Aramaic in light of new textual discoveries.[146] He draws his profile for Old Aramaic from a variety of inscriptions—including the Ben-Hadad and Zakkur Stelae, the Sefire Treaty Inscriptions, and the Hadad (Panamuwa) Stele—but gives special attention to the Tel Fakariyah Inscription, discovered in 1979. Stefanovic's basic argument is that the Aramaic of Daniel is aligned with Old Aramaic more than with later Aramaic. His approach is clearly apologetic, which unfortunately often clouds his analysis.[147]

Stefanovic focuses on grammar (orthography, phonology, and morphology) as well as syntax; he does not provide any substantial discussion of vocabulary. Regarding orthography and phonology, Stefanovic argues that vowel letters occasionally appear in Old Aramaic so that their presence in Daniel does not necessarily indicate a late date. For morphology, Stefanovic observes a few similarities between Old Aramaic and Daniel's Aramaic (e.g., use of precative

---

142. Vasholz, "Philological Comparison of the Qumran Job Targum," 92–94; idem, "Qumran and the Dating of Daniel," 318; Archer, "Aramaic of the 'Genesis Apocryphon,'" 163–67; cf. Kutscher, "Language of the 'Genesis Apocryphon,'" 1–35; Machiela, *Dead Sea Genesis Apocryphon*, 134–42; Fitzmyer, *Genesis Apocryphon of Qumran Cave 1*, 25–37. Stephen A. Kaufman dates the *Genesis Apocryphon* to the first century CE ("Job Targum," 325–27). He does so because he assumes that Daniel dates to the second century BCE and that there must be enough time between Daniel and the *Genesis Apocryphon*.

143. Archer, "Aramaic of the 'Genesis Apocryphon,'" 161–69.

144. Vasholz, "Philological Comparison of the Qumran Job Targum," 94–97; idem, "Qumran and the Dating of Daniel," 318–19; cf. Muraoka, "Aramaic of the Old Targum of Job," 441–42; Sokoloff, *Targum to Job*, 9–26; Ploeg, Woude, and Jongeling, *Targum de Job*, 3–4.

145. Vasholz, "Philological Comparison of the Qumran Job Targum," 97–101; idem, "Qumran and the Dating of Daniel," 320.

146. Stefanovic, *Aramaic of Daniel*. This work originated as Stefanovic's PhD dissertation completed at Andrews University in 1987.

147. Cf. Choi, review of *The Aramaic of Daniel in the Light of Old Aramaic*, 469–70.

-לְ) but also acknowledges that there are many differences. Finally, regarding syntax Stefanovic finds several parallels with the Tel Fakariyah Inscription and argues—like Kutscher—that Daniel's Aramaic exhibits Mesopotamian features (e.g., free word order).

9.4.3.3 Jongtae Choi

Finally, the most substantial, up-to-date analysis of Daniel's Aramaic is Jongtae Choi's PhD dissertation, completed at Trinity Evangelical Divinity School under the supervision of Gleason L. Archer, Jr.[148] Like Rowley, Choi's goal is to clarify the chronological relationship between the various Aramaic dialects and the Aramaic of Daniel. However, Choi incorporates many Aramaic texts not considered by Rowley, including the Dead Sea Scrolls. Choi compares all these Aramaic texts in electronically tagged format. Thus, Choi's study is much more comprehensive than Rowley's.

Choi begins with an investigation of Biblical Aramaic's orthography and phonology.[149] Contrary to Rowley, he finds that the most significant phonological changes take place between Old Aramaic and Imperial Aramaic, not between Imperial Aramaic and Biblical Aramaic. Thus, Biblical Aramaic aligns with Imperial Aramaic and Middle Aramaic in terms of its use of later *dalet*, *tav, ayin, tet,* and *sin* for earlier *zayin, shin, qoph, tsade,* and *samek*. Furthermore, although Choi recognizes that final *he* gradually shifted to *aleph* in Aramaic, he finds no definite alignment of Biblical Aramaic with other dialects in these terms.

Choi next analyzes the morphology of Biblical Aramaic.[150] He finds that Daniel's Aramaic seems to be later than that of Ezra's. For example, regarding pronominal suffixes, Choi argues that Ezra's Aramaic reflects a time when both older (e.g., כֹם-) and newer (e.g., כֹון-) forms were still used, whereas Daniel reflects a later stage of Aramaic in which only the younger form was used. Nevertheless, Choi contends that Biblical Aramaic on the whole aligns more closely with Imperial Aramaic than it does later dialects. For example, the absence of final *nun* in the third-person masculine plural *qtl* in Biblical Aramaic corresponds with Imperial Aramaic whereas final *nun* is absent at Qumran.

Choi also finds little evidence to separate Biblical Aramaic—including Daniel—from Imperial Aramaic in terms of syntax.[151] He demonstrates that Rowley's conclusions are incorrect on several syntactical issues including the

---

148. Choi, "Aramaic of Daniel."
149. Choi, "Aramaic of Daniel," 31–80.
150. Choi, "Aramaic of Daniel," 81–178.
151. Choi, "Aramaic of Daniel," 179–218.

usage of the preposition -לְ with infinitives and in dating formulae, which instead align Biblical Aramaic with Imperial Aramaic. Choi also points out that the relative pronoun זְי/דְי only has a retrospective function in Old Aramaic, Imperial Aramaic, and Biblical Aramaic, once again aligning Biblical Aramaic earlier rather than later. In terms of word order, Choi confirms Kutscher's argument that Biblical Aramaic's word order follows the relatively free pattern of eastern Imperial Aramaic texts.

Finally, Choi examines Biblical Aramaic's non-Aramaic words.[152] He notes that Akkadian and Persian loanwords occur frequently in Biblical Aramaic but rarely occur in the Aramaic of the Dead Sea Scrolls. The types of loanwords found in Biblical Aramaic reflect the setting in which Biblical Aramaic was written. For Choi, Biblical Aramaic must have been composed in Mesopotamia rather than Palestine. Furthermore, because at least two Greek words are attested in Imperial Aramaic, Choi rejects Rowley's argument that Daniel's Greek loanwords require a late date for the book.

In light of all these findings, Choi concludes that Biblical Aramaic more closely aligns with Imperial Aramaic than it does later Middle Aramaic. Choi argues that Ezra's mixture of early and late forms, contrasted with Daniel's tendency to use late forms, indicates that Daniel dates later than Ezra. But Daniel nevertheless aligns with Imperial Aramaic and therefore cannot be dated to the second century BCE.[153] The only late feature—which Choi finds in both Ezra and Daniel—is the orthography and phonology. For Choi, this is easily explained through scribal updating. Choi places these orthographical revisions no later than the fourth century BCE in Palestine, whereas Biblical Aramaic itself originated earlier in Mesopotamia as indicated by its word order and foreign loanwords.[154]

9.4.4 Evaluation

Scholarship on dating Biblical Aramaic has come a long way since the turn of the twentieth century. Discoveries of new Aramaic texts have expanded the Aramaic corpus drastically, giving a fuller picture of the Aramaic language during the first millennium BCE. This has refined our understanding of the Aramaic dialects. A particularly noteworthy development along these lines, one that put to rest Driver's and Rowley's argument that Biblical Aramaic originated in Palestine, was Schaeder's proof that first millennium BCE Aramaic did not distinguish between eastern and western dialects as later Aramaic did.

---

152. Choi, "Aramaic of Daniel," 219–30.
153. Choi, "Aramaic of Daniel," 231–34.
154. Choi, "Aramaic of Daniel," 234–35.

Expansion of the Aramaic corpus has permitted more accurate comparison of Biblical Aramaic with other Aramaic dialects. This, in turn, has permitted significant refinement of Driver's and Rowley's conclusion that Biblical Aramaic dated to the fourth and third centuries BCE. The efforts of Kutscher, Kitchen, Coxon, and especially Choi have corrected this picture. As a result, it is now clear that Biblical Aramaic—including Daniel's Aramaic—falls within the dialect of Imperial Aramaic. Furthermore, it is likely that certain features of Biblical Aramaic betray a Mesopotamian origin.

Nevertheless, as comprehensive as Choi's study is, it is not as comprehensive as it could be. Choi did not include the Palestinian Targums, which would have helped to provide a fuller picture of Middle Aramaic. Choi's data for the Elephantine Papyri were also somewhat incomplete because he did not have access to the entire authoritative *Textbook of Aramaic Documents from Egypt*.[155] Furthermore, important new Aramaic texts have been discovered since Choi completed his study in 1994, such as the cache of Imperial Aramaic texts discovered at Bactria.[156] Reevaluation of the data, including the Palestinian Targums and newly discovered Imperial Aramaic texts, would probably not change Choi's basic conclusions. However, it would help to further nuance our understanding of Biblical Aramaic's alignment with other Aramaic dialects.

Integration of sociolinguistics is another area that needs growth. As I noted earlier, increased attention to these issues represents an advance for scholarship on dating Biblical Hebrew texts. However, scholars dealing with the date of Biblical Aramaic have not paid much attention to sociolinguistics. Rather, their explorations have tended to assume that any difference between Biblical Aramaic and other Aramaic dialects should be explained chronologically. So, more attention needs to be given to the sociolinguistic context of language variation and linguistic change. Kutscher has paved the way by explaining some of Biblical Aramaic's features (e.g., word order) in light of its plausible socio-cultural context. However, in the future hopefully more attention will be given to sociolinguistics's possible role.

Moving forward, scholars investigating Biblical Aramaic's date need to be aware of their own presuppositions. Kitchen has rightly stated: "In dealing with the book of Daniel, theological presuppositions are apt to colour even the treatment and dating of its Aramaic."[157] This is evident in the work of critical scholars like Rowley, whose theological presuppositions preclude him from accepting an early composition for the book of Daniel. Theological bias

---

155. Porten and Yardeni, *Textbook of Aramaic Documents*.
156. Naveh and Shaked, *Aramaic Documents from Ancient Bactria*.
157. Kitchen, "Aramaic of Daniel," 32.

is also evident in the work of some conservative scholars, especially Stefanovic, who significantly misjudges and misrepresents data because of his beliefs on Daniel's date. Both Kitchen and Choi do a much better job of evaluating the data objectively, even as they hold to an early date of composition for the book. Hopefully, future scholarship on this topic will follow their lead by balancing commitment to Scripture with objective analysis of the data.

9.5 THE WAYS FORWARD

The dating of Biblical Hebrew and Biblical Aramaic texts has stirred up much debate, especially in recent years. Yet, even as the status quo has been challenged, progress has been made on several fronts. Especially noteworthy are the advances in theory and method.[158] Hebrew Bible scholars have begun to articulate theories of language change that are grounded in modern linguistics and that incorporate sociolinguistics. The diachrony debate has also resulted in the refinement of statistical methods for measuring language change and linguistic variation.

As Hebrew Bible scholars continue to refine their theory, methodology, and analysis, they will do well to learn from other disciplines. Arabic potentially offers much for comparison in terms of the coexistence of written and spoken dialects. Outside the realm of Semitics, Hebrew Bible scholars can potentially learn much from Indo-European philology, which is much more developed than Semitic philology. Furthermore, as I already noted, the linguistic dating of medieval European literature is analogous in many ways to the dating of biblical texts, but what Hebrew Bible scholars can potentially learn is not limited merely to theory and method. Recent advances in linguistic dating of medieval European texts like *Beowulf* have also been accompanied by discussion of how one's presuppositions and expectations of data tie in with linguistic dating.[159] It seems that Hebrew Bible scholars would profit from Indo-Europeanists' insights on both the opportunities and limits of linguistic dating.[160]

On this note, another area to be addressed is *LDBT*'s notion of textual fluidity. This concept is part of a larger trend known as the "New Philology."[161] This movement reacts against classical philology by claiming that all textual traditions are meaningful, not merely a means to reconstructing a hypothetical

---

158. Cf. Naudé and Miller-Naudé, "Historical Linguistics, Editorial Theory, and Biblical Hebrew," 834, 860–62.

159. E.g., Fulk, "On Argumentation in Old English Philology," 1–26.

160. Cf. Klein, "Historical Linguistics and Biblical Hebrew," 865–80.

161. Cf. Lied and Lundhaug, *Snapshots of Evolving Traditions*.

original text. This directly impacts the debate because textual fluidity is alleged to undermine the stability that diachronic analysis requires. This issue is complex and interrelated with ancient Near Eastern scribal culture and textual criticism. Some scholars have attempted to address these other issues, especially as they relate to the canon of the Hebrew Bible,[162] but more work needs to be done from the perspective of historical linguistics and diachronic dating.

I am confident that, moving forward, these and other important issues will continue to be explored by scholars. But I also hope that teachers, students, and pastors familiarize themselves with the debate along the way. Because the date of a text's composition directly relates to its historical-cultural background, a better understanding of linguistic dating can only enhance our exegesis of Scripture.

9.6 Further Reading

Choi, Jongtae. "The Aramaic of Daniel: Its Date, Place of Composition and Linguistic Comparison with Extra-Biblical Texts." PhD diss., Trinity Evangelical Divinity School, 1994.

Forbes, A. Dean. "The Diachrony Debate: A Tutorial on Methods." *JSem* 25 (2016): 881–926.

Gianto, Agustinus. "Archaic Biblical Hebrew." Pages 19–29 in vol. 1 of *A Handbook of Biblical Hebrew*. Edited by W. Randall Garr and Steven E. Fassberg. 2 vols. Winona Lake, IN: Eisenbrauns, 2016.

Hendel, Ronald S. and Jan Joosten. *How Old Is the Hebrew Bible? A Linguistic, Textual, and Historical Study*. ABRL. New Haven: Yale University Press, 2018.

Hornkohl, Aaron D. "Biblical Hebrew: Periodization." *EHLL* 1:315–25.

———. "Transitional Biblical Hebrew." Pages 31–42 in vol. 1 of *A Handbook of Biblical Hebrew*. Edited by W. Randall Garr and Steven E. Fassberg. 2 vols. Winona Lake, IN: Eisenbrauns, 2016.

Hurvitz, Avi. "Biblical Hebrew, Late." *EHLL* 1:329–38.

Kitchen, Kenneth A. "The Aramaic of Daniel." Pages 31–79 in *Notes on Some Problems in the Book of Daniel*. Edited by Donald J. Wiseman. London: Tyndale Press, 1965.

Lam, Joseph and Dennis Pardee. "Standard/Classical Biblical Hebrew." Pages 1–18 in vol. 1 of *A Handbook of Biblical Hebrew*. Edited by W. Randall Garr and Steven E. Fassberg. 2 vols. Winona Lake, IN: Eisenbrauns, 2016.

Mandell, Alice. "Biblical Hebrew, Archaic." *EHLL* 1:325–29.

Miller-Naudé, Cynthia L. and Ziony Zevit, eds. *Diachrony in Biblical Hebrew*. LSAWS 8. Winona Lake, IN: Eisenbrauns, 2012.

---

162. Cf. Toorn, *Scribal Culture*; Walton and Sandy, *Lost World of Scripture*.

Morgenstern, Matthew. "Late Biblical Hebrew." Pages 43–54 in vol. 1 of *A Handbook of Biblical Hebrew*. Edited by W. Randall Garr and Steven E. Fassberg. 2 vols. Winona Lake, IN: Eisenbrauns, 2016.

Naudé, Jacobus A. "The Complexity of Language Change: The Case of Ancient Hebrew." *Southern African Linguistics and Applied Language Studies* 30 (2012): 395–411.

Naudé, Jacobus A. and Cynthia L. Miller-Naudé. "Historical Linguistics, Editorial Theory, and Biblical Hebrew: The Current State of the Debate." *JSem* 25 (2016): 833–64.

Rezetko, Robert and Ian Young. "Currents in the Historical Linguistics and Linguistic Dating of the Hebrew Bible." *HIPHIL Novum* 5.1 (2019): 3–95.

———. *Historical Linguistics and Biblical Hebrew: Steps Toward an Integrated Approach.* Society of Biblical Literature Ancient Near Eastern Monographs 9. Atlanta: Society of Biblical Literature, 2014.

Walker, Larry L. "Notes on Higher Criticism and the Dating of Biblical Hebrew." Pages 35–52 in *A Tribute to Gleason Archer*. Edited by Walter C. Kaiser, Jr. and Ronald F. Youngblood. Chicago: Moody, 1986.

Young, Ian, Robert Rezetko, and Martin Ehrensvärd. *Linguistic Dating of Biblical Texts*. 2 vols. Bible World. London: Equinox, 2008.

CHAPTER 10

TEACHING *and* LEARNING *the* LANGUAGES *of the* HEBREW BIBLE

Learning how to teach languages from those who have devoted their professional lives to that project can only increase our success at bringing students closer to the text that is the center of our concern.

—FREDERICK E. GREENSPAHN[1]

10.1 INTRODUCTION

In her 2015 presidential address to the National Association of Professors of Hebrew, Cynthia Miller-Naudé lamented several challenges facing the study of Biblical Hebrew today.[2] The rapidly changing landscape of education has prompted many institutions to lower or even remove their curriculum requirements for Biblical Hebrew. Students often wonder whether learning Biblical Hebrew is ultimately worth the time and effort required to achieve proficiency. Accordingly, it is not uncommon for Biblical Hebrew courses to suffer from low enrollment. These difficulties are only exacerbated by the fact that many students who do complete a full Biblical Hebrew sequence fail to retain the language when they face the realities of life and ministry after graduation.

In such a challenging climate, it is crucial that instructors of Biblical Hebrew and Biblical Aramaic show students and academic institutions how firsthand knowledge of the biblical languages is more than worth the time and energy

---

1. Greenspahn, "Why Hebrew Textbooks Are Different."
2. Miller-Naudé, "Presidential Perspective," 1–3.

required to master them. The key to accomplishing this is a commitment to successful pedagogy. Instructors of Biblical Hebrew and Biblical Aramaic must engage their students effectively and bring about lasting acquisition of the languages, not merely transference of knowledge about the languages. Only then will pastors and scholars be empowered to use Hebrew and Aramaic fruitfully for exegesis and ministry.

This chapter discusses the teaching and learning of Biblical Hebrew and Biblical Aramaic. I address developments within the traditional approach to teaching Biblical Hebrew and Biblical Aramaic, explore the emergence of the communicative approach as a more effective form of pedagogy, and discuss several strategies for retaining the biblical languages. Throughout I focus primarily on Biblical Hebrew because most institutions offer Hebrew more regularly than Aramaic and also because the vast majority of educational resources are geared at learning Hebrew.

10.2 Fresh Ideas for Traditional Methods

The vast majority of Biblical Hebrew and Biblical Aramaic textbooks on the market today adopt what is known as the Grammar-Translation Method.[3] This method, familiar to many, is characterized by explicit, systematic teaching of grammar and vocabulary in the student's native language. Content is reinforced and tested by means of memorization, translation, parsing exercises, and simple vocabulary quizzes.[4]

It is unfortunate that so many textbooks continue to follow the Grammar-Translation Method. This is especially true because Second Language Acquisition research indicates that it is one of the least effective methods of promoting language acquisition in use today; it lacks rationale and justification in the scholarly literature on Second Language Acquisition.[5] Yet, a few notable developments have emerged over the past few decades with respect to textbooks and technology. I discuss these advances before turning to the emergence of more pedagogically sound methods for teaching the biblical languages.

10.2.1 Textbooks

The first development in teaching the biblical languages with the Grammar-Translation Method regards textbooks. The basic lesson content of most biblical

---

3. Noonan, "Recent Teaching Grammars for Biblical Hebrew," 104–5.
4. Hadley, *Teaching Language in Context*, 106–7.
5. Hadley, *Teaching Language in Context*, 107–8.

language textbooks remains the same as it has long been.[6] Yet recent biblical language textbooks have incorporated more and more supplemental material to reinforce the basic lesson content. Some supplemental materials, such as paradigms and Hebrew-to-English or English-to-Hebrew glossaries, have been around for years, but many recent grammars include workbooks and student exercises with answer keys.[7] This trend essentially began with the publication of Gary D. Pratico and Miles V. Van Pelt's *Basics of Biblical Hebrew Grammar* and Van Pelt's *Basics of Biblical Aramaic*, modeled on the hybrid inductive-deductive approach of William D. Mounce's *Basics of Biblical Greek Grammar*. The inclusion of workbooks, student exercises, and answer keys is important because they provide the student with plenty of exercises whose answers can be checked immediately. Nevertheless, most current workbooks and student exercises stick with the traditional approach of translating from Hebrew or Aramaic to English, with very few incorporating other activities.[8]

Another advancement in traditional grammars is the incorporation of authentic biblical texts. Generally speaking, biblical language textbooks tend to incorporate more and more authentic biblical material as lessons progress.[9] This is an important development because being able to read the biblical text provides the student with ongoing motivation for learning Biblical Hebrew and Biblical Aramaic. Even still, only a few traditional grammars, such as Brian Webster's *Reading Biblical Hebrew*, incorporate biblical texts early on by including English glosses. Avoidance of biblical texts at a textbook's beginning is probably provoked by the students' minimal knowledge of the biblical languages at the beginning of a course. Nevertheless, the inclusion of authentic biblical texts should be a top priority because it helps motivate the student and build confidence. Furthermore, Webster's textbook demonstrates that this can be done effectively.

Alongside traditional grammar textbooks, some advances have also been made in the area of vocabulary resources. Larry A. Mitchel's classic, *A Student's Vocabulary for Biblical Hebrew and Aramaic*, has recently been re-typeset and made accessible to a new generation of Hebrew and Aramaic students. An especially welcome resource is J. David Pleins's *Biblical Hebrew Vocabulary by Conceptual Categories*. This innovative book arranges Hebrew vocabulary by semantic domain rather than frequency. Such an arrangement helps students to expand their knowledge of Hebrew vocabulary beyond basic glosses. It does

---

6. Noonan, "Recent Teaching Grammars for Biblical Hebrew," 102–3.
7. Noonan, "Recent Teaching Grammars for Biblical Hebrew," 99–100.
8. Noonan, "Recent Teaching Grammars for Biblical Hebrew," 104–5.
9. Noonan, "Recent Teaching Grammars for Biblical Hebrew," 104–6.

so by facilitating connections with words in similar semantic domains, helping students to see the links between Hebrew words and real-world contexts.

10.2.2 Technology

The second development in teaching the biblical languages with the Grammar-Translation Method regards technology. Education in general has seen many technological developments in recent years. Similar to all technological advances, which can have both positive and negative effects, these developments have the potential either to facilitate or to hinder learning Biblical Hebrew and Biblical Aramaic.

Use of technology for classroom presentation is a topic familiar to most and therefore requires little comment. The learning possibilities provided by PowerPoint and other audio-visual presentation methods are vast, not least of which is the ability to better engage students. What is important to point out, however, is that use of this technology must be accompanied by attention to pedagogical method. Classroom technology is a wonderful asset, but it is merely a pedagogical tool and does not guarantee effective instruction.[10]

Also well known to many is the rapid expansion of online education. Numerous institutions have developed online biblical language courses using learning management systems such as Canvas, Blackboard, and Moodle. Fully packaged online course modules, such as those available through BibleMesh,[11] are also available for purchase. The important question once again, however, is how to use these resources effectively. Being skills-based, rather than content-based, Biblical Hebrew and Biblical Aramaic are best taught under the apprenticeship model. Replicating this pedagogical approach online is difficult, although instructors can help their online students to succeed by assuming a role like that of a learning coach.[12]

The topic of digital supplements is perhaps less well-known and deserving of some comment. Very few biblical language textbooks following the Grammar-Translation Method include some kind of digital supplement.[13] Webster's *Reading Biblical Hebrew* has an accompanying website that includes grammar illustrations, parsing practice, practice reading, and vocabulary flashcards. Pratico and Van Pelt's *Basics of Biblical Hebrew Grammar* and Van Pelt's *Basics of Biblical Aramaic* similarly have an e-workbook, accompanying video lectures, online answer keys, and audio recordings of vocabulary. These resources

---

10. Morse, "Learning and Retention of Biblical Languages," 45–46.
11. http://courses.zondervanacademic.com/biblical-languages/hebrew.
12. Harlow, "Succesfully Teaching Biblical Languages Online," 13–24.
13. Noonan, "Recent Teaching Grammars for Biblical Hebrew," 100.

provide students with multiple avenues for learning outside the classroom and are therefore a welcome addition to biblical language pedagogy. Nevertheless, the incorporation of digital supplements remains largely untapped. Future textbooks should be designed for use on devices, complete with hyperlinked material such as interactive materials, audio, and supplemental videos.[14]

Education-based websites independent of biblical language textbooks can also benefit teachers and students. Some websites are geared toward providing free instruction in Biblical Hebrew, such as the website Hebrew for Christians.[15] Other websites provide resources for reinforcing grammar and vocabulary. A good example of such a website is Quizlet.[16] Quizlet enables instructors to create online vocabulary flashcards accompanied by audio and images, aiding students in making a form-meaning connection without interference from their native language. Students can keep track of their vocabulary-learning progress by means of the flashcards, but they can also learn Hebrew and Aramaic vocabulary by means of other activities built into Quizlet. These include matching activities and even different games by which students can compete against their classmates. All this provides additional motivation for learning Biblical Hebrew and Biblical Aramaic.

Finally, Bible software packages such as Accordance and Logos bring welcome technological advances for learning Biblical Hebrew and Biblical Aramaic. Bible software is perhaps most useful beginning with the second year of language learning when students move into advanced reading and exegesis of Hebrew and Aramaic texts. Reading courses can be enhanced by projecting the Bible software's original text for the whole class to see; with each student watching, the instructor can easily pull up resources such as grammars or lexicons and search for words or forms, providing hands-on experience with these resources. The instructor might also require an assignment in which students search for a particular syntactic construction so they can discover for themselves what that construction means.

However, Bible software has the potential to hinder the learning of Biblical Hebrew and Biblical Aramaic, and therefore it must be used wisely. One danger is overreliance on the software's English glosses and parsing information, which naturally weakens one's memorization and internalization of the biblical languages. Another danger is that Bible software is unable to unlock the elements of Hebrew and Aramaic that cannot be parsed, such as the contextual nuance of words; it is for this reason that biblical language tools classes

---

14. Callaham, "Rethinking Biblical Hebrew Instruction," 256–57.

15. http://www.hebrew4christians.com/.

16. https://www.quizlet.com/.

(i.e., classes that teach students about the biblical languages and how to use basic tools for exegesis) are ultimately inadequate substitutes for reading Hebrew and Aramaic. As noted below, similar perils exist when using Bible software for retention purposes.

10.3 NEW METHODS FOR TEACHING THE BIBLICAL LANGUAGES

Despite the overall popularity of the Grammar-Translation Method, a growing number of language instructors are seeking more effective ways to help students learn. Their explorations have led them to Communicative Language Teaching, a more recent approach to teaching foreign languages that finds its basis in modern research on Second Language Acquisition. Teaching the biblical languages communicatively has become a common topic of academic conferences and scholarly publications. Several Biblical Hebrew grammars based on a communicative approach have even emerged. In the discussion that follows, I focus on Biblical Hebrew because most applications of Communicative Language Teaching to the languages of the Hebrew Bible have focused on Biblical Hebrew, not Biblical Aramaic.

10.3.1 Communicative Language Teaching

Communicative Language Teaching developed during the latter half of the twentieth century, in part as a response to the Grammar-Translation Method's emphasis on Structuralism. As its name implies, Communicative Language Teaching focuses on language's potential to communicate rather than on mastery of linguistic structures. Practically speaking, this means that language teachers utilize real-world tasks—especially speaking, listening, writing, and reading—in the classroom. These tasks are conducted in the second language as much as possible in order to increase student proficiency. The use of real-world tasks like this facilitates connections with real life, provides motivation for learning, and minimizes explicit grammar instruction (which unnecessarily encumbers a student's ability to process new material).[17]

The communicative approach includes a variety of different methods, including Total Physical Response, Total Physical Response Storytelling, Content-Based Instruction, and Processing Instruction. Total Physical Response, based on the assumption that students learn a second language the same way they learned their first language, requires students to respond to verbal commands

---

17. Hadley, *Teaching Language in Context*, 116–18.

given by the instructor.[18] Total Physical Response Storytelling is similar but also incorporates reading and writing to supplement the auditory focus of simple Total Physical Response.[19] Content-Based Instruction, or Immersion, places students in environments characterized by use of the second language, forcing them to use it rather than their first language.[20] Finally, Processing Instruction provides the student with comprehensible and meaningful input in the second language through real-world, relevant communication, often in the form of classroom activities. This method has proved particularly effective in the teaching of different languages.[21]

Most modern language programs adopt the communicative approach because it has been proven very effective.[22] For this reason, some instructors of ancient languages, including Greek and Latin, have adopted the communicative approach in their classrooms.[23] Similarly, in recent years a growing number of Biblical Hebrew instructors have sought to incorporate Communicative Language Teaching in various ways. I now sketch these developments, following in many aspects Scott J. McQuinn's important survey.[24]

10.3.2 Textbooks

One of the primary evidences of interest in Communicative Language Teaching is the emergence of Biblical Hebrew (but not yet Biblical Aramaic) textbooks that seek to incorporate a communicative approach. The most noteworthy textbooks in this vein are Randall Buth's *Living Biblical Hebrew*, John A. Cook and Robert D. Holmstedt's *Beginning Biblical Hebrew*, Paul Overland's *Learning Biblical Hebrew Interactively*, and Hélène M. Dallaire's *Biblical Hebrew: A Living Language*.[25]

10.3.2.1 Randall Buth's *Living Biblical Hebrew*

Randall Buth was the first to apply Communicative Language Teaching to Biblical Hebrew (and Biblical Koine Greek). He received his PhD in Semitic Languages from the University of California, Los Angeles and served as a Bible translator and translation consultant in Africa until he moved to Israel. There, he founded the Biblical Language Center, where he and his team offer Biblical

---

18. Asher, "Children's First Language as a Model," 133–39.
19. Ray and Seely, *Fluency through TPR Storytelling.*
20. Brinton, Snow, and Wesche, *Content-Based Second Language Instruction.*
21. VanPatten, *Input Processing and Grammar Instruction*; idem, *Processing Instruction.*
22. Richards and Rodgers, *Approaches and Methods in Language Teaching*, 83–84.
23. Cf. Gruber-Miller, *When Dead Tongues Speak.*
24. McQuinn, "Principled Communicative Methodology," 88–116.
25. McQuinn, "Principled Communicative Methodology," 88–104.

Hebrew language courses based on the ulpan immersion model. An outgrowth of Buth's immersion classes is his *Living Biblical Hebrew*, published as two parts with accompanying online modules.

Part one of *Living Biblical Hebrew* consists of about 1000 illustrations accompanied by audio that describes the images. The words, phrases, and events depicted in the illustrations gradually become more complex; only toward the end are students explicitly introduced to grammatical principles that they learned implicitly through the illustrations. Part two consists of short dialogues that prepare the student to read the Hebrew Bible. The dialogues accomplish this goal by introducing both vocabulary and grammar inductively. Passages from the book of Jonah, with audio and annotations, reinforce the material learned from the dialogues.

10.3.2.2 John A. Cook and Robert D. Holmstedt's *Beginning Biblical Hebrew*

John A. Cook and Robert D. Holmstedt both graduated from the University of Wisconsin–Madison, where they received their doctorates and began to develop their own methodology for the teaching of Biblical Hebrew. They continued to refine their approach as they taught Hebrew at their respective institutions: Cook at Asbury Theological Seminary and Holmstedt at the University of Toronto. Then, in 2013 they together published *Beginning Biblical Hebrew: A Grammar and Illustrated Reader*. As claimed in the preface, their textbook possesses several distinctives "grounded in modern methods for teaching languages."[26]

Beginning Biblical Hebrew features simple chapters with a minimal amount of grammar; more advanced topics or topics requiring detailed explanation (such as weak verbs) are relegated to the book's appendixes. This facilitates the presentation of grammar in small chunks and leaves more space for text-based exercises. The chapter exercises consist of traditional translation and parsing activities but also call students to write in Hebrew and complete small-group activities. An accompanying illustrated reader, which includes a variety of creative activities as well as color comic-strip presentations of the biblical text, is the most distinctive feature of *Beginning Biblical Hebrew*. A website with additional resources supplements the textbook,[27] and further materials (e.g., an instructor's manual, sample quizzes, and lesson plans) are available from the publisher for instructors.[28]

---

26. Cook and Holmstedt, *Beginning Biblical Hebrew*, 9.
27. http://www.beginningbiblicalhebrew.com/.
28. http://www.bakerpublishinggroup.com/books/beginning-biblical-hebrew/342630/esources.

10.3.2.3 Paul Overland's *Learning Biblical Hebrew Interactively*

Paul Overland, who currently teaches for Ashland Theological Seminary in Ohio, was raised within a bilingual context in Japan. Recalling how he learned Japanese by immersion and faced with students struggling to learn Hebrew via the Grammar-Translation Method, Overland began to explore the communicative approach. His investigations eventually prompted him to spearhead a workshop known as the Cohelet (Communicative Hebrew Learning and Teaching) Project, which developed and field-tested communicative materials for the Hebrew classroom.[29] Overland subsequently adapted many of the Cohelet Project materials into his own textbook, *Learning Biblical Hebrew Interactively*, which seeks to be "an SLA-oriented introductory textbook for Biblical Hebrew."[30]

In accordance with this goal, *Learning Biblical Hebrew Interactively* provides numerous output activities (e.g., conversations, writing activities, and games) in addition to traditional grammar explanations. Each lesson centers on a serialized adaptation of the book of Jonah, which reinforces the module's grammar and vocabulary, and more than forty articles throughout provide connections to the cultural context of Biblical Hebrew. A supplementary website provides a full set of instructional videos, PowerPoint presentations of each Jonah episode, audio files of vocabulary, and communicative-based assessments.[31]

10.3.2.4 Hélène M. Dallaire's *Biblical Hebrew: A Living Language*

Hélène M. Dallaire teaches for Denver Seminary in Colorado. She became interested in the communicative approach to teaching Biblical Hebrew after studying Modern Hebrew at an ulpan in Israel. Her ulpan experience convinced her that the best way to learn a language is to actively engage with it in a dynamic, interactive way. This realization prompted her to author her own textbook, *Biblical Hebrew: A Living Language*, first published in 2016. According to the preface, the textbook "is designed for teachers who wish to use a *blended* approach in classroom instruction."[32]

Each chapter begins with a brief devotional song followed by a cartoon entitled "Micah, Tamar, and Rabbi Shlomo," which serves as a review of the previous chapter's content. Then various in-class exercises and activities are interwoven in the midst of the chapter's grammar explanations, which utilize

---

29. https://sites.google.com/a/ashland.edu/cohelet/.

30. Overland, *Learning Biblical Hebrew Interactively*, 1:xii. Overland has also published *Millim: Words for Conversation in the Biblical Hebrew Classroom*. This helpful resource, which can supplement *Learning Biblical Hebrew Interactively*, lists many words and phrases for conversing in Biblical Hebrew.

31. http://www.learningbiblicalhebrewinteractively.com/.

32. Dallaire, *Biblical Hebrew*, i. The emphasis is original.

color to mark important features like vowel patterns. Dallaire provides homework exercises for each chapter, many of which entail writing in Hebrew in addition to the typical Hebrew-to-English translation. A website with teaching and visual vocabulary PowerPoints, assessments, and teaching suggestions for each chapter supplements the textbook.[33]

10.3.3 Institutes and Biblical Language Programs

In addition to textbooks, the emergence of several institutes and language programs reflect growing interest in teaching the biblical languages communicatively. The most important of these are the Biblical Language Center, the Institute for Biblical Languages and Translation, and Polis: The Jerusalem Institute of Languages and Humanities.[34]

10.3.3.1 Biblical Language Center

As noted earlier, Randall Buth founded the Biblical Language Center as a venue for teaching the biblical languages through immersion. This approach seeks to imitate the way that young children learn language, in other words, hearing and using Biblical Hebrew in context. Each Biblical Hebrew class is led by two instructors, which provides the repetition necessary for language learning and enables teachers to use each other as pedagogical props. Total Physical Response and Total Physical Response Storytelling represent the two primary teaching techniques used, creating a full immersion experience. The result is that more than 90 percent of the Biblical Language Center's classroom time consists of the spoken biblical language. Assigned reading and listening from Buth's *Living Biblical Hebrew* and its accompanying audio reinforce the day's content and prepare students for the next class.[35]

10.3.3.2 The Institute for Biblical Languages and Translation

The Institute for Biblical Languages and Translation regularly offers intensive workshops in Biblical Hebrew Fluency and Pedagogy that are available to instructors.[36] For those that wish to go deeper, the Institute also offers two different programs that count for Hebrew credit. The first program is a one-month intensive course, taught almost exclusively (approximately 90 percent) in Biblical Hebrew by means of oral teaching methods.[37] The second program

---

33. http://www.biblicalhebrew-livinglanguage.com/.
34. McQuinn, "Principled Communicative Methodology," 105–10.
35. https://www.biblicallanguagecenter.com/methodology/.
36. https://iblt.institute/programs/intensives/biblical-hebrew-fluency-and-pedagogy-workshop/.
37. https://iblt.ac/programs/intensives/introduction-to-biblical-hebrew/.

is an eight-month-long course designed to equip participants with the skills necessary for translating the Hebrew Bible. Similar to the Biblical Language Center's program, class sessions are structured around communicative activities like Total Physical Response, Teaching Proficiency through Reading and Storytelling, and Role Playing.[38]

10.3.3.3 Polis: The Jerusalem Institute of Language and Humanities

Polis was founded to reconnect western civilization with both its Judeo-Christian and classical Greco-Roman heritage. To this end, Polis offers reading fluency training in ancient languages, including Greek, Latin, Hebrew, Arabic, and Aramaic. Polis teaches these languages via the "Polis Method." This method consists of full immersion in the target language, using Total Physical Response, interactive narrative and stories, props, and songs. No speaking in one's native language is allowed. The end result, according to Polis, is that after two intensive summer courses students are able to read and understand simple ancient texts without a dictionary.[39] This includes Polis's Biblical Hebrew course, which fully immerses participants in Biblical Hebrew and requires they listen, speak, read, and write in the language.[40]

10.3.4 Other Voices

Lastly, several other voices promote the communicative teaching of Biblical Hebrew. At the institutional level, many different instructors have successfully implemented the communicative approach in their biblical language courses. Among them are Paul Ferris (Bethel University), Lee Fields (Mid-Atlantic Christian University), Jennifer Noonan (Columbia International University), and Brian Schultz (Fresno Pacific University). These and other like-minded individuals regularly participate in sessions on applied linguistics at the annual Society of Biblical Literature and Evangelical Theological Society meetings. Their sessions on applied linguistics and the biblical languages regularly discuss various aspects of Communicative Language Teaching in the Hebrew classroom. The high attendance rates of these sessions attest to a growing interest in the communicative approach to teaching the biblical languages.

10.3.5 Evaluation

As already noted, research demonstrates the superiority of Communicative Language Teaching to the Grammar-Translation Method for modern languages.

---

38. https://iblt.ac/programs/school-of-biblical-hebrew/.
39. http://www.polisjerusalem.org/polis-method.
40. http://www.polisjerusalem.org/biblical-hebrew-language-course.

Anecdotal evidence likewise points to the many benefits of teaching the biblical languages communicatively, both in terms of the learning experience it creates and the results it produces.[41] Given its many benefits, we should not be surprised by the recent emergence of textbooks and institutes affirming the communicative approach. Especially encouraging among these are Buth's *Living Biblical Hebrew* and Overland's *Learning Biblical Hebrew Interactively*, which out of all recent textbooks best incorporate principles of Second Language Acquisition.[42] All in all, recent interest in applying Communicative Language Teaching to the biblical languages is both a welcome and promising development.[43]

Yet, the communicative approach to Biblical Hebrew remains a relatively new field and faces several challenges. In particular, the great diversity of applications of Second Language Acquisition insights to teaching the biblical languages reveals the need for collaboration and further research on this topic. There is no common body of resources or research available for instructors seeking to implement the communicative approach into their own teaching. This has resulted in an inconsistent application of Communicative Language Teaching to Biblical Hebrew. There is therefore great need for a common body of research that shows how Second Language Acquisition research can be applied to teaching the biblical languages.[44] Empirical research is also needed to establish the benefits of and best practices for teaching Biblical Hebrew communicatively.[45] Such research will, undoubtedly, also empower instructors as they continue to develop a linguistically informed methodology for Biblical Hebrew pedagogy.

A closely related challenge is the general lack of training in communicative instruction. Currently, few instructors of Biblical Hebrew have specific training in applying communicative methods to the Biblical Hebrew classroom. This trend, however, is changing. Many of the institutes and language programs discussed above provide opportunity for instructors to learn how to teach

---

41. For example, the results of the Cohelet project, reported at the 2008 annual meeting of the National Association of Professors of Hebrew and in the journal *Foreign Language Annals*, were primarily positive. All the instructors and more than two-thirds of the students who participated reported that learning Biblical Hebrew by Communicative Language Teaching was effective and preferable to the Grammar-Translation Method. See Overland, Fields, and Noonan, "Communicative Principles," 583–98.

42. McQuinn, "Principled Communicative Methodology," 104. Cook and Holmstedt's *Beginning Biblical Hebrew* and Dallaire's *Biblical Hebrew* have many different various—and praiseworthy—elements characteristic of the communicative approach. But, on the whole they are largely structured around the traditional Grammar-Translation method and therefore are less valuable than Buth's *Living Biblical Hebrew* and Overland's *Learning Biblical Hebrew Interactively*.

43. Cf. Noonan, "Teaching Biblical Hebrew," 326–34.

44. McQuinn, "Principled Communicative Methodology," 114–16.

45. For an example of such a study, see Noonan, "Using Processing Instruction to Teach Biblical Hebrew Grammar."

communicatively. Perhaps the best option is the Biblical Language Center, which hosts regular training workshops for Biblical Hebrew that are available to instructors.[46] Many instructors have already gone through the Biblical Language Center's ulpan in order to learn how to teach Biblical Hebrew communicatively.[47] Similarly, since the Cohelet Project, Overland has held several workshops to train Biblical Hebrew teachers in the communicative approach.[48] Hopefully, as more instructors receive training in teaching Biblical Hebrew communicatively, they will be able to replicate the necessary skills in others.

Institutional realities present an additional challenge. This obstacle is not necessarily specific to the communicative approach because any approach to teaching Biblical Hebrew—not just Communicative Language Teaching—requires sufficient time and resources. In an era when many schools are lowering and even removing biblical language requirements, institutions are reluctant to devote time and resources to Biblical Hebrew language learning. However, instructors can offer creative solutions to work around these hurdles. Technology offers one possible way out through the capability of blended learning environments, such as the flipped classroom.[49] The creation of a Biblical Hebrew language lab, akin to language labs in most other foreign language programs, could facilitate communicative learning, as could the hosting of various Biblical Hebrew social events.[50] Speaking from my own experience, I meet weekly with my students for lunch to practice reading and speaking Biblical Hebrew, and I coordinate various social events—such as an annual Passover Seder and Hanukkah party—under the auspices of Eta Beta Rho, a national Hebrew honor society connected with the National Association of Professors of Hebrew.[51] These activities encourage communicative learning and generate interest in Biblical Hebrew on campus.

10.4 RETAINING BIBLICAL HEBREW AND BIBLICAL ARAMAIC

The last topic I address in this chapter is retention. Retention is important because students learn the biblical languages not merely to know them, but to use them. Furthermore, given the amount of time and effort required to learn Biblical Hebrew and Biblical Aramaic, it would be a shame not to keep them!

---

46. https://www.biblicallanguagecenter.com/workshops/.
47. Randall Buth, email message to author, December 22, 2016.
48. Paul Overland, email message to author, December 22, 2016.
49. Sigrist, "Overcoming Obstacles."
50. Cf. Streett, "Immersion Greek."
51. http://www.naphhebrew.org/eta-beta-rho.

The best way to retain the biblical languages is to learn them well the first time. A solid foundation in Biblical Hebrew and Biblical Aramaic makes reading the biblical text easy and enjoyable, which in turn facilitates retention. Beyond this, however, there are various strategies for retaining the biblical languages. In an essay entitled "Keeping Your Hebrew Healthy," Dennis Magary helpfully divides these strategies into two basic categories: review and use.[52]

Review of vocabulary and grammar is necessary because one cannot achieve reading fluency without a solid grasp of them. To maintain vocabulary, Magary recommends tackling approximately twenty-five words each week.[53] Electronic resources such as Quizlet, mentioned above, prove very helpful in this regard, but print resources such as Miles V. Van Pelt and Gary D. Pratico's *The Vocabulary Guide to Biblical Hebrew and Aramaic* remain useful. To retain grammar, Magary suggests reading through any one of the standard grammars, with the reading set at the pace required by comprehension.[54]

The second key to retaining the biblical languages is reading the biblical text. The old adage "use it or lose it" certainly applies to Biblical Hebrew and Biblical Aramaic, and regular reading of the Hebrew Bible is the best way to refresh the memory and reinforce the knowledge and skills one has already learned. Reading of the biblical text should alternate between fast-paced, sectional readings and slow-paced, close readings in order to build reading confidence and the ability to interact carefully with the text. As Magary points out, audio readings can serve as a helpful supplement and reinforcement of one's own visual reading.[55] An excellent resource for this is the ASI Hebrew Bible, originally produced by Audio Scriptures International, and now available through multiple websites online.[56] Another helpful resource for listening to the text of the Old Testament is the BSI Hebrew Audio Bible, a dramatized reading of the Hebrew Bible (complete with different voice actors for the narrator and characters, as well as sound effects and music) produced by the Bible Society in Israel.[57]

To read the biblical text, one must select a text edition such as *Biblia Hebraica Stuttgartensia* or its partially completed successor, *Biblia Hebraica Quinta*. However, even with a solid grasp of vocabulary, one is bound to encounter words not yet learned. Thus, a welcome development of recent

---

52. Magary, "Keeping Your Hebrew Healthy," 29–55.
53. Magary, "Keeping Your Hebrew Healthy," 34–37.
54. Magary, "Keeping Your Hebrew Healthy," 37–42.
55. Magary, "Keeping Your Hebrew Healthy," 43.
56. See, for example, http://www.aoal.org/hebrew_audiobible.htm.
57. http://haktuvim.co.il/en/study/Gen.1.1.

years is the emergence of several reader's Bibles, including *A Reader's Hebrew Bible* (edited by A. Phillip Brown II and Bryan W. Smith) and *Biblia Hebraica Stuttgartensia: A Reader's Edition* (edited by Donald R. Vance, George Athas, and Yael Avrahami). The former glosses all words occurring fewer than one-hundred times whereas the latter, based entirely on the text of *Biblia Hebraica Stuttgartensia*, glosses all words occurring fewer than seventy times and also parses all weak verbs. Resources such as these are to be preferred over interlinear Bibles or electronic editions of the biblical text found in Bible software packages. The latter make it all too easy to over rely on English glosses and parsing information and are therefore not helpful tools for retaining Biblical Hebrew and Biblical Aramaic, despite any usefulness they might have otherwise.

Especially effective for retaining proficiency in the biblical languages is Hendrickson's Two Minutes a Day Biblical Languages Series. Edited by Jonathan G. Kline, this series includes two volumes for Biblical Hebrew (*Keep Up Your Biblical Hebrew in Two Minutes a Day*) and one volume for Biblical Aramaic (*Keep Up Your Biblical Aramaic in Two Minutes a Day*). Each of these volumes contains 365 one-verse passages from the Hebrew Bible. For each passage the Hebrew or Aramaic text of each verse is presented first in full and secondly divided into phrases, accompanied by an English translation. Each passage, furthermore, intentionally introduces one (for Hebrew) or two (for Aramaic) new vocabulary words. The new words are presented in order of decreasing frequency so that the reader has reviewed the most common 730 Hebrew words upon completion of both Hebrew volumes and all the Hebrew Bible's 716 Aramaic words after reading the Aramaic volume. Thus, Kline's *Keep Up Your Biblical Hebrew* and *Keep Up Your Biblical Aramaic* serve as valuable tools for maintaining reading proficiency as well as vocabulary.

Other helpful resources for reading practice include devotionals such as Heinrich Bitzer's *Light on the Path* or its sequel, *More Light on the Path* by David W. Baker and Elaine A. Heath. The recent *Devotions on the Hebrew Bible: 54 Reflections to Inspire & Instruct*, edited by Milton Eng and Lee M. Fields, is also a helpful collection of Hebrew devotionals that keeps the reader engaged with Biblical Hebrew while showing the value and relevance of knowing the language. Unlike the devotionals by Bitzer and Baker and Heath, *Devotions on the Hebrew Bible* is dedicated exclusively to Biblical Hebrew, and its selections intentionally attempt to present a wide variety of insights from representative samples of the entire Hebrew Bible.

Another helpful resource along these lines is H. H. Hardy II's *Exegetical Gems from Biblical Hebrew: A Refreshing Guide to Grammar and Interpretation*. This book presents thirty different topics related to Biblical Hebrew and shows their relevance for biblical interpretation by applying them to specific passages. As such, it provides excellent motivation and encouragement to keep up one's Hebrew ability. Furthermore, because each chapter presents in systematic fashion the key concepts for the topic it covers, *Exegetical Gems from Biblical Hebrew* provides ample opportunity for reviewing the essentials of Hebrew grammar.

Finally, some online resources for retaining Biblical Hebrew exist. These include the websites Daily Dose of Hebrew created by Mark Futato (Reformed Theological Seminary)[58] and Hebrew Day by Day created by Gary E. Schnittjer (Cairn University).[59] Both websites contain helpful reviews of Biblical Hebrew grammar. Individuals can also subscribe to daily Hebrew videos. Five days per week, subscribers are sent a link to a short video that walks through the grammar and exegesis of a single Hebrew verse.

10.5 The Ways Forward

Attention to biblical language pedagogy is more important than ever as institutions decrease their commitment to Biblical Hebrew and Biblical Aramaic, as students question the value of learning the biblical languages, and as those who have learned the biblical languages struggle to retain them. If Biblical Hebrew and Biblical Aramaic teaching is to remain viable, instructors must learn to teach their students effectively and bring about lasting acquisition of these languages. Aiding biblical language students in this way ultimately helps the study of Hebrew and Aramaic as well as the exegesis, teaching, and preaching of the Hebrew Bible.

Some important innovations have taken place within the traditional approach to teaching Biblical Hebrew and Biblical Aramaic. Nevertheless, the most promising way forward is found in application of Communicative Language Teaching principles to biblical language instruction. Individuals such as Randall Buth and Paul Overland have laid a solid foundation for the communicative teaching of Biblical Hebrew, and others continue to build on their approach. Combined with successful approaches to retention, the communicative approach can help the next generation of students to use Biblical Hebrew and Biblical Aramaic more effectively in their exegesis and ministry. The teaching of the biblical languages, therefore, has a bright future.

---

58. http://dailydoseofhebrew.com/.
59. http://hebrewdaybyday.com/.

10.6 FURTHER READING

Baker, David W. "Studying the Original Texts: Effective Learning and Teaching of Biblical Hebrew." Pages 161–72 in *Make the Old Testament Live: From Curriculum to Classroom*. Edited by Richard S. Hess and Gordon J. Wenham. Grand Rapids: Eerdmans, 1998.

Callaham, Scott N. "Rethinking Biblical Hebrew Instruction." Pages 235–58 in *The Unfolding of Your Words Gives Light: Studies in Biblical Hebrew in Honor of George L. Klein*. Edited by Ethan C. Jones. University Park, PA: Eisenbrauns, 2018.

Greenspahn, Frederick E. "Why Hebrew Textbooks Are Different from Those for Other Languages." *SBL Forum*. July, 2005. http://www.sbl-site.org/publications/article.aspx?ArticleId=420.

Harlow, Joel. "Successfully Teaching Biblical Languages Online at the Seminary Level: Guiding Principles of Course Design and Delivery." *Teaching Theology & Religion* 10 (2007): 13–24.

Magary, Dennis R. "Keeping Your Hebrew Healthy." Pages 29–55 in *Preaching the Old Testament*. Edited by Scott M. Gibson. Grand Rapids: Baker Books, 2006.

McKenzie, Tracy. "Teaching Biblical Hebrew to Congregational Leaders: A Personal Reflection on Its Challenges and Potential Ways Forward." Pages 259–71 in *The Unfolding of Your Words Gives Light: Studies in Biblical Hebrew in Honor of George L. Klein*. Edited by Ethan C. Jones. University Park, PA: Eisenbrauns, 2018.

McQuinn, Scott J. "Toward a Principled Communicative Methodology for Teaching the Biblical Languages." MA thesis, Fresno Pacific University, 2017.

Morse, MaryKate. "Enhancing the Learning and Retention of Biblical Languages for Adult Students." *Teaching Theology & Religion* 7 (2004): 45–50.

Noonan, Jennifer E. "Recent Teaching Grammars for Biblical Hebrew: A Review and Critique." *ATJ* 43 (2011): 99–118.

———. "Teaching Biblical Hebrew." Pages 317–35 in *"Where Shall Wisdom Be Found?" A Grammatical Tribute to Professor Stephen A. Kaufman*. Edited by Hélène M. Dallaire, Benjamin J. Noonan, and Jennifer E. Noonan. Winona Lake, IN: Eisenbrauns, 2017.

Overland, Paul, Lee M. Fields, and Jennifer E. Noonan. "Can Communicative Principles Enhance Classical Language Acquisition?" *Foreign Language Annals* 44 (2011): 583–98.

CONCLUSION

Properly using the languages opens doors of biblical discovery that would otherwise remain locked and provides interpreters with accountability that they would not otherwise have.

—JASON DEROUCHIE[1]

I began this book by presenting an all-too common dilemma: the study of Biblical Hebrew and Biblical Aramaic is necessary for those who want to interpret the Hebrew Bible faithfully, but those reading the Hebrew Bible in its original languages face difficulty in grasping the linguistic study of the Hebrew Bible. In this book I have sought to remedy this problem by providing an accessible introduction to the world of Biblical Hebrew and Biblical Aramaic scholarship. My aim is that this book will introduce students, pastors, professors, and scholars to current issues of interest on these languages so they know why these issues are important for understanding the Hebrew Bible.

My reason for all this is simple: the quality of exegesis is directly related to knowledge of the biblical languages, which is in turn directly dependent on one's engagement with scholarship on those languages. Every student, pastor, professor, and scholar who wants to understand and proclaim the Hebrew Bible as effectively as possible must therefore be familiar with the basic issues discussed in this book. We ignore recent developments in Biblical Hebrew and Biblical Aramaic scholarship to our own peril. As stated by Martin Luther: "We will not long preserve the gospel without the languages. . . . If through our neglect we let the languages go (which God forbid!), we shall . . . lose the gospel."[2]

---

1. DeRouchie, "Profit of Employing the Biblical Languages," 50.
2. Luther, "To the Councilmen of All Cities," 360.

Furthermore, not only does engagement with Biblical Hebrew and Biblical Aramaic scholarship ensure our exegesis is as faithful as possible, it also brings joy. I hope that, as a result of this book, you have come to appreciate and even enjoy scholarship on the biblical languages. Hopefully Biblical Hebrew and Biblical Aramaic scholarship no longer seems as intimidating as it once did and instead comes to be an object of fascination and delight.

It is an exciting time to study Biblical Hebrew and Biblical Aramaic. Continued developments in linguistics and an ever-increasing understanding of the Semitic languages have established Hebrew and Aramaic study on solid footing. Many important advances that impact our exegesis of the Hebrew Bible are taking place, and readers of Hebrew and Aramaic are increasingly interested in the application of linguistic scholarship to interpreting the Hebrew Bible. Having come now to the end, I invite you, the reader, to continue your study of Biblical Hebrew and Biblical Aramaic so that you may be equipped for exegesis and ministry the best you can be.

BIBLIOGRAPHY

Adam, Klaus-Peter. "A (Socio-)Demonstrative Meaning of the Hitpael in Biblical Hebrew." *ZAH* 25–28 (2012–2015): 1–23.

Adams, William James, Jr. "An Investigation into the Diachronic Distribution of Morphological Forms and Semantic Features of Extra-Biblical Hebrew Sources." PhD diss., University of Utah, 1987.

———. "Language Drift and the Dating of Biblical Passages." *HS* 18 (1977): 160–64.

Adamska-Sałaciak, Arleta. "Explaining Meaning in Bilingual Dictionaries." Pages 144–60 in *The Oxford Handbook of Lexicography*. Edited by Philip Durkin. Oxford Handbooks in Linguistics. Oxford: Oxford University Press, 2016.

Aitken, James K. "Context of Situation in Biblical Lexica." Pages 181–201 in *Foundations for Syriac Lexicography III: Colloquia of the International Syriac Language Project*. Edited by Janet Dyk and Wido T. van Peursen. Perspectives on Syriac Linguistics 4. Piscataway, NJ: Gorgias, 2008.

Akmajian, Adrian, Ann Kathleen Farmer, Lee Bickmore, Richard A. Demers, and Robert M. Harnish. *Linguistics: An Introduction to Language and Communication*. 7th ed. Cambridge, MA: MIT Press, 2017.

Albright, William F. "A Catalogue of Early Hebrew Lyric Poems (Psalm LXVIII)." *HUCA* 23 (1950–1951): 1–39.

———. "The Earliest Forms of Hebrew Verse." *JPOS* 2 (1922): 69–86.

———. "Ivory and Apes of Ophir." *AJSL* 37 (1920–1921): 144–45.

———. "The Oracles of Balaam." *JBL* 63 (1944): 207–33.

———. "Some Additional Notes on the Song of Deborah." *JPOS* 2 (1922): 284–85.

———. "Some Remarks on the Song of Moses in Deuteronomy XXXII." *VT* 9 (1959): 339–46.

Alinei, Mario. "The Problem of Dating in Linguistics." Translated by Svetislav Kostić. *Quaderni di semantica: rivista internazionale di semantica teorica e applicata* 25 (2004): 211–32.

Allan, Keith, ed. *The Oxford Handbook of the History of Linguistics*. Oxford: Oxford University Press, 2013.

Alonso Schökel, Luís, Víctor Morla-Asensio, and Vicente Collado. *Diccionario bíblico hebreo-español*. Madrid: Trotta, 1994.

Amos, Ashley Crandell. *Linguistic Means of Determining the Dates of Old English Literary Texts.* Medieval Academy Books 90. Cambridge, MA: Medieval Academy of America, 1980.

Andersen, Francis I. *The Sentence in Biblical Hebrew.* Janua Linguarum Series Practica 231. The Hague: Mouton, 1974.

Andersen, Henning. "Markedness Theory—The First 150 Years." Pages 11–46 in *Markedness in Synchrony and Diachrony.* Edited by Olga Mišeska Tomić. Trends in Linguistics: Studies and Monographs 39. Berlin: Mouton de Gruyter, 1989.

Andersen, T. David. "The Evolution of the Hebrew Verbal System." *ZAH* 13 (2000): 1–66.

Andrason, Alexander. "The BH *weqatal*: A Homogenous Form with No Haphazard Functions (Part 1)." *JNSL* 37.2 (2011): 1–26.

———. "The BH *weqatal*: A Homogenous Form with No Haphazard Functions (Part 2)." *JNSL* 38.1 (2012): 1–30.

———. "The Biblical Hebrew Verbal System in Light of Grammaticalization: The Second Generation." *HS* 52 (2011): 19–51.

———. "Biblical Hebrew *wayyiqtol*: A Dynamic Definition." *JHebS* 11.8 (2011): 1–58. http://www.jhsonline.org.

———. "Future Values of the *qatal* and Their Conceptual and Diachronic Logic: How to Chain Future Senses of the *qatal* to the Core of Its Semantic Network." *HS* 54 (2013): 7–38.

———. "The Gnomic *qatal*." *Orientalia Suecana* 61 (2012): 5–53.

———. "Making It Sound—The Performative *qatal* and Its Explanation." *JHebS* 12.8 (2012): 1–58. http://www.jhsonline.org.

———. "An Optative Indicative? A Real Factual Past? Toward a Cognitive-Typological Approach to the Precative *qatal*." *JHebS* 13.4 (2013): 1–41. http://www.jhsonline.org.

———. "The Panchronic *yiqtol*: Functionally Consistent and Cognitively Plausible." *JHebS* 10.10 (2010): 1–63. http://www.jhsonline.org.

———. *El sistema verbal hebreo en su contexto semítico: una visión dinámica.* Instrumentos para el estudio de la Biblia 24. Estella: Verbo Divino, 2013.

Andrews, Edna. *Markedness Theory: The Union of Asymmetry and Semiosis in Language.* Roman Jackobsen Series in Linguistics and Philology. Durham, NC: Duke University Press, 1990.

Archer, Gleason L., Jr. "The Aramaic of the 'Genesis Apocryphon' Compared with the Aramaic of Daniel." Pages 160–69 in *New Perspectives on the Old Testament.* Edited by J. Barton Payne. Evangelical Theological Society Symposium Series 3. Waco, TX: Word, 1970.

Arnold, Bill T. "The Use of Aramaic in the Hebrew Bible: Another Look at Bilingualism in Ezra and Daniel." *JNSL* 22.2 (1996): 1–16.

Arnold, Mark A. "Categorization of the Hitpaʿēl of Classical Hebrew." PhD diss., Harvard University, 2005.

Aronoff, Mark and Janie Rees-Miller, eds. *The Handbook of Linguistics.* 2nd ed. Blackwell Handbooks in Linguistics. Malden, MA: Wiley-Blackwell, 2017.

Ashdowne, Richard. "Dictionaries of Dead Languages." Pages 350–66 in *The Oxford Handbook of Lexicography*. Edited by Philip Durkin. Oxford Handbooks in Linguistics. Oxford: Oxford University Press, 2016.

Asher, James. "Children's First Language as a Model for Second Language Learning." *Modern Language Journal* 56 (1972): 133–39.

Bailey, Nicholas A. and Stephen H. Levinsohn. "The Function of Preverbal Elements in Independent Clauses in the Hebrew Narrative of Genesis." *JOTT* 5 (1992): 179–207.

Baker, David W. "Studying the Original Texts: Effective Learning and Teaching of Biblical Hebrew." Pages 161–72 in *Make the Old Testament Live: From Curriculum to Classroom*. Edited by Richard S. Hess and Gordon J. Wenham. Grand Rapids: Eerdmans, 1998.

Baker, David W. and Elaine A. Heath. *More Light on the Path: Daily Scripture Readings in Hebrew and Greek*. Grand Rapids: Baker Books, 1998.

Bandstra, Barry. "Word Order and Emphasis in Biblical Hebrew Narrative: Syntactic Observations on Genesis 22 from a Discourse Perspective." Pages 109–23 in *Linguistics and Biblical Hebrew*. Edited by Walter R. Bodine. Winona Lake, IN: Eisenbrauns, 1992.

Bar-Asher, Elitzur Avraham. "סימוני לשון במגילת רות [Linguistic Markers in the Book of Ruth]." *Shnaton* 18 (2008): 25–42.

Barco del Barco, Javier del. *Profecía y sintaxis: el Uso de las formas verbales en los Profetas Menores preexílicos*. Textos y estudios "Cardenal Cisneros" 69. Madrid: Consejo Superior de Investigaciones Científicas, 2003.

Bar-Magen, M. "המלה 'נא' במקרא [The Word 'נָא' in the Bible]." *Beit Mikra* 25 (1980): 163–71.

Barr, James. *Comparative Philology and the Text of the Old Testament*. 2nd ed. Winona Lake, IN: Eisenbrauns, 1987.

———. "Etymology and the Old Testament." Pages 1–28 in *Language and Meaning: Studies in Hebrew Language and Biblical Exegesis: Papers Read at the Joint British-Dutch Old Testament Conference Held at London, 1973*. OtSt 19. Leiden: Brill, 1974.

———. "Hebrew Lexicography." Pages 103–26 in *Studies on Semitic Lexicography*. Edited by Pelio Fronzaroli. Quaderni di semitistica. Florence: Istituto di Linguistica e di Lingue Orientali, Università di Firenze, 1973.

———. "Hebrew Lexicography: Informal Thoughts." Pages 137–51 in *Linguistics and Biblical Hebrew*. Edited by Walter R. Bodine. Winona Lake, IN: Eisenbrauns, 1992.

———. "Limitations of Etymology as a Lexicographical Instrument in Biblical Hebrew." *Transactions of the Philological Society* 81 (1983): 41–65.

———. "Semantics and Biblical Theology: A Contribution to the Discussion." Pages 11–19 in *Congress Volume: Uppsala, 1971*. Edited by Pieter de Arie Hendrik Boer. VTSup 22. Leiden: Brill, 1972.

———. *The Semantics of Biblical Language*. Oxford: Oxford University Press, 1961.

———. "Semitic Philology and the Interpretation of the Old Testament." Pages 31–64 in *Tradition and Interpretation: Essays by Members of the Society for Old Testament Study*. Edited by G. W. Anderson. Oxford: Clarendon, 1979.

———. "Three Interrelated Factors in the Semantic Study of Ancient Hebrew." *ZAH* 7 (1994): 33–44.

Battistella, Edwin L. *The Logic of Markedness*. Oxford: Oxford University Press, 1996.

———. *Markedness: The Evaluative Superstructure of Language*. SUNY Series in Linguistics. Albany, NY: State University of New York Press, 1990.

Bauer, Hans and Pontus Leander. *Grammatik des biblisch-Aramäischen*. Halle: Niemeyer, 1927.

———. *Historische Grammatik der hebräischen Sprache des Alten Testamentes: Einleitung, Schriftlehre, Laut-und Formenlehre*. Halle: Niemeyer, 1922.

Baumgartner, Walter. "Das Aramäische im Buche Daniel." *ZAW* 45 (1927): 81–133.

Bean, Albert Fredrick. "A Phenomenological Study of the Hithpaʿel Verbal Stem in the Hebrew Old Testament." PhD diss., Southern Baptist Theological Seminary, 1976.

Beckman, John C. "Toward the Meaning of the Biblical Hebrew Piel Stem." PhD diss., Harvard University, 2015.

Beekman, John and John Callow. *Translating the Word of God*. Grand Rapids: Zondervan, 1974.

Beekman, John, John Callow, and Michael Koposec. *The Semantic Structure of Written Communication*. 5th ed. Dallas: Summer Institute of Linguistics, 1981.

Beneš, Eduard. "Die Verbstellung im Deutschen, von der Mitteilungsperspektive her betrachtet." *Philologica Pragensia* 5 (1962): 6–19.

Benton, Richard C. "Aspect and the Biblical Hebrew Niphal and Hitpael." PhD diss., University of Wisconsin–Madison, 2009.

———. "Verbal and Contextual Information: The Problem of Overlapping Meanings in the Niphal and Hitpael." *ZAW* 124 (2012): 385–99.

Berchman, Robert M. *Porphyry Against the Christians*. Studies in Platonism, Neoplatonism, and the Platonic Tradition 1. Leiden: Brill, 2006.

Bergen, Robert D., ed. *Biblical Hebrew and Discourse Linguistics*. Dallas: Summer Institute of Linguistics, 1994.

———. "Discourse Analysis: Biblical Hebrew." *EHLL* 1:746–49.

———. "Text as a Guide to Authorial Intention: An Introduction to Discourse Criticism." *JETS* 30 (1987): 327–36.

Bergey, Ronald L. "The Book of Esther: Its Place in the Linguistic Milieu of Post-Exilic Biblical Hebrew Prose: A Study in Late Biblical Hebrew." PhD diss., Dropsie College, 1983.

———. "Late Linguistic Features in Esther." *JQR* 75 (1984): 66–78.

———. "Post-Exilic Hebrew Linguistic Developments in Esther: A Diachronic Approach." *JETS* 31 (1988): 161–68.

Bergsträsser, Gotthelf. *Einführung in die semitischen Sprachen: Sprachproben und grammatische Skirren*. Munich: Huber, 1928.

Bergsträsser, Gotthelf, Wilhelm Gesenius, Mark Lidzbarski, and Emil Kautzsch. *Hebräische Grammatik*. 2 vols. Leipzig: Vogel, 1918–1929.

Bergström, Ulf. "Temporality and the Semantics of the Biblical Hebrew Verbal System." PhD diss., Uppsala Universitet, 2014.

Berman, Joshua A. "The Narratological Purpose of Aramaic Prose in Ezra 4:8–6:18." *AS* 5 (2007): 165–91.

Bernius, Elaine A. "When Foreigners Speak: Job—A Study in Dialectology." PhD diss., Hebrew Union College–Jewish Institute of Religion, 2013.

Bertholdt, Leonhard. *Historisch kritische Einleitung in sämmtliche kanonische und apokryphische Schriften des alten und neuen Testaments.* 6 vols. Erlangen: Palm, 1812–1819.

Biber, Douglas and Susan Conrad. *Register, Genre, and Style.* Cambridge Textbooks in Linguistics. Cambridge: Cambridge University Press, 2009.

Bicknell, Belinda Jean. "Passives in Biblical Hebrew." PhD diss., University of Michigan, 1984.

Birkeland, Harris. *Akzent und Vokalismus im Althebräischen mit Beiträgen zur vergleichenden semitischen Sprachwissenschaft.* Skrifter utgitt av Det Norske videnskapsakademi i Oslo, 2: Historisk-filosofisk klasse 3. Oslo: Dybwad, 1940.

Bitzer, Heinrich. *Light on the Path: Daily Readings in Hebrew and Greek.* Grand Rapids: Baker Books, 1982.

Bjøru, Øyvind. "Diathesis in the Semitic Languages: Exploring the *Binyan* System." MA thesis, University of Oslo, 2012.

———. "Transitivity and the Binyanim." Pages 48–63 in *Proceedings of the Oslo-Austin Workshop in Semitic Linguistics: Oslo, May 23 and 24, 2013.* Edited by Lutz Edzard and John Huehnergard. AKM 88. Wiesbaden: Harrassowitz, 2014.

Blake, Frank R. "The Form of Verbs after *Waw* in Hebrew." *JBL* 65 (1946): 51–57.

———. "The Hebrew Waw Conversive." *JBL* 63 (1944): 271–95.

———. *A Resurvey of Hebrew Tenses, with an Appendix: Hebrew Influence on Biblical Aramaic.* Scripta Pontificii Instituti Biblici 103. Rome: Pontifical Biblical Institute, 1951.

Blau, Joshua. "הרהוריו של ערביסטן על השתלשלות עברית המקרא וסעיפיה" [An Arabicist's Reflections on the Development of the Hebrew Bible and Its Divisions]." *Leš* 60 (1997): 21–32.

Blevins, James P. "American Descriptivism ('Structuralism')." Pages 419–37 in *The Oxford Handbook of the History of Linguistics.* Edited by Keith Allan. Oxford: Oxford University Press, 2013.

Block, Daniel I. *Ruth.* ZECOT 8. Grand Rapids: Zondervan, 2015.

Blois, Reinier de. "Cognitive Linguistic Approaches to Biblical Hebrew." *EHLL* 1:471–73.

———. "New Tools and Methodologies for Biblical Lexicography." Pages 203–16 in *Foundations for Syriac Lexicography III: Colloquia of the International Syriac Language Project.* Edited by Janet Dyk and Wido T. van Peursen. Perspectives on Syriac Linguistics 4. Piscataway, NJ: Gorgias, 2008.

———. "A Semantic Dictionary of Biblical Hebrew." *Bulletin of the United Bible Societies* 194–195 (2002): 275–95.

———. "Semantic Domains for Biblical Greek: Louw and Nida's Framework Evaluated from a Cognitive Perspective." Pages 265–78 in *Foundations for Syriac Lexicography III: Colloquia of the International Syriac Language Project.* Edited by Janet Dyk and Wido T. van Peursen. Perspectives on Syriac Linguistics 4. Piscataway, NJ: Gorgias, 2008.

———. "Semantic Domains for Biblical Hebrew." Pages 209–29 in *Bible and Computer: The Stellenbosch AIBI-6 Conference: Proceedings of the Association internationale Bible et informatique, "From Alpha to Byte," University of Stellenbosch, 17–21 July, 2000.* Edited by Johann Cook. Leiden: Brill, 2002.

———. "Towards a New Dictionary of Biblical Hebrew based on Semantic Domains." PhD diss., Vrije Universiteit, 2000.

Bodine, Walter R., ed. *Discourse Analysis of Biblical Literature: What It Is and What It Offers.* SemeiaSt. Atlanta: Scholars Press, 1995.

———. *Linguistics and Biblical Hebrew.* Winona Lake, IN: Eisenbrauns, 1992.

———. "Linguistics and Biblical Studies." *ABD* 4:327–33.

Boman, Thorleif. *Hebrew Thought Compared with Greek.* Translated by Jules L. Moreau. New York: Norton, 1960.

Bompiani, Brian A. "Is Genesis 24 a Problem for Source Criticism?" *BSac* 164 (2007): 403–15.

———. "Style Switching in the Jacob and Laban Narratives." *HS* 55 (2014): 43–57.

———. "Style Switching in the Speech of Transjordanians." *HS* 57 (2016): 51–71.

———. "Style-Switching: The Representation of the Speech of Foreigners in the Hebrew Bible." PhD diss., Hebrew Union College–Jewish Institute of Religion, 2012.

Bornemann, Robert. *Grammar of Biblical Hebrew.* Lanham, MD: University Press of America, 1998.

Botha, Philippus J. "The Measurement of Meaning: An Exercise in Field Semantics." *JSem* 1 (1989): 3–22.

Böttcher, Julius Friedrich. *Ausführliches Lehrbuch der hebräischen Sprache.* Edited by Ferdinand Mühlau. 2 vols. Leipzig: Barth, 1866–1868.

Botterweck, G. Johannes, Helmer Ringgren, and Heinz-Josef Fabry, eds. *Theological Dictionary of the Old Testament.* Translated by Geoffrey W. Bromiley, David E. Green, Douglas W. Stott, and John T. Willis. 15 vols. Grand Rapids: Eerdmans, 1974–2006.

Boutflower, Charles. *In and Around the Book of Daniel.* London: SPCK, 1923.

Boyd, Steven W. "The *Binyanim* (Verbal Stems)." Pages 85–125 in *"Where Shall Wisdom Be Found?" A Grammatical Tribute to Professor Stephen A. Kaufman.* Edited by Hélène M. Dallaire, Benjamin J. Noonan, and Jennifer E. Noonan. Winona Lake, IN: Eisenbrauns, 2017.

———. Review of *The Function of the Niphʿal in Biblical Hebrew in Relationship to Other Passive-Reflexive Verbal Stems and to the Puʿal and Hophʿal in Particular,* by P. A. Siebesma. *JAOS* 114 (1994): 669–71.

———. "A Synchronic Analysis of the Medio-Passive-Reflexive in Biblical Hebrew." PhD diss., Hebrew Union College–Jewish Institute of Religion, 1993.

Boyle, Milton L., Jr. "Infix-*t* Forms in Biblical Hebrew." PhD diss., Boston University, 1969.

Brenner, Athalya. "On the Semantic Field of Humour, Laughter and the Comic in the Old Testament." Pages 39–58 in *On Humour and the Comic in the Hebrew Bible.* Edited by Yehuda T. Radday and Athalya Brenner. JSOTSup 92. Sheffield: Almond Press, 1990.

Bresnan, Joan. "The Passive in Lexical Theory." Pages 3–86 in *The Mental Representation of Grammatical Relations*. Edited by Joan Bresnan. MIT Press Series on Cognitive Theory and Mental Representation. Cambridge, MA: MIT Press, 1988.

Bridge, Edward J. "The Use of Slave Terms in Deference and in Relation to God in the Hebrew Bible." PhD diss., Macquarie University, 2010.

Bright, John. "The Apodictic Prohibition: Some Observations." *JBL* 92 (1973): 185–204.

Brinton, Donna, Marguerite Ann Snow, and Marjorie Bingham Wesche. *Content-Based Second Language Instruction*. Boston: Heinle & Heinle, 1989.

Brockelmann, Carl. *Grundriss der vergleichenden Grammatik der semitischen Sprachen*. 2 vols. Berlin: Reuther & Reichard, 1908–1913.

———. "Die 'Tempora' des Semitischen." *Zeitschrift für Phonetik und allgemeine Sprachwissenschaft* 5 (1951): 133–54.

Brown, A. Phillip, II and Bryan W. Smith. *A Reader's Hebrew Bible*. Grand Rapids: Zondervan, 2008.

Brown, Francis, S. R. Driver, and Charles A. Briggs. *A Hebrew and English Lexicon of the Old Testament, with an Appendix Containing the Biblical Aramaic, based on the Lexicon of William Gesenius as Translated by Edward Robinson*. Oxford: Clarendon, 1906.

Brown, Gillian and George Yule. *Discourse Analysis*. Cambridge Textbooks in Linguistics. Cambridge: Cambridge University Press, 1983.

Brown, Penelope and Stephen C. Levinson. *Politeness: Some Universals in Language Usage*. Studies in Interactional Sociolinguistics 4. Cambridge: Cambridge University Press, 1987.

Brown, Roger and Albert Gilman. "The Pronouns of Power and Solidarity." Pages 253–76 in *Style in Language*. Edited by Thomas A. Sebeok. Cambridge, MA: MIT Press, 1960.

Brown, Roger and Marguerite Ford. "Address in American English." *Journal of Abnormal and Social Psychology* 62 (1961): 375–85.

Burney, C. F. *The Book of Judges with an Introduction and Notes*. London: Rivingtons, 1918.

———. *Notes on the Hebrew Text of the Books of Kings*. Oxford: Clarendon, 1903.

Burton, Marilyn E. *The Semantics of Glory: A Cognitive, Corpus-Based Approach to Hebrew Word Meaning*. SSN 68. Leiden: Brill, 2017.

Buth, Randall. "Functional Grammar, Hebrew and Aramaic: An Integrated, Textlinguistic Approach to Syntax." Pages 77–102 in *Discourse Analysis of Biblical Literature: What It Is and What It Offers*. Edited by Walter R. Bodine. SemeiaSt. Atlanta, GA: Scholars Press, 1995.

———. "The Hebrew Verb in Current Discussions." *JOTT* 5 (1992): 91–105.

———. *Living Biblical Hebrew*. 3 vols. Jerusalem: Biblical Language Center, 2007.

———. "Word Order in Aramaic from the Perspectives of Functional Grammar and Discourse Analysis." PhD diss., University of California, Los Angeles, 1987.

———. "Word Order in the Verbless Clause: A Generative-Functional Approach." Pages 89–108 in *The Verbless Clause in Biblical Hebrew: Linguistic Approaches*. Edited by Cynthia L. Miller-Naudé. LSAWS 1. Winona Lake, IN: Eisenbrauns, 1999.

Bütikofer, Christa. "Lord of the Languages: Code-Switching and Multilingualism in Tolkien's *Lord of the Rings*." MA thesis, University of Bern, 2011.

Butler, Christopher S. *Structure and Function: A Guide to Three Major Structural-Functional Theories.* 2 vols. Studies in Language Companion Series 63–64. Amsterdam: Benjamins, 2003.

Buxtorf, Johann. *Epitome grammaticae hebraeae, breviter et methodice ad publicum scholarum usum proposita.* Leiden: Luchtmans, 1613.

———. *Tiberias sive commentarius masorethicus triplex: historicus, didacticus, criticus ad illustrationem operis Biblici Basileensis conscriptus.* Basel: König, 1620.

Callaham, Scott N. "Mood and Modality: Biblical Hebrew." *EHLL* 2:687–90.

———. "Rethinking Biblical Hebrew Instruction." Pages 235–58 in *The Unfolding of Your Words Gives Light: Studies in Biblical Hebrew in Honor of George L. Klein.* Edited by Ethan C. Jones. University Park, PA: Eisenbrauns, 2018.

Callow, Kathleen. *Discourse Considerations in Translating the Word of God.* Grand Rapids: Zondervan, 1974.

Campanini, Saverio. "Christian Hebraists: Renaissance Period." *EHLL* 1:440–49.

Campbell, Constantine R. *Advances in the Study of Greek: New Insights for Reading the New Testament.* Grand Rapids: Zondervan, 2015.

Campbell, Edward F., Jr. *Ruth: A New Translation with Introduction, Notes, and Commentary.* AB 7. Garden City, NY: Doubleday, 1975.

Campbell, Lyle. *Historical Linguistics: An Introduction.* 3rd ed. Cambridge: MIT Press, 2013.

———. "The History of Linguistics: Approaches to Linguistics." Pages 97–117 in *The Handbook of Linguistics.* Edited by Mark Aronoff and Janie Rees-Miller. 2nd ed. Blackwell Handbooks in Linguistics. Malden, MA: Wiley-Blackwell, 2017.

Cantineau, Jean. "Essai d'une phonologie de l'hébreu biblique." *BSL* 46 (1950): 82–122.

Carnie, Andrew, Sheila Ann Dooley, and Heidi Harley, eds. *Verb First: On the Syntax of Verb-Initial Languages.* Linguistik Aktuell/Linguistics Today. Amsterdam: Benjamins, 2005.

Carson, D. A. *Exegetical Fallacies.* 2nd ed. Grand Rapids: Baker Books, 1996.

Chafe, Wallace L. "Givenness, Contrastiveness, Definiteness, Subjects, Topics and Point of View." Pages 27–55 in *Subject and Topic.* Edited by Charles N. Li. New York: Academic Press, 1976.

Chambers, J. K. "Studying Language Variation: An Informal Epistemology." Pages 1–15 in *The Handbook of Language Variation and Change.* Edited by J. K. Chambers and Natalie Schilling. 2nd ed. Blackwell Handbooks in Linguistics. Malden, MA: Wiley-Blackwell, 2013.

Chambers, J. K. and Peter Trudgill. *Dialectology.* 2nd ed. Cambridge Textbooks in Linguistics. Cambridge: Cambridge University Press, 1998.

Charlap, Luba R. "Grammarians: Medieval Italy." *EHLL* 2:88–94.

Choi, Jongtae. "The Aramaic of Daniel: Its Date, Place of Composition and Linguistic Comparison with Extra-Biblical Texts." PhD diss., Trinity Evangelical Divinity School, 1994.

———. Review of *The Aramaic of Daniel in the Light of Old Aramaic*, by Zdravko Stefanovic. *JETS* 38 (1995): 469–70.

Chomsky, Noam. *The Minimalist Program*. Current Studies in Linguistics 28. Cambridge, MA: MIT Press, 1995.

———. *Syntactic Structures*. Janua Linguarum Series Minor 4. The Hague: Mouton, 1957.

Christiansen, Bent. "A Linguistic Analysis of the Biblical Hebrew Particle *nā'*: A Test Case." *VT* 59 (2009): 379–93.

Claasen, W. T. "The Declarative-Estimative Hiph'il." *JNSL* 2 (1972): 5–16.

———. "The Hiph'il Verbal Theme in Biblical Hebrew." PhD diss., University of Stellenbosch, 1971.

———. "On a Recent Proposal as to Distinction between Pi'el and Hiph'il." *JNSL* 1 (1971): 3–10.

Clines, David J. A. "The Challenge of Hebrew Lexicography Today." Pages 87–98 in *Congress Volume: Ljubljana, 2007*. Edited by André Lemaire. VTSup 133. Leiden: Brill, 2010.

———, ed. *Dictionary of Classical Hebrew*. 8 vols. Sheffield: Sheffield Phoenix, 1993–2011.

Cohen, Ohad. *The Verbal Tense System in Late Biblical Hebrew Prose*. Translated by Avi Aronsky. HSS 63. Winona Lake, IN: Eisenbrauns, 2013.

Colasuonno, Maria Maddalena. "Linguistic Variation in Ancient Hebrew (1000 BCE–200 CE)." PhD diss., University of Naples, 2015.

———. "Sociolinguistics." *EHLL* 3:581–84.

———. "Some Considerations on the Problem of Diglossia in Biblical Hebrew." *AION* 76 (2016): 124–45.

Comrie, Bernard. *Aspect: An Introduction to the Study of Verbal Aspect and Related Problems*. Cambridge Textbooks in Linguistics. Cambridge: Cambridge University Press, 1976.

———. *Tense*. Cambridge Textbooks in Linguistics. Cambridge: Cambridge University Press, 1985.

Cook, Edward M. "Word Order in the Aramaic of Daniel." *Afroasiatic Linguistics* 9.3 (1986): 1–16.

Cook, John A. "Actionality (*Aktionsart*): Pre-Modern Hebrew." *EHLL* 1:25–28.

———. "Aspect: Pre-Modern Hebrew." *EHLL* 1:201–5.

———. "Current Issues in the Study of the Biblical Hebrew Verbal System." *Kleine Untersuchungen zur Sprache des Alten Testaments und seiner Umwelt* 17 (2014): 79–108.

———. "The Finite Verbal Forms in Biblical Hebrew Do Express Aspect." *JANES* 30 (2006): 21–35.

———. "The Hebrew Verb: A Grammaticalization Approach." *ZAH* 14 (2001): 117–43.

———. "The Semantics of Verbal Pragmatics: Clarifying the Roles of *wayyiqtol* and *weqatal* in Biblical Hebrew Prose." *JSS* 49 (2004): 247–73.

———. *Time and the Biblical Hebrew Verb: The Expression of Tense, Aspect, and Modality in Biblical Hebrew*. LSAWS 7. Winona Lake, IN: Eisenbrauns, 2012.

———. "Verbal Valency: The Intersection of Syntax and Semantics." Pages 53–86 in *Contemporary Examinations of Classical Languages (Hebrew, Aramaic, Syriac, and Greek): Valency, Lexicography, Grammar, and Manuscripts*. Edited by Timothy Martin Lewis, Alison G. Salvesen, and Beryl Turner. Perspectives on Linguistics and Ancient Languages 8. Piscataway, NJ: Gorgias, 2017.

Cook, John A. and Robert D. Holmstedt. *Beginning Biblical Hebrew: A Grammar and Illustrated Reader*. Grand Rapids: Baker Academic, 2013.

———. *Linguistics for Hebraists*. LSAWS. University Park, PA: Eisenbrauns, forthcoming.

Cotrozzi, Stefano. *Expect the Unexpected: Aspects of Pragmatic Foregrounding in Old Testament Narratives*. LBHOTS 510. London: T&T Clark, 2010.

Cotterell, Peter and Max Turner. *Linguistics and Biblical Interpretation*. Downers Grove, IL: InterVarsity Press, 1989.

Coulmas, Florian. *Sociolinguistics: The Study of Speakers' Choices*. 2nd ed. Cambridge: Cambridge University Press, 2013.

Coxon, Peter W. "The Distribution of Synonyms in Biblical Aramaic in the Light of Official Aramaic and the Aramaic of Qumran." *RevQ* 9 (1978): 497–512.

———. "Greek Loan-Words and Alleged Greek Loan Translations in the Book of Daniel." *TGUOS* 25 (1973–1974): 24–40.

———. "A Morphological Study of the *h*-Prefix in Biblical Aramaic." *JAOS* 98 (1978): 416–19.

———. "The Problem of Consonantal Mutations in Biblical Aramaic." *ZDMG* 129 (1979): 8–22.

———. "The Syntax of the Aramaic of *Daniel*: A Dialectal Study." *HUCA* 48 (1977): 107–22.

Creason, Stuart Alan. "Semantic Classes of Hebrew Verbs: A Study of *Aktionsart* in the Hebrew Verbal System." PhD diss., University of Chicago, 1995.

Cremer, Hermann. *Biblisch-theologisches Wörterbuch der neutestamentlichen Gräcität*. Gotha: Perthes, 1866.

Croft, William. *Typology and Universals*. 2nd ed. Cambridge Textbooks in Linguistics. Cambridge: Cambridge University Press, 2002.

Croft, William and D. Alan Cruse. *Cognitive Linguistics*. Cambridge Textbooks in Linguistics. Cambridge: Cambridge University Press, 2004.

Cross, Frank Moore, Jr. and David Noel Freedman. "The Blessing of Moses." *JBL* 67 (1948): 191–210.

———. "A Royal Song of Thanksgiving: II Samuel 22 = Psalm 18." *JBL* 72 (1953): 15–34.

———. "The Song of Miriam." *JNES* 14 (1955): 237–50.

———. *Studies in Ancient Yahwistic Poetry*. 2nd ed. Biblical Resource Series. Grand Rapids: Eerdmans, 1997.

Cryer, Frederick H. "The Problem of Dating Biblical Hebrew and the Hebrew of Daniel." Pages 185–98 in *In the Last Days: On Jewish and Christian Apocalyptic and Its Period*. Edited by Knud Jeppesen, Kirsten Nielsen, and Bent Rosendal. Aarhus: Aarhaus University Press, 1994.

Crystal, David. *The Cambridge Encyclopedia of Language*. 3rd ed. Cambridge: Cambridge University Press, 2010.

———. *A Dictionary of Linguistics and Phonetics*. 6th ed. Malden, MA: Blackwell, 2008.

Dallaire, Hélène M. *Biblical Hebrew: A Living Language*. 2nd ed. North Charleston, SC: CreateSpace, 2017.

———. *The Syntax of Volitives in Biblical Hebrew and Amarna Canaanite Prose*. LSAWS 9. Winona Lake, IN: Eisenbrauns, 2014.

Dan, Barak. "*Binyanim*: Biblical Hebrew." *EHLL* 1:354–62.

Davies, Philip R. "Biblical Hebrew and the History of Ancient Judah: Typology, Chronology and Common Sense." Pages 150–63 in *Biblical Hebrew: Studies in Chronology and Typology*. Edited by Ian Young. JSOTSup 369. London: T&T Clark, 2003.

———. *In Search of "Ancient Israel."* 2nd ed. JSOTSup 148. Sheffield: Sheffield Academic, 1999.

Dawson, David Allan. *Text-Linguistics and Biblical Hebrew*. JSOTSup 177. Sheffield: Sheffield Academic, 1994.

De Beaugrande, Robert and Wolfgang U. Dressler. *Introduction to Text Linguistics*. Longman Linguistics Library 26. London: Longman, 1981.

DeCaen, Vincent. "Ewald and Driver on Biblical Hebrew 'Aspect': Anteriority and the Orientalist Framework." *ZAH* 9 (1996): 129–51.

———. "Hebrew Linguistics and Biblical Criticism: A Minimalist Programme." *JHebS* 3.6 (2001): 1–32. http://www.jhsonline.org.

———. "On the Placement and Interpretation of the Verb in Standard Biblical Hebrew Prose." PhD diss., University of Toronto, 1995.

———. "A Unified Analysis of Verbal and Verbless Clauses within Government-Binding Theory." Pages 109–31 in *The Verbless Clause in Biblical Hebrew: Linguistic Approaches*. Edited by Cynthia L. Miller-Naudé. LSAWS 1. Winona Lake, IN: Eisenbrauns, 1999.

Delgado, José Martínez. "Lexicography: Middle Ages." *EHLL* 2:510–14.

———. "Phonology in Medieval Grammatical Thought." *EHLL* 3:122–30.

Dempster, Stephen G. "Linguistic Features of Hebrew Narrative: A Discourse Analysis of Narrative from the Classical Period." PhD diss., University of Toronto, 1985.

DeRouchie, Jason S. *A Call to Covenant Love: Text Grammar and Literary Structure in Deuteronomy 5–11*. Gorgias Biblical Studies 30. Piscataway, NJ: Gorgias, 2007.

———. *How to Understand and Apply the Old Testament: Twelve Steps from Exegesis to Theology*. Phillipsburg, NJ: P&R, 2017.

———. "The Profit of Employing the Biblical Languages: Scriptural and Historical Reflections." *Them* 37.1 (2012): 32–50.

Diakonoff, I. M. *Afrasian Languages*. Translated by A. A. Korolev and V. I. Porkhomovskiĭ. 2nd ed. Languages of Asia and Africa. Moscow: Nauka, 1988.

Di Giulio, Marco. "Discourse Marker: Biblical Hebrew." *EHLL* 1:757–58.

———. "Mitigating Devices in Biblical Hebrew." *Kleine Untersuchungen zur Sprache des Alten Testaments und seiner Umwelt* 8–9 (2008): 33–62.

Dik, Simon C. *The Theory of Functional Grammar.* Edited by Kees Hengeveld. 2nd ed. 2 vols. Functional Grammar Series 20–21. Berlin: Mouton de Gruyter, 1997.

Dombrowski, Bruno W. W. "Some Remarks on the Hebrew Hithpaʿel and Inversative -*t*- in the Semitic Languages." *JNES* 21 (1962): 220–23.

Dooley, Robert A. and Stephen H. Levinsohn. *Analyzing Discourse: A Manual of Basic Concepts.* Dallas: SIL International, 2001.

Doron, Edit. "Word Order in Hebrew." Pages 41–56 in *Research in Afroasiatic Grammar: Papers from the Third Conference on Afroasiatic Languages, Sophia Antipolis, France, 1996.* Edited by Jacqueline Lecarme, Jean Lowenstamm, and Ur Shlonsky. Amsterdam Studies in the Theory and History of Linguistic Science, Series IV: Current Issues in Linguistic Theory 202. Amsterdam: Benjamins, 2000.

Dressler, Wolfgang U. *Studien zur verbalen Pluralität: Iterativum, Distributivum, Durativum, Intensivum in der allgemeinen Grammatik, im Lateinischen und Hethitischen.* Österreichische Akademie der Wissenschaften: Philosophisch-Historische Klasse 259/1. Vienna: Böhlau, 1968.

Driver, G. R. "The Aramaic of the Book of Daniel." *JBL* 45 (1926): 110–19.

———. "Colloquialisms in the Old Testament." Pages 232–39 in *Mélanges Marcel Cohen: études de linguistique, ethnographie et sciences connexes offertes par ses amis et ses élèves à l'occasion de son 80ème anniversaire, avec des articles et études inédits de Marcel Cohen.* Edited by David Cohen. Janua Linguarum Series Maior 27. The Hague: Mouton, 1970.

Driver, S. R. *The Book of Daniel.* Cambridge Bible for Schools and Colleges 23. Cambridge: Cambridge University Press, 1900.

———. *An Introduction to the Literature of the Old Testament.* International Theological Library. Edinburgh: T&T Clark, 1891.

———. *A Treatise on the Use of the Tenses in Hebrew and Some Other Syntactical Questions.* 3rd ed. Oxford: Clarendon, 1892.

Dryer, Matthew S. "The Greenbergian Word Order Correlations." *Language* 68 (1992): 81–138.

———. "Word Order." Pages 61–131 in *Clause Structure.* Edited by Timothy Shopen. 2nd ed. Vol. 1 of *Language Typology and Syntactic Description.* 3 vols. Cambridge: Cambridge University Press, 2007.

Durkin, Philip. *The Oxford Guide to Etymology.* Oxford: Oxford University Press, 2009.

Emerton, J. A. "Comparative Semitic Philology and Hebrew Lexicography." Pages 1–24 in *Congress Volume: Cambridge, 1995.* Edited by J. A. Emerton. VTSup 66. Leiden: Brill, 1997.

———. "The Hebrew Language." Pages 171–99 in *Text in Context: Essays by Members of the Society for Old Testament Study.* Edited by Andrew D. H. Mayes. Oxford: Oxford University Press, 2000.

Endo, Yoshinobu. *The Verbal System of Classical Hebrew in the Joseph Story: An Approach from Discourse Analysis.* SSN 32. Assen: Van Gorcum, 1996.

Eng, Milton and Lee M. Fields, eds. *Devotions on the Hebrew Bible: 54 Reflections to Inspire and Instruct.* Grand Rapids: Zondervan, 2015.

Erteschik-Shir, Nomi. *Information Structure: The Syntax-Discourse Interface.* Oxford Surveys in Syntax and Morphology 3. Oxford: Oxford University Press, 2009.

Eskhult, Mats. *Studies in Verbal Aspect and Narrative Technique in Biblical Hebrew Prose.* Acta Universitatis Upsaliensis: Studia Semitica Upsaliensia 12. Stockholm: Almqvist & Wiksell, 1990.

Estelle, Bryan D. "Esther's Strategies of Becoming משכיל עבד." *HS* 53 (2012): 61–88.

———. "Know Before Whom You Stand: The Language of Deference in Some Ancient Aramaic and Hebrew Documents." PhD diss., Catholic University of America, 2001.

———. "The Use of Deferential Language in the Arsames Correspondence and Biblical Aramaic Compared." *Maarav* 13 (2006): 43–74.

Ewald, Heinrich. *Kritische Grammatik der hebräischen Sprache.* Leipzig: Hahnsche Buchhandlung, 1827.

Exter Blokland, A. F. den. *In Search of Text Syntax: Towards a Syntactic Text-Segmentation Model for Biblical Hebrew.* Applicatio 14. Amsterdam: Uitgeverij, 1995.

Farrier, Susan E. "A Linguistic Dating of the Oxford *Chanson de Roland.*" PhD diss., Cornell University, 1985.

Fassberg, Steven E. "The Lengthened Imperative קָטְלָה in Biblical Hebrew." *HS* 40 (1999): 7–13.

———. "What Is Late Biblical Hebrew?" *ZAW* 128 (2016): 1–15.

———. סוגיות בתחביר המקרא [*Studies in Biblical Syntax*]. Jerusalem: Magnes, 1994.

Fehri, Abdelkader Fassi. "Verbal Plurality, Transitivity, and Causativity." Pages 151–85 in *Research on Afroasiatic Grammar II: Selected Papers from the Fifth Conference on Afroasiatic Languages, Paris, 2000.* Edited by Jacqueline Lecarme. Amsterdam Studies in the Theory and History of Linguistic Science, Series IV: Current Issues in Linguistic Theory 241. Amsterdam: Benjamins, 2003.

Ferguson, Charles A. "Diglossia." *Word* 15 (1959): 325–40.

———. "Diglossia Revisited." *Southwest Journal of Linguistics* 10 (1991): 214–34.

Fidjestøl, Bjarne. *The Dating of Eddic Poetry.* Edited by Odd Einar Haugen. Bibliotheca Arnamagnæana 41. Copenhagen: Reitzel, 1999.

Fillmore, Charles J. "The Case for Case." Pages 1–90 in *Universals in Linguistic Theory.* Edited by Emmon Bach and Robert Thomas Harms. New York: Holt, Reinhart, & Winston, 1968.

———. "Scenes-and-Frames Semantics." Pages 55–81 in *Linguistic Structures Processing.* Edited by Antonio Zampolli. Fundamental Studies in Computer Science 5. Amsterdam: North Holland, 1977.

Firbas, Jan. "On Defining the Theme in Functional Sentence Perspective." *Travaux linguistiques de Prague* 1 (1964): 267–80.

Fishman, Joshua A. "Who Speaks What Language to Whom and When." *La Linguistique* 2 (1965): 67–88.

Fitzmyer, Joseph A. *The Genesis Apocryphon of Qumran Cave 1 (1Q20): A Commentary.* 3rd ed. BibOr 18/B. Rome: Pontifical Biblical Institute, 2004.

———. "The Phases of the Aramaic Language." Pages 57–84 in *A Wandering Aramean: Collected Aramaic Essays*. SBLMS 25. Missoula, MT: Scholars Press, 1979.

Floor, Sebastiaan Jonathan. "From Information Structure, Topic, and Focus, to Theme in Biblical Hebrew Narrative." DLitt thesis, University of Stellenbosch, 2004.

———. "From Word Order to Theme in Biblical Hebrew Narrative: Some Perspectives from Information Structure." *JSem* 12 (2003): 197–236.

Forbes, A. Dean. "The Diachrony Debate: A Tutorial on Methods." *JSem* 25 (2016): 881–926.

———. "The Diachrony Debate: Perspectives from Pattern Recognition and Meta-Analysis." *HS* 53 (2012): 7–42.

Fox, Michael V. "Words for Folly." *ZAH* 10 (1997): 4–15.

———. "Words for Wisdom." *ZAH* 6 (1993): 149–65.

Fredericks, Daniel C. "Diglossia, Revelation, and Ezekiel's Inaugural Rite." *JETS* 41 (1998): 189–99.

———. "A North Israelite Dialect in the Hebrew Bible? Questions of Methodology." *HS* 37 (1996): 7–20.

Freidin, Robert. "Noam Chomsky's Contribution to Linguistics: A Sketch." Pages 439–67 in *The Oxford Handbook of the History of Linguistics*. Edited by Keith Allan. Oxford: Oxford University Press, 2013.

Fried, Mirjam. "Word Order." Pages 289–300 in *Grammar, Meaning and Pragmatics*. Edited by Frank Brisard, Jan Ola Östman, and Jef Verschueren. Handbook of Pragmatics Highlights 5. Amsterdam: Benjamins, 2009.

Fulk, R. D. "Archaisms and Neologisms in the Language of *Beowulf*." Pages 267–88 in *Managing Chaos: Strategies for Identifying Change in English*. Edited by Christopher M. Cain and Geoffrey R. Russom. Vol. 3 of *Studies in the History of the English Language*. 7 vols. Topics in English Linguistics 53. Berlin: Mouton, 2007.

———. "*Beowulf* and Language History." Pages 19–36 in *The Dating of Beowulf: A Reassessment*. Edited by Leonard Niedorf. Cambridge: Brewer, 2014.

———. *A History of Old English Meter*. Middle Ages Series. Philadelphia: University of Pennsylvania Press, 1992.

———. "On Argumentation in Old English Philology, with Particular Reference to the Editing and Dating of *Beowulf*." *Anglo-Saxon England* 32 (2003): 1–26.

Fuller, Daniel P. "Hermeneutics: A Syllabus for NT 500." 6th ed. Pasadena, CA: Fuller Theological Seminary, 1983.

Furuli, Rolf. *A New Understanding of the Verbal System of Classical Hebrew: An Attempt to Distinguish between Semantic and Pragmatic Factors*. Oslo: Awatu, 2006.

Futato, Mark D. *Beginning Biblical Hebrew*. Winona Lake, IN: Eisenbrauns, 2003.

Gardner-Chloros, Penelope and Daniel Weston. "Code-Switching and Multilingualism in Literature." *Language and Literature* 24 (2015): 182–93.

Garr, W. Randall. "Denominal, Lexicalized *Hiphil* Verbs." Pages 51–58 in *Language and Nature: Papers Presented to John Huehnergard on the Occasion of His 60th Birthday*. Edited by Rebecca Hasselbach and Na'ama Pat-El. SAOC 67. Chicago: Oriental Institute of the University of Chicago, 2012.

———. *Dialect Geography of Syria-Palestine, 1000–586 B.C.E.* Philadelphia: University of Pennsylvania Press, 1985.

———. "The Semantics of ב״רן in the *Qal* and *Hiphil*." *VT* 63 (2013): 536–45.

Geeraerts, Dirk. "A Rough Guide to Cognitive Linguistics." Pages 1–28 in *Cognitive Linguistics: Basic Readings.* Edited by Dirk Geeraerts. Cognitive Linguistics Research 34. Berlin: Mouton de Gruyter, 2006.

———. *Theories of Lexical Semantics.* Oxford: Oxford University Press, 2010.

Geeraerts, Dirk and Hubert Cuyckens. "Introducing Cognitive Linguistics." Pages 3–21 in *The Oxford Handbook of Cognitive Linguistics.* Edited by Dirk Geeraerts and Hubert Cuyckens. Oxford Handbooks. Oxford: Oxford University Press, 2007.

Geniusiene, È. Sh. *The Typology of Reflexives.* Empirical Approaches to Language Typology 2. Berlin: Mouton de Gruyter, 1987.

Gentry, Peter J. "The System of the Finite Verb in Classical Biblical Hebrew." *HS* 39 (1998): 7–41.

Georgakopoulou, Alexandra and Dionysis Goutsos. *Discourse Analysis: An Introduction.* 2nd ed. Edinburgh: Edinburgh University Press, 2004.

Gerstenberger, Erhard S. *Wesen und Herkunft des "Apodiktischen Rechts."* Wissenschaftliche Monographien zum Alten und Neuen Testament 20. Neukirchen-Vluyn: Neukirchener Verlag, 1965.

Gervers, Michael, ed. *Dating Undated Medieval Charters.* Woodbridge: Boydell Press, 2000.

Gesenius, Wilhelm. *Gesenius' Hebrew Grammar.* Edited by Emil Kautzsch. Translated by A. E. Cowley. 2nd ed. Oxford: Clarendon, 1910.

———. *Hebräisch-deutsches Handwörterbuch über die Schriften des Alten Testaments mit Einschluß der geographischen Namen und der chaldäischen Wörter beym Daniel und Esra.* 2 vols. Leipzig: Vogel, 1810–1812.

———. *Hebräische Grammatik.* Halle: Renger, 1813.

———. *Hebräisches und aramäisches Handwörterbuch über das Alte Testament.* Edited by Rudolf Meyer and Herbert Donner. 18th ed. 7 vols. Berlin: Springer, 1987–2012.

———. *Hebräisches und chaldäisches Handwörterbuch über das Alte Testament.* 2 vols. Leipzig: Vogel, 1834.

———. *Thesaurus philologicus criticus linguae Hebraeae et Chaldaeae Veteris Testamenti.* Edited by Emil Rödiger. 4 vols. Leipzig: Vogel, 1829–1858.

Gianto, Agustinus. "Archaic Biblical Hebrew." Pages 19–29 in vol. 1 of *A Handbook of Biblical Hebrew.* Edited by W. Randall Garr and Steven E. Fassberg. 2 vols. Winona Lake, IN: Eisenbrauns, 2016.

———. "Variations in Biblical Hebrew." *Bib* 77 (1996): 494–508.

Gilman, Albert and Roger Brown. "Who Says 'Tu' to Whom." *ETC: A Review of General Semantics* 15 (1958): 169–74.

Givón, Talmy. "The Drift from VSO to SVO in Biblical Hebrew: The Pragmatics of Tense-Aspect." Pages 181–254 in *Mechanisms of Syntactic Change.* Edited by Charles N. Li. Austin: University of Texas Press, 1977.

Goddard, Burton L. "The Origin of the Hebrew Infinitive Absolute in the Light of Infinitive Uses in Related Languages and Its Use in the Old Testament." ThD thesis, Harvard Divinity School, 1943.

Goetze, Albrecht. "The So-Called Intensive of the Semitic Languages." *JAOS* 62 (1942): 1–8.

Goldenberg, Gideon. "The Contribution of Semitic Languages to Linguistic Thinking." *JEOL* 30 (1987–1988): 107–15.

Goldfajn, Tal. *Word Order and Time in Biblical Hebrew Narrative.* Oxford Theological Monographs. Oxford: Oxford University Press, 1998.

Gordon, Elizabeth and Mark Williams. "Raids on the Articulate: Code-Switching, Style-Shifting and Post-Colonial Writing." *Journal of Commonwealth Literature* 33 (1998): 75–96.

Graffi, Giorgio. "European Linguistics since Saussure." Pages 469–84 in *The Oxford Handbook of the History of Linguistics.* Edited by Keith Allan. Oxford: Oxford University Press, 2013.

Greenberg, Joseph H. *Language Typology: A Historical and Analytic Overview.* Janua Linguarum Series Minor 184. The Hague: Mouton, 1974.

———. *Language Universals, with Special Reference to Feature Hierarchies.* Janua Linguarum Series Minor 59. The Hague: Mouton, 1966.

———. "The Semitic 'Intensive' as Verbal Plurality: A Study of Grammaticalization." Pages 577–87 in vol. 1 of *Semitic Studies in Honor of Wolf Leslau on the Occasion of His Eighty-Fifth Birthday, November 14th, 1991.* Edited by Alan S. Kaye. 2 vols. Wiesbaden: Harrassowitz, 1991.

———. "Some Universals of Grammar with Particular Reference to the Order of Meaningful Elements." Pages 73–113 in *Universals of Language: Report of a Conference Held at Dobbs Ferry, N.Y., April 13–15, 1961.* Edited by Joseph H. Greenberg. 2nd ed. Cambridge, MA: MIT Press, 1966.

Greenfield, Jonas C. "Aramaic Studies and the Bible." Pages 110–30 in *Congress Volume: Vienna, 1980.* Edited by J. A. Emerton. VTSup 32. Leiden: Brill, 1981.

Greenspahn, Frederick E. "Why Hebrew Textbooks Are Different from Those for Other Languages." *SBL Forum.* July, 2005. http://www.sbl-site.org/publications/article.aspx?ArticleId=420.

Groom, Susan Anne. *Linguistic Analysis of Biblical Hebrew.* Carlisle: Paternoster, 2003.

Gropp, Douglas M. "The Function of the Finite Verb in Classical Biblical Hebrew." *HAR* 13 (1991): 45–62.

Gross, Walter. *Doppelt besetztes Vorfeld: syntaktische, pragmatische und übersetzungstechnische Studien zum althebräischen Verbalsatz.* BZAW 305. Berlin: de Gruyter, 2001.

———. "Is There Really a Compound Nominal Clause in Biblical Hebrew?" Pages 19–49 in *The Verbless Clause in Biblical Hebrew: Linguistic Approaches.* Edited by Cynthia L. Miller-Naudé. Translated by John Frymire. LSAWS 1. Winona Lake, IN: Eisenbrauns, 1999.

———. *Pendenskonstruktion im biblischen Hebräisch.* Arbeiten zu Text und Sprache im Alten Testament 27. St. Ottilien: EOS-Verlag, 1987.

————. "Die Position des Subjekts im hebräischen Verbalsatz, untersucht an den asyndetischen ersten Redesätzen in Gen, Ex 1–19, Jos–2Kön." *ZAH* 6 (1993): 170–87.

————. *Die Satzteilfolge im Verbalsatz alttestamentlicher Prosa: untersucht an den Büchern Dtn., Ri und 2Kön.* FAT 17. Tübingen: Mohr Siebeck, 1996.

————. "Das Vorfeld als strukturell eigenständiger Bereich des hebräischen Verbalsatzes." Pages 1–24 in *Syntax und Text: Beiträge zur 22. Internationalen Ökumenischen Hebräisch-Dozenten-Konferenz 1993 in Bamberg.* Edited by Hubert Irsigler. Arbeiten zu Text und Sprache im Alten Testament 40. St. Ottilien: EOS-Verlag, 1993.

————. "Zur syntaktischen Struktur des Vorfelds im hebräischen Verbalsatz." *ZAH* 7 (1994): 203–14.

Gruber, Jeffrey. "Studies in Lexical Relations." PhD diss., Massachusetts Institute of Technology, 1965.

Gruber-Miller, John, ed. *When Dead Tongues Speak: Teaching Beginning Greek and Latin.* Classical Resources Series 6. Oxford: Oxford University Press, 2006.

Guenther, Allen R. "A Diachronic Study of Biblical Hebrew Prose Syntax: An Analysis of the Verbal Clause in Jeremiah 37–45 and Esther 1–10." PhD diss., University of Toronto, 1977.

Gvozdanović, Jadranka. "Defining Markedness." Pages 47–66 in *Markedness in Synchrony and Diachrony.* Edited by Olga Mišeska Tomić. Trends in Linguistics: Studies and Monographs 39. Berlin: Mouton de Gruyter, 1989.

Gzella, Holger. "Language and Script." Pages 71–107 in *The Aramaeans in Ancient Syria.* Edited by Herbert Niehr. HdO 1/106. Leiden: Brill, 2014.

————. "Some General Remarks on Interactions between Aspect, Modality, and Evidentiality in Biblical Hebrew." *FO* 49 (2012): 225–32.

————. *Tempus, Aspekt und Modalität im Reichsaramäischen.* Veröffentlichungen der Orientalischen Kommission 48. Wiesbaden: Harrassowitz, 2004.

————. "Voice in Classical Hebrew against Its Semitic Background." *Or* 78 (2009): 292–325.

Hackett, Jo Ann and John Huehnergard. "On Revising and Updating BDB." Pages 227–34 in *Foundations for Syriac Lexicography III: Colloquia of the International Syriac Language Project.* Edited by Janet Dyk and Wido T. van Peursen. Perspectives on Syriac Linguistics 4. Piscataway, NJ: Gorgias, 2008.

Hadley, Alice Omaggio. *Teaching Language in Context.* 3rd ed. Boston: Heinle & Heinle, 2001.

Hall, Kira and Mary Bucholtz. *Gender Articulated: Language and the Socially Constructed Self.* New York: Routledge, 1995.

Halliday, M. A. K. *Halliday's Introduction to Functional Grammar.* Edited by Christian M. I. M. Matthiessen. 4th ed. London: Routledge, 2014.

————. "Notes on Transitivity and Theme in English: Part 2." *Journal of Linguistics* 3 (1967): 199–244.

Halliday, M. A. K., Angus McIntosh, and Peter Strevens. *The Linguistic Sciences and Language Teaching.* Longman Linguistics Library. London: Longman, 1964.

Halliday, M. A. K. and Ruqaiya Hasan. *Cohesion in English*. English Language Series 9. London: Longman, 1976.

———. *Language, Context, and Text: Aspects of Language in a Social-Semiotic Perspective*. 2nd ed. Language Education. Oxford: Oxford University Press, 1989.

Hanson, Paul D. *The Dawn of Apocalyptic: The Historical and Sociological Roots of Jewish Apocalyptic Eschatology*. 2nd ed. Philadelphia: Fortress, 1979.

Hardy, H. H., II. *Exegetical Gems from Biblical Hebrew: A Refreshing Guide to Grammar and Interpretation*. Grand Rapids: Baker Academic, 2019.

Harlow, Joel. "Successfully Teaching Biblical Languages Online at the Seminary Level: Guiding Principles of Course Design and Delivery." *Teaching Theology & Religion* 10 (2007): 13–24.

Harris, Kenneth Laing. "An Examination of the Function of the Pi'el in Biblical Hebrew." PhD diss., University of Liverpool, 2005.

Harris, Zellig S. "Discourse Analysis." *Language* 28 (1952): 1–30.

———. "Linguistic Structure of Hebrew." *JAOS* 61 (1941): 143–67.

Hatav, Galia. "Anchoring World and Time in Biblical Hebrew." *Journal of Linguistics* 40 (2004): 491–526.

———. *The Semantics of Aspect and Modality: Evidence from English and Biblical Hebrew*. Studies in Language Companion Series 34. Amsterdam: Benjamins, 1997.

———. "Tense: Biblical Hebrew." *EHLL* 3:736–40.

Hävernick, Heinrich Andreas Christoph. *Neue kritische Untersuchungen über das Buch Daniel*. Hamburg: Perthes, 1838.

Hawkins, John A. *Word Order Universals*. Quantitative Analyses of Linguistic Structure. New York: Academic Press, 1983.

Hayes, Christine Elizabeth. "Word Order in Biblical Aramaic." *Journal of the Association of Graduates in Near Eastern Studies* 1.2 (1990): 2–11.

Heimerdinger, Jean-Marc. *Topic, Focus and Foreground in Ancient Hebrew Narratives*. JSOTSup 295. Sheffield: Sheffield Academic, 1999.

Heine, Bernd and Heiko Narrogk, eds. *The Oxford Handbook of Linguistic Analysis*. 2nd ed. Oxford Handbooks in Linguistics. Oxford: Oxford University Press, 2015.

Heller, Roy L. *Narrative Structure and Discourse Constellations: An Analysis of Clause Function in Biblical Hebrew Prose*. HSS 55. Winona Lake, IN: Eisenbrauns, 2004.

Hendel, Ronald S. "In the Margins of the Hebrew Verbal System: Situation, Tense, Apsect, Mood." *ZAH* 9 (1996): 152–81.

Hendel, Ronald S. and Jan Joosten. *How Old Is the Hebrew Bible? A Linguistic, Textual, and Historical Study*. ABRL. New Haven: Yale University Press, 2018.

Hengstenberg, Ernst Wilhelm. *Die Authentie des Daniel und die Integrität des Sacharjah*. Vol. 1 of *Beiträge zur Einleitung ins Alte Testament*. 3 vols. Berlin: Oehmigke, 1831.

Hess, Natalie. "Code Switching and Style Shifting as Markers of Liminality in Literature." *Language and Literature* 5 (1996): 5–18.

Hill, Andrew E. "The Book of Malachi: Its Place in Post-Exilic Chronology Linguistically Reconsidered." PhD diss., University of Michigan, 1981.

———. "Dating Second Zechariah: A Linguistic Reexamination." *HAR* 6 (1982): 105–34.

———. "Dating the Book of Malachi: A Linguistic Reexamination." Pages 77–89 in *The Word of the Lord Shall Go Forth: Essays in Honor of David Noel Freedman in Celebration of His Sixtieth Birthday.* Edited by Carol L. Meyers and Michael O'Connor. American Schools of Oriental Research Special Volume Series 1. Winona Lake, IN: Eisenbrauns, 1983.

Hirschfeld, Hartwig. *Literary History of Hebrew Grammarians and Lexicographers, Accompanied by Unpublished Texts.* Jews' College Publications 9. London: Oxford University Press, 1926.

Hock, Hans Henrich. *Principles of Historical Linguistics.* 2nd ed. Berlin: Mouton de Gruyter, 1991.

Hock, Hans Henrich and Brian D. Joseph. *Language History, Language Change, and Language Relationship: An Introduction to Historical and Comparative Linguistics.* 2nd ed. Trends in Linguistics: Studies and Monographs 218. Berlin: Mouton de Gruyter, 2009.

Hogue, Timothy. "Return from Exile: Diglossia and Literary Code-Switching in Ezra 1–7." *ZAW* 130 (2018): 54–68.

Hoijer, Harry. "The Sapir-Whorf Hypothesis." Pages 92–105 in *Language in Culture: Conference on the Interrelations of Language and Other Aspects of Culture.* Edited by Harry Hoijer. Comparative Studies of Cultures and Civilizations. Chicago: University of Chicago Press, 1954.

Holladay, William L., ed. *A Concise Hebrew and Aramaic Lexicon of the Old Testament, based upon the Work of Ludwig Koehler and Walter Baumgartner.* Grand Rapids: Eerdmans, 1971.

Holmstedt, Robert D. "Constituents at the Edge in Biblical Hebrew." *Kleine Untersuchungen zur Sprache des Alten Testaments und seiner Umwelt* 17 (2014): 110–58.

———. "Investigating the Possible Verb-Subject to Subject-Verb Shift in Ancient Hebrew: Methodological First Steps." *Kleine Untersuchungen zur Sprache des Alten Testaments und seiner Umwelt* 15 (2013): 3–31.

———. *The Relative Clause in Biblical Hebrew.* LSAWS 10. Winona Lake, IN: Eisenbrauns, 2016.

———. "The Relative Clause in Biblical Hebrew: A Linguistic Analysis." PhD diss., University of Wisconsin–Madison, 2002.

———. *Ruth: A Handbook on the Hebrew Text.* Baylor Handbook on the Hebrew Bible. Waco, TX: Baylor University Press, 2010.

———. "The Typological Classification of the Hebrew of Genesis: Subject-Verb or Verb-Subject." *JHebS* 11.14 (2011): 1–39. http://www.jhsonline.org.

———. "Word Order and Information Structure in Ruth and Jonah: A Generative Typological Analysis." *JSS* 54 (2009): 111–39.

———. "Word Order in the Book of Proverbs." Pages 135–54 in *Seeking Out the Wisdom of the Ancients: Essays Offered to Honor Michael V. Fox on the Occasion of His Sixty-Fifth Birthday.* Edited by Ronald L. Troxel, Kelvin G. Friebel, and Dennis R. Magary. Winona Lake, IN: Eisenbrauns, 2005.

Holmstedt, Robert D. and Alexander T. Kirk. "Subversive Boundary Drawing in Jonah: The Variation of אשר and שַ as Literary Code-Switching." *VT* 66 (2016): 542–55.

Holtz, Shalom E. "Lexicography: Biblical Hebrew." *EHLL* 2:507–10.

Hornkohl, Aaron D. *Ancient Hebrew Periodization and the Language of the Book of Jeremiah: The Case for a Sixth-Century Date of Composition.* Studies in Semitic Languages and Linguistics 72. Leiden: Brill, 2014.

———. "Biblical Hebrew: Periodization." *EHLL* 1:315–25.

———. "Biblical Hebrew Tense-Aspect-Mood, Word Order and Pragmatics: Some Observations on Recent Approaches." Pages 27–56 in *Studies in Semitic Linguistics and Manuscripts: A Liber Discipulorum in Honour of Professor Geoffrey Khan.* Edited by Nadia Vidro, Ronny Vollandt, and Esther-Miriam Wagner. Acta Universitatis Upsaliensis: Studia Semitica Upsaliensia 30. Uppsala: Uppsala Universitet, 2018.

———. "The Pragmatics of the X+Verb Structure in the Hebrew of Genesis: The Linguistic Functions and Associated Effects and Meanings of Intra-Clausal Fronted Constituents." MA thesis, Hebrew University, 2003.

———. "Transitional Biblical Hebrew." Pages 31–42 in vol. 1 of *A Handbook of Biblical Hebrew.* Edited by W. Randall Garr and Steven E. Fassberg. 2 vols. Winona Lake, IN: Eisenbrauns, 2016.

Hospers, J. H. "Some Remarks about the So-Called Imperative Use of the Infinitive Absolute (*Infinitivus pro Imperativo*) in Classical Hebrew." Pages 97–102 in *Studies in Hebrew and Aramaic Syntax Presented to Professsor J. Hoftijzer on the Occasion of His Sixty-Fifth Birthday.* Edited by Karel Jongeling, Hendrika L. Murre-van den Berg, and Lucas van Rompay. Studies in Semitic Languages and Linguistics 17. Leiden: Brill, 1991.

Hovav, Malka Rappaport. "Lexical Semantics." *EHLL* 2:499–504.

Huehnergard, John. "The Early Hebrew Prefix-Conjugations." *HS* 29 (1988): 19–23.

———. "On the Etymology of the Hebrew Relative *šɛ-*." Pages 103–25 in *Biblical Hebrew in Its Northwest Semitic Setting: Typological and Historical Perspectives.* Edited by Steven E. Fassberg and Avi Hurvitz. Winona Lake, IN: Eisenbrauns, 2006.

Hughes, James A. "Another Look at the Hebrew Tenses." *JNES* 29 (1970): 12–24.

———. "The Hebrew Imperfect with *Waw* Conjunctive and Perfect with *Waw* Consecutive and Their Interrelationship." MA thesis, Faith Theological Seminary, 1955.

———. "Some Problems of the Hebrew Verbal System with Particular Reference to the Uses of the Tenses." PhD diss., University of Glasgow, 1962.

Hunziker-Rodewald, Regine. "The Gesenius/Brown-Driver-Briggs Family." Pages 219–26 in *Foundations for Syriac Lexicography III: Colloquia of the International Syriac Language Project.* Edited by Janet Dyk and Wido T. van Peursen. Perspectives on Syriac Linguistics 4. Piscataway, NJ: Gorgias, 2008.

———. "KAHAL—the Shorter HALAT: A Hebrew Lexicon Project in Process." Pages 243–49 in *Foundations for Syriac Lexicography III: Colloquia of the International Syriac Language Project.* Edited by Janet Dyk and Wido T. van Peursen. Perspectives on Syriac Linguistics 4. Piscataway, NJ: Gorgias, 2008.

Hurvitz, Avi. "Biblical Hebrew, Late." *EHLL* 1:329–38.

———. "Can Biblical Texts Be Dated Linguistically? Chronological Perspectives in the Historical Study of Biblical Hebrew." Pages 143–60 in *Congress Volume: Oslo, 1998*. Edited by André Lemaire and Magne Saebø. VTSup 80. Leiden: Brill, 2000.

———. "The Chronological Significance of Aramaisms in Biblical Hebrew." *IEJ* 18 (1968): 234–40.

———. "The Historical Quest for 'Ancient Israel' and the Linguistic Evidence of the Hebrew Bible: Some Methodological Observations." *VT* 47 (1997): 301–15.

———. "The Language of the Priestly Source and Its Historical Setting—The Case for an Early Date." Pages 83–94 in *Proceedings of the Eighth World Congress of Jewish Studies, Jerusalem, August 16–21, 1981: Panel Sessions: Bible Studies and Hebrew Language*. Jerusalem: World Union of Jewish Studies, 1983.

———. "Linguistic Criteria for Dating Problematic Biblical Texts." *Hebrew Abstracts* 14 (1973): 74–79.

———. "The 'Linguistic Dating of Biblical Texts': Comments on Methodological Guidelines and Philological Procedures." Pages 265–79 in *Diachrony in Biblical Hebrew*. Edited by Cynthia L. Miller-Naudé and Ziony Zevit. LSAWS 8. Winona Lake, IN: Eisenbrauns, 2012.

———. *A Linguistic Study of the Relationship between the Priestly Source and the Book of Ezekiel: A New Approach to an Old Problem*. CahRB 20. Paris: Gabalda, 1982.

———. "The Recent Debate on Late Biblical Hebrew: Solid Data, Experts' Opinions, and Inconclusive Arguments." *HS* 47 (2006): 191–220.

———. "The Usage of שש and בוץ in the Bible and Its Implication for the Date of P." *HTR* 60 (1967): 117–21.

———. "בחנים לשוניים לזהוי מזמורים מאוחרים בספר תהילים" [Linguistic Investigations into the Indentification of Late Psalms in the Book of Psalms]." PhD diss., Hebrew University, 1966.

———. בין לשון ללשון: לתולדות לשון המקרא בימי בית שני [*Between Languages: The History of the Biblical Language during the Second Temple Period*]. Jerusalem: Mosad Bialik, 1972.

———. "הוויכוח הארכאולוגי-היסטורי על קדמות הספרות המקראית לאור המחקר הבלשני של העברית [The Archaeological-Historical Debate on the Antiquity of the Hebrew Bible in the Light of Linguistic Research of the Hebrew Language]." Pages 34–46 in הפולמוס על האמת ההיסטורית במקרא [*Controversy over the Historicity of the Bible*]. Edited by Lee I. Levine and Amihai Mazar. Jerusalem: Merkaz Dinur, 2001.

———. מבראשית לדברי הימים: פרקים בהיסטוריה הלשונית של העברית המקראית. [*From Genesis to Chronicles: Chapters in the Linguistic History of Biblical Hebrew*]. Asuppot 15. Jerusalem: Bialik Institute, 2017.

Hurvitz, Avi, Leeor Gottlieb, Aaron D. Hornkohl, and Emmanuel Mastéy. *A Concise Lexicon of Late Biblical Hebrew: Linguistic Innovations in the Writings of the Second Temple Period*. VTSup 160. Leiden: Brill, 2014.

Ikeda, Jun. "ユダとイスラエル: 列王記に見る言葉のちがい [Judah and Israel: Regional Linguistic Varieties Found in the Book of Kings]." *Seishogaku ronshū* 34 (2002): 1–21.

————. "聖書ヘブライ語における言語変種: 概観とケーススタディ [Linguistic Varieties in Biblical Hebrew: An Overview and a Case Study]." *Kyōto Sangyō Daigaku Kokusai Gengo Kagaku Kenykūjo shohō* 21 (2000): 179–204.

————. "聖書ヘブライ語に見られる地域差について [Regional Dialects in Biblical Hebrew]." *Bungei gengo kenkyū* 38 (2000): 1–16.

Imbayarwo, Taurai. "A Biblical Hebrew Lexicon for Translators Based on Recent Developments in Theoretical Lexicography." DLitt thesis, University of Stellenbosch, 2008.

Isačenko, Alexander V. Грамматический строй русского языка в сопоставлении с словацким: морфология [*The Grammatical Structure of the Russian Language in Comparison with Slovakian: Morphology*]. 2 vols. Klassiki otechestvennoĭ filologii. Moscow: Iazyki slavianskoi kulʹtury, 2003.

Ives, Sumner. "A Theory of Literary Dialect." *Tulane Studies in English* 2 (1950): 137–82.

————. "A Theory of Literary Dialect." Pages 144–77 in *A Various Language: Perspectives on American Dialects*. Edited by Juanita V. Williamson and Virginia M. Burke. New York: Holt, Reinhart, & Winston, 1971.

Jakobson, Roman. "Signe zéro." Pages 143–52 in *Mélanges de linguistique offerts à Charles Bally sous les auspices de la Faculté des lettres de l'Université de Genève par des collègues, des confrères, des disciples reconnaissants*. Geneva: Georg, 1939.

————. "Zur Struktur des russichen Verbums." Pages 74–84 in *Charisteria Guilelmo Mathesio Quinquagenario: a discipulis et circuli linguistici Pragensis sodalibus oblata*. Prague: Pražský linguistický kroužek, 1932.

Jankowsky, Kurt R. "Comparative, Historical, and Typological Linguistics since the Eighteenth Century." Pages 635–54 in *The Oxford Handbook of the History of Linguistics*. Edited by Keith Allan. Oxford: Oxford University Press, 2013.

Jenni, Ernst. "Aktionsarten und Stammformen im Althebräischen: Das Piʿel in verbesserter Sicht." *ZAH* 13 (2000): 67–90.

————. "Faktitiv und Kausativ von ʾbd ʾzugrunde gehen.ʾ" Pages 143–57 in *Hebräische Wortforschung: Festschrift zum 80. Geburtstag von Walter Baumgartner*. Edited by Benedikt Hartmann, Ernst Jenni, E. Y. Kutscher, Victor Maag, I. L. Seeligmann, and Rudolf Smend. VTSup 16. Leiden: Brill, 1967.

————. *Das hebräische Piʿel: Syntaktisch-semasiologische Untersuchung einer Verbalform im Alten Testament*. Zürich: EVZ-Verlag, 1968.

————. "Höfliche bitte im Alten Testament." Pages 3–16 in *Congress Volume: Basel, 2001*. Edited by André Lemaire. VTSup 92. Leiden: Brill, 2002.

————. "Nifʿal und Hitpaʿel im Biblisch-Hebräischen." Pages 131–303 in vol. 3 of *Studien zur Sprachwelt des Alten Testaments*. Edited by Hanna Jenni. 3 vols. Stuttgart: Kohlhammer, 2012.

————. "Toward the Function of the Reflexive-Passive Stems in Biblical Hebrew." Pages 13–20 in *The Unfolding of Your Words Gives Light: Studies in Biblical Hebrew in Honor of George L. Klein*. Edited by Ethan C. Jones. University Park, PA: Eisenbrauns, 2018.

————. "Zur Funktion der reflexiv-passiven Stammformen im Biblisch-Hebräischen." Pages 61–70 in vol. 4 of *Proceedings of the Fifth World Congress of Jewish Studies, the Hebrew University, Mount Scopus-Givat Ram, Jerusalem, 3–11 August, 1969*. Edited by Pinchas Peli and Avigdor Shinan. 5 vols. Jerusalem: World Union of Jewish Studies, 1973.

Jenni, Ernst and Claus Westermann, eds. *Theological Lexicon of the Old Testament*. Translated by Mark E. Biddle. 3 vols. Peabody, MA: Hendrickson, 1997.

Jero, Christopher. "Tense, Mood, and Aspect in the Biblical Hebrew Verbal System." Pages 65–84 in *"Where Shall Wisdom Be Found?" A Grammatical Tribute to Professor Stephen A. Kaufman*. Edited by Hélène M. Dallaire, Benjamin J. Noonan, and Jennifer E. Noonan. Winona Lake, IN: Eisenbrauns, 2017.

————. "The Verbal System of Biblical Hebrew Poetry: The Morphosyntactic Role of Internal Aspect (*Aktionsart*)." PhD diss., Hebrew Union College–Jewish Institute of Religion, 2008.

Johnson, Marion R. "A Unified Temporal Theory of Tense and Aspect." Pages 145–75 in *Tense and Aspect*. Edited by Philip J. Tedeschi and Annie E. Zaenen. Syntax and Semantics 14. New York: Academic Press, 1981.

Johnson, Robert M., Jr. "The Words in Their Mouths: A Linguistic and Literary Analysis of the Dialogues in the Book of Ruth." PhD diss., Vanderbilt University, 1993.

Jongeling, Karel. "On the VSO Character of Hebrew." Pages 103–11 in *Studies in Hebrew and Aramaic Syntax Presented to Professsor J. Hoftijzer on the Occasion of His Sixty-Fifth Birthday*. Edited by Karel Jongeling, Hendrika L. Murre-van den Berg, and Lucas van Rompay. Studies in Semitic Languages and Linguistics 17. Leiden: Brill, 1991.

Joosten, Jan. "Diachronic Linguistics and the Date of the Pentateuch." Pages 327–44 in *The Formation of the Pentateuch: Bridging the Academic Cultures of Europe, Israel, and North America*. Edited by Jan Christian Gertz, Bernard M. Levinson, Dalit Rom-Shiloni, and Konrad Schmid. FAT 111. Tübingen: Mohr Siebeck, 2016.

————. "Do the Finite Verbal Forms in Biblical Hebrew Express Aspect?" *JANES* 29 (2002): 49–70.

————. "The Functions of the Semitic D Stem: Biblical Hebrew Materials for a Comparative-Historical Approach." *Or* 67 (1998): 202–30.

————. "Hebrew Thought and Greek Thought in the Septuagint: Fifty Years after Barr's *Semantics*." Pages 125–33 in *Reflections on Lexicography: Explorations in Ancient Syriac, Hebrew, and Greek Sources*. Edited by Richard A. Taylor and Craig E. Morrison. Perspectives on Linguistics and Ancient Languages 4. Piscataway, NJ: Gorgias, 2014.

————. "The Indicative System of the Hebrew Verb and Its Literary Exploitation." Pages 51–71 in *Narrative Syntax and the Hebrew Bible: Papers of the Tilburg Conference 1996*. Edited by Ellen J. van Wolde. BibInt 29. Leiden: Brill, 1997.

————. "Verbal System: Biblical Hebrew." *EHLL* 3:921–25.

————. *The Verbal System of Biblical Hebrew: A New Synthesis Elaborated on the Basis of Classical Prose*. JBS 10. Jerusalem: Simor, 2012.

Joüon, Paul. *Grammaire de l'hébreu biblique.* 2nd ed. Rome: Institut Biblique Pontifical, 1947.

Joüon, Paul and Takamitsu Muraoka. *A Grammar of Biblical Hebrew.* 2nd ed. SubBi 27. Rome: Pontificio Istituto Biblico, 2006.

———. *A Grammar of Biblical Hebrew.* 2 vols. SubBi 14. Rome: Pontificio Istituto Biblico, 1991.

Juhás, Peter. *Die biblisch-hebräische Partikel* נָא *im Lichte der antiken Bibelübersetzungen: Unter besonderer Berücksichtigung ihrer vermuteten Höflichkeitsfunktion.* SSN 67. Leiden: Brill, 2017.

Kaddari, Menaḥem Zevi. מילון העברית המקראית: אוצר לשון המקרא מאל"ף עד תי"ו. [*Dictionary of Biblical Hebrew: Thesaurus of the Language of the Bible, from aleph to tav*]. Ramat-Gan: University of Bar-Ilan, 2006.

Kaltner, John. "The Koehler-Baumgartner Family." Pages 235–42 in *Foundations for Syriac Lexicography III: Colloquia of the International Syriac Language Project.* Edited by Janet Dyk and Wido T. van Peursen. Perspectives on Syriac Linguistics 4. Piscataway, NJ: Gorgias, 2008.

Kamp, Hans and Uwe Reyle. *From Discourse to Logic: Introduction to Modeltheoretic Semantics of Natural Language, Formal Logic and Discourse Representation Theory.* Studies in Linguistics and Philosophy 42. Dordrecht: Kluwer, 1993.

Kaufman, Stephen A. "Aramaic." Pages 114–30 in *The Semitic Languages.* Edited by Robert Hetzron. New York: Routledge, 1997.

———. "The Classification of the North West Semitic Dialects of the Biblical Period and Some Implications Thereof." Pages 41–57 in *Proceedings of the Ninth World Congress of Jewish Studies, Jerusalem, 4–12 August, 1985: Division D: Panel Sessions, Hebrew and Aramaic Languages.* Jerusalem: Magnes, 1988.

———. "An Emphatic Plea for Please." *Maarav* 7 (1991): 195–98.

———. "The Job Targum from Qumran." *JAOS* 93 (1973): 317–27.

———. "Languages (Aramaic)." *ABD* 1:173–78.

———. Review of *Diachrony in Biblical Hebrew,* eds. Cynthia L. Miller-Naudé and Ziony Zevit. *RBL* (July 29, 2014). http://www.bookreviews.org/.

———. "Semitics: Directions and Re-Directions." Pages 273–82 in *The Study of the Ancient Near East in the Twenty-First Century: The William Foxwell Albright Centennial Conference.* Edited by Jerrold S. Cooper and Glenn M. Schwartz. Winona Lake, IN: Eisenbrauns, 1996.

Kautzsch, Emil. *Grammatik des Biblisch-Aramäischen, mit einer Kritischen Erörterung der aramäischen Wörter im Neuen Testament.* Leipzig: Vogel, 1884.

Kawashima, Robert S. "Stylistics: Biblical Hebrew." *EHLL* 3:643–50.

Kedar-Kopfstein, Benjamin. *Biblische Semantik: Eine Einfuhrung.* Stuttgart: Kohlhammer, 1981.

Keenan, Edward L. "Passive is Phrasal (not Sentential or Lexical)." Pages 181–213 in *Lexical Grammar.* Edited by Teun Hoekstra, Harry van der Hulst, and Michael Moortgat. Publications in Language Sciences 3. Dordrecht: Foris, 1981.

Kelley, Page H. *Biblical Hebrew: An Introductory Grammar.* Edited by Timothy G. Crawford. 2nd ed. Grand Rapids: Eerdmans, 2018.

Kemmer, Suzanne. *The Middle Voice.* Typological Studies in Language 23. Amsterdam: Benjamins, 1993.

Khan, Geoffrey, ed. *Encyclopedia of Hebrew Language and Linguistics.* 4 vols. Leiden: Brill, 2013.

Kim, Dong-Hyuk. *Early Biblical Hebrew, Late Biblical Hebrew, and Linguistic Variability: A Sociolinguistic Evaluation of the Linguistic Dating of Biblical Texts.* VTSup 156. Leiden: Brill, 2013.

Kim, Young Bok. "Hebrew Forms of Address: A Sociolinguistic Analysis." PhD diss., University of Chicago, forthcoming.

Kitchen, Kenneth A. "The Aramaic of Daniel." Pages 31–79 in *Notes on Some Problems in the Book of Daniel.* Edited by Donald J. Wiseman. London: Tyndale Press, 1965.

Klaiman, M. H. "Middle Verbs, Reflexive Middle Constructions, and Middle Voice." *Studies in Language* 16 (1992): 35–61.

Klein, George Linam. "The Meaning of the Niphal in Biblical Hebrew." PhD diss., Annenberg Research Institute, 1992.

Klein, Jared S. "Historical Linguistics and Biblical Hebrew: An Indo-Europeanist's View." *JSem* 25 (2016): 865–80.

Klein, Wolfgang. "How Time Is Encoded." Pages 39–82 in *The Expression of Time.* Edited by Wolfgang Klein and Ping Li. Expression of Cognitive Categories 3. Berlin: de Gruyter, 2009.

———. *Time in Language.* Germanic Linguistics. London: Routledge, 1994.

Kline, Jonathan G., ed. *Keep Up Your Biblical Aramaic in Two Minutes a Day: 365 Selections for Easy Review.* Peabody, MA: Hendrickson, 2017.

———, ed. *Keep Up Your Biblical Hebrew in Two Minutes a Day: 365 Selections for Easy Review.* 2 vols. Peabody, MA: Hendrickson, 2017.

Koerner, Konrad. "Linguistics vs Philology: Self-Definition of a Field or Rhetorical Stance?" *Language Sciences* 19 (1997): 167–75.

Kofoed, Jens Bruun. "Using Linguistic Difference in Relative Text Dating: Insights from Other Historical Linguistic Case Studies." *HS* 2006 (2006): 93–114.

Kogan, Leonid. "Semitic Etymology in a Biblical Hebrew Lexicon: The Limits of Usefulness." Pages 83–102 in *Biblical Lexicology: Hebrew and Greek: Semantics—Exegesis—Translation.* Edited by Jan Joosten, Regine Hunziker-Rodewald, and Eberhard Bons. BZAW 443. Berlin: de Gruyter, 2015.

Köhler, Ludwig and Walter Baumgartner. *The Hebrew and Aramaic Lexicon of the Old Testament.* Translated by M. E. J. Richardson. 2 vols. Leiden: Brill, 2001.

König, Eduard. *Historisch-kritisches Lehrgebaude der hebraischen Sprache, mit steter Beziehung auf Qimchi und die anderen Auctoritaten.* 3 vols. Leipzig: Hinrichs, 1897.

Koskela, Anu. "Homonyms in Different Types of Dictionaries." Pages 457–71 in *The Oxford Handbook of Lexicography.* Edited by Philip Durkin. Oxford Handbooks in Linguistics. Oxford: Oxford University Press, 2016.

Kotzé, Zacharias. "The Cognitive Linguistic Methodology for the Study of Metaphor in the Hebrew Bible." *JNSL* 31 (2005): 107–17.

Kouwenberg, N. J. C. *The Akkadian Verb and Its Semitic Background.* LANE 2. Winona Lake, IN: Eisenbrauns, 2010.

———. *Gemination in the Akkadian Verb*. SSN 32. Assen: Van Gorcum, 1997.

Kuryłowicz, Jerzy. "Verbal Aspect in Semitic." *Or* 42 (1973): 114–20.

Kutscher, E. Y. "Aramaic." Pages 347–412 in *Linguistics in South West Asia and North Africa*. Edited by Thomas A. Sebeok. Vol. 6 of *Current Trends in Linguistics*. 14 vols. The Hague: Mouton, 1970.

———. *A History of the Hebrew Language*. Edited by Raphael Kutscher. 2nd corrected ed. Jerusalem: Magnes, 1984.

———. "The Language of the 'Genesis Apocryphon': A Prelimary Study." Pages 1–35 in *Aspects of the Dead Sea Scrolls*. Edited by Chaim Rabin and Yigael Yadin. ScrHier 4. Jerusalem: Magnes, 1958.

———. "הארמית המקראית—ארמית מזרחית היא או מערבית? [Biblical Aramaic—Is It Eastern or Western?]." Pages 123–27 in קיץ תש"ז, הכינוס העולמי למדעי היהדות [*World Congress of Jewish Studies, Summer 1947*]. Jerusalem: Magnes, 1952.

Kwon, Sung-dal. "성서 아람어의 어순에 관한 연구 [A Study on the Word Order in Biblical Aramaic]." *Sŏnggyŏng wŏnmun yŏn'gu* 41 (2017): 52–74.

Labov, William. *Principles of Linguistic Change*. 3 vols. Language in Society 20, 29, 39. Oxford: Blackwell, 1994–2010.

———. *The Social Stratification of English in New York City*. Urban Languages Series 1. Washington, DC: Center for Applied Linguistics, 1966.

Lakoff, George. *Women, Fire, and Dangerous Things: What Categories Reveal about the Mind*. Chicago: University of Chicago Press, 1987.

Lakoff, George and Henry Thompson. "Introducing Cognitive Grammar." *Proceedings of the Annual Meeting of the Berkeley Linguistics Society* 1 (1975): 295–313.

Lakoff, George and Mark Johnson. *Metaphors We Live By*. Chicago: University of Chicago Press, 1980.

Lakoff, Robin. *Language and Woman's Place*. Harper Colophon Books. New York: Harper & Row, 1975.

Lam, Joseph and Dennis Pardee. "Standard/Classical Biblical Hebrew." Pages 1–18 in vol. 1 of *A Handbook of Biblical Hebrew*. Edited by W. Randall Garr and Steven E. Fassberg. 2 vols. Winona Lake, IN: Eisenbrauns, 2016.

Lambdin, Thomas O. *Introduction to Biblical Hebrew*. New York: Scribner, 1971.

Lambert, Mayer. "De l'emploi du nifal en hébreu." *REJ* 41 (1900): 196–214.

———. *Traité de grammaire hébraïque*. 2nd ed. Hildesheim: Gerstenberg, 1972.

Lambrecht, Knud. *Information Structure and Sentence Form: Topic, Focus, and the Mental Representations of Discourse Referents*. Cambridge Studies in Linguistics 71. Cambridge: Cambridge University Press, 1994.

Lamprecht, Adriaan. *Verb Movement in Biblical Aramaic*. Acta Academica Supplementum. Bloemfontein: University of the Free State, 2001.

Langacker, Ronald W. *Cognitive Grammar: A Basic Introduction*. Oxford: Oxford University Press, 2008.

Leemhuis, Frederik. *The D and H Stems in Koranic Arabic: A Comparative Study of the Function and Meaning of the faʿʿala and ʾafala Forms in Koranic Usage*. Publications of the Netherlands Institute of Archaeology and Arabic Studies in Cairo 2. Leiden: Brill, 1977.

Lehrer, Adrienne. *Semantic Fields and Lexical Structure.* North Holland Linguistic Series 11. Amsterdam: North Holland, 1974.

Lengerke, Cäsar von. *Das Buch Daniel: verdeutscht und ausgelegt.* Königsberg: Bornträger, 1835.

Li, Fengxiang. "An Examination of Causative Morphology from a Cross-Linguistic and Diachronic Perspective." Pages 344–59 in *Part One: The General Session.* Edited by Lise M. Dobrin, Lynn Nichols, and Rosa M. Rodriquez. Vol. 1 of *Papers from the 27th Regional Meeting of the Chicago Linguistic Society, 1991.* 2 vols. Chicago: Chicago Linguistic Society, 1993.

Li, Tarsee. *The Verbal System of the Aramaic of Daniel: An Explanation in the Context of Grammaticalization.* Studies in the Aramaic Interpretation of Scripture 8. Leiden: Brill, 2009.

Lieber, Laura S. "An Ephraimite Yankee in King David's Court: Regional Dialect in the Book of Judges." Rabbinic thesis, Hebrew Union College–Jewish Institute of Religion, 1999.

Lieberman, Stephen J. "The Afro-Asiatic Background of the Semitic N-Stem: Towards the Origin of the Stem-Afformatives of the Semitic and Afro-Asiatic Verb." *BO* 53 (1986): 577–628.

Lied, Liv Ingeborg and Hugo Lundhaug, eds. *Snapshots of Evolving Traditions: Jewish and Christian Manuscript Culture, Textual Fluidity, and New Philology.* TUGAL 175. Berlin: de Gruyter, 2017.

Linder, Josef. "Das Aramäische im Buche Daniel." *ZKT* 59 (1935): 503–45.

Lode, Lars. "Postverbal Word Order in Biblical Hebrew: Structure and Function." *Semitics* 9 (1984): 113–64.

———. "Postverbal Word Order in Biblical Hebrew: Structure and Function, Part Two." *Semitics* 10 (1989): 24–38.

Longacre, Robert E. "Analysis of Preverbal Nouns in Biblical Hebrew Narrative." *JOTT* 5 (1992): 208–24.

———, ed. *Discourse Grammar: Studies in Indigenous Languages of Colombia, Panama, and Ecuador.* 3 vols. Summer Institute of Linguistics Publications in Linguistics and Related Fields 52. Dallas: Summer Institute of Linguistics, 1976.

———. "Discourse Perspective on the Hebrew Verb: Affirmation and Restatement." Pages 177–89 in *Linguistics and Biblical Hebrew.* Edited by Walter R. Bodine. Winona Lake, IN: Eisenbrauns, 1992.

———. *The Grammar of Discourse.* 2nd ed. Topics in Language and Linguistics. New York: Plenum, 1996.

———. *Joseph: A Story of Divine Providence: A Text Theoretical and Textliniguistic Analysis of Genesis 37 and 39–48.* 2nd ed. Winona Lake, IN: Eisenbrauns, 2003.

———. "Left Shifts in Strongly VSO Languages." Pages 331–54 in *Word Order in Discourse.* Edited by Pamela Downing and Michael P. Noonan. Typological Studies in Language 30. Amsterdam: Benjamins, 1995.

Longacre, Robert E. and Andrew C. Bowling. *Understanding Biblical Hebrew Verb Forms: Distribution and Function across Genres.* SIL International Publications in Linguistics 151. Dallas: SIL International, 2015.

Lowery, Kirk E. "The Theoretical Foundations of Hebrew Discourse Grammar." Pages 103–30 in *Discourse Analysis of Biblical Literature: What It Is and What It Offers*. Edited by Walter R. Bodine. SemeiaSt. Atlanta: Scholars Press, 1995.

———. "Toward a Discourse Grammar of Biblical Hebrew." PhD diss., University of California, Los Angeles, 1985.

Lunn, Nicholas P. *Word-Order Variation in Biblical Hebrew Poetry: Differentiating Pragmatic Poetics*. Paternoster Biblical Monographs. Carlisle: Paternoster, 2006.

Luther, Martin. "To the Councilmen of All Cities in Germany that They Establish and Maintain Christian Schools." Pages 340–78 in *The Christian in Society II*. Edited by Walther I. Brandt. Translated by Albert T. W. Steinhauser. Luther's Works 45. Philadelphia: Muhlenberg, 1962.

Lyons, John. *Semantics*. 2 vols. Cambridge: Cambridge University Press, 1977.

MacDonald, J. "Some Distinctive Characteristics of Israelite Spoken Hebrew." *BO* 32 (1975): 162–75.

MacDonald, Peter J. "Discourse Analysis and Biblical Interpretation." Pages 153–75 in *Linguistics and Biblical Hebrew*. Edited by Walter R. Bodine. Winona Lake, IN: Eisenbrauns, 1992.

Machen, J. Gresham. "Westminster Theological Seminary: Its Purpose and Plan." *The Presbyterian* 99 (October 10 1929): 6–9.

Machiela, Daniel A. *The Dead Sea Genesis Apocryphon: A New Text and Translation with Introduction and Special Treatment of Columns 13–17*. STDJ 79. Leiden: Brill, 2009.

Magary, Dennis R. "Keeping Your Hebrew Healthy." Pages 29–55 in *Preaching the Old Testament*. Edited by Scott M. Gibson. Grand Rapids: Baker Books, 2006.

Mallinson, Graham and Barry J. Blake. *Language Typology: Cross-Linguistic Studies in Syntax*. North Holland Linguistic Series. Amsterdam: North Holland, 1981.

Malone, Joseph L. *Tiberian Hebrew Phonology*. Winona Lake, IN: Eisenbrauns, 1993.

Maman, Aharon. "Morphology in the Medieval Rabbanite Grammatical Tradition." *EHLL* 2:712–21.

Mandell, Alice. "Biblical Hebrew, Archaic." *EHLL* 1:325–29.

Mangum, Douglas, ed. *The Lexham Theological Wordbook*. Bellingham, WA: Lexham, 2014.

Mangum, Douglas and Joshua R. Westbury, eds. *Linguistics and Biblical Exegesis*. Lexham Methods Series 2. Bellingham, WA: Lexham, 2017.

Mann, William C. and Sandra A. Thompson. "Relational Propositions in Discourse." *Discourse Processes* 9 (1986): 57–90.

———. "Rhetorical Structure Theory: Toward a Functional Theory of Text Organization." *Text: An Interdisciplinary Journal for the Study of Discourse* 8 (1988): 243–81.

Marti, Karl. *Kurzgefasste Grammatik der biblisch-aramäischen Sprache, Literatur, Paradigmen, Texte und Glossar*. Berlin: Reuther & Reichard, 1896.

Matheus, Frank. *Ein jegliches hat seine Zeit: Tempus und Aspekt im biblisch-hebräischen Verbalsystem*. Kleine Untersuchungen zur Sprache des Alten Testaments und seiner Umwelt: Beihefte 1. Kamen: Spenner, 2011.

Matthews, Victor H. *More than Meets the Ear: Discovering the Hidden Contexts of Old Testament Conversations.* Grand Rapids: Eerdmans, 2008.

Mazars, Paul. "Sens et usage de l'hitpael dans le Bible hébraïque." *Divinitas* 12 (1968): 351–64.

McFall, Leslie. *The Enigma of the Hebrew Verbal System: Solutions from Ewald to the Present Day.* Historic Texts and Interpreters in Biblical Scholarship 2. Sheffield: Almond Press, 1982.

McGregor, William B. *Linguistics: An Introduction.* 2nd ed. London: Bloomsbury Academic, 2015.

McKenzie, Tracy. "Teaching Biblical Hebrew to Congregational Leaders: A Personal Reflection on Its Challenges and Potential Ways Forward." Pages 259–71 in *The Unfolding of Your Words Gives Light: Studies in Biblical Hebrew in Honor of George L. Klein.* Edited by Ethan C. Jones. University Park, PA: Eisenbrauns, 2018.

McQuinn, Scott J. "Toward a Principled Communicative Methodology for Teaching the Biblical Languages." MA thesis, Fresno Pacific University, 2017.

McWhorter, John H. *The Language Hoax: Why the World Looks the Same in Any Language.* Oxford: Oxford University Press, 2014.

Merwe, Christo H. J. van der. "Biblical Hebrew Lexicology: A Cognitive Linguistic Perspective." *Kleine Untersuchungen zur Sprache des Alten Testaments und seiner Umwelt* 6 (2006): 87–112.

———. "Discourse Linguistics and Biblical Hebrew Grammar." Pages 13–49 in *Biblical Hebrew and Discourse Linguistics.* Edited by Robert D. Bergen. Dallas: Summer Institute of Linguistics, 1994.

———. "Explaining Fronting in Biblical Hebrew." *JNSL* 25 (1999): 173–86.

———. "Lexical Meaning in Biblical Hebrew and Cognitive Semantics: A Case Study." *Bib* 87 (2006): 85–95.

———. "A Major Step towards a Better Understanding of Biblical Hebrew Word Order." Review of *Die Satzteilfolge im Verbalsatz alttestamentlicher Prosa: untersucht an den Büchern Dtn., Ri und 2Kön*, by Walter Gross. *JNSL* 25 (1999): 277–300.

———. "An Overview of Hebrew Narrative Syntax." Pages 1–20 in *Narrative Syntax and the Hebrew Bible: Papers of the Tilburg Conference 1996.* Edited by Ellen J. van Wolde. BibInt 29. Leiden: Brill, 1997.

———. "A Short Survey of Major Contributions to the Grammatical Description of Old Hebrew since 1800 A.D." *JNSL* 13 (1987): 161–90.

———. "Some Recent Trends in Biblical Hebrew Linguistics: A Few Pointers towards a More Comprehensive Model of Language Use." *HS* 44 (2003): 7–24.

———. "Towards a Principled Working Model for Biblical Hebrew Lexicography." *JNSL* 30.1 (2004): 119–37.

Merwe, Christo H. J. van der and Eep Talstra. "Biblical Hebrew Word Order: The Interface of Information Structure and Formal Features." *ZAH* 15–16 (2002–2003): 68–107.

Merwe, Christo H. J. van der, Jacobus A. Naudé, and Jan H. Kroeze. *A Biblical Hebrew Reference Grammar.* Biblical Languages: Hebrew 3. Sheffield: Sheffield Academic, 1999.

———. *A Biblical Hebrew Reference Grammar.* 2nd ed. London: Bloomsbury T&T Clark, 2017.

Michaelis, Johann David. *Grammatica Chaldaica.* Göttingen: Deiterich, 1771.

Miller-Naudé, Cynthia L. "Presidential Perspective." *Iggeret* 87 (2015): 1–3.

———. *The Representation of Speech in Biblical Hebrew Narrative: A Linguistic Analysis.* 2nd ed. HSM 55. Winona Lake, IN: Eisenbrauns, 2003.

Miller-Naudé, Cynthia L. and Ziony Zevit, eds. *Diachrony in Biblical Hebrew.* LSAWS 8. Winona Lake, IN: Eisenbrauns, 2012.

Mitchel, Larry A. *A Student's Vocabulary for Biblical Hebrew and Aramaic.* Updated ed. Grand Rapids: Zondervan, 2017.

Mithun, Marianne. "Is Basic Word Order Universal?" Pages 15–61 in *Pragmatics of Word Order Flexibility.* Edited by Doris L. Payne. Typological Studies in Language 22. Amsterdam: Benjamins, 1992.

Moers, Gerald, Kai Widmaier, and Antonia Giewekemeyer, eds. *Dating Egyptian Literary Texts.* Lingua Aegyptia: Studia monographica 11. Hamburg: Widmaier, 2013.

Montgomery, James A. *A Critical and Exegetical Commentary on the Book of Daniel.* ICC. Edinburgh: T&T Clark, 1927.

Moomo, David O. "The Meaning of the Biblical Hebrew Verbal Conjugation from a Crosslinguistic Perspective." DLitt thesis, University of Stellenbosch, 2004.

Morgenstern, Matthew. "Late Biblical Hebrew." Pages 43–54 in vol. 1 of *A Handbook of Biblical Hebrew.* Edited by W. Randall Garr and Steven E. Fassberg. 2 vols. Winona Lake, IN: Eisenbrauns, 2016.

Morrison, Craig E. "Courtesy Expressions: Biblical Hebrew." *EHLL* 1:633–35.

Morse, MaryKate. "Enhancing the Learning and Retention of Biblical Languages for Adult Students." *Teaching Theology & Religion* 7 (2004): 45–50.

Moshavi, Adina. "Word Order: Biblical Hebrew." *EHLL* 3:991–98.

———. *Word Order in the Biblical Hebrew Finite Clause: A Syntactic and Pragmatic Analysis of Preposing.* LSAWS 4. Winona Lake, IN: Eisenbrauns, 2010.

Moshavi, Adina and Tania Notarius, eds. *Advances in Biblical Hebrew Linguistics: Data, Methods, and Analyses.* LSAWS 12. Winona Lake, IN: Eisenbrauns, 2017.

———. "Biblical Hebrew Linguistics: Perspectives on Data and Method." Pages 1–24 in *Advances in Biblical Hebrew Linguistics: Data, Methods, and Analyses.* Edited by Adina Moshavi and Tania Notarius. LSAWS 12. Winona Lake, IN: Eisenbrauns, 2017.

Mounce, William D. *Basics of Biblical Greek Grammar.* 4th ed. Grand Rapids: Zondervan, 2019.

Moyer, Clinton J. "Literary and Linguistic Studies in *Sefer Bilʿam* (Numbers 22–24)." PhD diss., Cornell University, 2009.

Muraoka, Takamitsu. "The Aramaic of the Old Targum of Job from Qumran Cave XI." *JJS* 25 (1974): 425–33.

———. "A Case of Diglossia in the Book of Jonah?" *VT* 62 (2012): 129–31.

———. *Emphatic Words and Structures in Biblical Hebrew.* Leiden: Brill, 1985.

———. "A New Dictionary of Classical Hebrew." Pages 87–101 in *Studies in Ancient Hebrew Semantics.* Edited by Takamitsu Muraoka. AbrNSup 4. Leuven: Peeters, 1995.

Murphy, M. Lynne. *Lexical Meaning*. Cambridge Textbooks in Linguistics. Cambridge: Cambridge University Press, 2010.

Naudé, Jacobus A. "The Complexity of Language Change: The Case of Ancient Hebrew." *Southern African Linguistics and Applied Language Studies* 30 (2012): 395–411.

———. "Diachrony in Biblical Hebrew and a Theory of Language Change and Diffusion." Pages 61–82 in *Diachrony in Biblical Hebrew*. Edited by Cynthia L. Miller-Naudé and Ziony Zevit. LSAWS 8. Winona Lake, IN: Eisenbrauns, 2012.

———. "Government and Binding." *EHLL* 2:72–76.

———. "Linguistic Dating of Biblical Hebrew Texts: The Chronology and Typology Debate." *JNSL* 36 (2010): 1–22.

———. "A Syntactic Analysis of Dislocations in Biblical Hebrew." *JNSL* 16 (1990): 115–30.

———. "The Transitions of Biblical Hebrew in the Perspective of Language Change and Diffusion." Pages 189–214 in *Biblical Hebrew: Studies in Chronology and Typology*. Edited by Ian Young. JSOTSup 369. London: T&T Clark, 2003.

Naudé, Jacobus A. and Cynthia L. Miller-Naudé. "Historical Linguistics, Editorial Theory, and Biblical Hebrew: The Current State of the Debate." *JSem* 25 (2016): 833–64.

Naveh, Joseph and Shaul Shaked, eds. *Aramaic Documents from Ancient Bactria (Fourth Century BCE) from the Khalili Collections*. London: Khalili Family Trust, 2012.

Nedialkov, V. P. and Sergei Jaxontov. "The Typology of Resultative Constructions." Pages 3–62 in *Typology of Resultative Constructions*. Edited by V. P. Nedialkov and Bernard Comrie. Typological Studies in Language 12. Amsterdam: Benjamins, 1988.

Nerhlich, Brigitte and David D. Clarke. "Cognitive Linguistics and the History of Linguistics." Pages 589–607 in *The Oxford Handbook of Cognitive Linguistics*. Edited by Dirk Geeraerts and Hubert Cuyckens. Oxford Handbooks. Oxford: Oxford University Press, 2007.

Newman, Paul. *Nominal and Verbal Plurality in Chadic*. Publications in African Languages and Linguistics 12. Dordrecht: Foris, 1990.

———. "Pluractional Verbs: An Overview." Pages 185–209 in *Verbal Plurality and Distributivity*. Edited by Patricia Cabredo Hofherr and Brenda Laca. Linguistische Arbeiten 546. Berlin: De Gruyter, 2012.

Niccacci, Alviero. "On the Hebrew Verbal System." Pages 117–37 in *Biblical Hebrew and Discourse Linguistics*. Edited by Robert D. Bergen. Dallas: Summer Institute of Linguistics, 1994.

———. *Sintassi del verbo ebraico nella prosa biblica classica*. SBFA 23. Jerusalem: Franciscan Printing Press, 1986.

———. *The Syntax of the Verb in Classical Hebrew Prose*. Translated by Wilfred G. E. Watson. JSOTSup 86. Sheffield: JSOT Press, 1990.

Nida, Eugene Albert and Charles R. Taber. *The Theory and Practice of Translation*. Helps for Translators 7. Leiden: Brill, 1969.

Noegel, Scott B. "Dialect and Politics in Isaiah 24–27." *AuOr* 12 (1994): 177–92.

Noonan, Benjamin J. "Daniel's Greek Loans in Dialectal Perspective." *BBR* 28 (2018): 575–603.

———. *Non-Semitic Loanwords in the Hebrew Bible: A Lexicon of Language Contact.* LSAWS 14. University Park, PA: Eisenbrauns, 2019.

Noonan, Jennifer E. "Recent Teaching Grammars for Biblical Hebrew: A Review and Critique." *ATJ* 43 (2011): 99–118.

———. "Teaching Biblical Hebrew." Pages 317–35 in *"Where Shall Wisdom Be Found?" A Grammatical Tribute to Professor Stephen A. Kaufman.* Edited by Hélène M. Dallaire, Benjamin J. Noonan, and Jennifer E. Noonan. Winona Lake, IN: Eisenbrauns, 2017.

———. "Using Processing Instruction to Teach Biblical Hebrew Grammar." PhD diss., Hebrew Union College–Jewish Institute of Religion, 2009.

Notarius, Tania. *The Verb in Archaic Biblical Poetry: A Discursive, Typological, and Historical Investigation of the Tense System.* Studies in Semitic Languages and Linguistics 68. Leiden: Brill, 2013.

Nuyts, Jan. "Cognitive Linguistics and Functional Linguistics." Pages 543–65 in *The Oxford Handbook of Cognitive Linguistics.* Edited by Dirk Geeraerts and Hubert Cuyckens. Oxford Handbooks. Oxford: Oxford University Press, 2007.

O'Connor, Michael. "Discourse Linguistics and the Study of Biblical Hebrew." Pages 17–42 in *Congress Volume: Basel, 2001.* Edited by André Lemaire. VTSup 92. Leiden: Brill, 2002.

———. "Semitic Lexicography: European Dictionaries of Biblical Hebrew in the Twentieth Century." Pages 173–212 in *Semitic Linguistics: The State of the Art at the Turn of the Twenty-First Century.* Edited by Shlomo Izre'el. IOS 20. Winona Lake, IN: Eisenbrauns, 2002.

Ólafsson, Sverrir. "On Diglossia in Ancient Hebrew and Its Graphic Representation." *FO* 28 (1992): 193–205.

Olsen, Mari Broman. *A Semantic and Pragmatic Model of Lexical and Grammatical Aspect.* Outstanding Dissertations in Linguistics. New York: Garland, 1997.

Olshausen, Justus. *Lehrbuch der hebräischen Sprache.* 2 vols. Brunswick: Vieweg, 1861.

Overland, Paul. *Learning Biblical Hebrew Interactively.* 2nd ed. 2 vols. Sheffield: Sheffield Academic, 2016.

———. *Millim: Words for Conversation in the Biblical Hebrew Classroom.* 2nd ed. Ha'arets: Hebrew and Aramaic Accessible Resources for Exegetical and Theological Studies. Wilmore, KY: GlossaHouse, 2016.

Overland, Paul, Lee M. Fields, and Jennifer E. Noonan. "Can Communicative Principles Enhance Classical Language Acquisition?" *Foreign Language Annals* 44 (2011): 583–98.

Palmer, Frank Robert. *Mood and Modality.* 2nd ed. Cambridge Textbooks in Linguistics. Cambridge: Cambridge University Press, 2001.

Paltridge, Brian. *Discourse Analysis: An Introduction.* 2nd ed. Continuum Discourse Series. London: Continuum, 2012.

Park, Sung Jin. *Typology in Biblical Hebrew Poetic Meter: A Generative Metrical Approach.* Lewiston, NY: Mellen, 2017.

Pat-El, Na'ama. "Israelian Hebrew: A Re-Evaluation." *VT* 67 (2017): 227–63.

Patton, Matthew H. and Frederic Clarke Putnam. *Basics of Hebrew Discourse: A Guide to Working with Hebrew Prose and Poetry.* Edited by Miles V. Van Pelt. Grand Rapids: Zondervan, 2019.

Payne, Geoffrey. "Functional Sentence Perspective: Theme in Biblical Hebrew." *SJOT* 1 (1991): 62–82.

Peckham, J. Brian. "Tense and Mood in Biblical Hebrew." *ZAH* 10 (1997): 139–68.

Pennington, Jonathan T. "Setting aside 'Deponency': Rediscovering the Greek Middle Voice in New Testament Studies." Pages 181–203 in *The Linguist as Pedagogue: Trends in the Teaching and Linguistic Analysis of the Greek New Testament.* Edited by Stanley E. Porter and Mathew Brook O'Donnell. New Testament Monographs 11. Sheffield: Sheffield Phoenix, 2009.

Person, Raymond F., Jr. *The Deuteronomic History and the Book of Chronicles: Scribal Works in an Oral World.* AIL 6. Atlanta: Society of Biblical Literature, 2010.

———. "Linguistic Variation Emphasized, Linguistic Variation Denied." Pages 119–25 in *The Archaeology of Difference: Gender, Ethnicity, Class, and the "Other" in Antiquity: Studies in Honor of Eric M. Meyers.* Edited by Douglas R. Edwards and C. Thomas McCoullough. AASOR 60–61. Boston: American Schools of Oriental Research, 2007.

Peters, Kurtis. *Hebrew Lexical Semantics and Daily Life in Ancient Israel: What's Cooking in Biblical Hebrew?* BibInt 146. Leiden: Brill, 2016.

Petyt, K. M. *The Study of Dialect: An Introduction to Dialectology.* Language Library. London: Deutsch, 1980.

Phua, Chiew Phen. "Dating the Chapters in *Guanzi*: Evidence from Historical Linguistics Perspective." MPhil thesis, Hong Kong University of Science and Technology, 2002.

Pike, Kenneth L. *Language in Relation to a Unified Theory of the Structure of Human Behavior.* 2nd ed. Janua Linguarum Series Maior 24. The Hague: Mouton, 1967.

Pinker, Steven. *The Language Instinct: The New Science of Language and Mind.* New York: Morrow, 1994.

Pleins, J. David. *Biblical Hebrew Vocabulary by Conceptual Categories: A Student's Guide to Nouns in the Old Testament.* Grand Rapids: Zondervan, 2017.

Ploeg, J. P. M. van der, A. S. van der Woude, and Bastiaan Jongeling. *Le Targum de Job de la grotte XI de Qumrân.* Leiden: Brill, 1971.

Poebel, Arno. *Studies in Akkadian Grammar.* AS 9. Chicago: University of Chicago Press, 1939.

Polak, Frank H. "Language Variation, Discourse Typology, and the Socio-Cultural Background of Biblical Narrative." Pages 301–38 in *Diachrony in Biblical Hebrew.* Edited by Cynthia L. Miller-Naudé and Ziony Zevit. LSAWS 8. Winona Lake, IN: Eisenbrauns, 2012.

———. "Linguistic and Stylistic Aspects of Epic Formulae in Ancient Semitic Poetry and Biblical Narrative." Pages 285–304 in *Biblical Hebrew in Its Northwest Semitic Setting: Typological and Historical Perspectives.* Edited by Steven E. Fassberg and Avi Hurvitz. Winona Lake, IN: Eisenbrauns, 2006.

———. "The Oral and the Written: Syntax, Stylistics and the Development of Biblical Prose Narrative." *JANES* 26 (1998): 59–105.

———. "Parler de la langue: Labov, Fishman et l'histoire de l'hébreu biblique." Pages 13–37 in *Le Proche-Orient ancien à la lumière des sciences sociales*. Edited by Madalina Vârtejanu-Joubert. Yod 18. Paris: Publications langues O', 2013.

———. "Sociolinguistics: A Key to the Typology and the Social Background of Biblical Hebrew." *HS* 47 (2006): 115–62.

———. "Sociolinguistics and the Judean Speech Community in the Achaemenid Empire." Pages 589–628 in *Judah and the Judeans in the Persian Period*. Edited by Oded Lipschits and Manfred Oeming. Winona Lake, IN: Eisenbrauns, 2006.

———. "Style Is More Than the Person: Sociolinguistics, Literary Culture and the Distinction between Written and Oral Narrative." Pages 38–103 in *Biblical Hebrew: Studies in Chronology and Typology*. Edited by Ian Young. JSOTSup 369. London: T&T Clark, 2003.

———. "The Style of the Dialogue in Biblical Prose Narrative." *JANES* 28 (2001): 53–95.

———. "מעמד הדוברים ומבנה הדו-שיח בסיפורי המקרא [On Dialogue and Speaker Status in Biblical Narrative]." *Beit Mikra* 48 (2002–2003): 1–18, 97–119.

———. "תמורות ותקופות בלשון הסיפורת במקרא: חלק ראשון [Development and Periodization of Biblical Prose Narrative]." *Beit Mikra* 43 (1997–1998): 30–52, 142–60.

Polzin, Robert. *Late Biblical Hebrew: Toward a Historical Typology of Biblical Hebrew Prose*. HSM 12. Missoula, MT: Scholars Press, 1976.

Porten, Bezalel and Ada Yardeni. *Textbook of Aramaic Documents from Ancient Egypt*. 4 vols. Texts and Studies for Students. Winona Lake, IN: Eisenbrauns, 1986–1999.

Porter, Stanley E. *Verbal Aspect in the Greek of the New Testament*. Studies in Biblical Greek 1. New York: Lang, 1989.

Pratico, Gary D. and Miles V. Van Pelt. *Basics of Biblical Hebrew Grammar*. 3rd ed. Grand Rapids: Zondervan, 2019.

Rabin, Chaim. "An Arabic Phrase in Isaiah." Pages 303–9 in *Studi sull'Oriente e la Bibbia: Offerti al P. Giovanni Rinaldi nel 60° compleanno da allievi, colleghi, amici*. Genoa: Studio e vita, 1967.

———. "Hebrew." Pages 304–46 in *Linguistics in South West Asia and North Africa*. Edited by Thomas A. Sebeok. Vol. 6 of *Current Trends in Linguistics*. 14 vols. The Hague: Mouton, 1970.

Rainey, Anson F. "The Ancient Hebrew Prefix Conjugation in Light of Amarna Canaanite." *HS* 27 (1986): 4–19.

Rattray, Susan. "The Tense-Mood-Aspect System of Biblical Hebrew, with Special Emphasis on 1 and 2 Samuel." PhD diss., University of California, Berkeley, 1992.

Ray, Blaine and Contee Seely. *Fluency through TPR Storytelling: Achieving Real Language Acquisition in School*. 2nd ed. Berkeley, CA: Command Performance Language Institute, 1998.

Regt, Lénart J. de. *A Parametric Model for Syntactic Studies of a Textual Corpus, Demonstrated on the Hebrew of Deuteronomy 1–30*. 2 vols. SSN 23. Assen: Van Gorcum, 1988.

———. "Participant Reference in Discourse: Biblical Hebrew." *EHLL* 3:30–33.

Reichenbach, Hans. *Elements of Symbolic Logic.* New York: Macmillan, 1947.

Rendsburg, Gary A. "Addressee-Switching." *EHLL* 1:34–35.

———. "Biblical Hebrew: Dialects and Linguistic Variation." *EHLL* 1:338–41.

———. "A Comprehensive Guide to Israelian Hebrew: Grammar and Lexicon." *Orient* 38 (2003): 5–35.

———. "Diglossia: Biblical Hebrew." *EHLL* 1:724–25.

———. *Diglossia in Ancient Hebrew.* AOS 72. New Haven: American Oriental Society, 1990.

———. "Kabbîr in Biblical Hebrew: Evidence for Style-Switching and Addressee-Switching in the Hebrew Bible." *JAOS* 112 (1992): 649–51.

———. "Linguistic Variation and the 'Foreign' Factor in the Hebrew Bible." *IOS* 15 (1996): 177–90.

———. "Northern Hebrew through Time: From the Song of Deborah to the Mishnah." Pages 339–59 in *Diachrony in Biblical Hebrew.* Edited by Cynthia L. Miller-Naudé and Ziony Zevit. LSAWS 8. Winona Lake, IN: Eisenbrauns, 2012.

———. "Some False Leads in the Identification of Late Biblical Hebrew Texts: The Cases of Genesis 24 and 1 Samuel 2:27–36." *JBL* 121 (2002): 23–46.

———. "The Strata of Biblical Hebrew." *JNSL* 17 (1991): 81–99.

———. "Style-Switching." *EHLL* 3:633–36.

———. "Style-Switching in Biblical Hebrew." Pages 65–85 in *Epigraphy, Philology and the Hebrew Bible: Methodological Perspectives on Philological and Comparative Study of the Hebrew Bible in Honor of Jo Ann Hackett.* Edited by Jeremy M. Hutton and Aaron D. Rubin. ANEM 12. Atlanta: Society of Biblical Literature, 2015.

Revell, E. J. "The Conditioning of Word Order in Verbless Clauses in Biblical Hebrew." *JSS* 34 (1989): 1–24.

———. *The Designation of the Individual: Expressive Usage in Biblical Narrative.* CBET 14. Kampen: Kok Pharos, 1996.

———. "The System of the Verb in Standard Biblical Prose." *HUCA* 60 (1989): 1–37.

———. "Thematic Continuity and the Conditioning of Word Order in Verbless Clauses." Pages 297–319 in *The Verbless Clause in Biblical Hebrew: Linguistic Approaches.* Edited by Cynthia L. Miller-Naudé. LSAWS 1. Winona Lake, IN: Eisenbrauns, 1999.

Rezetko, Robert. "The Spelling of 'Damascus' and the Linguistic Dating of Biblical Texts." *SJOT* 24 (2010): 110–28.

Rezetko, Robert and Ian Young. "Currents in the Historical Linguistics and Linguistic Dating of the Hebrew Bible." *HIPHIL Novum* 5.1 (2019): 3–95.

———. *Historical Linguistics and Biblical Hebrew: Steps Toward an Integrated Approach.* ANEM 9. Atlanta: Society of Biblical Literature, 2014.

Rezetko, Robert and Martijn Naaijer. "An Alternative Approach to the Lexicon of Late Biblical Hebrew." *JHebS* 16.1 (2016): 1–39. http://www.jhsonline.org.

Richards, Jack C. and Theodore S. Rodgers. *Approaches and Methods in Language Teaching: A Description and Analysis.* 3rd ed. Cambridge Language Teaching Library. Cambridge: Cambridge University Press, 2014.

Robar, Elizabeth. "Grounding: Biblical Hebrew." *EHLL* 2:151–56.

———. *The Verb and the Paragraph in Biblical Hebrew: A Cognitive-Linguistic Approach.* Studies in Semitic Languages and Linguistics 78. Leiden: Brill, 2015.

Robertson, David A. *Linguistic Evidence in Dating Early Hebrew Poetry.* SBLDS 3. Missoula, MT: Society of Biblical Literature, 1972.

Robins, Robert H. *A Short History of Linguistics.* 4th ed. Longman Linguistics Library. London: Routledge, 1997.

Rocine, Bryan M. *Learning Biblical Hebrew: A New Approach Using Discourse Analysis.* Macon, GA: Smyth & Helwys, 2000.

Römer, Thomas. "How to Date Pentateuchal Texts: Some Case Studies." Pages 357–70 in *The Formation of the Pentateuch: Bridging the Academic Cultures of Europe, Israel, and North America.* Edited by Jan Christian Gertz, Bernard M. Levinson, Dalit Rom-Shiloni, and Konrad Schmid. FAT 111. Tübingen: Mohr Siebeck, 2016.

Rooker, Mark F. *Biblical Hebrew in Transition: The Language of the Book of Ezekiel.* JSOTSup 90. Sheffield: JSOT Press, 1990.

Rosch, Eleanor. "On the Internal Structure of Perceptual and Semantic Categories." Pages 111–44 in *Cognitive Development and the Acquisition of Language.* Edited by Timothy E. Moore. New York: Academic Press, 1973.

———. "Principles of Categorization." Pages 27–48 in *Cognition and Categorization.* Edited by Eleanor Rosch and Barbara B. Lloyd. Hillsdale, NJ: Erlbaum, 1978.

Rosén, Haiim B. "On the Use of the Tenses in the Aramaic of Daniel." *JSS* 6 (1961): 183–203.

Rosenbaum, Michael. *Word-Order Variation in Isaiah 40–55: A Functional Perspective.* SSN 36. Assen: Van Gorcum, 1997.

Rosenthal, Franz. *A Grammar of Biblical Aramaic.* PLO 5. Wiesbaden: Harrassowitz, 1961.

———. *A Grammar of Biblical Aramaic.* 7th ed. PLO 5. Wiesbaden: Harrassowitz, 2006.

Ross, Allen P. *Introducing Biblical Hebrew.* Grand Rapids: Baker Academic, 2001.

Ross, John Robert. "The Penthouse Principle and the Order of Constituents." Pages 397–422 in *You Take the High Node and I'll Take the Low Node: Papers from the Comparative Syntax Festival, The Differences between Main and Subordinate Clauses, 12 April 1973.* Edited by Claudia W. Corum, Thomas Cedric Smith-Stark, and Ann Weiser. Chicago: Chicago Linguistic Society, 1973.

Rothstein, Susan. *Structuring Events: A Study in the Semantics of Lexical Aspect.* Explorations in Semantics. Oxford: Blackwell, 2004.

Rowley, H. H. *The Aramaic of the Old Testament: A Grammatical and Lexical Study of Its Relations with Other Early Aramaic Dialects.* London: Oxford University Press, 1929.

Rubino, Carl. "Reduplication: Form, Function, and Distribution." Pages 11–29 in *Studies on Reduplication.* Edited by Bernhard Hurch. Empirical Approaches to Language Typology 28. Berlin: Mouton de Gruyter, 2005.

Rundgren, Frithiof. *Das althebräische Verbum: Abriss der Aspektlehre.* Stockholm: Almqvist & Wiksell, 1961.

Runge, Steven E. and Joshua R. Westbury, eds. *Lexham Discourse Hebrew Bible.* Bellingham, WA: Lexham, 2012.

———, eds. *Lexham High Definition Old Testament*. Bellingham, WA: Lexham, 2012.

Runnalls, Graham A. "The Linguistic Dating of Middle French Texts with Special Reference to the Theatre." *Modern Language Review* 71 (1976): 757–61.

Russom, Geoffrey R. "Dating Criteria for Old English Poems." Pages 245–65 in *A Millennial Perspective*. Edited by Donka Minkova and Robert P. Stockwell. Vol. 1 of *Studies in the History of the English Language*. 7 vols. Topics in English Linguistics 39. Berlin: Mouton, 2002.

Ryder, Stuart A. *The D-Stem in Western Semitic*. Janua Linguarum Series Practica 131. The Hague: Mouton, 1974.

Sáenz-Badillos, Angel. *A History of the Hebrew Language*. Translated by John F. Elwolde. Cambridge: Cambridge University Press, 1993.

Sampson, Geoffrey. *Schools of Linguistics*. Stanford, CA: Stanford University Press, 1980.

Sande, Axel van de. *Nouvelle perspective sur le système verbal de l'hébreu ancien: les formes *qatala, *yaqtul et *yaqtulu*. Publications de l'Institut orientaliste de Louvain 57. Leuven: Peeters, 2008.

Saussure, Ferdinand de. *Cours de linguistique générale*. Edited by Charles Bally and Albert Sechehaye. Lausanne: Payot, 1916.

———. *Course in General Linguistics*. Edited by Charles Bally and Albert Sechehaye. Translated by Wade Baskin. New York: Philosophical Library, 1959.

Sawyer, John F. A. *Semantics in Biblical Research: New Methods of Defining Hebrew Words for Salvation*. SBT 24. London: SCM Press, 1972.

Schaeder, Hans Heinrich. *Iranische Beiträge I*. Schriften der Königsberger gelehrten Gesellschaft, geisteswissenschaftliche Klasse 6/5. Halle: Niemeyer, 1930.

Schlesinger, Kalman. "Zur Wortfolge im hebräischen Verbalsatz." *VT* 3 (1953): 381–90.

Schneider, Wolfgang. *Grammatik des biblischen Hebräisch: ein Lehrbuch*. Munich: Claudius, 1974.

Schniedewind, William M. "Prolegomena for the Sociolinguistics of Classical Hebrew." *JHebS* 5.6 (2004): 1–32.

———. *Social History of Hebrew: Its Origins through the Rabbinic Period*. ABRL. New Haven: Yale University Press, 2013.

Schniedewind, William M. and Daniel Sivan. "The Elijah-Elisha Narratives: A Test Case for the Northern Dialect of Hebrew." *JQR* 87 (1997): 303–37.

Schroeder, Nicolaus Wilhelm. *Institutiones ad fundamenta linguae Hebraeae*. Groningen: Bolt, 1772.

Schultens, Albert. *Institutiones ad fundamenta linguae Hebraea: quibus via panditur ad ejusdem analogiam restituendam & vindicandam in usum collegii domestici*. Leiden: Luzac, 1737.

Scow, C. L. *A Grammar for Biblical Hebrew*. 2nd ed. Nashville: Abingdon, 1995.

Sérandour, Arnaud. "Remarques sur le bilinguisme dans le livre d'Esdras." Pages 131–44 in *Mosaïque de langues, mosaïque culturelle: le bilinguisme dans le Proche-Orient ancien: actes de la table-ronde du 18 novembre 1995 organisée par l'URA 1062 'Etudes sémitiques.'* Edited by Françoise Briquel-Chatonnet. Antiquitées sémitiques 1. Paris: Maisonneuve, 1996.

Seuren, Pieter A. M. *Western Linguistics: An Historical Introduction.* Oxford: Blackwell, 1998.

Shankara Bhat, D. N. *The Prominence of Tense, Aspect, and Mood.* Studies in Language Companion Series 49. Amsterdam: Benjamins, 1999.

Shead, Stephen L. *Radical Frame Semantics and Biblical Hebrew: Exploring Lexical Semantics.* BibInt 108. Leiden: Brill, 2011.

Shepherd, Michael B. *The Verbal System of Biblical Aramaic: A Distributional Approach.* StBibLit 116. New York: Lang, 2008.

Shimasaki, Katsuomi. *Focus Structure in Biblical Hebrew: A Study of Word Order and Information Structure.* Bethesda, MD: CDL, 2002.

———. "Information Structure: Biblical Hebrew." *EHLL* 2:279–83.

Shippey, T. A. *J.R.R. Tolkien: Author of the Century.* Boston: Houghton Mifflin, 2000.

Shulman, Ahouva. "Imperative and Second Person Indicative Forms in Biblical Hebrew Prose." *HS* 42 (2001): 271–87.

———. "The Particle נָא in Biblical Hebrew Prose." *HS* 40 (1999): 57–82.

———. "The Use of Modal Verb Forms in Biblical Hebrew Prose." PhD diss., University of Toronto, 1996.

Siebesma, P. A. *The Function of the Niphʿal in Biblical Hebrew in Relationship to Other Passive-Reflexive Verbal Stems and to the Puʿal and Hophʿal in Particular.* SSN 28. Assen: Van Gorcum, 1991.

Siewierska, Anna. "Functional and Cognitive Grammars." Pages 485–501 in *The Oxford Handbook of the History of Linguistics.* Edited by Keith Allan. Oxford: Oxford University Press, 2013.

———. *Word Order Rules.* Croom Helm Linguistics Series. London: Croom Helm, 1988.

Sigrist, David Joseph. "Overcoming Obstacles: Proposed Technological Solutions for Perceived Problems with Ancient Language Learning through Communicative Methods." Paper presented at the annual meeting of the Society of Biblical Literature. Atlanta, GA, November 22, 2015.

Silva, Moisés. *Biblical Words and Their Meaning: An Introduction to Lexical Semantics.* 2nd ed. Grand Rapids: Zondervan, 1994.

———. *God, Language, and Scripture: Reading the Bible in the Light of General Linguistics.* Foundations of Contemporary Interpretation 4. Grand Rapids: Zondervan, 1990.

Silzer, Peter J. and Thomas J. Finley. *How Biblical Languages Work: A Student's Guide to Learning Hebrew and Greek.* Grand Rapids: Kregel, 2004.

Sinclair, Cameron. "The Valence of the Hebrew Verb." *JANES* 20 (1991): 63–81.

Smith, Carlota S. *The Parameter of Aspect.* Studies in Linguistics and Philosophy 43. Dordrecht: Kluwer, 1997.

Smith, Colin J. "With an Iron Pen and a Diamond Tip: Linguistic Peculiarities in the Book of Jeremiah." PhD diss., Cornell University, 2003.

Smith, Scobie Philip. "The Question of Diglossia in Ancient Hebrew." Pages 37–52 in *Diglossia and Other Topics in New Testament Linguistics.* Edited by Stanley E. Porter. JSNTSup 193. Sheffield: Sheffield Academic, 2000.

Sokoloff, Michael. *The Targum to Job from Qumran Cave XI.* Bar-Ilan Studies in Near Eastern Languages and Cultures. Ramat-Gan: Bar-Illan University Press, 1974.

Song, Jae Jung. *Word Order.* Research Surveys in Linguistics. Cambridge: Cambridge University Press, 2012.

Speiser, E. A. "The Durative Hitpaʿel: A *tan*-Form." *JAOS* 75 (1955): 118–21.

———. "The 'Elative' in West-Semitic and Akkadian." *JCS* 6 (1952): 81–92.

———. "Studies in Semitic Formatives." *JAOS* 56 (1936): 22–46.

Stabnow, David K. "A Discourse Analysis Perspective on the Syntax of Clauses Negated by לא in the Primary History." PhD diss, Westminster Theological Seminary, 2000.

Stade, Bernhard. *Lehrbuch der hebräischen Grammatik.* Leipzig: Vogel, 1879.

Stauder, Andréas. *Linguistic Dating of Middle Egyptian Literary Texts.* Lingua Aegyptia: Studia Monographica 12. Hamburg: Widmaier, 2013.

Stefanovic, Zdravko. *The Aramaic of Daniel in the Light of Old Aramaic.* JSOTSup 129. Sheffield: JSOT Press, 1992.

Stein, Adolf. *Der Stamm des Hithpael im Hebräischen.* Leipzig: Drugulin, 1893.

Stein, David E. S. "The Grammar of Social Gender in Biblical Hebrew." *HS* 49 (2008): 7–26.

Strack, H. L. *Grammatik des Biblisch-Aramäischen mit den nach Handschriften berichtigten Texten und einem Wörterbuch.* 6th ed. Munich: Beck, 1921.

Streck, Michael P. *Die akkadischen Verbalstämme mit ta-Infix.* AOAT 303. Münster: Ugarit-Verlag, 2003.

Streett, Daniel R. "Immersion Greek: Developing the Necessary Support Structure (Basics of Greek Pedagogy, Pt. 9)." καὶ τὰ λοιπά. September 29, 2011. https://danielstreett.com/2011/09/29/immersion-greekdeveloping-the-necessary-support-structure-basics-of-greek-pedagogy-pt-9/.

Swanson, James. *A Dictionary of Biblical Languages: Hebrew Old Testament.* 2nd ed. Oak Harbor, WA: Logos Research Systems, 2001.

Talmy, Leonard. "Force Dynamics as a Generalization over 'Causative.'" Pages 67–85 in *Languages and Linguistics: The Interdependence of Theory, Data, and Application.* Edited by Deborah Tannen and James E. Alatis. Georgetown University Round Table on Languages and Linguistics. Washington, DC: Georgetown University Press, 1986.

———. "Force Dynamics in Language and Cognition." Pages 409–70 in *Concept Structuring Systems.* Vol. 1 of *Toward a Cognitive Semantics.* 2 vols. Language, Speech, and Communication. Cambridge, MA: MIT Press, 2000.

Talshir, David. "The Habitat and History of Hebrew during the Second Temple Period." Pages 251–75 in *Biblical Hebrew: Studies in Chronology and Typology.* Edited by Ian Young. JSOTSup 369. London: T&T Clark, 2003.

Talstra, Eep. "Hebrew Syntax: Clause Types and Clause Hierarchy." Pages 180–93 in *Studies in Hebrew and Aramaic Syntax Presented to Professsor J. Hoftijzer on the Occasion of His Sixty-Fifth Birthday.* Edited by Karel Jongeling, Hendrika L. Murre-van den Berg, and Lucas van Rompay. Studies in Semitic Languages and Linguistics 17. Leiden: Brill, 1991.

———. "Text Grammar and the Hebrew Bible 1: Elements of a Theory." *BO* 35 (1978): 168–74.

———. "Text Grammar and the Hebrew Bible 2: Syntax and Semantics." *BO* 39 (1982): 26–38.

———. "Text Linguistics: Biblical Hebrew." *EHLL* 1:755–60.

Tannen, Deborah. *Gender and Discourse.* Oxford: Oxford University Press, 1996.

Taylor, John R. "Cognitive Linguistics and Autonomous Linguistics." Pages 566–88 in *The Oxford Handbook of Cognitive Linguistics.* Edited by Dirk Geeraerts and Hubert Cuyckens. Oxford Handbooks. Oxford: Oxford University Press, 2007.

———. *Linguistic Categorization.* 3rd ed. Oxford Textbooks in Linguistics. Oxford: Oxford University Press, 2003.

Téné, David, Aharon Maman, and James Barr. "Linguistic Literature, Hebrew." *EncJud* 13:29–61.

Tesnière, Lucien. *Éléments de syntaxe structurale.* Paris: Klinksiek, 1959.

Thompson, Jeremy P. and Wendy Widder. "Major Approaches to Linguistics." Pages 87–133 in *Linguistics and Biblical Exegesis.* Edited by Douglas Mangum and Joshua R. Westbury. Lexham Methods Series 2. Bellingham, WA: Lexham, 2017.

Thomson, Christopher J. "What Is Aspect? Contrasting Definitions in General Linguistics and New Testament Studies." Pages 13–80 in *The Greek Verb Revisited: A Fresh Approach for Biblical Exegesis.* Edited by Steven E. Runge and Christopher J. Fresch. Bellingham, WA: Lexham, 2016.

Tilahun, Gelila, Andrey Feuerverger, and Michael Gervers. "Dating Medieval English Charters." *Annals of Applied Statistics* 6 (2012): 1615–40.

Tisdall, William St. Clair. "The Book of Daniel: Some Linguistic Evidence Regarding Its Date." *Journal of the Transactions of the Victoria Institute* 53 (1921): 206–55.

———. "Egypt and the Book of Daniel: Or What Say the Papyri?" *The Expositor* 22 (1921): 340–57.

Toews, Brian G. "A Discourse Grammar of the Aramaic in the Book of Daniel." PhD diss., University of California, Los Angeles, 1993.

Tolkien, J. R. R. *The Fellowship of the Ring: Being the First Part of the Lord of the Rings.* 2nd ed. Boston: Houghton Mifflin, 1988.

Tomlin, Russel S. *Basic Word Order: Functional Principles.* Croom Helm Linguistics Series. London: Croom Helm, 1986.

Toorn, Karel van der. *Scribal Culture and the Making of the Hebrew Bible.* Cambridge: Harvard University Press, 2007.

Torrey, Charles C. "The Aramaic Portions of Ezra." *AJSL* 24 (1908): 209–81.

Trier, Jost. *Der deutsche Wortschatz im Sinnbezirk des Verstandes: Die Geschichte eines Sprachlichen feldes.* Germanische Bibliothek, Abteilung 2: Untersuchungen und Texte 31. Heidelberg: Winter, 1931.

Tropper, Josef. "Althebräisches und semitisches Aspektsystem." *ZAH* 11 (1998): 153–90.

———. "Lexikographische Untersuchungen zum Biblisch-Aramäischen." *JNSL* 23.2 (1997): 105–28.

Trosborg, Anna. "Text Typology: Register, Genre and Text Type." Pages 3–23 in *Text, Typology and Translation*. Edited by Anna Trosborg. Benjamins Translation Library 26. Amsterdam: Benjamins, 1997.

Trubetskoĭ, Nikolaĭ Sergeevich. *N.S. Trubetzkoy's Letters and Notes*. Edited by Roman Jakobson. Janua Linguarum Series Maior 47. The Hague: Mouton, 1975.

———. "La phonologie actuelle." *Journal de psychologie normale et pathologique* 30 (1933): 219–46.

———. "Die phonologischen Systeme." Pages 96–116 in vol. 4 of *Réunion phonologique internationale tenue à Prague, 18–21/XII 1930*. Pražský linguistický kroužek: Travaux 4. Prague: Jednota československých matematiků a fysiků, 1931.

Ullendorff, Edward. "Is Biblical Hebrew a Language?" *BSOAS* 34 (1971): 241–55.

Valle Rodríguez, Carlos del. "Grammarians: Medieval Spain." *EHLL* 2:94–101.

Vance, Donald R., George Athas, and Yael Avrahami. *Biblia Hebraica Stuttgartensia: A Reader's Edition*. Peabody, MA: Hendrickson, 2015.

VanGemeren, Willem A., ed. *New International Dictionary of Old Testament Theology and Exegesis*. 5 vols. Grand Rapids: Zondervan, 1997.

VanPatten, Bill. *Input Processing and Grammar Instruction in Second Language Acquisition*. Second Language Learning. Norwood, NJ: Ablex, 1996.

———, ed. *Processing Instruction: Theory, Research, and Commentary*. Second Language Acquisition Research. Mahwah, NJ: Erlbaum, 2004.

Van Pelt, Miles V. *Basics of Biblical Aramaic: Complete Grammar, Lexicon, and Annotated Text*. Grand Rapids: Zondervan, 2011.

Van Pelt, Miles V. and Gary D. Pratico. *The Vocabulary Guide to Biblical Hebrew and Aramaic*. 2nd ed. Grand Rapids: Zondervan, 2019.

Van Steenbergen, Gerrit Jan. "Hebrew Lexicography and Worldview: A Survey of Some Lexicons." *JSem* 12 (2003): 268–313.

Van Valin, Robert D. "Functional Linguistics: Communicative Functions and Language Structure." Pages 141–57 in *The Handbook of Linguistics*. Edited by Mark Aronoff and Janie Rees-Miller. 2nd ed. Blackwell Handbooks in Linguistics. Malden, MA: Wiley-Blackwell, 2017.

———. "Semantic Macroroles in Role and Reference Grammar." Pages 62–82 in *Semantische Rollen*. Edited by Rolf Kailuweit and Martin Hummel. Tübinger Beiträge zur Linguistik 472. Tübingen: Narr, 2004.

Vasholz, Robert I. "A Philological Comparison of the Qumran Job Targum and Its Implications for the Dating of Daniel." DTh thesis, University of Stellenbosch, 1976.

———. "Qumran and the Dating of Daniel." *JETS* 21 (1978): 315–21.

Vendler, Zeno. "Verbs and Times." *The Philosophical Review* 66 (1957): 143–60.

Verheij, Arian J. C. *Bits, Bytes, and Binyanim: A Quantitative Study of Verbal Lexeme Formations in the Hebrew Bible*. OLA 93. Leuven: Peeters, 2000.

———. "Stems and Roots: Some Statistics Concerning the Verbal Stems in the Hebrew Bible." *ZAH* 5 (1990): 64–71.

Vern, Robyn C. *Dating Archaic Biblical Hebrew Poetry: A Critique of the Linguistic Arguments*. PSHC 10. Piscataway, NJ: Gorgias, 2011.

Voigt, Rainer Maria. "Derivatives und flektives ṯ im Semitohamitischen." Pages 85–107 in *Proceedings of the Fourth International Hamito-Semitic Congress, Marburg, 20–20 September, 1983.* Edited by Hermann Jungraithmayr and Walter W. Müller. Amsterdam Studies in the Theory and History of Linguistic Science, Series IV: Current Issues in Linguistic Theory 44. Amsterdam: Benjamins, 1987.

Waldman, Nahum M. *The Recent Study of Hebrew: A Survey of the Literature with Selected Bibliography.* Bibliographica Judaica 10. Cincinnati: Hebrew Union College Press, 1989.

Walker, Larry L. "Notes on Higher Criticism and the Dating of Biblical Hebrew." Pages 35–52 in *A Tribute to Gleason Archer.* Edited by Walter C. Kaiser, Jr. and Ronald F. Youngblood. Chicago: Moody, 1986.

Waltke, Bruce K. and Michael O'Connor. *An Introduction to Biblical Hebrew Syntax.* Winona Lake, IN: Eisenbrauns, 1990.

Walton, John H. "Principles for Productive Word Study." *NIDOTTE* 1:161–71.

Walton, John H. and D. Brent Sandy. *The Lost World of Scripture: Ancient Literary Culture and Biblical Authority.* Downers Grove, IL: IVP Academic, 2013.

Wang, Ting. "The Use of the Infinitive Absolute in the Hebrew Bible." PhD diss., Hebrew Union College–Jewish Institute of Religion, 2003.

Wasow, Thomas. "Generative Grammar: Rule Systems for Describing Sentence Structure." Pages 119–39 in *The Handbook of Linguistics.* Edited by Mark Aronoff and Janie Rees-Miller. 2nd ed. Blackwell Handbooks in Linguistics. Malden, MA: Wiley-Blackwell, 2017.

Watts, John D. W. "Infinitive Absolute as Imperative and the Interpretation of Exodus 20 8." *ZAW* 33 (1962): 141–45.

Webster, Brian L. *The Cambridge Introduction to Biblical Hebrew.* Cambridge: Cambridge University Press, 2009.

———. *Reading Biblical Hebrew: Introduction to Grammar.* 2nd ed. Belmont, MI: DigiScroll, 2017.

Weingreen, Jacob. "The Piʿel in Biblical Hebrew: A Suggested New Concept." *Hen* 5 (1983): 21–29.

Weinrich, Harald. *Tempus: Besprochene und erzählte Welt.* Sprache und Literatur 16. Stuttgart: Kohlhammer, 1964.

Wendland, Ernst R. "The Discourse Analysis of Hebrew Poetry: A Procedural Outline." Pages 1–27 in *Discourse Perspectives on Hebrew Poetry in the Scriptures.* Edited by Ernst R. Wendland. United Bible Society Monograph Series 7. New York: United Bible Societies, 1994.

Widder, Wendy. "Linguistic Fundamentals." Pages 11–49 in *Linguistics and Biblical Exegesis.* Edited by Douglas Mangum and Joshua R. Westbury. Lexham Methods Series 2. Bellingham, WA: Lexham, 2017.

———. "Linguistic Issues in Biblical Hebrew." Pages 135–60 in *Linguistics and Biblical Exegesis.* Edited by Douglas Mangum and Joshua R. Westbury. Lexham Methods Series 2. Bellingham, WA: Lexham, 2017.

———. *"To Teach" in Ancient Israel: A Cognitive Linguistic Study of a Biblical Hebrew Lexical Set.* BZAW 456. Berlin: De Gruyter, 2014.

Williams, Edwin. "Argument Structure and Morphology." *The Linguistic Review* 1 (1981): 81–114.

Williams, Ronald J. *Williams' Hebrew Syntax.* Edited by John C. Beckman. 3rd ed. Toronto: University of Toronto Press, 2007.

Williamson, H. G. M. "Semantics and Lexicography: A Methodological Conundrum." Pages 327–39 in *Biblical Lexicology: Hebrew and Greek: Semantics—Exegesis—Translation.* Edited by Jan Joosten, Regine Hunziker-Rodewald, and Eberhard Bons. BZAW 443. Berlin: de Gruyter, 2015.

Wilson, Robert Dick. "The Aramaic of Daniel." Pages 261–306 in *Biblical and Theological Studies by the Members of the Faculty of Princeton Theological Seminary Published in Commemoration of the One Hundreth Anniversary of the Founding of the Seminary.* New York: Scribner, 1912.

Wilt, Timothy. "A Sociolinguistic Analysis of *nā'*." *VT* 46 (1996): 237–55.

Winther-Nielsen, Nicolai. *A Functional Discourse Grammar of Joshua: A Computer-Assisted Rhetorical Structure Analysis.* ConBOT 40. Stockholm: Almqvist & Wiksell, 1995.

Wolde, Ellen J. van. *Reframing Biblical Studies: When Language and Text Meet Culture, Cognition, and Context.* Winona Lake, IN: Eisenbrauns, 2009.

Wood, Esther Jane. "The Semantic Typology of Pluractionality." PhD diss., University of California, Berkeley, 2007.

Wright, Richard M. "Further Evidence for North Israelite Contributions to Late Biblical Hebrew." Pages 129–48 in *Biblical Hebrew: Studies in Chronology and Typology.* Edited by Ian Young. JSOTSup 369. London: T&T Clark, 2003.

———. *Linguistic Evidence for the Pre-Exilic Date of the Yahwistic Source.* LHBOTS 419. London: T&T Clark, 2005.

Yakubovich, Ilya S. "Information Structure and Word Order in the Aramaic of the Book of Daniel." Pages 373–96 in *Narratives of Egypt and the Ancient Near East: Literary and Linguistic Approaches.* Edited by Fredrik Hagen, John Johnston, Wendy Monkhouse, Kathryn Piquette, John Tait, and Martin Worthington. OLA 189. Leuven: Uitgeverij Peeters, 2011.

Yiyi, Chen. "Israelian Hebrew in the Book of Proverbs." PhD diss., Cornell University, 2000.

Yoo, Yoon Jong. "Israelian Hebrew in the Book of Hosea." PhD diss., Cornell University, 1999.

Young, Ian. "Ancient Hebrew without Authors." *JSem* 25 (2016): 972–1003.

———, ed. *Biblical Hebrew: Studies in Chronology and Typology.* JSOTSup 369. London: T&T Clark, 2003.

———. *Diversity in Pre-Exilic Hebrew.* FAT 5. Tübingen: Mohr Siebeck, 1993.

———. "Evidence of Diversity in Pre-Exilic Judahite Hebrew." *HS* 38 (1997): 7–20.

———. "The 'Northernisms' of the Israelite Narratives in Kings." *ZAH* 8 (1995): 63–70.

———. "What Do We Actually Know about Ancient Hebrew?" *Australian Journal of Jewish Studies* 27 (2013): 11–31.

Young, Ian, Robert Rezetko, and Martin Ehrensvärd. *Linguistic Dating of Biblical Texts*. 2 vols. Bible World. London: Equinox, 2008.

Zanella, Francesco. *The Lexical Field of the Substantives of "Gift" in Ancient Hebrew*. SSN 54. Leiden: Brill, 2010.

Zevit, Ziony. *The Anterior Construction in Classical Hebrew*. SBLMS 50. Atlanta: Scholars Press, 1998.

———. "Talking Funny in Biblical Henglish and Solving a Problem of the *yaqtul* Past Tense." *HS* 29 (1988): 25–33.

Zorell, Franz. *Lexicon hebraicum et aramaicum: Veteris Testamenti*. Rome: Pontifical Biblical Institute, 1954.

Zuber, Beat. *Das Tempussystem des biblischen Hebräisch: eine untersuchung am Text*. BZAW 164. Berlin: de Gruyter, 1986.

Zuo, Jeremiah Xiufu. *The Biblical Hebrew Word Order Debate: A Testing of Two Language Typologies in the Sodom Account*. GlossaHouse Thesis Series 3. Wilmore, KY: GlossaHouse, 2017.

Zwyghuizen, Jill E. "Time Reference of Verbs in Biblical Hebrew Poetry." PhD diss., Dallas Theological Seminary, 2012.

SCRIPTURE INDEX

SUBJECT INDEX

AUTHOR INDEX